LOCATIONS OF LITERARY MODERNISM

Region and Nation in British and American Modernist Poetry

In this collection, an international team of contributors contest the conventional critical view of modernism as a transnational or supranational entity. They examine relationships between modernist poetry and place, and foreground issues of region and space, nation and location in the work of poets such as Ezra Pound, Wallace Stevens and Marianne Moore. The book brings the work of major canonical writers into juxtaposition with more neglected modernists such as Basil Bunting and Dylan Thomas, writers whose investment in the concepts of region and nation, it is argued, contributed to their relative marginalisation. These essays offer a fresh perspective on contemporary revaluations of modernism through their investigation of some of the Anglo-American locations of modernism, and reassess the regional and national affiliations of modernist poetry. *Locations of Literary Modernism* maps a topography of poetic modernism that is quite different from what has hitherto been accepted as comprehensive.

ALEX DAVIS is Lecturer in English at University College Cork and is co-editor of *Modernism and Ireland: The Poetry of the 1930s* (1995). He is the author of *A Broken Line: Denis Devlin and Irish Poetic Modernism* (2000).

LEE M. JENKINS is Lecturer in English at University College Cork and is the author of *Wallace Stevens: Rage for Order* (1999).

LOCATIONS OF LITERARY MODERNISM

Region and Nation in British and American Modernist Poetry

EDITED BY

ALEX DAVIS and LEE M. JENKINS

PUBLISHED BY THE PRESS SYNDICATE OF THE UNIVERSITY OF CAMBRIDGE
The Pitt Building, Trumpington Street, Cambridge, United Kingdom

CAMBRIDGE UNIVERSITY PRESS
The Edinburgh Building, Cambridge, CB2 2RU, UK   http://www.cup.cam.ac.uk
40 West 20th Street, New York, NY 10011–4211, USA   http://www.cup.org
10 Stamford Road, Oakleigh, Melbourne 3166, Australia

© Cambridge University Press 2000

First published 2000

Printed in the United Kingdom at the University Press, Cambridge

Typeset in Baskerville 11/12.5pt [VN]

A catalogue record for this book is available from the British Library

Library of Congress cataloguing in publication data
Locations of literary modernism: region and nation in British and American modernist poetry / edited by Alex Davis and Lee M. Jenkins.
p. cm.
Includes bibliographical references and index.
ISBN 0 521 78032 2
1. English poetry – 20th century – History and criticism.   2. Modernism (Literature) – Great Britain,   3. American poetry – 20th century – History and criticism.   4. National characteristics, American, in literature.   5. National characteristics, British, in literature.   6. Modernism (Literature) – United States.   7. Regionalism in literature.   8. Nationalism in literature.   9. Setting (Literature) I. Davis, Alex. II. Jenkins, Lee M. (Lee Margaret)
PR605.M63 L63   2000
821'.9109112–dc21   99–086099   CIP

ISBN 0 521 78032 2 hardback

For Donal and Vivienne

Contents

PART TWO. AN AMERICAN PLACE

Notes on contributors

PETER BROOKER is Professor of Modern Literature and Culture at University College, Northampton. He has written extensively on aspects of modernism, postmodernism and contemporary theory. He is the editor of *Modernism/Postmodernism* (Longman, 1992), *New York Fictions: Modernity, Postmodernism, The New Modern* (Longman, 1996) and *Cultural Theory* (Arnold, 1998). A volume of essays, *Modernity and Metropolis*, is forthcoming.

RICHARD CADDEL is Director of the Basil Bunting Poetry Centre, University of Durham. He is editor of *Complete Poems of Basil Bunting* (Oxford University Press, 1994), and of *Sharp Study and Long Toil: Basil Bunting, Durham University Journal Special Supplement* (1995); he is the co-author of *Basil Bunting: A Northern Life* (Basil Bunting Poetry Centre, 1997), and is the co-editor of *OTHER British and Irish Poetry since 1970* (Wesleyan University Press, 1998).

ROBERT CRAWFORD is Professor of Modern Scottish Literature at the University of St Andrews. Publications include *Devolving English Literature*, 2nd edn (Edinburgh University Press, 2000); he co-edited *The Penguin Book of Poetry from Britain and Ireland since 1945* (1998), and the new *Penguin Book of Scottish Verse* (2000). His collections of poetry include *A Scottish Assembly* (Chatto, 1990), *Talkies* (Chatto, 1992), *Masculinity* (Cape, 1996) and *Spirit Machines* (Cape, 1999).

THOMAS DILWORTH, a Killam Fellow, is Professor of English at the University of Windsor, Ontario. Publications include *The Shape of Meaning in the Poetry of David Jones* (University of Toronto Press, 1988), which won the British Council Prize in the Humanities. Professor Dilworth is currently writing Jones' authorised biography for Jonathan Cape.

JOHN GOODBY lectures in English at the University of Wales, Swansea. Publications include numerous articles on Anglo-Irish poetry, and *From Stillness into History: Irish Poetry 1950–1995* (Manchester University Press, 2000). His collection of poems, *A Birmingham Yank*, was published by Ark in 1999.

FIONA GREEN is a Fellow of Corpus Christi College, Cambridge. She is currently completing a book on intertextuality in twentieth-century American poetry.

PETER NICHOLLS is Professor in the School of English and American Studies at the University of Sussex. Publications include *Ezra Pound: Politics, Economics and Writing* (Macmillan, 1984), and *Modernisms* (Macmillan, 1995).

STAN SMITH is Professor of English at Nottingham Trent University. Publications include *W. H. Auden* (Basil Blackwell, 1985), *W. B. Yeats: A Critical Introduction* (Gill and Macmillan, 1990), *The Origins of Modernism: Eliot, Pound, Yeats and the Rhetorics of Renewal* (Harvester, 1994).

GEOFF WARD is Professor of English at the University of Dundee. Publications include *Statutes of Liberty: The New York School of Poets* (Macmillan, 1993). He is currently writing a critical biography of John Ashbery.

CHRISTOPHER WIGGINTON is completing a doctorate at the University of Wales, Swansea, on the poetry of Dylan Thomas and Louis MacNeice. He is the author of several articles on twentieth-century British poetry; with John Goodby he is co-editing the *New Casebook* on Dylan Thomas, and in 1998, organised *Under the Spelling Wall*, the Dylan Thomas Swansea Conference.

ALEX DAVIS lectures in English at University College Cork. He is the co-editor of *Modernism and Ireland: The Poetry of the 1930s* (Cork University Press, 1995) and author of *A Broken Line: Denis Devlin and Irish Poetic Modernism* (University College Dublin Press, 2000). He is currently editing Denis Devlin's uncollected poems for Dedalus Press.

LEE M. JENKINS lectures in English at University College Cork. She has published articles on American and Irish modernist poetry and on African American writing, and is the author of *Wallace Stevens: Rage for Order* (Sussex Academic Press, 1999).

Preface

We would like to thank Ray Ryan for his editorial enthusiasm and commitment, the two readers for Cambridge University Press who helped us to shape this book, the staff at Inter-Library Loans at University College Cork, Peter Flynn for his technical assistance, Leigh Mueller for her careful copy-editing, and John Loftus for compiling the index. Above all, we thank the contributors to this book, for their trust in us and in this project.

ALEX DAVIS AND LEE M. JENKINS

Introduction

Locating modernisms: an overview

Alex Davis and Lee M. Jenkins

Recent theoretical debate has served to enhance our understanding of the plural bases of poetic modernism, and yet the construction of modernism as an international, urban and yet placeless, phenomenon remains, for the most part, a critical given. Peter Nicholls' *Modernisms* is one recent critical enterprise which has sought to overturn 'the one-dimensional view of modernism' which 'is with us still' as 'a sort of monolithic ideological formation'.[1] Accordingly, *Modernisms*, as the title of Nicholls' book suggests, proposes a survey of the diverse and often mutually antagonistic avant-gardes which jostle for space beneath the umbrella term of 'modernism'. Nicholls' is a welcome and important intervention in studies of modernism, offering as it does a polysemous approach to its polysemous subject, and thus avoiding the limitations imposed by reading those poets we broadly classify as 'modernist' retrospectively, through the New Critical tenets which have canonised one strain of modernism (Eliot's), at the expense of other modernisms which do not prove so tractable to New Critical paradigms. (The importance of seeing modernism outside the New Critical paradigm is pressing, too, for those contemporary poets who view themselves as the inheritors of, in Charles Bernstein's words, 'a set of radical modernist concerns that are still relevant to current poetic and political practice, just as they are still unacceptable to the official cultural apparatus'. Bernstein targets 'literary canon makers from the New Critics to Helen Vendler' as promoting a 'type of gutted modernism' over and above a range of avant-garde modernist approaches.)[2] As Peter Brooker argues, 'we have to recognise a plurality of modernisms which sought to innovate on different artistic and cultural fronts, and to understand too the process by which a selective modernism came to represent a standard and orthodoxy and thus marginalise other work'.[3] Yet if the New Critical rubric of text over context which, despite interventions to the contrary, is, as Nicholls acknowledges, 'with us still', puts up barriers to

3

understanding the diversity of poetic modernism, so too does the tendency of accepting too quickly and uncritically the commonplace that modernism is a transnational or even supranational entity. In a headnote in the reader *Modernism* called 'A Geography of Modernism', the editors, Malcolm Bradbury and James McFarlane, comment that 'one of the more striking features of modernism is its wide geographical spread, its multiple nationality . . . Yet each of the contributing countries has its own cultural inheritance . . . which impose[s] distinctively national emphases upon modernism and leave[s] any account which relies on a single national perspective misleadingly partial'.[4]

The point is surely a valid one – Irish versions of modernism may not be congruent with Russian versions, and so on. Yet to stress both the quiddity of a particular 'cultural inheritance' *and* the danger of relying on single national perspectives may be to run the risk of each part of this seemingly balanced equation cancelling out the other. It may be 'partial' and 'misleading' to pass too quickly over individual 'national' (or regional) emphases within modernism[5] – Dada is often described as the epitome of modernist internationalism, and yet the demise of Zurich Dada was according to national fracture lines.[6] The present collection of essays examines relationships between modernist poetry and place, and suggests that issues of region, of nation, of location in modernist poetics may be explored with profit.

As the editors of *Locations of Literary Modernism*, we must begin by mapping out our terrain, defining our terms of exploration, and defending the territorial boundaries of our collection. Our terrain, those locations of modernism which these essays explore, is necessarily a circumscribed one, and we are aware that our concentration upon the British Isles and the United States is at the expense of attention to other modernising locations such as Latin America and Paris. Our focus, then, is English-language modernist poetry (although not always poetry written in standard English). The two other principal boundaries of this collection are generic and chronological. Although spatial questions are by no means peculiar to the lyric, the focus of *Locations of Literary Modernism* is modernist poetry. If our second, chronological, boundary is more elastic, this reflects the elasticity of the chronology of modernism. Querying the idea that there is a modernist 'moment', we suggest instead that modernism is an unfinished project, and so the essays collected here range from high modernism to the late work of modernist poets such as Pound, and from putatively 'post-modern' poets such as O'Hara to the poets of the Harlem Renaissance, who write at the temporal apogee of modernism, but who also write in a tangential and often revisionary relationship to the white modernisms of their time. Yet Langston Hughes, who came to prominence as a poet at the time of the Harlem Renaissance, extends the temporal bounds of modernism too: his sequence *Montage of a Dream Deferred* was published in 1951 to coincide with and help to form the modernist jazz aesthetic which, as Peter Brooker points out, did not emerge until the 1940s and 1950s, well after the high point of the Harlem Renaissance itself. This is why, in his essay on Hughes for this collection, Brooker discusses a 'modernism deferred'.[7]

These essays offer an exploration, both necessarily and deliberately selective, of the interface between modernist poetry and place – and if 'place', like our titular term 'locations', suggests neutral territory, other terms used in this collection – 'region' and 'nation' – may be more problematically aligned with the various ideologies associated with regionalism and nationalism. That modernism and nationalism need not be mutually incompatible is vividly demonstrated by the example of the Irish Literary Revival. The Celticism of the Revival represents a form of cultural nationalism; its rummaging through mythology and its veneration of a pre-modern existence glimpsed in life on the Western seaboard constitute a familiar variant on that strain of high modernism antipathetic to modernity. As Terry Eagleton has suggestively argued: 'Both nationalism and modernism eclipse the prosaic time of modernity, placing this whole epoch in brackets by the power of a thought which, in striving for some post-bourgeois form of life, finds its models for this in a pre-bourgeois world'.[8] Ireland's lack of a developed industrial base (with the exception of Belfast) gave added impetus to this form of modernist nationalism, in which the rural Celt stands opposed to the mercantile Anglo-Saxon, though the absence of the new technologies, as Eagleton continues, may go some way to explaining the absence of an Irish avant-garde. Elsewhere, agrarian economies convulsively transformed by industrial development produced avant-garde artistic experimentation wedded to national self-awareness. As Marjorie Perloff observes, 'Both the Italian and the Russian versions of Futurism found their roots in economically backward countries that were experiencing rapid industrialisation – the faith in dynamism and national expansion associated with capitalism in its early phase'.[9]

The neutrality of our covering term 'locations' is designed not to occlude but rather to cater for and respect the asymmetries between the terms of our subtitle, 'region' and 'nation', between the particularities of region and the abstractions of nation: as this introductory essay goes on to show, issues raised by nationality do not simply run parallel to those raised by region or regionalism. Although nation and region are not seen, here, as interchangeable signs of the 'local', the purpose of this book is less to contribute to ongoing debates to do with the ideologies of locus than it is to highlight the heretofore underexplored interrelations, affiliations and antitheses which emerge when we, in various senses, 'place' the work of modernist poets. The essays here both reexamine canonical modernist poets through the focus of place, and bring into sometimes provocative juxtaposition with these major poets the work of other modernist poets whose investments in region or in nation have contributed to their relative peripheralisation.

Such peripheralisation or marginalisation was deliberately courted by a number of the poets discussed in the chapters which follow: looking at Hugh MacDiarmid in the context of Montrose in the 1920s, Robert Crawford argues that on a 'micro level', this small town is 'a key location of modernism' because it offered MacDiarmid, and the poet Edwin Muir, 'a sense of empowering marginality'. Similarly, Richard Caddel discusses Basil Bunting's 'Northumbrian version of modernism', which, Caddel shows, looks to old Welsh poetry as a 'cultural signifier of location'. In his essay on the 'terra informis' of David Jones, Jones' authorised biographer Thomas Dilworth explores the psychological roots of the Spenglerian antithesis between the rural and the urban, between culture and civilisation, which, for Jones, is figured in the Yeatsian masks or desired opposites which are at play in Wales versus London. For John Goodby and Christopher Wigginton, Welsh modernism has suffered as a result of the critical over-attention paid to Faber poet Jones: in a bid to rectify this imbalance, Goodby and Wigginton conceive Dylan Thomas' 'negotiations of constructions of Welshness' as a reworking of modernism. Read here in terms of a hybrid 'interstitial writing', Thomas emerges as the proponent of 'Surregionalism', 'a provincial simulacrum of surrealism'. According to Stan Smith's revisionary reading of the uses of topography in Edward Thomas, Auden and Yeats, Thomas' 'England' is 'a peculiarly disjunct, decentred terrain', to be differentiated generationally and in terms of class from Auden's 'anxious border country' and from the 'artifice' which is Yeats' Ireland. Irish modernist poets of the thirties are Alex Davis' focus, in an essay which explores the reactions of Samuel Beckett, Denis Devlin, Brian Coffey, Thomas MacGreevy, as well as Austin Clarke and Louis MacNeice, to both Yeats' Ireland, 'terrible and gay', and the more mundane realities of the Irish Free State in that decade.

Moving to our American locations of modernism: Peter Nicholls' analysis of 'Pound's places' maps those 'traces of poetic energies' which Pound found in 'actual landscape[s]' like the Midi, places which operated for Pound as 'sites of intermingled temporalities', foregrounding the 'visionary locations' of the *Cantos*. Lee Jenkins' chapter suggests that the ironised localism of Wallace Stevens' early poetry gives way to descriptions without places, as the poet retreats into the autotelic world of the poem in a time of war – only to return, late in his career, to a sense of his own American region. Fiona Green also discusses the American lyric poem at the time of the Second World War, linking Marianne Moore's version of the crystalline, sealed space of the poem to that of Stevens, and exploring Moore and Elizabeth Bishop in relation to 'the effect of geographical location on the development of American poetry in wartime'. Geoff Ward's chapter focuses on the cultural cartography, as well as the urban locus, of the New York School, offering the grouping of the New York poets as a significant location of modernism, in which New York City acts as a 'fulcrum' and as 'a multi-dimensional context' for the work of Ashbery, O'Hara and Schuyler. Finally, Peter Brooker's chapter on Langston Hughes identifies Harlem not only as a physical place on the grid map of Manhattan, but also as a locus of 'a utopian belongingness'. Conceptualising Harlem in terms of 'spatial hybridity', Brooker explores both the differing and the interrelated significances the 'permeable heteropolis' of Harlem has had for blacks and whites.

The arrangement of these chapters may suggest an arch-form, a rising out of the particular, and a falling back into it. The first two chapters, on MacDiarmid and Bunting, describe an intensely local poetics, in which strange vocabulary itself becomes a metaphor for the uniqueness of place; and the two final chapters, on O'Hara and Langston Hughes, also describe the strong specificities of New York streets. In between, the essays posit certain surrogations of the local, usurpation of particular place names by more general themes, so that the chapter on Jones describes a poet dominated by rural places, yet a poet for whom these rural places become lost in generality or in myth; the chapter on Dylan Thomas suggests localism giving way to a parody of the same; and according to the theme of the eviction of the particular by the general in Stan Smith's chapter, all of England becomes a vast allegory. When, in the second half of the book, the venue shifts from Britain to America, there is a reorientation in the small facts of places.

The chapters collected as *Locations of Literary Modernism* do not propose a single, seamless, thesis. The collection as a whole respects and attempts to represent the heterogeneous nature of the modernisms it examines – and it is not our intention to attempt to define a localist-modernist counter-canon over and against an internationalist-modernist canon: if it is the case, as we suggest, that margins can be empowering, this does not preclude the centre, or the international, as a place of power. The overview of the locations of modernism, which comprises the remainder of this Introduction, prefigures the purview of this book in suggesting some of the correspondences and divergences which emerge when modernist poetry is examined from the perspective of place.

In his article 'Geoliterature' in a recent edition of *Poetry Ireland Review*, J. C. C. Mays points to a new phenomenon within American literary and cultural production, based on the conception of 'landscape as a text which is itself to be read'. 'The notion of geoliterature', Mays explains, 'is that the place itself . . . might be a text.' Emerson and Whitman had suggested something similar in the mid nineteenth century; but Mays' article expresses his sense of surprise and discovery, while attending a recent Modern Languages Association conference, at the burgeoning enterprise of contemporary 'geoliterature' (and, presumably, its inevitable corollary of 'geocriticism') in the United States – and certainly there appears at present to be a plethora of books, essays and anthologies of poetry which intersect in various ways with 'geoliterature', 'ethnopoetics', 'bioregionalism' and other movements concerned with the relationship between writing and place. A possible explanation for this is offered by one of the contributors to a collection of essays entitled *Regionalism Reconsidered*. Francesco Lorrigio suggests that the increasing incidence of global fragmentation – such as the break-up of the former Yugoslavia and the Soviet Bloc – has prompted a revival of interest in 'literary regionalism' (a view shared by Richard Caddel in his chapter for the present volume when he writes of Basil Bunting's 'deliberately marginal voice' which 'resonates strongly in the emerging fragmented and marginalised cultures of Europe today'); while David Jordan, the editor of *Regionalism Reconsidered*, argues that all 'notions of cultural homogeneity' are in any case becoming outmoded, in the face of the contemporary contexts of multiculturalism and environmentalism.[10]

'Regionalism' has long been a contested term, within America anyway. Robert Penn Warren argued in the thirties that 'Regionalism . . . we may take in its more practical aspects as . . . a belated recognition of the fairly obvious fact that a circle cannot have a center without having a

circumference'. Wendell Berry, like Penn Warren a champion of regional writing, will, however, have no truck with the tag 'regionalism'
and the associations he says the term has with the supposedly minor
genre of 'local color' and with an attitude of condescension toward
people who are odd enough to choose to live outside the major urban
centres.[11] Reconsiderations of regionalism and region, such as those
proposed in Jordan's book, offer us Berry and the poet Gary Snyder as
the gurus and forerunners of new critical perspectives which, to use
Michael Kowalewski's words, recognise and exploit 'the potential influence of geography in shaping new art forms' while, according to Lorrigio, such new perspectives must privilege space over time.[12] If this is
the case, however, these perspectives aren't really new: the priority of
space over time – and the priority of the local over the universal –
underpin the aesthetic of Charles Olson, while Olson's aesthetic derives,
in significant part, from the cultural localism of William Carlos Williams.[13] In other words, a number of the issues raised by recent regionalist critical enterprises such as Jordan's are issues which emerge and are
foregrounded in modernist poetics.

Hugh MacDiarmid believed that only through a vigorous cultural
and political nationalism could a viable *inter*nationalism be achieved –
hence his poem 'Second Hymn to Lenin', where from his base of
operations in Scotland the poet engages in an inter-national dialogue
with his addressee in the Soviet Union – in demotic Scots. As Scottish
nationalist and cultural and ideological internationalist, MacDiarmid's
stance courts inevitable and almost comic paradox – he was expelled
from the Scottish National Party for being a Communist and expelled
from the Communist Party for his nationalist beliefs. But the balancing
act MacDiarmid could not quite sustain in his public life as radical he
achieves with greater finesse in the modernism/(inter)nationalism axis
of his poetry. His early lyrics, written in Scots, can be seen as a
nationalist gesture, and are MacDiarmid's attempt – an attempt which
has suggestive analogues in the use of black dialect in the work of some
Harlem Renaissance writers – to retrieve a specific and a marginalised
national identity from the homogenising effect of the dominant culture.
Yet MacDiarmid's early lyrics are also a *modernist* gesture, because his
Scots is what MacDiarmid would later term *synthetic* Scots – essentially
an invented language. So, for MacDiarmid as for Eliot (national) 'Tradition' is something actively to be *made*, constructed, not something to be
passively inherited. After the forays into (synthetic) Scots of his first two
volumes of lyrics, MacDiarmid would turn to other synthetic language-

systems – to the discourse of science in his masterly riposte to Eliot, the poem 'On a Raised Beach', and then to the eclectic 'braidbinding', to use MacDiarmid's own term, of his later 'world language' poems.

Despite the considerable efforts of Robert Crawford, a critic powerfully adequate to the often considerable demands of MacDiarmid's work, MacDiarmid remains a marginalised figure in discussions of poetic modernism; and, according to received ideas about the internationalism of modernist writing, modernism and ideas of nation are still for the most part seen as separate and antithetical phenomena: the positing of the kind of single, unitary selfhood which is often associated with nationalism is seen to be at odds with the shifting ideas of subjectivity and fragmentation of the self which we associate with modernism.

From the commonplace that modernism is an inter- or supra-national movement in the arts, it is a short step to the formalist assertion that the only *site* of poetic modernism is the site of the inviolate and well-wrought modernist text itself. Recognising and exploring tensions *between* the international circulation of ideas in the modernist period, and the countervailing claims of nation and region in modernist poetics constitutes a new challenge to formalist definitions of modernism. The exploration of such tensions brings poets as various as those discussed in the following chapters – writers who are diverse in terms of their regional and national belongings as well as in terms of poetic practice – into often provocative juxtaposition with one another, suggesting new locations on and possible re-locations – in terms of interplay between central and peripheral modernist poets and poetics – of the modernist map. Robert Crawford, in the exploration of 'Modernism as Provincialism' in his *Devolving English Literature*, has demonstrated that such tensions may be explored with profit, pointing out that 'it was the un-English provincials' (Pound, Eliot, MacDiarmid) 'and their traditions which contributed most to the . . . phenomenon which we now know as modernism'. Crawford goes on to argue that 'A cursory account of modernism stresses its cosmopolitanism and internationalism, presenting it as a facet of "high" metropolitan culture. But there is also another, equally important, side of modernism that is demotic and crucially "provincial"'.[14]

For Crawford, the cosmopolitan and provincial aspects of modernism are complementary, not antithetical – a view which is queried in this collection of essays by John Goodby and Christopher Wigginton, who argue that Crawford's configuration of province and cosmopolis offers 'a too-easy overcoming of very real and material differences of class, gender'. Yet Crawford's point is endorsed by the symbiosis of modernism and region we find in the fiction of William Faulkner; and in terms of modernist poetics, a conjunction between modernism and place, modernism and region, invites suggestive if seldom explored conjunctions between poets as seemingly diverse – at least in terms of their politics – as MacDiarmid, David Jones and Charles Olson. MacDiarmid's idea of approaching the international via the national finds an analogue in Olson's approach to world consciousness via the local in *The Maximus Poems*.[15] MacDiarmid and David Jones inhabited different ideological worlds, MacDiarmid sponsoring a nationalist socialism, and Jones a right-wing Catholicism. Yet MacDiarmid would hail Jones as the greatest native English poet of the twentieth century, and would denounce Philip Larkin's editorship of the 1974 *Oxford Book of English Verse* for its exclusion of Jones.[16] The experimental poetics of both MacDiarmid and Jones are rooted in a sense of place, and this connection, if we juxtapose MacDiarmid's poem 'On a Raised Beach' with 'Rite and Fore-Time' from Jones' *The Anathemata*, is further grounded in a shared geological lexicon:

> foraminous cavo-rilievo of the world,
> Deictic, fiducial stones. Chiliad by chiliad
> What bricole piled you here, stupendous cairn?
>
> ('On a Raised Beach')

> This is how Cronos reads the rubric, *frangit per medium*, when
> he breaks his ice like morsels, for the therapy and fertility
> of the land-masses.
> Or before
>   from Eden-dales, or torn from the becked fells
>   transmontane
>   transmarine
> the barrier-making flood-gravels
> the drumlined clays and the till-drift
>   had bye-wayed and delta'd the mainway
> for Tanat and Vyrnwy.   ('Rite and Fore-Time')[17]

The British modernism of David Jones and Basil Bunting makes good Guilbaut's claim of 'an elite international avant-garde art held in a fructifying relationship with a strong-felt sense of place'.[18] Jones' modernism is not an adjunct to his Welsh nationalism, or vice versa; the two are deeply meshed. As Tony Conran has argued, modernism in Welsh and Anglo-Welsh writing is bound to the new nationalism, directing its energies against *buchedd* culture in the name of 'the old Wales of the *traddodiad*', as revived by John Morris-Jones, T. Gwynn Jones and Ifor Williams.[19] David Jones' work, though written as a partial 'outsider', and from the 'megalopolis' of London, deploys a reactionary modernist concern with cultural 'deposits', and their retrieval in fragmentary form, in the service of the new nationalism. Nevertheless, Wales in Jones' writings is also metonymic of *any* locale or region, the particularity of which is threatened by the levelling effects of a dominant cultural and political centre. In this respect, his nationalism shades into regionalism and into a defence of, in Drew Milne's words, 'a *materia poetica* determined by place, forged in exile from the placeless cosmopolis'.[20] In Jones, therefore, the notions of nation and region are, in a sense, interchangeable, both terms denoting a 'place' or ground to which the rootless artist is drawn. Furthermore, his belief in national and regional uniqueness is closely related to his protest at a society in which the deformations of instrumental reason have produced individuals for whom the particular has been crushed under the universality of conceptual thought.

Basil Bunting shares Jones' wilful provincialism, and to not unrelated ends. As Donald Westling has observed, Bunting's Northumbria, conveyed most powerfully in *Briggflatts*, represents the claims not just of region but also 'whatever is marginal, local, plural, adulterated and inconvenient'.[21] Such an emphasis on the heterogeneous recalls Jones' representations of Wales, or 'Celticity', in, for example, 'The Tutelar of the Place', in *The Sleeping Lord and Other Fragments*. Further from home, it also chimes with Charles Olson's Gloucester in *The Maximus Poems*, a 'polis' that is heterogeneous rather than homogeneous, and which becomes the locus for an attack on 'mercantilism' and 'statism' very much in the spirit of his slightly older British contemporaries. Indeed, Olson's desire to be 'an historian as Herodotus was',[22] suggests an openness to myth as relevant to historical undertaking very much in the spirit of Jones' and Bunting's deployment of Welsh and Northumbrian legend in their evocations of a region's past.

Exile from one's native place, as Malcolm Bradbury has argued, is a precondition for much modern writing, and experimental modernists ranging from Pound and Eliot to Joyce to the Lost Generation have sought to disentangle themselves from the nets of nation and nationality.[23] Dis-placement may have been a prerequisite for the Lost Generation, and yet many expatriate modernist writers were as energised by their place of origin as by their self-imposed exile from it. For the Lost

Generation writer, as for many theorists of modernism, one's identity *as writer* may seem to be predicated upon an erasure of national identity. Malcolm Cowley describes the Lost Generation in *Exile's Return* as 'homeless citizens of the world . . . adhering to a theory of art which held that the creative artist is absolutely independent of all localities, nations or classes', and he points to the names of the little magazines associated with the Lost Generation – *transition*, *Secession* and, 'to make a clean sweep of it', *Broom*. Cowley's words accord with Lukacs' claim that 'transcendental homelessness' is 'the epitome of modernity' and Steiner's belief that modernism is 'a strategy of permanent exile', a condition of 'unhousedness' or 'extraterritoriality'. Yet many of the Lost Generation, like Henry James before them, chose to write about America *in absentia* – so, as Leslie Fiedler has argued, the mountains of Hemingway's Spain become a version of the American West, as Hemingway exports and reverses the direction of the American pioneer spirit to give it, in *The Sun Also Rises*, a European trajectory.[24]

Antithetical to but parallel with the Lost Generation's exodus out of America in the twenties, was the manufacture by Mencken, Van Wyck Brooks and others of an indigenous American literary history or 'tradition' with little room for what Louis Untermeyer would have dismissed as the 'Frenchified' influence of European or Euro-American innovation. Mencken may have launched attacks on the cultural inadequacies of the American scene, but was equally forthright in his denunciation of overweening European influence on American culture and in his advocacy of an indigenous American civilisation – Mencken acted as mentor to a number of the Harlem Renaissance poets.[25] And yet the formation of 'usable pasts' in the twenties isn't confined to these emergent American literary histories, but is common, if in divergent forms, to the idea of 'Tradition' which animates Eliot's modernism and to MacDiarmid's appropriation of a (synthetic) Scots, as well as to the confluence of national tradition and modernist innovation found in both the Irish Literary Revival and the Harlem Renaissance. Parallels between black America's bid for cultural nationhood and the earlier Irish struggle for political and cultural self-determination were made at the time of the New Negro Renaissance of the twenties by the principal architect and theorist of that movement, Alain Locke, who contended that 'Harlem has the same role to play for the New Negro as Dublin has had for the New Ireland'.[26] Similar connections were also made by Van Wyck Brooks between Ireland and the *New Republic*, the American journal founded in 1914 to promote political and cultural nationalism. Brooks was enthusiastic about the Irish Literary Renaissance and its aim of 'a national purpose and a literature . . . along the lines of its own racial genius', and he saw Ireland and America as participating in a common drive to break free of English influence.[27] Ireland again provides 'a parallel' for Southern Agrarian writers like Robert Penn Warren: as John Burt has suggested, 'the Agrarians recognised something of their own circumstances in the cultural tradition of the Irish Renaissance' and Warren found in Ireland, and its 'different tradition and a rich folklife, facing the big modern machine', a background against which Agrarian thought could be formulated.[28]

T. S. Eliot may perhaps be cited as specimen internationalist at the expense of the regionalist in him: poems such as 'East Coker' and 'Landscapes' suggest regional affiliations. The 'strong brown god' of 'The Dry Salvages' is usually taken as the Mississippi of Eliot's St Louis childhood, while the poem's title refers to a group of rocks off the coast of Cape Ann – although Charles Olson accused Eliot of 'stealing Dry Salvages from me'. A resident of Gloucester, Cape Ann, Olson resented Eliot's appropriation of a local place-name, especially since Eliot uses this local reference with no sense of the texture, the significance, of this locale: as Ralph Maud writes, 'in this poem ['The Dry Salvages'] purporting to be about Cape Ann, is there anything, Olson would want to ask, of the real Gloucester? Does Eliot know what having to do with fish really involves, in economic and human terms? . . . Olson's point of contention is particularity.'[29] As Crawford argues, Eliot 'both left behind and carried with him "the roots that clutch"', and yet he effectively sloughed off his American national identity as a prelude to his entry into the modern literary world, making the London of *The Waste Land* the international and urban locus of his brand of poetic modernism.[30] Eliot's London is a textual rather than a temporal or, despite the specificity of the poem's reference to street names and London landmarks, a geographical phenomenon. Eliot's London is a series of shifting elisions of time and place, where you may meet Smyrna merchants and fifth-century BC Greek soldiers who may also be American cowboys. National and temporal boundaries are dissolved by Eliot's Tardis-poem, his mobile time-machine, as it goes about its business of replacing national definition with intra-national superimposition and of dissolving a strongly particularised London into urban hallucination – 'Jerusalem Athens Alexandria / Vienna London' – and yet all these cities are 'Unreal'. For Eliot, the modernist cityscape is a composite 'Unreal City', a description, to paraphrase Wallace Stevens, without a place, a site in which the alienation of the modern urban experience – an alienation heightened for the 'metoikos' or 'resident alien' that Eliot was – becomes both an analogue and a model for the cultural fragmentation of the modernist era.

Other strands within modernism, however, suggest that the opposite can be the case.[31] A poet of the Harlem Renaissance like Langston Hughes uses montage, collage and the experimental contours of the modernist epic to conceptualise the modern urban locus not as an 'Unreal City' but as a jiving city, a place for celebration as much as for lamentation, a place for culture to cohere as much as to fragment, a site of social interaction as much as of alienation. The writers of the Harlem Renaissance did not see themselves as a lost generation, and they did not respond to New York as returning members of the Lost Generation responded to it as, to use Malcolm Cowley's phrase, 'the homeland of the uprooted'.[32] Many of the Harlem Renaissance writers *were* uprooted, refugees from a rural South afflicted by disenfranchisement and the boll weevil; but the push from the South to Harlem and the Northern cities involved a vision of collectivity and community alien to Lost Generation *angst* and invective against modern industrial America. Where the Lost Generation railed against America's championship of industry at the expense of the arts, black America looked to the industrial North for economic opportunity and to economic viability as the base for artistic expression. The African American push from the South to the Northern urban centres offers a different inflection to white versions of the relationship between modernity, modernism and the city: as Alain Locke put it, the exodus out of the still quasi-feudal South was 'a deliberate flight not only from countryside to city, but from mediaeval America to modern'.[33]

Locke described Manhattan in the twenties as a 'race capital', offering an upbeat corrective to the Spenglerian diagnosis of New York as the prototypical modern 'world-city', the equivalent of what was, to David Jones, the 'megalopolis that wills death': Spengler's 'world-city' is a place of deadening conformity which 'disenfranchises' the 'entire motherland of its own Culture', making the rest of the nation mere 'provinces' and polarising humanity into '*only cosmopolitans and provincials*'.[34] With the contrast between Locke and Spengler in mind, we can contrast these lines about Harlem from Hughes' improvisational sequence *Montage of a Dream Deferred* with Eliot's Spenglerian as well as

Dantean evocation of London at the end of 'The Burial of the Dead':

> What's the use
> in Harlem?
> What's the use?
> What's the Harlem
> use in Harlem
> what's the lick?
>
> *Hey!*
> *Baba-re-bop!*
> *Mop!*
> *On a be-bop kick!*   (*Montage*)

> Unreal City,
> Under the brown fog of a winter dawn,
> A crowd flowed over London Bridge, so many,
> I had not thought death had undone so many.
> Sighs, short and infrequent, were exhaled,
> And each man fixed his eyes before his feet.   (*The Waste Land*)[35]

Eliot's 'City' is involved in the Spenglerian eternal recurrence of the same, where what recurs is despair and enervation. Hughes' Harlem, alternatively, possesses a dialogical energy which is absent from the first person monologue of the Eliot passage but which is, as Ralph Ellison and others have observed, an integral part of the tragi-comic nature of the blues, from initial despondency and weariness to the upbeat tempo of '*be-bop*'.[36] The lines from Hughes quoted above are not, of course, intended as a rebuttal of a wasteland ethos: yet despite Ann Douglas' claim that *The Waste Land* was not 'the crucial text of the day' for Renaissance Harlem, re-workings of the wasteland theme *do* appear in Harlem Renaissance poetry – in, for instance, Claude McKay's 'The Desolate City', published the year after Eliot's poem.[37] In more general terms, a parallel emerges between the cultural nationalisms of Harlem and MacDiarmid's Scotland, when we compare Hughes' celebration of the modern city with MacDiarmid's positive 'translations' of *The Waste Land* in his poem 'On a Raised Beach', in which the poet insists that 'This is no heap of broken images', and in his earlier sequence *A Drunk Man Looks at the Thistle*.[38] Crawford comments on the contrast between MacDiarmid's 'thistlescape' and Eliot's wasted city that, 'such a difference in poetic attitude comes not merely from temperamental differences, but from the simple fact that MacDiarmid, on the eve of his campaign for a Scottish Renaissance, had to see rebirth as hopeful'.[39]

In poem-sequences like *Montage of a Dream Deferred*, as well as in shorter, individual lyrics, Langston Hughes proposes a black version of modernism which is oppositional to, at the same time that it feeds, the psychological need for blackness and for the 'primitive' evinced by some white modernisms – Carl Van Vechten's *Nigger Heaven*, for instance, attempts to recreate the pulse of the African jungle in the heart of New York City; and the dark energies of Gatsby's Manhattan are externalised in the image of the 'three modish negroes, two bucks and a girl' who in 'haughty rivalry' pass Gatsby's cream-coloured Rolls-Royce in their black limousine, causing Fitzgerald's narrator to think, 'Anything can happen now.'[40]

It's worth thinking about what can happen, how our ideas of modernism can alter, when Hughes' Harlem is juxtaposed with Eliot's 'Unreal City', and when the ambivalent nationhood of the Lost Generation or Van Vechten's primitivist idyll are juxtaposed with the ways in which black America negotiated ideas of nationhood in the era of modernism. Where W. E. B. Du Bois sponsored the idea of a 'Talented Tenth', a minority of black intellectuals and artists who by their endeavours would ameliorate and, in Renaissance jargon, 'uplift' the situation of all black Americans, Marcus Garvey conceived of black nationhood in more concrete terms, with his ill-fated plan of relocating the 'nation within a nation' of black America to West Africa. Despite their considerable differences – Du Bois referred to Garvey as the most dangerous man in America – what these opposed versions of black America and nation have in common is an impulse toward self-determination. As Nathan Huggins has observed, 'self-determination, an aim of the Allies in the war, became a slogan in the 1920s. Black intellectuals saw in the Yugoslavs, Czechs and Irish a clue to their own emancipation . . . They, too, were a people to be defined.' As Ann Douglas comments, 'The conjunction of the two movements, nationalism abroad and Negro independence at home, was conspicuous.'[41]

However we construe black American nationhood at the time of the Harlem Renaissance, the subject of a black *modernism* is fractured by ideological and critical disagreement. In his *Modernism and the Harlem Renaissance*, Houston Baker strategically conflates 'modernism' with modernity, in order to challenge the – white – historical belongings of the 'modernism' tag. Baker argues that for black America, 'modernism' is identical with a modernity (for Baker, modernity involves a potential for black agency) which is emblematised in the figure of Booker T. Washington and his attempts to move black America up from slavery.

Baker contends that the Harlem Renaissance should be seen not in terms of formal experimentation, but instead and exclusively as an art 'of national self-definition' and as 'national cultural expression'. In Baker's thesis, and in a chiasmus redolent of the rhetoric of Frederick Douglass, 'the mastery of form' entails 'the deformation of mastery'. Baker illustrates this with reference to the work of the Harlem Renaissance poet Countee Cullen, who, known as the 'black Keats', worked within traditional forms. Baker's point is that:

If the younger generation was to proffer 'artistic' gifts, such gifts had first to be recognizable as 'artistic' by Western, formal standards, and not simply as unadorned or primitive *folk* creations . . . It seems inconceivable that . . . the congregation of Reverend Frederick Cullen's Salem Methodist Episcopal church in Harlem would have responded positively if, after the father's announcement of his son's accomplishments as a *poet*, the young Countee had produced sounds such as 'April is the cruellest month . . .'

According to Baker, it was 'the black spokesperson's necessary task' to employ 'audible extant forms in ways that move clearly *up*, masterfully and resoundingly away from slavery'.[42] Baker's argument that African-American modernism is 'radically opposed' to 'British, Anglo-American and Irish modernisms' courts a critical segregation which enables most discussions of poetic modernism to omit black writers entirely. Hughes' *Montage of a Dream Deferred* is a case in point: as Weinberger says, this is 'a work which, like all of Hughes's poetry, is inexplicably still primarily discussed in the context of African-American, and not American modernist writing'.[43] This is not to suggest, however, that black poetic modernism should simply be absorbed into a catch-all category of 'American modernist writing'[44]: on the contrary, it may be profitable to see an oppositional relationship *between modernisms* here, with black modernism 'signifying' upon white modernisms to create its own artistic space.[45]

Another counter to Baker's position is that taken by Ann Douglas in the thesis of her recent *Terrible Honesty*, of a 'complex and double empowerment; at the moment that America-at-large was separating itself culturally from England and Europe, black America, in an inevitable corollary movement, was recovering its own heritage from the dominant white culture'. Douglas points to the 'patterns of unmistakable influence and looser analogy' which 'speak volumes about the degree to which . . . black and white metropolitans stood on shared ground'. It may be that 'shared ground' is too sanguine a term for a black–white relationship which was laden with tension in the modernist era. Interconnections there are, but as Douglas herself points out, 'in America, whites may borrow from blacks with impunity, but negro use of white materials is always suspect'. In relation to the desires of some white modernisms for an energising blackness and 'primitivism', Douglas notes that: 'It is one thing to be in search of the "primitive", as white artists of the 1920s were; another thing to be told, as the black New Yorkers were, that you *are* the primitive, the savage "id" of Freud's new psychoanalytic discourse.'[46]

Alain Locke could turn white modernism's desire for the 'primitive' to black account, as in his contribution to *The New Negro*, the essay 'The Legacy of the Ancestral Arts', where Locke discusses the significance of African art forms to modernist painting, and claims that African models alone can save white art from 'sterility'.[47] Locke attempts to translate the status of Africa and the 'primitive' from that of mere *materia poetica* into a form of agency; but that white modernism remained in the driving seat is evident from the relationship between Langston Hughes and Mrs Osgood Mason, the wealthy white patroness of Hughes and other Harlem writers like Zora Hurston. In a poem published in 1939 entitled 'Poet to Patron', Hughes explores the relationship between black poetry and white money: the poem's conclusion is that

> A factory shift's better,
> A week's meagre pay.
> Than a perfumed note asking
> *What poems today?*[48]

For Mrs Mason, Hughes was a representative 'primitive', a regenerative force in the modern wasteland, where only 'pagan' rituals could save or replace a white civilisation 'in the throes of death'.[49] Malcolm Cowley makes the same point less apocalyptically in *Exile's Return*:

it was in New York and other large cities that this escape into primitivism was carried furthest and assumed a dozen different forms. It was expressed, for example, in the enthusiasm of tired intellectuals for Negro dances and music, the spirituals, the blues, Black Bottom and *Emperor Jones*; time and again one was told that the Negroes had retained a direct virility that the whites had lost through being overeducated.[50]

The politico-cultural ethos of the Harlem Renaissance is obviously different in kind from that of the separatist nationalism proposed by the Black Arts movement of the 1960s, and yet the contrast with Black Arts should not serve to cancel the declaration of nationhood or 'nationalist assertion'[51] of twenties Harlem. As has been suggested, the modernism of the Harlem Renaissance was engaged in an *oppositional relationship* with white modernisms, just as the nationalist animus of Harlem can be compared *and* contrasted with other American cultural nationalisms of the period – for instance, that of the *New Republic*, mentioned above.[52]

America in the modernist period was also the site of ideological conflicts between versions of cultural nationalism and versions of cultural *localism*. The Southern Agrarian movement, for instance, militated against a national American literature, and insisted that American literature should be redefined along regional lines. This is the argument put forward by the Agrarian Donald Davidson: 'Regionalism is a name for a condition under which the national American literature exists as a literature: that is, its constant tendency to decentralize rather than to centralize.' This opposition to a national literature pits the Agrarians of the rural South against the urban circle associated with the *New Republic*; yet Agrarian rhetoric shares with the rhetoric of the *New Republic* intellectuals a common invective against Lost Generation mores – compare, for instance, Van Wyck Brooks' comment that 'I was convinced . . . that a man without a country could do nothing of importance' with Davidson's apology for regionalism, that 'Without its background he [the American writer] is a homeless exile in the wilderness of modern life.' David Jordan suggests that Southern Agrarianism can be linked to *regionalismo* movements in South America in the 1920s and 1930s, movements which also opposed modern cosmopolitanism: *vide* Davidson's insistence that local art forms stand in opposition to eclectic internationalism, 'offering an alternative to the prevailing trend toward "rootlessness"' – Davidson here prefiguring Gary Snyder's more recent 'bioregional' challenge to the American 'delusion . . . that we exist as rootless intelligence without layers of localized contexts'.[53]

Nevertheless, the South of the Agrarians could largely be defined as such in opposition to the metropolitan centre, the New York of the *New Republic* writers: as Davidson argued, 'Regionalism . . . is in large measure a protest . . . against the false nationalism that the metropolitans have been disseminating.' Davidson rails against the condescension shown by the Eastern seaboard for the provinces and for the South – a condescension which, he suggests, is mired in political and historical, as well as cultural, ignorance: Davidson complains, for instance, that 'the Scottsboro attorneys, the shock troops of Dayton and Gastonia asked no questions about the genius of place'. For John Crowe Ransom 'the genius of place', or, to use Ransom's own phrase 'the aesthetic of regionalism', is predicated on what he calls the presence of the 'darkey', as 'one of the bonds that make a South out of all the Southern regions'. Ransom states that: 'The peculiar institution of slavery set this general area apart from the rest of the world, gave a spiritual continuity to its many regions, and strengthened them under the reinforcement of "sectionalism", which is regionalism on a somewhat extended scale.'

Donald Davidson argues that 'The weakness of New York is that in becoming a world-city and *entrepreneur* between Europe and the American hinterland, it broke the ties, intellectual and sentimental, that might have bound it to America.' Instead, Davidson suggests, 'New York was strategically placed as a port of entry for the Europeanisms with which it felt a closer communion than with the Americanisms of the hinterland.'[54] This may be so, but Davidson's argument is misleadingly partial: given views like those of Ransom on slavery and 'spiritual continuity', and the role of the 'darkey' in Southern self-definition, it isn't surprising that the *black* American self-definition and assertion of cultural identity of the twenties should have been formulated in the city, in the metropolitan centre which, in Agrarian terms, is schematically opposed to the rural hinterland.[55]

Another version of American cultural localism in the modernist era, and one which stands in contradistinction to that of the Agrarians, is the aesthetic proposed by William Carlos Williams, a bringing of the experimental techniques of European modernist art back home to forge his conception of a 'local' poetics, a poetry based in the sense of the American *place* (as opposed to the American Puritan version of America as *idea*), that Williams defines in his *In the American Grain*. Williams shared with the painter Marsden Hartley a localised sensibility – but one which did not exclude European artistic movements. David Bennett offers a useful distinction between Williams' brand of cultural localism and *New Republic* style cultural nationalism, explaining that 'a nationalist literature' – of the kind defined by the *New Republic* – 'was by definition a literature of representations': that is, a literature that promoted social realism. 'It was in programmatic opposition to the social realism of the cultural nationalists', Bennett says, 'that the expatriate American avant-gardiste magazine *transition* mounted its aggressive campaign of "non-representational" writing.' This campaign undertook 'to win for the literary medium the same autonomy, the same freedom from the obligation to re-present, that abstractionist movements in painting had already won for the visual arts'. Williams,

'the American who stayed at home, that member of the Lost Generation who never got lost', was one of *transition*'s firmest apologists – as
Bennett again points out, 'The poem and the New World, both governed by the imperative not to imitate, became virtually synonymous for
Williams in the 1920s.'[56]

In Bennett's opinion, Williams' localism finds a parallel in Joyce's use
of place: 'Like the Irish Joyce whose "break up" of the English language
Williams both defended and (in the name of beginning again) re-
pudiated as an example for American writing, Williams saw himself as
beginning again with a "borrowed" language in a locale whose identity
had already been defined by an alien culture.' For Bennett, this links 'the
modernist imperative' to 'the post-colonial imperative' in the work of
Williams and Joyce, as 'the reinvention of language' is central to both.[57]
If such be the case, then the modernism of the Irish Literary Revival as a
whole, not just that of Joyce, is a post-colonial literature to the extent
that the Revivalists explore the interactions between national and/or
regional identity and literary form. David Lloyd has argued the case for
a proto-modernist and modernist line of Irish writing, running from
James Clarence Mangan to Joyce and Beckett, that questions the
identarian thinking of romantic nationalism through formal means as
much as thematic declarations.[58] Yet the relationship between nationalism, localism and modernism in Irish poetry is more complex than
Lloyd's thesis allows. Yeats' early cultural nationalism is imbued with an
insistence on the importance of international influences on a healthy
national literature, culminating in Yeats' attempt to bring together
Celticism and symbolism in his *fin-de-siècle* collection *The Wind Among the
Reeds*. His extensive cultural polemics of the 1890s through the early
years of the Abbey Theatre are an index of his desire to overcome
sectarian ideologies informing the definition and construction of a
national literature in terms of not only content, but also form. While
Yeats campaigned vigorously for a popular literature drawing upon the
Irish ballad tradition, his own writing in the last decade of the nineteenth century becomes preoccupied with its own increasingly hermetic
medium. The stories collected in *The Secret Rose* and *The Tables of the Law
and The Adoration of the Magi* are Irish in subject matter, covering Irish
history from ancient times to the present, but are constructed and
ordered with an eye to their apocalyptic and occult symbolism; an
attention to form that extends to the complex relationship between
Althea Gyle's cover-design for the first edition of *The Secret Rose* and
the sacred book central to the volume's concluding story, 'Rosa

Alchemica'.[59] Likewise, the density and obscurity of Yeats' material in *The Wind Among the Reeds* spawns a body of notes to the collection that prefigures Eliot's annotations to *The Waste Land*. Yeats' oeuvre by the time of the 1908 *Collected Works* can thus be viewed as striving to find a balance between an aestheticist or high modernist concern with form-as-content and the drive to create or 'revive' a national literature. It is in this context that the Revival's idealisation of the West and of the Irish peasantry should be viewed. The primitivism of the Revival is, of course, a nationalist assertion of an essential difference between the Irish and the English; yet, as a number of critics have observed, it is equally recognisable as a high modernist reaction to nineteenth-century positivism and myths of 'progress' in favour of a return to archaic well-springs of knowledge and culture.[60] To this extent, the modernism and nationalism of the Revival are inextricably interwoven, a fact which constitutes a powerful counterargument to the over-easy identification of modernism and an internationalist mindset. Ireland thus proved attractive to non-Irish writers for whom it constituted less a geographical entity than an imaginative space free from the encroachments of modernity. The career of the English decadent poet Lionel Johnson exhibits the attraction of Irish nationalism conceived as more an extension of *fin-de-siècle* aestheticism than a coherent ideological stance. As Seamus Deane observes: 'Whistler's London was not sufficiently twilit; Yeats' Ireland had more of the tremulous glimmer so beloved of the decadent school.'[61] Johnson – a friend of Yeats who contributed to the Revival's polemical battles of the 1890s, wrote an elegy for Parnell and chose the title *Ireland, with Other Poems* for his collection of 1897 – illustrates the aesthetic appeal of Ireland to a poetics transitional to modernism.

Further, the cultural primitivism of the Revival is inseparable, in Yeats and other Protestant writers of the Revival, from a more or less conscious sense of political and social marginalisation.[62] It granted writers whose Anglo-Irish background distanced them from the majority of the population a compensatory and wish-fulfilling rejection of those forces that were rapidly rendering them a social and political anachronism. Yet that marginalisation finds expression in the little-remarked regionalism of the Revival, in which feelings of insecurity within an emergent modern nation are partially neutralised by identification with locality as opposed to nation. In this context, it is relevant to consider Yeats' ambivalent admiration for the regionalism of the nineteenth-century poet William Allingham, whose attachment to the town of his birth clearly found an echo in Yeats' nostalgia for the Sligo of his youth: 'To feel the entire fascination of his poetry, it is perhaps necessary to have spent one's childhood, like the present writer, in one of those little seaboard Connaught towns. He has expressed that curious devotion . . . that is not national, but local, a thing at once more narrow and idyllic. He sang Ballyshannon and not Ireland.'[63] The attraction of region as a means of rooting one's art within place, and thus subduing the feelings of alienation from nation that prompt such localism, is to be seen in Yeats' 1904 revisions to his *Stories of Red Hanrahan*. Assisted by Augusta Gregory, Yeats recast these stories 'In the beautiful country speech of Kiltartan', in order to bring them 'nearer to the mind of the country places where Hanrahan and his like wandered and are remembered'.[64] Gregory's Kiltartanese replaces the Paterian prose of the original tales, yet it is equally stylised, a self-conscious reproduction of local dialect that in its preoccupation with the literary medium betrays an anxiety to be 'nearer' the elusive genius of place. It thus displaces rather than overcomes the Revivalist fidelity to romantic nationalism's spirit of the nation. It is thus no surprise that Yeats' regionalist yearnings, in the early essay on Allingham, do not fully quell his commitment to a poetry touched by nationalism and influenced by symbolism: 'In greater poets everything has relation to the national life or to profound feeling; nothing is an isolated artistic moment; there is a unity everywhere, everything fulfils a purpose that is not its own; the hailstone is a journeyman of God, and the grass blade carries the universe upon its point'.[65] The half-quotations from Blake (whom, incidentally, Yeats claimed was of Irish descent) are indicative of the importance of the symbolic imagination to a national literature, through the organic 'unity' common to the literary symbol and the nation. However, Yeats' gravitation over the 1890s to the example of Villiers de l'Isle Adam's *Axël*, and other manifestations of French and Belgian symbolism, illustrates his contrary adherence to *fin-de-siècle* aestheticism, and the symbolic artist's alienation from sociopolitical determinants. Yeats' mature modernism has its origins in the fruitful contradictions of his early meditations on literature and nationality, exemplifying David Harvey's contention that, in modernism, 'The tensions between internationalism and nationalism, between globalism and parochialist ethnocentrism, between universalism and class privileges, were never far from the surface.'[66]

These tensions surface in several later Irish modernist poets whose work is usually seen as closer to that of Joyce than that of Yeats. Thomas MacGreevy, whose admiration for Joyce can be gauged by his contribution to *Our Exagmination Round His Factification for Incamination of Work in*

Progress,[67] brings together, in his 1934 *Poems*, a sensibility informed by both the European avant-garde and Irish nationalism. Critics have tended to view these two aspects of his work as, to some degree, incompatible, and have further suggested that the tension between them was, finally, detrimental to his poetic productivity. This said, the combination of experimental form and a strong sense of national identity links MacGreevy's work to that of many modernist writers and artists, before and after the First World War, from the Futurists to Dada. In this respect, MacGreevy's poetic needs to be held against Beckett's better-known antipathy toward cultural nationalism, formulated as early as 1934, in a pseudonymous article for the *Bookman*, 'Recent Irish Poetry'.[68] Beckett's denunciation of the 'antiquarianism' of the Irish Literary Revival, and its progeny, is a polemic subsequently continued in Brian Coffey's vigorous denunciation of Yeats and his influence on Irish poetry, and in the pages of the neo-modernist Irish journal, the *Lace Curtain* (1969–78), on the editorial policy of which, from the early 1970s, Coffey exerted a shaping influence. From 'Recent Irish Poetry' to the *Lace Curtain* (which, significantly, saw the first reprinting of Beckett's 1934 essay) a polemic is mounted that, roughly put, construes the formal developments of modernism, its response to that which Beckett memorably calls 'the breakdown of the object', as an irrelevance to a poetry committed to the representation of land and nation. If, as argued above, the Literary Revival's Celticism, though the product of eighteenth- and nineteenth-century 'antiquarianism', is a part of European modernism,[69] still, Beckett is right to see that its tropes ran the risk of ossifying into lifeless conventions, to the extent that the avant-garde's deconstructive response to high modernism, as evinced elsewhere in Europe, does not occur in Ireland. Rather, a powerfully realist dismantling of Revivalist and Irish Ireland idealisations of nation takes place, of which Patrick Kavanagh's *The Great Hunger* stands as the poetic counterpart to the fictions of Seán Ó Faolain and Frank O'Connor.

Nevertheless, modernist poetry in Ireland after the Revival pursues its own dialogue with nation and nationalism; breaking with 'antiquarianism' it does not sever its connections with Ireland. Beckett's firm rejection of cultural nationalism, particularly in his earlier writings, relies heavily on allusions to Ireland. A number of his poems, as Lawrence Harvey has documented, have Irish settings;[70] while in his fiction – from *More Pricks than Kicks* and *Murphy*, and through *Watt* to the post-war *Trilogy* – such references to recognisable location become more coded, but are discernible as late as the 1980s work *Company*. The presence of Ireland in

Beckett's oeuvre allows us to see the extent to which his modernism is informed, at its inception, by an engagement with the ideologically repressive and coercive forces of the Irish Free State (and, later, the Republic of Ireland) in as interrogative a fashion as that of the late Yeats. Likewise, the poetry of Coffey remains preoccupied with the matter of Ireland, especially in his 1962 *Missouri Sequence*. Nationality, in Coffey, provides one spur to his complex meditations on the social and cultural grounds that inform and partially direct the individual's existential choices and metaphysical commitments. Similarly, Denis Devlin's poetry is coloured, though more directly, by post-revolutionary Ireland, for which state he served as a diplomat from the mid 1930s to the late 1950s. Devlin's uneasy flirtation with the pre-war avant-garde, and his subsequent development of a poetic comparable to that of the New Critical poetics of Allen Tate and Robert Penn Warren, should be read in the context of Ireland's passage from revolution through internecine war to, by the time of the Emergency, neutrality. Devlin's trajectory, from his dabblings with a 'revolution of the word' to a modernism committed to an autotelic structure, provides an oblique reflection – on the level of form, rather than that of content – of his response to questions of national autonomy and Ireland's place within an increasingly unstable Europe in the decades immediately succeeding independence.

Challenging Marshall Berman's famous account of modernism and modernisation, in *All That Is Solid Melts Into Air*, as casting modernism in too narrowly uniform a fashion, Perry Anderson has identified the 'multiplicity of Modernisms' in Europe before 1914 as 'a cultural force-field "triangulated" by three decisive co-ordinates'. Firstly, 'the codification of a highly formalized *academicism* in the visual and other arts, which itself was institutionalized within official regimes of states and society still massively pervaded, often dominated, by aristocratic or landowning classes that were . . . still setting the political and cultural tone in country after country of pre-First World War Europe'; secondly, the 'emergence within these societies of the key technologies or inventions of the second industrial revolution; that is, telephone, radio, automobile, aircraft, and so on'; and thirdly, 'the imaginative proximity of social revolution'.[71] From one standpoint, modernist artists found in the academicism of the *anciens régimes* a stultified culture against which to react, but the conservative values of which still harboured qualities modernism sought to redeem from the market place. From another standpoint, the emancipatory promise of the new technology provided a stimulus to creative thought and practice, as in the various futurisms of the pre-Great-War period. The 'haze of social revolution drifting across the horizon of this epoch'[72] added an apocalyptic dimension to the work of many modernists, deepening a sense of the critical urgency of intervening in the precarious future of European society. While the First World War irrevocably changed these coordinates, claims Anderson, 'it did not eliminate any of them; for another twenty years they lived on in a kind of hectic afterlife', with the aristocratic classes still influential in politics in Germany, France and Britain, and the social effects of mass production only beginning to become tangible in Germany and France. For Anderson, Europe, in this respect, was 'still over a generation behind America in the structure of its civilian industry and pattern of consumption on the eve of the Second World War'.[73] The problem with Anderson's reconstruction of the historical context for European modernism is that, contrary to its intentions, it signally *fails* to account for the very multiplicity of modernist movements it sets out to explain, Anderson's diversity of modernisms inhabiting what would appear to be a largely undifferentiated Europe. The variegated nature of European modernisms in this period can be traced more convincingly to the gradual and *uneven* corrosion of the *anciens régimes* as the aristocratic orders gave way to bourgeois societies. As Alex Callinicos maintains, 'the survivals of the agrarian order' after 1900 'have to be seen in the context of the progressive restructuring of European social formations to reflect the predominance of capital'.

For example, Britain's transformation to bourgeois society being completed before industrialisation, its relative paucity of modernism (which Anderson concedes), may be seen according to Callinicos to derive from precisely the absence of the kind of dislocations attendant upon industrialisation as experienced in, for instance, Russia. 'The uneven and incomplete nature of this development added to the dislocating and disruptive impact of industrialization', resulting in the differences between the various European modernisms.[74] British modernism is usually judged a tamer affair than its American or European counterparts: the subtleties of Forster and Woolf deriving in the last instance from precisely the absence of the social dislocations and disruptions Callinicos and others see as a necessary prerequisite to the historical avant-garde's restless experiments. Furthermore, it is frequently observed that, in Fredric Jameson's words, 'what we think of as the *English* canon are in fact social marginals of various kinds, when not

outright foreigners'.[75] Of the 'outright foreigners' Pound was central to
the formation of Vorticism, the short-lived English contribution to
avant-gardism prior to the First World War, the journal of which chose
to foreground the movement's relation to place: *Blast* erupted as the
'Review of the Great London Vortex', and, as Christopher Butler has
argued, 'raised great hopes for co-operative enterprise between the arts,
and indeed, in the minds of its promoters, for the status of London as a
modernist centre'.[76] Pound's role, and that of Wyndham Lewis and
others, was to promote a Renaissance in the arts, poetic and visual,
which depended on a cultural centre, a city-vortex corresponding to the
Italian city-states of the past: 'LONDON', in the words of the first issue of
Blast, 'IS *NOT* A PROVINCIAL TOWN'.[77] Vorticism thus positioned itself
against competing national and/or metropolitan avant-gardes elsewhere, its modernism reinforced, *Blast* suggested, by Britain's highly
developed industrial base, its privileged status as a nation-state that had
'made it new' before all others. London *is* modernity, the city is the
Vortex, a node of artistic energy that made good Pound's belief that 'all
civilisation has proceeded from cities and cenacles'.[78] As a site of
'civilisation' London is also possessed of the authority of tradition. Thus,
while Vorticism was derivative of Italian Futurism in its scornful attitude
toward the bourgeoisie and shock-tactic methods of disseminating its
ideas – *Blast*'s layout and design clearly owes much to Marinetti's
typographical experiments – the Great London Vortex was intended by
Pound and Lewis as the bringing together of modernity and tradition.
'LONDON' denotes such a fusion: it is a city-vortex in which the new is
contained and given order by the past, an apt location for Pound's and
Lewis' desire to 'combine', in Peter Nicholls' words, 'a Futurist sense of
dynamism with a rather different notion of bounded form', the latter the
bequest of the artistic tradition to the present moment.[79]

   Pound countered what he termed 'The Rage or Peevishness which
Greeted the First Number of Blast' with the comment: 'Throughout the
length and breadth of England and through three continents BLAST has
been REVILED by all save the intelligent. / WHY? / Because BLAST alone
has dared to show modernity its face in an honest glass.'[80] Of course,
Blast was more a fairground mirror than 'an honest glass'; furthermore,
it was not 'alone', as Pound claims, but one among the many responses
made by movements and individuals ('through three [*sic*] continents')
faced by modernity. The argument of this collection of essays is that
such responses and reactions can be profitably explored by attending to
the locations of modernism.

The foregoing discussion has offered a selective investigation of some of the Anglo-American locations of modernism: the chapters which follow map the terrain we have skirted here, and suggest, collectively, a topography of poetic modernism which contributes to, at the same time that it offers a fresh perspective on, contemporary revaluations of modernisms.

PART ONE

Obstinate isles: the Anglo-Celtic archipelago

CHAPTER I

MacDiarmid in Montrose

Robert Crawford

> A glance at the records of literary history shows – in contradistinction to the old sneer, 'Can any good thing come from Nazareth?' – that few indeed of our writers have been born and written their books in the great cities in comparison to the number belonging to – and preferring to continue working in – our small towns . . . In a very real sense in the 'Twenties Angus (and particularly Montrose) was the cultural centre of Scotland.[1]

Christopher Murray Grieve, who went on to write under the name Hugh MacDiarmid and a plethora of other pseudonyms, reacted enthusiastically to *Ulysses* and *The Waste Land* in 1922. Both works were important to his poetry. Again, he relished Wallace Stevens' *Harmonium* in 1924, and, whether as a reviewer for the *New Age* or for many other periodicals, he inveighed against 'provinciality of outlook' and was alert to the developments of international modernism.[2] My chapter starts with those reminders, because most of it will deal with MacDiarmid's particular location in small-town Scotland. There, without at all renouncing international concerns, he matured in various areas of his work through an interaction with the minutely local. He fused the immediate and vernacular with the transnational and synthetic practices of modernist writing. In so doing, he can be seen as developing an exemplary aesthetic of the local–international that is in some ways as bound up with participation in the events of a small community as is the work of Robert Burns.

To argue this involves reading against the grain of some of MacDiarmid's own pronouncements as well as those of a number of his critics. We know from several studies that MacDiarmid's is synthetically assembled modernist Scots verse, yet for many readers it still carries a tang of the rural and vernacular.[3] His spiky combination of intense involvement with the grain of local language, in the life of a small town and a small country, alongside his equally intense engagement with transnational literary currents makes MacDiarmid perhaps more attractive, daring and exemplary than other figures who, for all their anxious provincial provenance, gravitated effortlessly toward the established centres of power. When Seamus Heaney sensed in MacDiarmid a cherished 'fidelity' and noted 'the intimacy of the Scottish voice and the democratic style', he was partly mishearing the sometimes Stalinist accents of the Scottish poet; but he was also picking up on resonances too often ignored.[4]

MacDiarmid wrote most of his great Scots poetry in Montrose, and it may be that readers have to go to the map to check exactly where Montrose is. That in itself helps signal something of the remarkable nature of this poet's achievement. His 'location of modernism', this Scottish east-coast burgh situated between Dundee and Aberdeen, is beautiful, ordinary and provincial. Recalling Montrose in the 1930s, MacDiarmid seemed a little puzzled by the way in which it had nourished him; he called it 'a miniature Edinburgh', but that is hardly accurate; he liked the way it was 'so small and yet radiating out', yet he had also chafed there against intellectual confinement in a town whose local paper printed endless poetic effusions from 'the democratic butcher', and whose principal commitment to poetry took the form of annual, minutely detailed reporting of Suppers held in honour of Scotland's national bard whose statue stood between Grieve's home and workplace.[5] Suffice it to say that MacDiarmid's was one of those talents most energetically quickened by marginality. Glasgow and Edinburgh, London and Dublin were places to visit, to argue and hustle in. Montrose was somewhere to live in and to produce one's very best work.

His biographer Alan Bold has chronicled MacDiarmid's time in Montrose. Others have commented on it, but given that the poems of *Sangschaw* (1925), *Penny Wheep* (1926) and *A Drunk Man Looks at the Thistle* (1926), along with much other significant work, were written between 1919 and 1929 throughout a decade of residence and intense participation in the life of the town, the poet's time there has been insufficiently studied. A good deal of what follows cites seldom-quoted and never republished material from the 1920s *Montrose Review*, because I want to suggest just how fully and minutely MacDiarmid's best work evolved out of his participation in the life of Montrose and his connection with its institutions.

In the hot summer of August 1919 in his 'wee house' (now demolished) at 65 Market Street, St Andrews, Christopher Murray Grieve, newly returned to Scotland after his demobilisation from the Royal Army

Medical Corps, was beginning to bring to fruition his dream of a re-energised Scottish literature.[6] He wrote in July to his former teacher and literary mentor, George Ogilvie, to let him know that the firm of T. N. Foulis had accepted the proposal for Grieve's first published book, an anthology to be called *Northern Numbers*, aimed at 'displaying the best of the work available by living Scottish poets'.[7] Foulis was a firm based in Edinburgh and London, but also enjoying a Boston agent and some Australasian, Canadian and Danish distribution.[8] For the 27-year-old Grieve, eager to advance the publication of his own poetry and that of his friends in the company of older, better-known and poetically conservative Scottish writers such as John Buchan, Violet Jacob and Neil Munro, this opportunity represented a breakthrough. His letters from St Andrews in 1919 characteristically communicate a rush of energy – 'it is essential' to get 'selections . . . at the earliest possible moment'.[9]

As well as working on the poetry anthology and on his own verse, Grieve in St Andrews was writing out a fair copy of a 200,000-word novel covering his wartime experiences in Salonika, Marseilles and elsewhere. Most of this never saw the light of day, but a section of it appears to survive as 'A Four Years' Harvest' in MacDiarmid's first authored volume, *Annals of the Five Senses*, published a few years later in 1923. Glancing toward Bergson and recent scholarship of various kinds, incorporating verse quotations and delighting in vertiginous shifts, this writing has a protagonist whose 'mind was like a hayrick aflame'.[10] On the one hand it draws on Grieve's experiences of the feverish horrors of a war during which he had caught malaria, and on the other hand it tries effortfully to be modern. This is the Grieve who earlier in 1919 had planned a study of Conrad, written an 'essay in futurism' ('If *Blast* were still being issued it might appear there'), and claimed to be in contact with such figures as Valéry and Gide.[11] Yet just as Grieve was copying out his vast prose work, and making progress with his first anthology, the street outside his house in this small east-coast Scottish university town was busy with the setting up of stalls and entertainments for the Lammas Market, a traditional fair with 'stands, booths, shows, etc.', held each August on the cobbled streets of the mediaeval burgh.[12] With its origins in the harvest festival of the agricultural year, the Lammas Fair looked more to the world of the 'ploughman poet' Robert Burns (one of whose most famous celebratory songs begins 'It was upon a Lammas night') than to the world of aggressively post-*Blast*ian modernity.[13] Closed to traffic, MacDiarmid's part of Market Street played host to 'Houpla-stands . . . shooting-galleries, swing boats, and a variety of games of chance'. If one of the main attractions at the 1919 Market fair was a display of motor cars, then connecting post-World War I modernity to a much older way of life were 'An old fiddler who has visited St Andrews on market-days for many years and was playing his reels and strathspeys as spiritedly as ever, and another old man grinding "Home Sweet Home" on a rickety organ'. Between South Street and Market Street lines of dancers performed spirited reels.[14] This was the still identifiable folk world underlying earlier Scottish poems such as the St Andrews professor William Tennant's long, boisterous *ottava rima* depiction of Fife market revels in 'Anster Fair' (1812) or Burns' reelingly carnivalesque 'Tam o' Shanter' which famously begins 'As market-days are wearing late'.[15] To MacDiarmid, born and brought up in the small Scottish Borders town of Langholm with its own folk festival of the Common Riding, this world of the non-metropolitan community was familiar and became in some ways central to his best work. If such various European modernists as the Jules Laforgue of 'Pierrots', the Stravinsky of *Petrushka*, and the Satie and Picasso of *Parade* could be said to have drawn on aspects of the carnivalesque, then they did so in ways that were more mannered and refracted than MacDiarmid's experience of Scottish folk festivities. Yet the Scottish poet also developed a powerful will toward modernity and love of modernist techniques and textures.

A similar modernist ambition and jagged restlessness can be sensed in the first book by MacDiarmid's near-contemporary the Orcadian farmer's son Edwin Muir whose *We Moderns* (1918) was dedicated to A. R. Orage, that often 'anonymous and polypseudonymous' writer coveted for Scotland by the young C. M. Grieve.[16] Orage was editor of the *New Age*, where many of Muir's volume's contents had appeared as articles. Directed against 'a theory of art by the average man for the average man', *We Moderns* repeatedly invokes Nietzsche, and argues that 'Inequality is the source of all advancement.'[17] Yet, as the book's subtitle 'Enigmas and Guesses' suggests, Muir's Supermannish determination is in part very clever bluster. He is obsessed with 'What is Modern' and his book, published a year before Eliot's 'Tradition and the Individual Talent', is innovative, especially in the context of MacDiarmid and Scottish modernism:

It is time we erected a standard whereby to test what is modern. To be an adherent of all the latest movements – that is at most to be anarchistic, eclectic, inconsistent – call it what you will. Futurism, Realism, Feminism, Traditionalism may be all of them opposed or irrelevant to modernity. It is not sufficient that movements should be new – if they are ever new; the question is, To what end are they? If they are movements in the direction of emancipation, 'the elevation of the type Man', then they are modern; if they are not, then they are movements to be opposed or ignored by moderns. If modernism be a vital thing it must needs have roots in the past and be an essential expression of humanity: in short, it can only be a tradition. The true modern is a continuator of tradition as much as the Christian or the conservative: the true fight between progress and stagnation is always a fight between antagonistic *traditions*. To battle against tradition *as such* is, therefore, not the task of the modern; but rather to enter the conflict – an eternal one – for his tradition against its opposite: Nietzsche found for this antithesis the symbolism of Dionysus and Apollo. Does a tradition of modernity exist? Is there a 'modern spirit' not dependent upon time and place, and in all ages modern?[18]

Muir soon abandoned his battling Nietzschian stance, and his book was not reprinted after 1920; yet he hung on to his own copy, inscribed 'Edwin Muir, 1918', through many moves over several continents.[19] *We Moderns* seems to teeter between the Victorian milieu of, say, Matthew Arnold's 'On the Modern Element in Literature', and a much more aggressive, anti-popular stance of what Muir pioneeringly calls 'modernism'. His view of tradition prefigures that of T. S. Eliot.

Related tensions between modernist anti-popularism and interest in traditions (which, in the context of Scottish literature, often means popular traditions), between the language of the nineteenth century and earlier on the one hand and that of a determined modernity on the other, characterise the work of C. M. Grieve. His development shows that to be a Scottish modernist involves something of a contradiction in terms, a clash that sets high modernism's attraction to the anti-popular against the dominant, popular strand in much of the best-known Scottish writing of the eighteenth and nineteenth centuries. Such a clash became for MacDiarmid both empowering and destabilising, leading him toward a poetry and politics of brilliantly eccentric excess. A hugely ambitious writer, publishing his first article in A. R. Orage's Nietzsche-rich *New Age* in 1911 at the age of eighteen, Grieve was always eager to engage with cosmopolitan energies and international currents. Yet if, as I argued in *Devolving English Literature*, there is an aspect of modernism as a whole that is crucially provincial, then MacDiarmid's career and poetry exemplify this acutely.[20] For a good deal of the 1930s, when his most adventurous English-language work was written, MacDiarmid lived on the remote Shetland island of Whalsay, a fact that has attracted not inconsiderable comment.[21] Yet MacDiarmid's time in Montrose during the 1920s is in its way equally remarkable as, evolving his 'synthetic Scots' work, he darts about on a literary spectrum that runs from *The Waste Land* to 'Tam o' Shanter'. His work as small-town newspaperman, councillor, propagandist and political activist operates symbiotically with his literary and linguistic imaginings. C. M. Grieve, soon to become 'Hugh MacDiarmid', is the modernist at the Lammas Fair.

Soon, though not immediately, after he left St Andrews in the autumn of 1919 Grieve and his wife Peggy were living in the Angus town of Montrose where the poet (who had worked on local newspapers before the Great War) had obtained a job as chief reporter on the Liberal *Montrose Review*, one of Scotland's oldest weekly local papers. Local wisdom has it that he wrote most of the paper, and MacDiarmid recalled how he also wrote leaders for the Tory *Montrose Standard* 'without any difficulty at all'.[22] Being a newspaperman helped develop in Grieve various skills and techniques which were of use to him as a writer and campaigner alert to 'publicity value'.[23] 'Journalism', he argued in 1922, 'rightly conceived is a training in the understanding of public affairs and in the formulation and expression of opinion.'[24] The *Review* might also function as part of Grieve's literary proselytising. By early 1920, its readers were being reminded that 'It is not generally known that one of the most consistent and interested patrons of Montrose Library is Mrs Violet Jacob, the well-known poetess and novelist, and acknowledged to be Scotland's greatest exponent of the Doric.'[25] Violet Jacob, who had published several collections of poetry and novels, was one of the poets whose contributions Grieve secured for the first *Northern Numbers*.

From early in his Montrose residency, Grieve began to take part in and harness the energies of the local community. By 1 March 1920 he was singing the 'Red Flag' at the weekly meeting of the Montrose Branch of the Independent Labour Party, having opened that Monday's debate on Divorce Law reform. The same occasion saw Grieve elected Secretary of the Montrose ILP and voted a delegate to the Montrose and District Trades and Labour Council.[26] At the following week's meeting he was appointed one of three men 'to form a Committee to organize dramatic performance of short propagandist plays'.[27] There were various causes being fought in and around Montrose at the time. One long-running argument was over the licensing laws. Home to a large brewery and a substantial number of pubs as well as to examples of the Temperance Hotel, the Montrose area was well aware of the era of Prohibition.[28] 'Freedom! A drunk man free to annoy and molest others . . .!' exclaimed one local official in early 1920, and the theme of prohibitionist Pussyfooters versus liberalising Antipussyfooters runs on through the columns of the *Montrose Review* throughout the 1920s.[29] His local actions, his 'susceptibility to whisky' and his literary work make it clear which side the author of *A Drunk Man Looks at the Thistle* was on in such a debate.[30]

The Grieves were away from Montrose from the autumn of 1920 until April 1921, but on their return the *Montrose Review* became on many occasions a clear vehicle for the fledgeling poet's ploys. So, in May 1921 there appears over the initials 'B. L'. a complaint about how hard it is to find publishers for 'genuine artistic books unable to command more than a very limited sale – poetry, belles lettres, and the like'. This is followed by a laudatory review of Jane Findlater's *A Green Grass Widow and Other Stories* which praises the way

these tales, essentially national, deserve to stand beside Cumminghame-Grahame's [*sic*] Scottish sketches; and the difference, not only in art but in tone between them, and the tales of Barrie, Crockett, and Ian Maclaren is of great interest alike to the student of Scottish life or letters. They were windows behind which the clearest brain can delight to stand; whereas the 'Window in Thrums' would be smashed aside, its distorting panes scattered in all directions, by anyone determined to have a clear view to-day.

One wonders just how many Montrosians of the time would identify with 'the taste of a young reader who savours with quick gratitude every word written by Joseph Conrad, R. B. Cunninghame Graham, Aldous Huxley, Virginia Woolf, and the others in whom we all delight'. Many stylistic touches and gestures proclaim this unsigned review as Grieve's work, but what is most striking is the way in which he is arguing for a sometimes iconoclastic sensibility which can appreciate the work of the avant-garde writers just mentioned, but can nonetheless also savour the tales of such much more traditional Scottish writers as Violet Jacob and Jane Findlater: 'The enthusiasms of a disciple of Dorothy Richardson are all very well – provided they are counterbalanced by a solid respect for and appreciation of work such as this.'[31]

The three volumes of *Northern Numbers* which Grieve edited over the years 1920–2 demonstrate such a catholic sensibility, including some avant-garde work and a lot more conservative Scottish verse, so that 'certain Scottish poets of today' appear to sponsor younger poets of 'to-morrow!' As he acknowledged in the first, November 1920 volume, these Scottish anthologies were to an extent based on the example of

'what the "Georgian Poetry" series has done for a particular group of
mainly-English poets of our period'. Such a precedent seems an odd one
for an aspiring avant-garde writer to set, and little of the verse in *Northern
Numbers* seems very avant-garde in anything more than aspiration.
Grieve was aware that 'Group-poetry developments have been a
marked feature of recent British poetry publishing', but as the sole poet
to appear in all three of his *Northern Numbers* anthologies, he still seemed
something of a minor player in the band of writers whom he had
assembled.[32]

Already, though, Grieve was attempting to sculpt a sense of himself as
bound up with a group of authors bringing about a revival. As 'The
World of Books, A Literary Causerie' by 'B. L.' put it in the *Montrose
Review* for 3 June 1921, 'The revival – for it is a revival – of Regionalism
in British literature predicates for its success the discovery of some
effective solution to the great publishing problem.' This was the problem outlined by 'B. L.' in an earlier issue, and the most attractive
solution now advanced ('So far as poetry goes this is certainly the case') is
that of 'Group publication':

The method enables a number of young writers to reach a wider circle than any
one of them could command. It reinforces the attracting powers of a single
aspirant to literary honours with the power of a school. Each contributor
instead of remaining indefinitely a voice in the wilderness participates in a
movement in which the strength of each contributor has added to it the
additional force of a united action. Nor need group publication necessarily
imply any identity either in technique or ideation. It involves in the nature of it
no surrender of artistic freedom to any formula.[33]

This attitude to the group – that it was a useful mechanism for
promoting new work, for nurturing those who might otherwise be left
'in the wilderness', yet that it might also leave room for idiosyncratic
talent – characterises MacDiarmid's stance toward various associations
in which he participated, whether in life or letters, during his Montrose
years. These include 'the Scottish Renaissance group' as well as Montrose Council, political parties, local organisations and the international
Burns Federation. Groups provided sounding-boards and platforms.
While MacDiarmid contributed to several as organiser or supporter, he
also used them as punchbags or suppliers of ready antagonists against
whom to define his ideas. As he developed, he seems often to have
courted linguistic, geographical and political marginalisation, at the
same time as attempting to link his work to groups or movements which,

in the long term, he hoped would come to dominate the cultural and political map. Few poets have had such a determined strategic imagination.

In the 1921 *Montrose Review* the writer goes on to discuss a further application of group publication to the field of journals, 'the Chapbook idea' as exemplified by 'The Liverpool Chapbook':

The essence of such an undertaking lies in having a sufficiently good little group of local writers and artists capable of an expression of themselves on a certain level, and with such a significance in their work as is distinctively local, or at least regional. How many provincial centres in Great Britain can even attempt this? What would be the fate of such a project in Montrose? The Biblical test of the essential ten just men would fail. No ten writers of any ability at all exist even in Glasgow or Edinburgh – let alone Montrose.[34]

On 26 August 1922 Grieve launched from Montrose the monthly *Scottish Chapbook*. The magazine was published from the Grieves' recently built council house at 16 Links Avenue (alias 'The Scottish Poetry Bookshop'), and ran for fifteen months; it would be followed in May 1923 by the *Scottish Nation*, 'Scotland's only National Literary Paper, Edited by Councillor C. M. Grieve, Montrose', available 'from any local newsagent or direct from The "Review" Press, 97 High Street, Montrose'.[35] Contributors to these periodicals soon included Neil Gunn and Edwin Muir as well as C. M. Grieve / Hugh MacDiarmid, and articles from the *Scottish Nation* on such topics as 'The Evolution of Scottish Nationalism' appeared also in the *Montrose Review*.[36] So, however impossible a Montrose-based literary paper might have seemed to 'B. L.' in 1921, by 1922 it was an actuality. To decide what was impossible, and then to do it, is characteristic of Grieve, whose literary and political careers developed through a series of spectacular U-turns. Such a predictably unpredictable course also governed his relationships with the groups he created, and with his local community in Montrose. It is bound up with the evolution of his finest poetry.

Grieve threw himself into the life of Montrose with vigour. In June 1921 a column in the *Review* is championing the provision of first-class library facilities and arguing that 'a good going Literary and Debating Society' is 'badly needed in Montrose', alongside quality 'amateur theatricals'.[37] Later that year the Angus small-town paper began to champion such unlikely works as the Scot Douglas Ainslie's 1907 translation of Croce's *The Essence of Aesthetic* (later an enthusiasm of 'Hugh MacDiarmid'), as well as new poems in Scots by Violet Jacob such as her 'Tam i the Kirk' (another MacDiarmid favourite) which is rated as 'among the few supreme expressions in modern poetry of true Scottish genius'.[38] Grieve in 1921 had made a name for himself by attacking proposals from the Vernacular Circle of the London Burns Club to revive 'Braid Scots'. He noted that 'The intention in fact is to do something similar in Scotland for "Braid Scots" as the Irish nationalists have achieved in Ireland for the Irish Gaelic; and as our own Highlanders in Scotland have attempted with less success for Highland Gaelic.' While he protested himself 'as keenly nationalistic as the most enthusiastic London Burnsians', Grieve was extremely sceptical of this 'Braid Scots' movement. His propagandistic and self-aggrandising argument was not only conducted through the national press, but also within the Montrose community.[39] Indeed, it is arguable that the clearest signs of Grieve's evolving aesthetic develop through his engagement with local groups, and through his publicity-hungry work on the local paper. So, for instance, in December 1921 the *Montrose Review* carries a full report of an address given to the Montrose 'YMCA Literary and Debating Society' by 'Mr C. M. Grieve' on the subject of 'Contemporary Scottish Poetry'. Partly, Grieve's talk is clearly designed to bolster his *Northern Numbers* anthologies, since he included readings from a number of the poets included. More interesting is his account of his flyting with the Burns movement, and, in particular, the way in which he argues strongly against modern attempts to nurture artificially poetry in Scots. Yet toward the end he hesitates, then pivots round to a position which leaves open the possibility of major achievement in poetry in Scots. Grieve makes it clear that he has been arguing straightforwardly that:

the hand of the clock could not be put back, and that Scotland, having evolved tremendously in all human directions since 'Braid Scots' ceased to be used, 'Braid Scots' was no longer an adequate vehicle for the expression of the thoughts and feelings of a great industrial population who knew only a few phrases of it, and who had whole aspects (and in certain respects the most important aspects) to their lives for which 'Braid Scots' made no provision and had no resources of expression, and which did not exist at all in the far-off days when Scotland was primarily a rural country and 'Braid Scots' in this form or that (for there was no standard) its distinguishing dialect. Education has worked and is working its will and the vehicle of education in Scotland is, for the most part, the English language – and rightly so in my opinion. The English language is an infinitely ampler medium than the 'Braid Scots' ever was, and through it access can be had to a far wider and ever-widening public. Even if by reviving the Doric a few new literary tendencies were ultimately developed wherein would the advantage lie? They would only be intelligible to a comparatively small number at best; and no greater writer will willingly circumscribe his potential public, and the potential influence of his work, in the interests of a parochial philology. I do not deny the forcibleness, the grip, the verve, the picturesqueness of the 'Auld Scots Tongue' any more than I forget the qualities of Greek and Latin – but 'the old order changeth, giving place to new' and the day of the Doric is a dead day. It may sound callous, but my cry in this controversy was, 'Let the dead bury their dead' – we who can write have other duties to perform – the expression of the present, with all its tremendous problems and possibilities, its realities and hopes, and fears; and the endowment of the future . . . And yet I admit that even yet the Doric has its place. For literature is still being produced in the Doric. Even the merely linguistic influence of the great genius of Burns is unexhausted; but infinitely greater than that line which puzzles schoolboys in the 'Mouse' – 'A daimen-icker in a thrave' [–] is the spirit of his declaration, made not in the Doric, but in English, and yet with the true Scottish note in it:- 'A man's a man for a' that'. In literature as in life 'the letter killeth but the spirit giveth life'.[40]

Grieve here seems much keener on preserving the spirit of Burns than on using his Scots language.

Critics are used to repeating MacDiarmid's insistence on Dunbar rather than Burns as a poetic model, yet it was through a tangled engagement with Burns and his supporters that Grieve in Montrose moved toward producing MacDiarmid's Scots lyrics. The 'keenly nationalistic' Grieve is publicly evident in his 1922 letter to the *Montrose Review* campaigning 'for a Scottish Free State' and rallying local support for a proposed branch of the Scottish National League in Montrose whose 'sole object' would be 'the restoration of Scottish Independence', while a week later a substantial article in the paper also championed this cause as advocated by 'Mr Grieve', at the same time as sniping at 'the annual supper of Montrose Burns Club' and the way 'too many [Burnsites] have only a superficial knowledge of the man and his writings'.[41] Grieve by now was 'Councillor Grieve' of Montrose, arguing against wage reductions for council employees, making himself known in the local paper as 'an enthusiastic Home Ruler', and as 'secretary of the Montrose Branch of the League of Nations Union'; he was convinced that 'Nationalism and Internationalism presuppose and confirm each other.'[42] In Montrose, he recalled at the end of his life, 'I became immersed in local politics of all kinds, I became a Town Councillor and Magistrate and what not – a member of the Parish Council, a member of the Education Authority and that led to more and more public speaking.'[43] Here not only Hugh MacDiarmid the poet, but also

MacDiarmid the ubiquitous and often ferocious speaker and politician was trained and stepped on to the local, then the national, stage.

As a newspaperman, Grieve had contacts and outlets in the major as well as the minor media, yet the attention he gave to local affairs in Montrose is remarkable. He allied himself with men like the Home Ruler J. Spears Burt, headmaster in Ferryden, a working-class fishing community adjacent to Montrose, and the librarian James Christieson. Something of the excited debates in which Grieve participated may be sensed in the first work attributed to 'Hugh MacDiarmid', which appeared in the *Scottish Chapbook* in August and September 1922. This short dramatic piece, 'Nisbet, an Interlude in Post War Glasgow', centres round the demobbed poet Nisbet who is searching for a 'new beginning' but seems to have reached a stage of 'Brainlock' in his verse and is struggling to make headway in a climate of 'propaganda' involving 'the Scottish Home Rule Association and half-a-dozen other things'.[44] For Grieve himself in Montrose in 1922 a 'new beginning' that involved writing in Scots was bound up not only with his reception of *The Waste Land* and the poetry of T. S. Eliot (as I have argued elsewhere), but also with a new engagement with Burns and the Burns movement.[45]

Around the time he moved to Montrose, Grieve at the age of twenty-seven read Burns thoroughly for the first time.[46] Rather surprisingly, given his expressed hostility toward so many aspects of Burns Clubs, Grieve went in early September 1922 as the representative of the Montrose Burns Club to the annual conference of the Burns Federation, held that year in Birmingham. Instituted in 1908, Montrose Burns Club had as its Vice-President in 1922 Grieve's friend James Christieson and its special feature was an 'Annual songshaw for children's rendering of Burns' Works in song or recitation'.[47] The Scots word 'songshaw' or 'sangschaw' meant 'song festival' and was an early twentieth-century coinage associated with the Scottish National Song Society and the Burns movement. Hugh MacDiarmid's first collection of poems would bear the title *Sangschaw*; his second, 1926 collection would be called *Penny Wheep*, an expression meaning 'small beer' and one most familiar from a stanza of Burns' carnivalesque poem 'The Holy Fair',

> Leeze me on Drink! it gies us mair
> Than either School or Colledge:
> It kindles Wit, it waukens Lear,
> If pangs us fou o' Knowledge.
> Be't *whisky-gill* or *penny-wheep*,
> Or onie stronger potion,

It never fails, on drinkin deep,
To kittle up our *notion*,
By night or day.[48]

This stanza, called up by the title *Penny Wheep*, also forms an illuminating context for the title and trajectory of *A Drunk Man Looks at the Thistle*, in which it is quoted too. What these nods and winks suggest is how assiduously, for all his synthetically assembled and modernist-oriented Scots, MacDiarmid in Montrose was trying to woo local and international Burnsians by deploying phrases familiar from the works of the Bard, and by operating in the spirit (pun intended) of Burns.

At the 1922 Birmingham Grand Hotel dinner Thomas Amos, Honorary Secretary of the Burns Federation, paid tribute to 'the enterprise of Mr Grieve, of Montrose, in encouraging our rising bards by his publications, *Northern Numbers* and *The Scottish Chap Book* [*sic*]'.[49] In replying to the toast to Scottish Literature, Grieve made it clear that he was no stranger to Burns suppers; he was content to inhabit the traditional Burns supper rhetoric, using it to imply Burns' commitment to radical and nationalist politics. Councillor Grieve's Birmingham reply was reported to readers of the *Montrose Review*, who could perceive how their man attempted to connect the spirit of Burns with the sort of modern Scottish literature favoured by Grieve:

Scottish literature in particular Burns charged with an imperative obligation to concentrate in the love of liberty and the love of love on the solution of the great social problems of humanity – and Scottish literature to-day was striving and must continue to strive to exercise what the genius of Burns recognised as its paramount function, albeit even Burns did not conceive the difficulties and complications which had since arisen. Those who forgetful of the vast changes which had come to pass since Burns' day and of the ever-increasing complexity of our industrial civilisation, accused contemporary Scottish literature of being un-Scottish and un-Burnsian, were throwing away the substance alike of life and letters and grasping a shadow, and those who regarded Burns as the unsurpassable genius of our race implicitly accused Scotland of national decline. He for his part, while conscious of the immeasurable debt they owed to the past, looked to the present and the future . . . He believed in the future of Scottish literature just as he believed in the continuance of Scottish nationality. (Applause.)[50]

That applause marks Grieve's success in cultivating the Burns movement. In the chair at Birmingham was Dr Duncan McNaught, President of the Burns Federation, to whom Grieve dedicated a pious sonnet in 1923, hailing McNaught as a 'Moses' who 'hath established / A means to realise Burns' noblest dream' of 'Burns International' and 'eventual brotherhood'.[51] Just how far Grieve was working on linking himself to the Burns legacy is even clearer in the version of his Birmingham reply printed a few weeks later in the *Scottish Chapbook*. Here his speech concludes, 'I believe in the future of Scottish literature just as I believe in the continuance of Scottish nationality which our presence here on this occasion exemplifies; and of which such an accent as mine is surely an incorruptible witness.'[52] What is particularly odd in this act of bonding with Burns and the Burnsians is that Grieve makes no mention of the Scots language, the topic which had so exercised him in his controversy with the Vernacular Circle of the London Burns Club, and about which he had been so interestingly and passionately ambivalent in his December 1921 talk to the Montrose YMCA. The reason for Grieve's silence on this issue in September 1922 in Birmingham is surely that he was in the course of going through one of his characteristic about-turns.

For it was 30 September 1922 which saw the appearance of the first Scots lyrics by Hugh MacDiarmid. Grieve explained how 'a friend' drew his attention to Sir James Wilson's *Lowland Scotch as Spoken in the Lower Strathearn District of Perthshire* (1915), and how he then began to find in it words around which poems grew. This tale has often been repeated. Alan Bold shrewdly pointed out how one of these first two MacDiarmid poems, 'The Blaward and the Skelly', 'was clearly conceived as part of Grieve's plans to renew the Burnsian manner'.[53] This poem with its 'bonnier far was Nelly / Whom I shall see no more' is clearly sub-Burnsian as well as somewhat awkwardly in thrall to Wordsworth's Lucy poems. It is usually assumed, though, that the other September 1922 MacDiarmid poem, his great lyric 'The Watergaw', is quite magnificently unBurnsian. Certainly the way in which it synthetically assembles its most striking vocabulary from a few pages of Wilson's book goes beyond the artificiality of anything Burns did in putting together what Seamus Heaney has called 'Burns' art speech'.[54] Yet an English-language sonnet by Grieve also published in 1922 suggests that a particular passage from Burns was very deeply lodged in his mind. 'Introduzione alla Vita Mediocre' signals Grieve's strong identification with the poem's dedicatee, Italian novelist Arturo Stanghellini:

> The youth called straight from school to soldiering
> What sense of destiny and solitude
> Possessed! Lonely in all his world he stood
> His boyhood like a dream evanishing.[55]

It is salutary to recall the generally poor English-language poems which MacDiarmid published alongside his early Scots work. In the Stanghellini sonnet the word 'evanishing' finally scuppers the opening sentence. Yet to a Scottish ear that word has a particular provenance, for it occurs in a famous passage when the Scots of 'Tam o' Shanter' modulates into grandly resourced English-language moralising in a set of variations:

> But pleasures are like poppies spread,
> You seize the flower, its bloom is shed;
> Or like the snow falls in the river,
> A moment white – then melts for ever;
> Or like the borealis race,
> That flit ere you can point their place;
> Or like the rainbow's lovely form
> Evanishing amid the storm.[56]

This same passage surely underpins not the vocabulary but several key images brought together in MacDiarmid's 1922 masterpiece, 'The Watergaw', which presents one of Burns' best-known images, that of the rainbow whose form is 'Evanishing amid the storm'. Burns' poem shares with MacDiarmid's the image of falling snow presaging death, and where in the context of loss Burns has the flitting light of the aurora borealis, MacDiarmid has the 'foolish licht' of virtual extinction. It would be hard to find two more different poems than 'The Watergaw' and 'Tam o' Shanter', yet there is a vital cluster of images where they connect. Rainbows had become fit for modernism thanks to Burns' admirer D. H. Lawrence, but, for all MacDiarmid's interest in Lawrence, it is the snow-connected, storm-obscured rainbow of 'Tam o' Shanter' (a poem in which, crucially, stormy darkness is drawing on) that ghosts some of the imagery in MacDiarmid's lyric which, taking place on a wet evening at the cold end of July just before Lammas, features a shaky rainbow beyond the fall of wet snow, 'A watergaw wi' its chitterin' licht / Ayont the on-ding'.[57] It has become a valid commonplace that 'The Watergaw' exemplifies MacDiarmid's contention in 1923 that the Scottish Vernacular is 'instinct with . . . uncanny and pathological perceptions' and that 'word after word of Doric establishes a blood-bond more thrilling and vital than those deliberately sought after by writers such as D. H. Lawrence'.[58] Yet if for MacDiarmid in Montrose modernism evolved through a specific interaction with place, then the work of this modernist poet who sought to present himself as 'The Voice of Scotland' also developed through a constant dialogue and argument with the work and legacy of the poet most lauded in that place, Robert Burns.

There are many signs of MacDiarmid's success in this direction in the period just after his visit as Montrose delegate to the Birmingham Burns conference. At the 1924 Burns Federation meeting Thomas Amos was telling delegates that 'This Scottish renaissance, of which we see so many signs, has given hope that in the near future we may yet have an important Scottish author showing in his work the plasticity and colour of our dialect as a vehicle for literary expression.'⁵⁹ That same year the *Scotsman* newspaper picked up on claims advanced by C. M. Grieve and his supporter Professor Denis Saurat (who had written about a growing 'Scottish Renaissance') that MacDiarmid was 'a new Burns'.⁶⁰ The following year, introducing MacDiarmid's collection *Sangschaw*, the influential John Buchan, whose work had featured in *Northern Numbers*, and whose approval MacDiarmid had courted, presented even Mac-Diarmid's Scots language in terms of Burns: 'Since there is no canon of the vernacular, he makes his own, as Burns did, and borrows words and idioms from the old masters.'⁶¹ *Sangschaw* included a long, Scots poem, 'Ballad of the Five Senses', dedicated '*To Sir Robert Bruce, President of the Burns Federation, in appreciation of his efforts to foster a Scottish Literary Revival*'.⁶² MacDiarmid is usually presented in terms of his reaction against Burns. Even Alan Riach, who has done so much for readers of MacDiarmid by making possible the reprinting of much of his work in the Carcanet MacDiarmid 2000 edition, writes in his acute essay 'MacDiarmid's Burns' about the modern poet's charting 'a course *away from* Burns', but I think MacDiarmid's trajectory is less straightforward.⁶³ In the *New Age* in 1924, reviewing Buchan's Scots Vernacular anthology *The Northern Muse*, Grieve can certainly describe Burns' 'highest flights' as 'like the lamentable attempts of a hen at soaring; no great name in literature holds its place so completely from extra-literary causes as does that of Robert Burns'. Yet in that very same piece we may note Grieve's admiration of 'Burns at his best in such poems as "Tam o' Shanter"'.⁶⁴

'Tam o' Shanter' for MacDiarmid at this time had a particular link with Montrose. It was connected not so much by periodic articles in the *Montrose Review* which mention that its author had visited the town where he had relations, as through an early nineteenth-century poem in Hudibrastic heroic couplets, George Beattie's 'Jock o' Arnha'.⁶⁵ Mac-Diarmid several times argued in the early 1920s that this poem is not only a sort of expansion of 'Tam o' Shanter' which opens at Montrose Fair and is set in the Montrose countryside, but also 'a veritable tour-de-force, abounding in wanton humour, uncanny imaginings, and extraordinary ingenuities of rhyme and phrase; and has a gusto and abandon from start to finish rarely ˙encountered in any literature'.[66] I would suggest that alongside *The Waste Land* and the much more familiar Scottish poetry of Burns, this was a work which helped spur the wanton humour and uncanny imaginings of *A Drunk Man Looks at the Thistle*.

Beattie's Jock goes through a stormy night which affords him natural and supernatural adventures. While the plot is related to that of 'Tam o' Shanter', the form is much lengthier and looser, allowing for short interpolated poems, and for asides about other recent and contemporary poets. MacDiarmid's poem, with all its modernist rollercoasting, takes a similar tack and shares Beattie's mixture of contemporary and traditional allusion as well as Beattie's love of 'racy, old terms, many of them conveying subtle shades of significance incommunicable in English or any other language'.[67] The centenary of Beattie's suicide occurred in the summer of 1923 when a substantial article about him appeared in the *Montrose Review*, and a movement to restore the poet's gravestone below the cliffs at nearby St Cyrus (where the Grieves spent several summers) was started; a decade later MacDiarmid still remembered Beattie's poem as 'in the same category as Burns' "Tam o' Shanter"' and as having 'passages of imaginative force and verbal vigour not excelled by that masterpiece'; he also recalled Beattie's tombstone and his own 'share in organising the movement which led to its renovation'.[68] This campaign was going on during the time MacDiarmid was developing as a Scots lyricist, and Grieve, who by 1923 had read the standard memoir of Beattie, would have known too Beattie's eerie poem 'The Dream' which describes the dead rising from their graves in a Montrose churchyard. In October 1923, a month after Beattie's centenary, Grieve published his short story 'Some Day' which deals with the Montrose cemetery of Sleepyhillock and imagines 'RESURRECTION DAY at Sleepyhillock . . . a' the graves crackin' open an' the folk loupin' out'.[69] Earlier that year a report in the *Montrose Review* had stated 'Farmers, as a whole, are not blate.'[70] We can sense all these details from local affairs and literature nourishing one of MacDiarmid's finest early Scots lyrics, 'Crowdieknowe', where on the blowing of the last trumpet 'the deid come loupin' owre / The auld grey wa's' and where '*God's no blate gin he stirs up / The men o' Crowdieknowe*'.[71] In this poem from *Sangschaw* the cemetery is that of farmers from MacDiarmid's Borders boyhood, but the poem is surely brought to birth by what the poet has encountered through his life in Montrose.

What MacDiarmid did in Montrose on the micro-level spurred and reinforced his larger-scale operations. So his leading role in 1924 in organising the 'Montrose Parliamentary Society', which was inaugurated on 28 January 1924 and did not 'intend to model itself at all closely on the "Mother of Parliaments"', is of a piece with his developing, wider literary and political works.[72] Montrose was MacDiarmid's immediate launch-site. In the Parliamentary Debating Society he spoke on such topics as unemployment, Gandhi and India; his intellectualism was honed against popular resistance and sometimes incomprehension as 'questions involved were too academic and involved to be debatable in public'.[73] Yet as a local Councillor, Grieve confronted such day-to-day social problems as housing conditions and 'Too Many Beggars at Montrose' (he defended itinerant musicians and singers).[74] His participation in local affairs gave the poet a platform and let him attend such events as the Burns Federation conference and the 1924 debate on Scottish Home Rule at the Convention of Royal Burghs of Scotland held in Edinburgh in April 1924. There Grieve as a Montrose delegate moved that 'there should be established a Scottish Legislature and Executive for the control of Scottish affairs, and that this be sent to the Prime Minister, the Secretary for Scotland, and each of the Scottish Members of Parliament'.[75] No doubt having the power to report his own doings and speeches through the organ of the *Montrose Review* won him enemies as he developed the skills of media manipulation which he was to employ throughout his career; his relationship with his employer, the paper's proprietor, James Foreman, was a stormy one, and some in Montrose still remember Grieve as 'a horrible man'.[76] Again, we may sense how as artist and agitator MacDiarmid attempted locally and generally to forge a Scottish modernist poetry and aesthetic which might, in the dreamed future, gain power through its alignment with dominant cultural and political forces. His ambition and marginal vulnerability fuelled his work, yet (as in the case of Pound) also led toward a compensatory bullying which might have overtones of extremist politics. Few would have enjoyed his hectoring speech to local people on the Scottish Arts after a 1924 folk-song recital in Montrose, when he argued that the audience, who had been slow to join in the words of the songs, was

still wallowing in the slough of sordid individualism . . . That individualism was antagonistic to arts of every kind. It was a tragic thing that people should be thus unable to join together in song. It showed that something had atrophied in their hearts, shrivelling and restricting them, and depriving them of their natural freedom and vitality. It was especially sad that Mr Smith [the recitalist] should find it necessary to give explanations of famous old Scottish songs to a Scottish audience – and that these explanations should be so obviously necessary. These people were uprooted and out of touch with national traditions.[77]

One can just about feel the Montrosians wincing here, and sense the extremist rhetoric that would lead MacDiarmid, for all his socialist sympathies, to write such pieces as his 1923 'Programme for a Scottish Fascism' as '*the only thing that will preserve our distinctive national culture*'.[78] Yet it is also worth noting that this Montrose speech demonstrates Grieve's commitment to traditions of popular folksong in the period when MacDiarmid was constructing his synthetic Scots lyrics. It is out of a fusion of demotic tradition and uncompromisingly high art that MacDiarmid's Scots modernism grew.

Nor should we think of Montrose as furnishing MacDiarmid merely with a less informed, popular milieu against which to react. At the Montrose ILP meetings he could discuss Tagore and Gandhi with informed speakers; in the Burgh Hall he could praise Labour Radicalism and speak alongside the Secretary of State for Scotland.[79] Moreover, in Montrose in the 1920s Grieve found himself a member of an impressive community of artists resident in or visiting the burgh. In the summer and autumn of 1924 and at Christmas 1925, for instance, Willa and Edwin Muir were staying in Willa Muir's mother's house in the town centre and were in touch with Grieve. In October 1924 Edwin Muir published *Latitudes*, a volume of essays on topics ranging from Burns to Conrad, Dostoyevsky and Nietzsche.[80] He was completing for the Woolfs at the Hogarth Press his first volume of poems (some in Scots, some in English) and writing a series of articles on such contemporary writers as Joyce, Lawrence, Virginia Woolf and Eliot which would be collected in his 1926 book *Transition*, its preface signed 'E. M., Montrose, Scotland'; like *A Drunk Man*, *Transition* was dedicated to the composer Francis George Scott, for whom MacDiarmid wrote some of his finest lyrics. Grieve admired not only Muir's verse and his writing on European letters (examples of both had appeared from Montrose in the *Scottish Nation*) but also his essay on Burns. At the start of 1925 he was listing Muir as among the 'Scottish Renaissance' group – 'the least parochial of the whole group'; he was convinced that Muir 'has already the makings of a world-reputation' and he celebrated 'Muir's *will* that has lifted him out of our Scottish provincialism and is making him an international force'.[81] If MacDiarmid seemed to want to follow Muir in escaping provincialism, the two men also fuelled each other's work in the provincial town of Montrose.

Later accounts (by Willa Muir and others) post-date the bitter 1930s quarrel between MacDiarmid and Muir and so tend to downplay the two poets' closeness throughout the previous decade. In 1923 in response to a letter from Muir suggesting to MacDiarmid that 'a long poem in the language you are evolving would go tremendously', Mac-Diarmid dedicated to Muir his planned long poem 'Braid Scots', part of which would eventually form the verse-manifesto 'Gairmscoile' in *Penny Wheep*. Willa Muir was writing for the Woolfs *Women: An Inquiry* (1925) when she was in Montrose and her account of Grieve in *Belonging* is a useful corrective to his own strutting as it shows him very much supported by his cooking, washing and ironing spouse in the role of 'wee wifie'; it also recalls the way Grieve would come home drunk from *Review* duties such as attending 'farmers' dinners where whisky was the only drink'.[82] Yet Willa Muir's portrait of Grieve as drunk man, distant in sensibility from her own husband, is only partial. For, however temperamentally different from Grieve, the young Muir, eager to define 'the very essence of the Scottish spirit' as well as to engage with world literature, had many interests in common with the poet of *A Drunk Man*.[83] That the two finest Scottish poets of their generation should have been near-neighbours at this time, both writing for the *New Age* and other periodicals while concentrating on maturing their poetries and considering Scottish as well as other cultures, only emphasises how much Montrose can be seen as a key location of modernism, and how varied and challenging could be the society and ideas Grieve found there. If Edwin Muir at 81 High Street, Montrose, loved 'the landscape' but not 'the people', then Grieve (working along the road in Review Close at 97 High Street), for all his sometimes elitist rantings, was eager to play a full part in the community life.[84] Willa Muir was prepared to participate in town affairs; her 'brilliant analytical gifts' and her 'energy and enthusiasm' helped coach the Montrose Players' admired production of *A Midsummer Night's Dream* in early 1926.[85] However, her fine novel *Imagined Corners* (1935) presents Montrose as 'Calderwick' and deals sometimes sharply with the pulls between narrow provincialism and the yearning for imaginative release and wider horizons. Similar tensions energised MacDiarmid's work there, but the male poet seems to have found more stimulation among his hard-drinking farmers than did the female novelist who was only too keen to get away from the confining Scottish town of her upbringing.

Like Grieve, the Muirs attracted distinguished visitors to Montrose. These included the composer F. G. Scott (who helped edit *A Drunk Man*) and the educationalist A. S. Neill in whose thinking Grieve too was interested and who admired Grieve's work.[86] Grieve could discuss 'old Scots words' with Violet Jacob and modern literature with the Muirs, but these were not his only artistic contacts in the town. The sculptor William Lamb returned to his native Montrose in 1924 and, as the *Montrose Review* noted, was soon exhibiting in Edinburgh, London and Paris, winning admiration for his bronzes of male and female workers; stimulated by being part of a local artistic community committed to a Scottish Renaissance, Lamb sculpted Violet Jacob in 1925 and Hugh MacDiarmid in 1927.[87] Later Grieve's local contacts would include at 12 Links Avenue the Montrose-born novelist Tom MacDonald (who wrote as Fionn MacColla) and the splendid young Montrose painter Edward Baird whose 1927 *Figure Composition with Montrose behind* presents images of heroic workers in front of the local townscape and surrounding hills.[88] Other visitors included Compton Mackenzie, Neil Gunn (with whom MacDiarmid 'had many an all-night session'), the poet and sculptor Pittendrigh Macgillivray, critic Herbert Grierson, novelist Winifred Duke and nationalist intellectual Ruaraidh Erskine of Marr.[89]

MacDiarmid, then, was part of an artistic community in Montrose. Important stimulation came not just from contact with extraordinary locals, but also from his day-to-day journalistic work. In many ways the 1920s *Montrose Review* is typical of small community papers, particularly in the early twentieth century. Its pages are made up of a mixture of syndicated columns (on such topics as poultry and motoring), local news items (often bulletins on or from clubs and societies), lengthy reports of debates and speeches at council meetings and gatherings of Rotarians, Burns Clubs or similar bodies. In the 1920s, as today, to produce such a weekly paper with a tiny staff requires the submission from a variety of organisations of copy which the reporter–editor shapes and sometimes rewrites; reporting of such occasions as Burns Night addresses or council debates includes long direct quotations from speeches, as well as the reporter's own summaries and linking material. The published paper is, then, an amalgam of original, edited and quoted texts; the process of production is such that distinctions between these categories are frequently blurred. In short, there are strong formal connections between the production methods underlying the text of the *Montrose Review* and those underpinning the work of Hugh MacDiarmid.

MacDiarmid's journalistic training no doubt helped him maintain the remarkable volume of his prose output. Often his own prose has a syndicated quality; readers of the MacDiarmid 2000 edition may note how frequently ideas, words, references and phrases are recycled in various prose pieces. Especially in such works as *Scottish Eccentrics* (1936) or *Lucky Poet* (1943) vast chunks of quotations from his own and other authors' writings bulk out the text so that, despite flashes of MacDiarmidian pungency, the book often appears as much a hastily edited anthology as an original text. Even in MacDiarmid's earlier prose from the 1920s there is a great deal of quotation and of recycling from piece to piece as the author under a number of pseudonyms puts over similar points; at times it is as if MacDiarmid is writing all the letters in the correspondence column of a newspaper, and this technique, which can vitiate his prose, surely derives from his journalistic experience.

A very similar technique produces his later, largely English-language poetry, and has given rise to charges of plagiarism. These seem to me often wide of the mark, and I have argued elsewhere that the recasting of prose as poetry importantly recontextualises it, so that we are invited to read from an aesthetic standpoint different from that invited by, say, an encyclopaedia entry or an article in a scientific journal.[90] My main point, here, though, is that the sort of skills and techniques demanded by his work on the *Montrose Review* are also those applied with intuitive brilliance to the Scots poetry of the 1920s. At times it is as if MacDiarmid is 'reporting' the Scots dictionary, quoting not just words but lines and phrases, editing them into his own text so that the edited 'submitted copy' from the dictionary is rewritten by the editor for publication in the poem. The way this works in detail has been suggested by such critics as David Murison, Kenneth Buthlay and W. N. Herbert.[91] What they describe, surely, is not just the magpie acquisitiveness of the textually eclectic modernist poet such as T. S. Eliot, but also the compositional technique of the hard-pressed small-town journalist. Though one might call attention to Whitman's hoard of newspaper cuttings, to passages in Dos Passos, or to Joyce's 'Aeolus' section in *Ulysses*, MacDiarmid's work more than any of these represents the convergence of journalism and modernist high art.

MacDiarmid in Montrose was a poet with a full-time job. One of his triumphs was that he was able to allow that job (often, one suspects, at a subterranean level) to nourish his work as a creative artist; of his early Scots lyrics he recalled in 1977, 'I did them when I was going about my daily work.'[92] Practically, MacDiarmid's work in Montrose gave him access to review copies of books he could not have obtained otherwise, to printing facilities, and several channels of communication; it allowed him to report his own activities and those of his friends; it sharpened and sometimes goaded his political sensibilities. On a deeper level, Mac-Diarmid also accepted what his job and his Montrose base provided: a compositional method that was at once editorial and creative; a sense of a strong local culture whose major poetic preoccupation was the verse of Burns, yet which also included the work of contemporary writers and artists; immediate fora in which MacDiarmid was both determined and open enough to promote his ideas; and, lastly, a sense of empowering marginality which may have been bound up with pleasure in being a big fish in a small pond. All these come together in *A Drunk Man Looks at the Thistle*, a work that includes substantial translations from the work of other writers which MacDiarmid 'edits' into his own text. Appropriately for someone who had attended the Montrose Burns Club's supper in 1926 and who (again attempting to bond the Bard to his own work) was producing his own edition of Burns that year, MacDiarmid quotes from and engages with Burns throughout the poem.[93] Critics tend to concentrate on the attack on platitudinous Burns suppers with which the poem opens, but allusions to Burns and his works (particularly 'Tam o' Shanter') occur throughout, as Kenneth Buthlay's notes to his edition make clear. Burns, the poet most frequently quoted from or alluded to in *A Drunk Man*, holds his place alongside Schoenberg, T. S. Eliot, Nietzsche, Mallarmé and other figures who interested both Grieve and the author of *We Moderns*. The political arguments with which Councillor C. M. Grieve had become so familiar find their apotheosis in the poem. Its mention of the author's place of residence is brief (other verses may have been edited out here) and is not a flattering one,

> And in the toon that I belang tae
> – What tho'ts Montrose or Nazareth? –
> Helplessly the folk continue
> To lead their livin' death![94]

Nevertheless, what MacDiarmid is doing here is to universalise Montrose as typical of a modern malaise, at the same time as hinting by way of biblical allusion ('Can any good thing come out of Nazareth?') that from Montrose may come the salvation of modern Scotland.[95] The suggestion carries with it a blasphemous, Nietzschian and modernist arrogance in which MacDiarmid often delighted; yet in the context of 'locations of modernism' it is hard to deny that a good deal of the finest Scottish poetry of the twentieth century emerged with a brilliance whose afterburn is undiminished from the small coastal town of Montrose. MacDiarmid's liberating remoteness from metropolitan power developed a sense of marginal vulnerability that led to over-compensatory extremist harangues; this pattern would be exacerbated by his later residence on Whalsay. Yet, crucially, Montrose allowed MacDiarmid both to maintain contact with international literary developments, and to keep faith with the peculiar grain of Scottish and minutely local affairs, so that, spikily but compellingly, he developed into what Burns called 'The man of independant mind'.[96] Over several centuries small Scottish towns have often afforded the curbs, freedom and improbable incitement that nourishes the making of poetry. They still do.

CHAPTER 2

Bunting and Welsh

Richard Caddel

Basil Bunting seemed to delight in opposition: throughout his life he distanced himself from the literary and cultural authorities and establishments around him, preserving for himself a deliberately marginal voice which continues to resist easy classification. Like David Jones and Hugh MacDiarmid, he seems to stamp out a ground as an international modernist, with intense classical and local concerns. Like them, he drew deeply and consciously on the culture and languages of his homeplace, and like them his voice is often contrary to the 'centre' of British culture – a voice which resonates strongly in the emerging fragmented and marginalised cultures of Europe today, and which on occasion cries against the tenets of centralised economics.[1]

One recurrent thread in Bunting's later work is the exploration of Old Welsh poetry, which he was at pains to identify as part of the cultural heritage of his homeplace in Northeast England, incorporating its poetic within his own aims. This chapter seeks to trace this concern as it runs through Bunting's later work, and to demonstrate its importance for him as a technical component, which links directly and practically to its importance as the cultural signifier of location as he fuses linguistic device with his robustly asserted concern for place.

As preparatory material it will be useful to offer a brief account of the Old Welsh poetries concerned, as they relate to Bunting's reading and writing. Welsh scholars will be appalled at the generalisation and over-simplification which this entails – nevertheless, the following summary is offered as a reference-point, in the specific context of his Northeastern understanding of the matter.

Before any English or Anglo-Saxon poetry in the Northeast came the poets of the last Brythonic kingdoms of the North. Most notably, for us, these are Taliesin, who sang of the rulers of Rheged (roughly Cumbria and western lowland Scotland), and Aneirin, who sang of the Gododdin, whose kingdom at one time stretched from Edinburgh to the Tees –

57

the Bunting heartlands. Nennius mentions these poets at the same time, and in the same tones, as he mentions the princes who led the last British defences against the incoming waves of English: 'At that time Outigern then fought bravely against the English nation. Then Talhaearn Tad Awen was famed in poetry; and Aneirin and Taliesin and Bluchbard and Cian, known as Gueinth Guaut, were all simultaneously famed in British verse.'[2]

This is heroic poetry, oral and richly aurally textured. Ultimately it is a poetry of defeat – but also, significantly for Bunting and his readers, it is a poetry of the endangered margins seeking to re-affirm their identity in the same way that Bunting was to seek to re-affirm his own local identity.

By the end of the sixth century Urien of Rheged, Taliesin's patron, was dead, killed perhaps by a rival princeling while besieging Lindisfarne. The pride of the Gododdin, together with their leader Mynyddog Mwynfawr, lay dead at Catraeth (present day Catterick), to be mourned, one by singular one, by Aneirin. The remnants of these peoples slipped through the increasingly English-occupied territories – which were, in fact, about to become England – to join their cousins in Powys and Gwynedd and Dyfed. There, they remembered their homelands and their dead with remarkable consistency in poems which survived for hundreds of years, before they were written down (there is, of course, much debate about the exact time of composition and transcription of all dark age literature). They called themselves 'Cymry' – The People – but in the language of invading incomers they became 'Walischer' – the foreigners.

The authentic core of Taliesin's work survives in a manuscript which also contains the prophecies of a much later pseudo-Taliesin, and much else of philological and other interest; Aneirin's work is contained in the remarkably consistent 'Book of Aneirin' which dates from about 1250, and contains two partial versions of his elegies for the Gododdin, and little else. 'This is the Gododdin', says the rubric at the start of it: 'Aneirin sang it.' The language of this poetry is what we now call Old Welsh, and both collections of work survived and were shaped by centuries of oral transmission – a process revered by Bunting – before their earliest manuscript versions.

One of the pieces of marginalia in the 'Book of Aneirin' is a cradle-song, for a lad whose daddy's gone a-hunting, and who is clad in skins from previous hunting:

Pais Dinogad, fraith fraith,
O grwyn balaod ban wraith.
Chwid, chwid, chwidogaith!
Gochanwn, gochenyn wythgaith.
Pan elai dy dad di i helia,
Llath ar ei ysgwydd, llory yn ei law,
Ef gelwi gwn gogyhwg:
'Giff, Gaff, daly, daly, dwg, dwg!'
Ef lleddi bysg yng nghorwg
Mal ban lladd llew llywiwg.
Pan elai dy dad di i fynydd
Dyddygai ef pen iwrch, pen gwythwch, pen hydd,
Pen grugiar fraith o fynydd,
Pen pysg o Raedr Derwennydd.
O'r sawl yd gyrhaeddai dy dad di a'i gigwain,
O wythwch a llewyn a llwynain,
Nid angai oll ni fai oradain.[3]

Here we are linked directly with the country of Basil Bunting, twenti-eth-century Northumbrian. I quote the piece in full, not simply to propose some connection to my subject by way of 'Bye, Baby Bunting', but to draw attention to the place where daddy's gone fishing in his coracle: Raedr Derwennydd, the falls on the River Derwent. This gives a location for the poem, in the heart of Gododdin country prior to Anglian invasion: a number of scholars seem to agree that this is the River Derwent in County Durham, at the heart of Bunting's Northumbria. The earliest poetry of his part of the world, then, was Welsh. I also quote the poem in Welsh, as Bunting would do.[4] Here is Brian Swann recalling a visit to Basil Bunting in 1976:

Bunting rose to walk over to the bookcase behind me to reach down the Penguin Book of Welsh Verse. He read, in Welsh, a lovely kind of 7th Century lullaby called 'Raedr Derwennydd' – Bunting called it by its first words 'Pais dinogad'. He read, with the occasional bogging down in a Welsh word ('a hell of a one, that'). Then he read a translation ('that's bloody nonsense, that'). 'Now', he said, 'there's mention made of the falls of Derwent. And the only Derwent with falls is not in Wales but between Northumberland and Durham. The poet was a Northumbrian!' The voice was triumphant.[5]

I should perhaps add a pedantic note to this: Bunting might have read 'Pais dinogad' in Welsh from a variety of editions in 1976, but not the Penguin selection, which is purely in translation. We should note also that the ascription of the place is by no means as clear cut as Bunting suggests: the point is that Bunting not only accepted this placing, but went out of his way to assert it.

Bunting evidently drew on such models, to some extent, because they fitted his 'oppositional' and regional stance. 'A poet is just a poet', he told one interviewer, 'but I am a Northumbrian man. It has always been my home, even when I've been living elsewhere.'[6] In one sense, by promoting this identification he is simply deliberately drawing into his geographical and cultural world the poetic values which concern him (elsewhere he similarly adopts the Gawain poet – in the face of a good deal of contrary evidence – as a poet of the Northumbrian/Cumbrian uplands). Bunting talked more of the materials of Welsh poetry to Jonathan Williams in 1983:

There is, for instance, the unique figure of Aneirin, in the Brythonic or Proto-Welsh tradition of the 5th or 6th centuries AD. The repetition of the formula, with variations, is a very important part of a poem. Often he utters only two or three words in mourning the men in the Battle of Catraeth, but these words are very telling. There's a prose translation by Jackson of Edinburgh, which must be read with the Welsh opposite. It's a hard task. It is something I am extremely glad to have come across, but not until my old age, alas.

Heledd is perhaps no more than a century later. She laments the people at a battle near Shrewsbury. She has two or three poems in which she scores by the repetition of slightly varying refrains. Devastating poems, if you have any imagination. Not the sort of poem that goes down well at the present time. Some say she never existed. But the poems do.

> Stauell Gyndylan ys tywyll heno
>   heb dan heb wely
> wylaf wers tawaf wedy
>
> (Cynddylan's hall is dark tonight;
>   no fire, no bed.
> I'll weep awhile and then be still.)

This is a small sample of Heledd from *An Introduction to Welsh Poetry (From the Beginning to the Sixteenth Century)*, by Gwyn Williams, Faber & Faber, London, 1953. From there you must go to big libraries. It's a terrible thing. I get old, I get lost. I know so little about these things. And yet, they are important. How astonishingly tied together those words are, the rhymes, the alliteration. You have to use every scrap of your face to speak Welsh.[7]

Bunting came to invoke the physical realities of Old Welsh most self-evidently in section IV – the 'return home' section – of *Briggflatts*. We will note that each time that he lays practical emphasis in his poetry upon the use of Old Welsh sound systems, he does so in a context closely and consciously related to the idea of 'home'. In the following passage he stamps out a direct relationship between the sounds of Old Welsh and the history and linguistic culture of his Northumbria:

> I hear Aneurin number the dead, his nipped voice.
> Slight moon limps after the sun. A closing door
> stirs smoke's flow above the grate. Jangle
> to skald, battle, journey; to priest Latin is bland.
> Rats have left no potatoes fit to roast, the gamey tang
> recalls ibex guts steaming under a cold ridge,
> tomcat stink of a leopard dying while I stood
> easing the bolt to dwell on a round's shining rim.
> I hear Aneurin number the dead and rejoice,
> being adult male of a merciless species.
> Today's posts are piles to drive into the quaggy past
> on which impermanent palaces balance.
> I see Aneurin's pectoral muscle swell under his shirt,
> pacing between the game Ida left to rat and raven,
> young men, tall yesterday, with cabled thighs.
> Red deer move less warily since their bows dropped.
> Girls in Teesdale and Wensleydale wake discontent.
> Clear Cymric voices carry well this autumn night,
> Aneurin and Taliesin, cruel owls
> for whom it is never altogether dark, crying
> before rules made poetry a pedant's game.[8]

'You have to use every scrap of your face' to speak this poetry. For Bunting, it is a poetry of clashing consonants and patterned vowels (Aneurin/number/nipped/limps/sun; posts/piles/past/ /piles/palaces/balance) which is directly associated with life on the margins – the geographical margins of upland England, the oppositional margins between clear Cymric, jangled Saxon, bland Latin, day and night – and life and death. In the last interview he gave he continued to exemplify this principle:

You realise that a great deal of what people goggle at in *Briggflatts* is merely an undisciplined and indiscriminate use of Cynghanedd . . . Cynghanedd is of course all the things that hold poetry together by way of sound; various kinds of rhyme, real ordinary rhyme we are used to, the peculiar rhyme the Welsh like, when you come to the rhyme word and it doesn't rhyme but the next word rhymes instead, or when a rhyme goes in the middle of the next line, or the end of the line rhymes with the middle of the line before. And they like rhymes that don't have the same vowel, only the same consonants each side of it, and funny things like that, and a tremendous variety of possibilities in the alliteration and so on.[9]

Bunting was not the first English poet to discover Cynghanedd: Hopkins had tried them, as had Dorset poet William Barnes (elsewhere a stalwart of the nineteenth-century movement to revitalise the use of Old English) – in 'My Orcha'd in Linden Lea', for example, in consonant-patterned lines such as 'Do lean down low in Linden Lea'.[10] For both these, however, Bunting would have felt, their adherence to the literal definitions of the form had robbed them of the true energy which could be generated in a world 'before rules made poetry a pedant's game'. Bunting's interpretations of the spirit of Welsh assonance and patterned sound would be much less dogmatic, more responsive to his Northumbrian version of modernism. As such, of course, he is relating more to the structures of Old Welsh than to the artifice of mediaeval Cynghanedd: to the period, in other words, which in Bunting's terms produced Welsh poetry from Bunting's own region.

The earliest evidences of any concern for Welsh on Bunting's part date back to the 1930s, and are rooted firmly in the evolving poetics of modernism. Among the papers in the Louis Zukofsky collections in Austin, Texas, is a piece in Zukofsky's hand headed 'Bunting on Jones'.[11] It is not dated, but probably stems from the mid-thirties, when Bunting, Zukofsky, Pound and Selwyn Jones were engaged in a four-way exchange on the poetic techniques of different cultures. Bunting was the Persian correspondent, and wrote to Pound on 12 October 1935: 'I know no Welsh whatever and hardly even how they pronounce the more complicated consonants.'[12] 'Bunting on Jones' seems to summarise information gleaned from Jones via Bunting: after two pages of notes on Persian poetry (significantly, on the sound qualities of Persian), we reach a page and a bit on Cynghanedd, with some examples from Mediaeval Welsh, gleaned, presumably, from Selwyn Jones. In terms of Bunting's own poetry, nothing seems to have come of it at this stage, though it is perhaps worth noting that in 'Let them remember Samangan' (dated 1937)[13] – an ode differing from those around it in its use of sound-patterning – we may see an isolated, and to my mind rather artificial, sort of Cynghanedd:

> hideous children of cautious marriages,   c – m – j
> those who drink in contempt of joy.   c – m – j

I would suggest that at that time Bunting was not reading Welsh in great depth (his main work was on Persian at that stage), and had not followed through to any extent the information which he was passing on, which was in itself sketchy, only showing a small range of the dozen or so possible different types of Cynghanedd described in the *Oxford Companion to the Literature of Wales*.[14]

The Second World War brought Bunting into closer contact with Welsh servicemen, and his first direct experience of the (modern) language. In 1942 he travelled out to Persia on the troopship *Strathaird*, giving lectures on basic Persian to the officers. G. G. Evans, a Welsh aircraftman on board who struck up an acquaintance with Bunting, recalls their conversations as they watched the flying fish astern of the ship: literary conversations, in which Bunting talked about Persian, whilst Evans contributed information on Welsh: 'my part was to answer his questions about early Welsh literature'.[15] Later, Evans amplified this point: 'I explained to him the principles of the traditional Welsh metres, based on alliterative patterns . . . The other subject was the early Welsh poetry associated with Aneirin, Taliesin and Llywarch Hen . . . Certainly I spoke of Heledd.'[16]

The intense military activity of the following years – years of excitement and authority which Bunting frankly enjoyed – can only have reinforced the images of the Brythonic battle-poetry originating from his distant homeland: the seed, one might say, was sown *in absentia*, to begin to shoot on his return to the Northeast in the early 1950s. On 6 August 1953, deep in the process of rediscovering his homeworld, Bunting writes to Zukofsky: 'here's a book on Welsh poetry, from the library, mine for a fortnight, with at least some lines of Aneirin and Taliesin that belong with the best and straightest'.[17] This is the first occasion which I can find where he can show enthusiastic mention of a Welsh text which is before him, and, significantly, it points us to the earliest Welsh poets and poetry, before the intricacies of mediaeval construction and full-blown Cynghanned, 'before rules made poetry a pedant's game'.

Armed with instruction on the air and on the page, Bunting was ready to incorporate his understanding of Old Welsh into his own regional construct – to use the strategies of Old Welsh as part of a physical reconstruction of his reasserted homeplace in his own work. By 1969, lecturing to students in the University of Newcastle, he was keen to draw parallels between early English and Welsh metrics: 'The line of four stresses is not confined to English. There is something very like it in the oldest Welsh or proto-Welsh or British poem, the Gododdin of Aneurin [*sic*], though the stresses are less marked and alliteration is used more sparingly than in Beowulf.'[18]

It is time to consider the ways in which Old Welsh verse strategy constituted, according to Bunting, 'all the things that hold poetry together' – to give some sketchy account of the mechanics which attracted him, though they were often not described by scholars until after his death. To start with, early Welsh poetry became noted by some for its 'intensive use of consonance, various sorts of internal rhyme, and cymeriadau'.[19] One of the earliest forms of sound patterning, the alliteration of sequences of consonants within a line known as cyflythraeth, was already 'quite archaic and traditional' in Aneirin's time.[20] In its approach to patterning of sound, cyflythraeth may be seen as a kind of loose early version of cynghannedd, and obviously worth looking at in connection with Bunting. If we take the line from Taliesin, 'Vryen hwn anwawt eineuyd' (Cruel attacker, this Urien)[21] – a pattern emerges: 'un un nu nu' – and by one argument, the consonant patterning can be made even more remarkable by putting it into an older form of Welsh orthography:[22] 'Urbagen hunn hanmoc henhamid / n h n h nm h nh m'. And we should note that in either case, these patterns of sounds are closely related to those which Peter Quartermain has pointed out in Bunting's 'At Briggflatts Meetinghouse' (again, an assertion of his Northern place):[23]

> Boasts time mocks cumber Rome.
> b   sts t m   m   ks k mb   m

The definition of cymeriadau augments the point, and relates closely to Bunting's own statement of 'all the things that hold poetry together'. Cymeriadau are most concisely described as 'linking devices which use rhyme, alliteration, and verbal repetition'.[24] Elsewhere they are described as 'linking of lines in a verse of "cywydd" or "awdl" by beginning each line with the same letter or word, by alliteration, or rhyming the first word in each consecutive line, or by allowing the sense to extend from one line into another'.

As a further instance, we may give another example from Taliesin (poet of the Rheged, from the country around Brigflatts) at his most oppositional :

> kyscit lloegyr llydan nifer
> a leuver yn eu llygeit

a rei ny ffoynt hayach
a oedynt hyach no reit[25]

(sleep England's wide host / with light in their eyes / and those that fled not / were more brave than wise). Apart from the couplet rhyming, note the echoes which carry from 'niver' to 'leuver', and 'hayach' to 'hyach', and many other elements of sound-patterning: a use of rhyme strategies to promote conflict, rather than congruency. Again, we can directly match that piece of line-linking and echoing with another Northern landscape part of *Briggflatts*:

> Winter wrings pigment
> from petal and slough
> but thin light lays
> white next red on sea-crow wing,
> gruff sole cormorant
> whose grief turns carnival.
> Even a bangle of birds
> to bind sleeve to wrist
> as west wind waves to east
> a just perceptible greeting -
> sinews ripple the weave,
> threads flex, slew, hues meeting,
> parting in whey-blue haze.[26]

The sounds are laid next to each other in a manner which itself opposes the direct meaning of the passage: a perpetual motion of contrast, the half-rhyme of one line picking up the assonance of the next, or the one after that, without regard for syntax. My intention here is to do no more than suggest how close these early Welsh devices cyflyth-raeth and cymeriadau are to 'all the things that hold poetry together' as Bunting described them, and how he was to appropriate their essence to his own local constructions: 'lays . . . waves to east . . . weave . . . whey-blue haze'.

At this stage we could go to the countless further examples where Bunting, particularly in his later work, uses effects such as these – and usually relates them to his homeplace, the place (in his mind) where such devices were first developed. In the following late poem, a range of vowel- and consonant-groups are patterned and linked throughout the piece, in a manner for which one must use every part of the mouth:

> Stones trip Coquet burn;
> grass trails, tickles
> till her glass thrills.

The breeze she wears
lifts and falls back.
Where beast cool

in midgy shimmer
she dares me chase
under a bridge,

giggles, ceramic
huddle of notes,
darts from gorse

and I follow, fooled.
She must rest, surely;
some steep pool

to plodge or dip
and silent taste
with all my skin.[27]

The Coquet Burn, in central Northumberland (and the heart of Gododdin-country), is a location of recurring significance throughout Bunting's wandering life. He must have walked this valley on many occasions, particularly in the late 1920s when he was living in the nearby Simonside Hills – a period of his life which he recalled vividly in the writing of *Briggflatts*, at the point when 'Then is diffused in Now' in both personal and historical terms.[28] This Northumbrian-Cymric water-nymphette, perhaps, from the borderlands of the sixth or twentieth centuries, is presented in modern cyflythraeth which hark back to the earliest poetries voiced in this part of the world. It is, after all, only a few miles from Raedr Derwennydd to Coquet Burn.

CHAPTER 3

Antithesis of place in the poetry and life of David Jones

Thomas Dilworth

Integral to the poetry of David Jones is symbolic antithesis in which a rural place associated with cultural vitality is threatened by a large, engulfing, dehumanising city. The humane place is sometimes a small city – medieval London in *The Anathemata*, first-century Jerusalem in 'The Wall' and 'The Dream of Private Clitus' – but it is usually the countryside and often Celtic. The large city symbolises industrial–technological civilisation, which is inimical to humane culture. In all the later poetry, this 'megalopolis' is imperial Rome and, by analogy, modern inter-urban civilisation. The antithesis is, of course, a variation on the conventional pastoral polarity of town and country, but there is much more to it than that. Jones' spatial symbolism expresses an original and penetrating cultural theory, which is based on the Spenglerian distinction between culture and civilisation and his own discernment of the kinds of values that characterise each. Gratuitous values characterise culture; the single utilitarian value of efficiency characterises civilisation. Gratuitous acts such as good-night kisses and gratuitous objects such as birthday cakes are innately symbolic – and, in these instances, directly express love; utilitarian or pragmatic acts (fixing a faucet) and objects (a wrench) are not innately symbolic and, in themselves, express nothing. For Jones, a healthy society is one in which gratuitous values balance pragmatism.[1] He is convinced that modern life is dehumanising because pragmatism far outweighs the gratuitous values traditionally expressed in domestic rituals, in art and craft, and in religion. In other words, today human life is unbalanced in favour of civilisation at the expense of culture.

For Jones the utility of civilisation belongs predominantly to the city, the gratuitous values of culture to the country. Never in his vision of historical possibility is there, however, an idyllic escape to a rural paradise which ignores the influence of modern technology or pre-modern pragmatic need. In his poetry, the city threatens or consumes the country. This happens implicitly in his first published writing, *In Parenthesis* (1937), an epic poem of the Great War, which 'towers', as the novelist and poet Adam Thorpe writes in 1996, 'above any other prose or verse memorial of that war (indeed, of any war)'.[2] In this work, the antithesis of place mutates to opposition between nature and mechanised war, which is the city come to the country with a vengeance. Industrialised warfare in the shape of artillery pulverises the land, destroying human and vegetable life. Near the start of the poem, this is evident literally and by implication in the word 'mangolds' after the first shell-burst experienced by a platoon recently arrived in France and on its way to the trenches: 'Behind E Battery, fifty yards down the road, a great many mangolds, uprooted, pulped, congealed with chemical earth, spattered and made slippery the rigid boards leading to the emplacement. The sap of vegetables slobbered the spotless breech-block of No. 3 gun.'[3] Here vegetable sap is no mere metaphor but a sort of biological synecdoche implying the shedding of blood that occurs on a massive scale at the end of the poem in the attack on a wood during the Battle of the Somme.[4]

The threat to the country by the city is explicit and personal in *The Anathemata* (1952), Jones' *summa* and symbolic anatomy of Western culture, which, in 1970, W. H. Auden called 'probably the greatest long poem in English in this century'.[5] In this work, during the period of late republican Rome, the *latifundiae* or great estates of Roman capitalism gobble up independent family farms and the reformer

> Tiberius Gracchus
>   wept for the waste-land
> and the end of the beginnings
>   . . . and where I had a vineyard
> on a very fruitful hill fenced and watered
>   the syndicate's agent
> pays-off the ranch operatives
>   (his bit from the Urbs
> waits in the car).[6]

('Bit' is 1920s dismissive slang for a woman, a bit of fluff.) In 133 BC senatorial capitalists murdered Tiberius Gracchus, as they would subsequently murder his brother Gaius, for promoting land-reform legislation. It was a triumph for utility in the service of greed.

In itself, however, utility is amoral. There is nothing essentially wrong with it but it cannot express the fullness of humanity. Utility is, after all, the attribute we share with insects, although with them it is instinctual and not freely chosen. In *The Anathemata*, gratuity and utility attain synthesis in Western history only in sixth-century BC Greece and the early and high middle ages. The vital cultures of these periods are evident in the balance between technique (utility) and significance in sculpture. In Greece, it is 'the second Spring' after the devastating Dorian invasion (I clarify in square brackets terms that may be obscure):

> and a new wonder under heaven:
> man-limb stirs
> in the god-stones
> and the kouroi [youths]
> are gay and stepping it
> but stanced solemn
> . . .
> and the Delectable Korê [Maiden]
> by the radial flutes for her chiton [over-garment], the lineal, chiselled hair
> the contained rhythm of her
> is she Elenê Argive
> or is she transalpine Eleanore [of Aquitaine]
> or our own Gwenhwyfar [Guinevere]
> the Selenê of Thulê [moon]
> West-Helen? (91–2)

As the suggested identification of Helen of Troy with Guinevere implies, Jones sees the Homeric epics and the mediaeval romances (whose writing Eleanore of Aquitaine partly sponsored) as analogous achievements, each the literary manifestation of a vital culture. Jones goes on to suppose that the sculpture of ancient Greece may nearly have its match in the sculptures decorating the façades of mediaeval cathedrals:

> on west-portals
> in Gallia Lugdunensis [central France]
> when the Faustian [modern Western] lent is come
> and West-wood springs new
> (and Christ the thrust of it!)
> and loud sings West-cuckoo (92)

Ancient and mediaeval, these are periods of cultural spring or youth, according to Spengler's schema of cultural life-cycles. In these periods, culture more than balances civilisation, in contrast to the late civilisational phases of imperial Rome and the industrialised West – the latter a time when, during the Second World War, 'they strictly grid / quadrate and number on the sea-green *Quadratkarte* [gridmap] / . . . for the fratricides', England and Germany (115). All other meanings of space and the sea are subordinated to a killing efficiency. Whether in balance or not, significant gratuity and meaningless utility are perennially in tension. This is evident when ancient Athenean sailors who seemed doomed to drown 'all for thalassocracy' [maritime empire], pray to the love goddess, 'Maiden help yr own' (104). They serve an ancient Greek antecedent of British empire – which is pragmatism in the form of robbery – but their praying (and the loving for which sailors are notorious) restores a little the balance.[7]

The rural/urban antithesis was first noted by Elizabeth Ward, who saw that it also appears, in transmuted form, as contrast between past and present – the past being humane; the present, dehumanising.[8] Although she writes that the spatial and temporal versions of the antithesis are aspects of Jones' own private myth, they are obviously matters of broad consensus over the past three centuries. Both temporal and spatial versions of the antithesis inform the writing of nineteenth-century European intellectuals and poets. The temporal version is a dominant motif in all the great modernist writers, including T. S. Eliot, Ezra Pound and James Joyce in *Finnegans Wake*. With characteristic dismissiveness, Ward suggests that the source of the antithesis for Jones is 'barely assimilated memories, perhaps, of his early encounter with Catholic Distributist teaching'.[9] Jonathan Miles suggests that living some of the time between 1924 and 1927 in the borderland of the Welsh Marches informed the Celtic–rural side of the antithesis.[10] No doubt these and other experiences were influential, but an antithesis so pervasive must have deeper roots. This is especially true of David Jones, whose *materia poetica* was always well assimilated and, for him at least, richly resonant emotionally. In 1928 before beginning to write *In Parenthesis*, he was in complete agreement with Livingstone Lowes' description of Coleridge's creative process in *The Road to Xanadu*, particularly the essential importance of long years of subconscious assimilation and association of experiences prior to their emergence as images in art. Jones' writing always followed such a period of subconscious gestation. He began writing about the war ten years after its conclusion. His antithetical spatial symbolism originates not, as Ward suggests, from discussions he first experienced at the age of twenty-five nor partly, as Miles suggests, in temporary and intermittent relocation at the age of twenty-nine; it is rooted in Jones' earliest experiences of place. The antithesis between country and city first acquired meaning for him in his childhood, and part of that meaning included psychological associations with his parents. In this respect, his earliest personal experiences underlie and charge his poetry with feeling even though, in his work, he subordinates private feeling to aesthetic prerogatives of form and meaning.

In 1895 David Jones was born in Brockley, south-east of London. He grew up there. That makes him primarily English rather than, as he is often mistakenly considered, Welsh. Brockley was a place that then embodied both town and country. Not yet part of greater London, it was an unfinished housing development with its own postal address in Kent. The main thoroughfare, Brockley Road, was a stone's throw from the house where he was born and was paved and lined with shops, but in the field beside the house a neighbour raised chickens. The Jones family moved several times during his childhood but always within Brockley. Near the local District Railway station (Crofton Park) were remnants of a farm, including, here and there, a stile on which he climbed as a child to improve his view. There were large open fields, on some of which houses were being built. Further south, the area called Honor Oak Park was open country with fields of wheat. To the north was also open space, with, at Brockley Cross, a blacksmith's shop, where he liked watching the smith making horseshoes and shoeing horses and where he took his toy hoop to be soldered. Further north, the area of New Cross was open country. Most local streets were unpaved and not yet fronted with unbroken rows of houses. On holidays, his father hired an open carriage and took the family for rides in the country. He was impressed by how close this open other-world was to where he lived.[11]

The landscape of childhood is basic to a person's regional identity and spatial imagination, and in this semi-pastoral location his sense of place developed. A turning point in the gradual suburbanisation of Brockley was the cutting down of the rows of elms along Brockley Road in 1910 to make way for tram lines. When, in February 1911, electric trams replaced horse-drawn buses some felt 'sadness & annoyance', Jones remembered, 'while others talked of "the advantages of progress"'. With the passing years, the large areas of open fields diminished but did not disappear entirely until 1913, and even then he easily walked into the open country of western Kent, which he could still reach by foot in 1919.[12] (As a boy and as a young man, he was a habitual and energetic walker.) Not until he was fourteen did Brockley lose its feeling of being of, though no longer in, the country. Until then, it had unique magic, as all such places do, as a zone of metamorphosis. In retrospect it was a site of nostalgia and of experiential corroboration of what was happening throughout the Western world.

A living folk-remnant of receding rural life appeared at the door of the house each May Day until Jones was five or six: a man covered in branches and green leaves who mimed or danced and was called 'Jack o' the Green' or 'the Man in the Green'. Later, he read about this figure in *The Golden Bough* and learned that the Green Man originally personated a vegetation god in a fertility rite that ensured the return of spring. He alludes to this leafy figure near the end of *In Parenthesis* during the assault on a wood smashed by artillery and torn by machinegun-fire:

And now all the wood-ways live with familiar faces and your mate moves like Jack o' the Green: for this season's fertility gone unpruned   (168)

> they could quite easily train dark muzzles
> to fiery circuit
> and run with flame stabs to and fro among
> stammer a level traversing
> and get a woeful cross-section on
> stamen-twined and bruised pistiline
> steel-shorn of style and ovary
> leaf and blossoming
> with flora-spangled khaki pelvises
> and where rustling, where limbs thrust
>   from nurturing sun hidden,
> late-flowering dog-spray let fly like bowyers ash,
> disturbed for the movement
> for the pressing forward, bodies in the bower
> where adolescence walks the shrieking wood.   (170–1)

His final book of poetry, *The Sleeping Lord* (1974), is a collection of mid-length poems in which the antithesis is between rural cultures of the Latin and Celtic heartlands and the mega-civilisation of imperial Rome. In one of these poems entitled 'The Hunt', he again alludes to the Green Man while describing Arthur furiously riding as symbolic restorer of a proto-Welsh wasteland. You can hear the verbal equivalent of early-mediaeval visual Celtic interlace:

> for the thorns and flowers of the forest and the bright elm-shoots and the twisted tanglewood of stamen and stem clung and meshed him and starred him with variety
> and the green tendrils gartered him and briary-loops gallon him with splinter-spike and broken blossom twining his royal needlework
> . . .

he was caparison'd in the flora
             of the woodlands of Britain
and like a stricken numen of the woods
             he rode
with the trophies of the woods
             upon him
who rode
             for the healing for the woods
. . .
             the speckled lord of Prydain
in his twice-embroidered coat
             the bleeding man in the green[13]

Arthur is pursuing a mythic boar, the Twrch Trwyth who has wasted much of Ireland and Britain. The boar is an open symbol that may include, in the mythic timelessness of the poem, the effects of industrialisation. These effects are explicitly referred to in the final poem of the collection, in which the speaker asks whether a sleeping Arthur is angry 'where black-rimed Rhymni / soils her Marcher-banks', whether he sighs 'where the mountain-ash / droops her bright head / for the black pall of Merthyr', and whether 'grimed Ogwr' tosses 'on a fouled riple / his broken-heart flow' (92).

> Does the blind & unchoosing creature of sea know the marking and
> indelible balm from flotsomed sewage and the seaped valley-waste?
>   Does the tide-beasts' maw
>   drain down the princely tears
> with the mullocked slag-wash
>   of Special Areas?
> Can the tumbling and gregarious porpoises
> does the aloof and infrequent seal
>   that suns his puckered back
>   and barks from Pirus' rock
> tell the dole-tally of a drowned *taeog* [labourer] from a
> Gwledig's [King's] golden collar, refracted in Giltar shoal?
>   Or, is the dying gull
>   on her sea-hearse
> that drifts the oily bourne
>   to tomb at turn of tide
> her own stricken cantor?   (93)

'The dying gull' recalls the *Dying Gaul*, an ancient sculpture, and the centuries-long defeat of the Celtic peoples that it symbolised for Jones.[14]

A short walk from the boyhood houses of David Jones was 'the Hilly Fields', a green area almost a half-mile square rising high above the roofs of bordering houses. Atop this park he looked south into what were then the bare green hills of Kent. To the south-east he could see the towers of the Crystal Palace. From the north slope, he could see Blackheath and, beyond, the south-west slope of the hill of Greenwich Park. To the north-west on a clear day he could see the dome of St Paul's.[15] His mother and sometimes his elder brother and sister took him in a pram and then by the hand up onto the Hilly Fields. He came here with friends and by himself as a boy and, later, sometimes to visit his father who grew vegetables in an allotment here. This was his native hill, the height of his earliest imagining, the familiar prototype of the ancient hills with their maternal guardian spirits that he celebrated half a century later in 'The Tutelar of the Place', in which the guardian of a height is the local, rural manifestation of the Earth Mother: 'Tellus of the myriad names answers to but one name: From this tump she answers Jac o' the Tump only if he call Great-Jill-of-the-tump-that-bare-me, not if he cry by some new fangle moder of far gentes over the flud, fer-goddes name from anaphora of far folk won't woo her; she's a rare one for locality' (59). Religion, culture, locality: they belong together in a synthesis of gratuity that is threatened by, and resists the threat of, social and industrial technocracy.

From early childhood, the essential ambiguity of his developing native suburb had its extensions, for Jones, in London and Wales. These larger places took on for him dominant parental associations. The experience of London was predominantly maternal; that of Wales, paternal. This was only partly because his mother was a Londoner and his father a Welshman.

His mother was his primary guide through London. Like all middle-class married women then, she did no work in or outside the home and was free to take him on excursions, whereas his father worked in London and spent most of his free time doing church work as an Anglican lay preacher. Jones' mother took him on the black, smoky District Railway to London Bridge Station. In town they travelled by horse-drawn tram and omnibus. He loved the river and enjoyed watching the shipping. She took him to the zoo and public exhibitions in the Alexandra Palace, in Tottenham Court Road and, in 1902, to an exhibition of 'Youthful Art' at Queen Anne's Gate, where, at the age of seven, he had pictures on show. The following year, she took him for the first time to the British Museum. They visited his father at work in the office of the *Christian Herald* on Tudor Street off Fleet Street. They visited his maternal uncle, a paper-manufacturer, in Great St Thomas the

Apostle Street near the river, an area David would have remembered as having 'the atmosphere of Dickensian London'.[16] All his life he remembered this earlier, less crowded horse-drawn city, whose river still bore ships and barges under sail. The remembered, more humane city was for him a measure of the technological revolution his generation experienced, which brought losses as well as gains. As with all true modernists, his awareness of the new (which is what 'modern' means) was grounded in experience of the preceding age.

There is no human place without a history, and, from the start, his acquaintance with London had a historic dimension. Throughout his childhood, when he was home from school, sick or malingering, his mother spent long hours talking to him about her childhood in Rotherhithe, a then-prosperous area of London south of the Thames, east of Tower Bridge. She told him of the local tradition of the Danes led by Canute besieging London and outflanking London Bridge by digging a wide ditch from the site of Greenland Dock to Walworth. *The Anglo-Saxon Chronicle* for the year 1016 records the event but not, of course, the locations. Jones was impressed by the continuity of this oral tradition. The nearly millennium-long, living memory gave Rotherhithe, and London, personal life. When writing *The Anathemata*, he embodied this sense of the living city in the figure of the Lady of the Pool, who peddles lavender in London in the late middle ages but personifies the city from pre-Roman through Victorian times. His mother spoke of her father, Ebeneezer Bradshaw, a master mast and block maker who owned his own workshop east of Cherry-Garden Stairs with a yard running down to the river. During winter he rose at six, during summer at five, to do accounts and read the Bible, the Book of Common Prayer, and Milton before breakfast.[17] Though devoutly Church of England, he was a radical who gloried in descent from Bradshaw-the-regicide, the judge whose signature tops those on the warrant that brought 'the man Charles Stuart', as Eb Bradshaw called him, to his death.

Jones' mother told him how her father prided himself on his integrity as a workman. His main employment was to row out to a ship to make necessary repairs. He would refuse to begin unless the ship's master guaranteed enough time to finish properly. If a captain insisted on haste or offered extra money for a quick job to economise on heavy harbour-dues, Bradshaw would return with his men to shore. His integrity sometimes precipitated arguments, one of which occurred aboard a ship cargoed with sulphur from Sicily. Jones recreates his grandfather's half of the argument in the section in *The Anathemata* entitled 'Redriff' – the

Anglo-Saxon name for Rotherhithe that remained in use through the
eighteenth century. In the poem, the Sicilian captain offers a bribe for a
rushed job and Bradshaw protests

Not for a gratis load of the sound teak in
Breaker's Yard
            and that we could well do with.
Not for a dozen cords of Norweyan, red nor yaller, paid for,
carried and stacked.
Not for a choice of the best float of Oregon in the mast-pond.
Not for as many cubic fathoms of best Indies lignum vitae as 'ld stock us till we
re-sheave the blocks for master-bargees plying the Styx.
Not for a pickin' of all the bonded stuffs passed over the quays in a full working
week between the Bridge and Battlebridge Stairs
. . .
And, as for next Thor's Day's nighttide
            tell the Wop, to-go-to
                        Canute
if he can find him
            down at the Galley Wall.   (118–20)

The final reference here is to the area where Canute dug his ditch in
1016. Jones' mother also told him how Bradshaw's employment and the
family prosperity declined as wooden sailing vessels were replaced by
metal steamships. It was his first awareness of the momentous technological changes that were transforming the world and would later
preoccupy him as a writer.[18]

Jones mined memories of his mother's conversation when writing
'Redriff' and its longer companion section, 'The Lady of the Pool'. The
monologists in these sections are companion figures: Eb Bradshaw, a
protesting Protestant and father figure; the Lady of the Pool, a protec-
tive Catholic lover-and-mother figure. The religious contrast is true to
his parents: his father a very Low-Church, evangelical Anglican; his
mother a closet Anglo-Catholic. Jones writes that he got from his
mother

a pretty vivid impression of the now long vanished ways. Of the 'mast-ponds'
where great 'floes' of softwood from the Baltic were stored for use as masts &
spars. And not only of the immediate, busy life of the water-side but something
of the city itself on the further shore – the churches & parishes of the various
'wards' of the municipality – with St Paul's towering high above the rest and
'the Bridge' meant simply London Bridge . . . Certainly 'the Lady of the Pool'

section of *The Ana* could hardly have been written but for those childhood conversations with my mother. Of course, much else beside went to the making, but to a surprising degree, it depends, in odd ways, on what can only be called the handing on of an 'oral tradition' – though that was the last thing either of us had in mind.

'Whole sections' of 'The Lady of the Pool', he later said, 'are practically direct quotes from her, rounded off'.[19] His monologuing mother is the prototype of the mediaeval woman who is the Lady of the Pool.

He also had an immediate sense of this past through surviving relatives of his grandfather's generation, including Bradshaw's widow who lived with Jones' family till her death when Jones was twelve, in 1907. She and her contemporaries, his great aunts and uncles, who visited mostly on Sundays, were living relics of the era of the Crimean War, the digging of Brunel's Thames tunnel, and the Victorian heyday of the Pool of London – the Thames between Tower Bridge and Greenwich. Their conversation was coloured by the language of nautical commerce: 'bills of lading', 'sight drafts', 'brokerage', 'harbour dues', 'mast-ponds'. His elder relatives were, he later said, 'absolutely pure "Dickensian"'. They were also Dickensians and spoke of Dickens' characters as though of living acquaintances.[20] It was inevitable that Jones read Dickens as soon as he could and became steeped in the London of Dickens' imagining. After Dickens, it is Jones who most makes London present in his writing. This presence was achieved, as perhaps it must be, through personal or personally communicated experience. In childhood, largely through his mother and her relatives, he acquired nearly a century of such experience, including a texture of language, which he gives life to at the centre of *The Anathemata*.

In the years before and after the 1914–18 war, when he was an art student, he had a friend named Frank Medworth who lived in Rotherhithe, and Jones visited him and his family there. Rotherhithe then retained vestiges of its late-Victorian flavour. Some of the dilapidated large Georgian houses – formerly of sea-captains, merchants and ship-wrights – were still hung with tackle. Bowsprits of sailing vessels still extended over some of the Thames-side streets. There were pubs and a church frequented by Norwegian sailors. He and Medworth patronised a pub called The Paradise, in the street of the same name. (It was a Paradise that would be lost to the saturation bombing of south-east London during the Second World War.) He visited for the first time the childhood home of his mother. Walking about the area, remembering the stories of her girlhood and father, he haunted the past of his family.[21]

At Medworth's house in Rotherhithe, he met his friend's alleged great aunt, actually his grandmother. She had been mistress to a nobleman whose son she had borne and given to a sister, who subsequently married the supposed grandfather. 'Auntie', as they called her, was now in her sixties, a delightful woman, the best talker Jones had ever met. She entertained him and other visiting friends with uproarious stories of Edward VII and his circle. In *The Anathemata*, the Lady of the Pool, who symbolises London, is a Redriff Cockney. Medworth's aunt is one of her main sources. She was, as the Lady of the Pool is, a late middle-aged Cockney who had acquired much learning of the world in her youth while giving and receiving carnal knowledge.[22]

Before the 1914–18 war, while still an adolescent, Jones discovered and read John Stowe's *Survey of Elizabethan London*. The sites Stowe mentions were still largely recognisable, and Jones' sojourns to central London then and later were journeys also into an imagined past.[23] He walked through a city to which imagination gave a fifth dimension in which Shakespeare's Globe stood within sight of Southwark Cathedral and wooden, pre-Elizabethan timber-and-stucco buildings lined the labyrinthine streets of the City and the road across old London Bridge. The Walbrook still flowed open to the air, and the Roman forum stood on Ludgate Hill. He walked a city with its past imaginatively restored as it would be in 'The Lady of the Pool'.

In the early 1930s he grew to dislike London, an aversion that increased as he aged. Except during the Blitz, when much of the population was gone and the blackout at night allowed him to see the stars, he avoided the city whenever possible. His aversion was partly a symptom of agoraphobia, a neurotic consequence of prolonged exposure to enemy shell-fire during the war. But there were also objective practical and aesthetic reasons for dislike. For him, London was a city in contrast with its former self. To a degree, its past was imaginary, but it was also largely remembered, much of it by him personally. Elderly people I have interviewed attest to London's having been, in the 1920s and earlier, a much more humane and habitable city than it is now.

The rural aspect of his native Brockley had its extension in far-away Wales, which Jones associated with his father. Among Jones' earliest memories were his father singing in Welsh: 'Ar Hyd y Nos' ('All through the Night'), 'Aderyn Pur' ('The Pure Bird'), 'Dafydd y Garreg Wen' ('David of the White Rock') and the national anthem, 'Mae Hen Wlad Fynhadau' ('Land of My Fathers'). He sang movingly, filling his son with pride and 'a kind of awe'. Though his father could no longer speak

Welsh, he was proud of being a Welshman, and on St David's Day his wife made sure he was served leeks for supper. He told his son stories of his native Gwynedd (Flintshire), and, as he did, he conveyed a 'sense of "otherness"'.[24]

Jones first experienced Wales for himself during a family holiday in 1901 or 1902. His first sight of it was in the early dawn west of Chester. He woke and looked out of the train window: on his right the coastal flats of the estuary of the Dee, on the left the rising hills and, beyond, the mountains of North Wales appearing and disappearing in the mist. Seeing him awake, his father told him, 'Well, here you are now.' Near the end of his life, Jones wrote of this experience, 'the Rubicon had been passed. And so this was the land of which my father had so often spoken, and that's why he had said just then, "Well here you are now". This was . . . the first glimpse of a visual otherness and for me it was an otherness that, as is said of certain of the sacraments, is not patient of repetition but leaves an indelible mark on the soul.'[25]

This and subsequent family holidays in Wales were spent in and around Llandrillo-on-Rhos on the western-most point of Conwyn Bay. The family stayed with relatives whose house was beside wide open fields. It was a place with historic resonance. He and his cousins played on the sea margin in tiny St Trillos chapel, thought to have been built in the sixteenth century on the site of a sixth-century oratory. Inside was a shallow 'holy well' with a gravel bottom filled with cool fresh water. He thought it 'a marvellous thing' that this spring at the edge of the sea should be free of the taste of salt.[26] In the sea just east of the oratory was a fishing weir built in the twelfth century by Cistercian monks for salmon fishing and still in use. On his first visit, he met his Welsh grandfather – tall but bent and using a cane. He later associated him with the mediaeval Welsh figure of Llywarch Hen, his staff a third foot for him. He and his grandfather sat together on a bench by the sea near the chapel, looking at the weir. This chapel, its well, the fishing weir and his (to six- or seven-year-old David Jones) ancient Welsh-speaking grandfather formed in his imagination a significant constellation, linking him with an ancient past. A few years later he read the Taliesin story and associated the wattled weir at Rhos with Gwyddno's weir and his tall grandfather with King Maelgwyn the Tall, whose principal seat had been in Rhos.

Jones and his cousins went to the hill behind Rhos, called Bryn Euryn – Hill of Gold – for the colour of the gorse on its slopes. There they picnicked at Llys Euryn – the 'Golden Court' of Edryfed Fychan, who built a fortified manor house here in 1230. Edryfed had fought in the Crusades and was a baron and the chief minister of Llywelyn the Great. Owen Glendower burned the hall in 1409. The site was, as it remains today, a wild place, its ruins overgrown, unexcavated. The picnickers build a fire in the remains of the huge late-Gothic fire-place to boil water for tea. Walls stand to either side with breaches in them like rugged caves overgrown with ivy. At the age of 'eight or nine', Jones sat among these ruins thinking 'a lot' about Llywelyn the Great '& his chief minister Edryfed'. Further up the hill were the remains of a circular stone-age fort and a spectacular view of the craggy summits of the mountains of Snowdonia to the south and, to the north, the immense bay. It would be difficult to exaggerate the importance for Jones of this wild, unspoiled and, for him, enchanted place. It was the sensory-experiential ground in which his fascination with ancient Britain took root and grew. Spectacularly huge, this was another local mountain, one to shrink, by comparison, the Hilly Fields of Brockley. From visiting Rhos and, specifically, its seaside chapel and the ruins of Llys Euryn and from playing here, pretending to be an ancient Briton or a mediaeval Welshman, his imagination acquired permanent direction. If there were a single place from which his historical imagining flowed, this would be it.[27]

Because of the remembered past, the land had significance and was, itself, a poetic text. In 1910 his father took him to visit the vicar at Raegs-y-cae, a tiny hamlet five miles from Holywell. The vicar pointed out and named for him the local hills: Moel Famau – Hill of the Mothers; Moel-y-Crio – Hill of the Cry; Moel Arthur; and Moel Ffagnallt, which meant, he said, Hill of Dereliction.[28] They were names and shapes to conjure by: the Mothers were the ancient Celtic triune goddess and the human mothers who cried out in torment and cried inwardly in grief down the long ragged edge of Welsh history. For the rest of his life, these named heights served as a remembered poem-in-landscape, juxtaposing maternity, the cry of grief (for dead husbands and sons and for defeated Celtica), the silent desolation and the legend of Arthur. In this region, so long contested by the earls of Chester and the princes of Gwynedd that it was a cumulative Welsh Gettysburg, these hills symbolically mediated an association between Calvary, Arthur-as-Christ-figure and the history of Wales. As an adult, Jones realised that what these hills symbolised also marked the landscape of mortal life and its universal experience of decline and loss, cultural (during many periods including our own) and otherwise. In *The Anathemata* he commemorates these hills – with their evocations of Christian-

ity, pagan religion and primordial legend – as constituting 'vision lands'.
The primary reference is to Calvary:

> On to one of the mountains there
> > on an indicated hill
> not on any hill
> > but on Ariel Hill
> that is as three green hills of Tegeingl
> in one:
> > > the hill of the out-cry
> > > the hill of dereliction
> > > the *moel* of the *mamau*
> that is all help-heights
> the mount of the in-cries.
> Of which cry?
> > His, by whom all oreogenesis [mountain-making] is
> his hill-cry who cries from his own *oreos*.[Latin, 'mouth'; Greek, 'mountain']
> > > *Ante colles* [before the hills] he is and
> before the fleeting hills
> > > in changing order stood. (233)

Jones identified with Wales and with his father's people. He loved the
landscape, which he painted, one way or another, from childhood to
1961. He was obsessed – there is no other word for it – with Welsh
history. In his poetry and in his imagination Wales was not primarily a
modern nation or region, however; it was the localised mediaeval
residuum of all pre-Anglo-Saxon Britain, a Dark-Aged post-Roman
quasi-tribal Catholic society and culture which, of all historical societies
and cultures, most intrigued him. To him, the Welsh countryside, what
he called 'Welshness', and the Celtic past, which is continuous with that
of all Britain, constitutes a Yeatsian mask (or desired opposite) for
modern, urban technological society. This is largely what 'country'
means in his antithesis between country and city. It is an antithesis that
was influenced by his adolescent reading of Ruskin and Morris and his
post-war reading of Spengler. It is an antithesis basic to *The Sleeping Lord*
in the implied debate between an urban male Roman tribune and the
mythic female tutelar in the central, juxtaposed poems, 'The Tribune's
Visitation' and 'The Tutelar of the Place'. The antithesis is also basic, in
'The Dream of Private Clitus', to the contrast between a Roman
legionary's waking duty and his dream of being back on his parents'
farm on the lap of the Earth Mother. But initially Welsh rurality and the
Celtic past were things experienced personally, and that means imaginatively, in his most formative years.

The symbolic antithesis of city and country may also express and perhaps resolve an aspect of Jones' psychological (and to some extent Oedipal) relationship with his mother and father. She was possessive, dominant, nervous, aggressive – like the city she introduced her son to. His father was gentle, lovable, easy-going – in harmony with the country he drove into on holidays and in harmony with his native Wales, where he took the family on extended holidays. Jones loved both of his parents but was attached primarily to his mother. In compensation to his Welsh father for his closer attachment to his mother, at the age of seven he decided to be, or became convinced that he was, Welsh. Neither his brother (six years older) nor his sister (four years older) felt anything like his strong identification with Wales. One indication that this was, in fact, compensatory is that its expression involved the dropping of his baptismal first name, 'Walter', which had been his mother's choice, and its replacement by his middle name, 'David', which had been his father's choice for his son's first name. Consciously, Jones renounced the name 'Walter' solely because of its Saxon origin. From the age of 'eight or nine' he would answer only to 'David'.[29]

It seems likely that on some level of consciousness he subtly sustains, elaborates and alters his relationships with his parents through his poetry and that this involves the shifting antithesis between the dominating, all-consuming city and the gentler, endangered countryside. This symbolic negotiation of his relationship with his parents would, however, take considerable subtlety to articulate without reductionist distortion and is anyway barely traceable. In 'The Hunt', for instance, proto-Welsh Arthur, the saviour figure and therefore a father figure, is identified with the forest he rides through by being tangled in its vegetation to resemble the Green Man. His symbolic opposite is not, however, a female or a city but a mythic boar (i.e., male), who is in Jones' source (in 'Kilhwch and Olwen' in *The Mabinogion*) a metamorphosed king. Since Rome has fallen, there is no city but only a tribal unity, the riding war-band, divided by social and psychological differences but emotionally unified, if only for the moment, by common purpose. At the heart of *The Anathemata*, the Lady of the Pool symbolises London (and also Britain), but the London she represents is a humane place, where Augustine's City of God coexists in considerable harmony with the secular city. That is one reason why she tells time 'by tax-chandler's Black Exchecky Book' and 'Archie's piscopal *Ordo*' (127) – the other reason being that the calendar then actually was set by cross-checking between the *Black Book of the Exchequer* and the ecclesiastical *Ordo*. London is a city but also pastoral, wet with 'wells, rills, shares, bourns, stremlets, ponds, apart from the great tidal river' (126 n.7). The Lady of the Pool symbolises the city in all its past ages, which include the Celtic proto-British past. And, though she is in some sense a woman alone, she is talking to a sea captain, recalls trysts with former lovers, and, on a mythic level, represents the Earth Mother in communion with 'the fathering figures' in cosmic marriage (163). In this female figure, Jones most completely resolves Oedipal tension by marrying on various levels: mother to father, city to country, and London to Celtic Britain. Involved in this marrying is the Lady's most unlikely prototype – for, in addition to Jones' mother and Medworth's aunt and fictional females, including the Wife of Bath, she has for a prototype Winston Churchill as heard by Jones on the wireless during the Second World War.[30] Among the attributes that Churchill and the Lady share is corpulence. And Churchill also provides a further link between her and Jones' maternal grandfather, Eb Bradshaw, the prototype of the Lady's speaking male counterpart. Bradshaw and Churchill spoke in the same home-county accent, dropping the 'g's at the end of words and pronouncing 'gels' instead of 'girls'.[31] Oedipal tension is resolved internally, in the wedding of symbolically male and female aspects of the psyche, which makes a person balanced and whole. (Jones had great respect for Jung, who believed that a single person incorporates a male *animus* and a female *anima*.) There is nothing simplistically moral about these sexual binaries. Femininity is not equated with goodness, nor masculinity with evil. The Lady of the Pool impersonates (and disapproves of) an allegorical siren whom she imagines and who represents post-mediaeval London and Britain, dangerous to humanity because she subordinates human life to commercial and military imperialism. This siren is Britannia, wearing the armour of imperial Athena, the patroness of ancient thalassocracy, just as she did until recently on the British penny. In addition to experience in childhood and psychological tension, London is female here because of objective cultural convention in which cities are identified with females such as Athena and Roma.

Jones sometimes follows symbolic convention and expresses one aspect of childhood experience and tension by identifying rural countryside and humane values with maternal figures. At the conclusion of *In Parenthesis*, the Queen of the Woods appears among the dead as the feminine principle complimenting their masculinity by revealing the innate and secret goodness of these men. She is the dryad of the forest, delivering benign judgments and floral decorations to the fallen. She is the Earth Mother receiving them.

> The Queen of the Woods has cut bright boughs of various
> flowering.
>   These knew her influential eyes. Her awarding hands can
> pluck for each their fragile prize.
>   She speaks to them according to precedence. She knows
> what's due to this elect society. She can choose twelve
> gentle-men. She knows who is most lord between the high
> trees and on the open down.
>   Some she gives white berries
>   some she gives brown
>   Emil has a curious crown it's
>   made of golden saxifrage.
>   Fatty wears sweet-briar,
> he will reign with her for a thousand years.
>   For Balder she reaches high to fetch his.
>   Ulrich smiles for his myrtle wand.
>   That swine Lillywhite has daisies to his chain – you'd hard-
> ly credit it.
>   She plaits torques of equal splendour for Mr Jenkins and
> Billy Crower.
>   Hansel with Gronwy share dog-violets for a palm, where
> they lie in serious embrace beneath the twisted tripod.
>   Siôn gets St John's Wort – that's fair enough.
>   Dai Great-coat, she can't find him anywhere – she calls
> both high and low, she had a very special one for him.
>   Among this July noblesse she is mindful of December wood
> – when the trees of the forest beat against each other because
> of him [the last Welsh prince, Llewelyn, slain 2 December 1282].
>   She carries to Aneirin-in-the-nullah a rowan sprig, for the
> glory of Guenedota [North Wales]. You couldn't hear what she said to
> him, because she was careful for the Disciplines of the Wars.   (185–6)

She is Nature, in its leafy, flowery opposition to industrialised war. She is also a representative of gratuitous Western culture, for her garlands have significance to those familiar with the language of flowers. Daisies for one soldier symbolise love, for example, and dog-violets for two others symbolise steadfastness in suffering.

The country, cultural values and the mother also combine in 'The Lady of the Pool'. But the combination is easier to see in 'The Tutelar of the Place', where the antagonists of the Tutelar are 'dux of far folk . . .

the men who plan, the *mercatores* . . . the *negotiatores* . . . the *missi'* –
imperial Roman terms for 'the agents' of large centralised government
who enumerate for purposes of taxation and 'impose . . . uniformities
and liquidate . . . diversities'. All work for 'the Ram', a male dictator
identified with the military engine that breaks walls and gates and levels
houses. He dominates 'in all times of *Gleichschaltung'* – the Nazi term for
coordination of all aspects of culture – 'in the days of the central
economies' (63).

The associations of the feminine with the city and the masculine with
the country are reversed in this poem largely for symbolic effectiveness.
But the reversal is deeply possible emotionally because of the root
ambiguity of Brockley in 1895–1913. The rural as well as urban aspects
of the place were associated with the mother who did not go into the
City to work and who took him up onto the Hilly Fields. Of course, this
reversal also suits the tradition by which country is female. Shortly after
the 1914–18 war, he became aware of the Earth Mother through reading
cultural anthropology, including Frazer's *The Golden Bough*. In the late
1920s he read and fell in love with the 'Anna Livia Plurabelle' chapter of
Finnegans Wake. That was the first great manifestation of the female
fertility goddess in modern literature. The Queen of the Woods is the
second.

Femininity is not synonymous here with virtue, for allied with the
masculine (and, of course, phallic) Ram is 'the Ram's wife' (63). This is
none of the simplistic moralism of extreme ideological feminism. Yet in
the years preceding the Second World War, Jones did see the imbalance
in contemporary society symbolically in terms of gender. In 1942, he
writes, 'It is to be hoped that this masculine emphasis is at all events
tempered by the saving skepticism of the female mind; there is a danger
of Juno being put into a concentration camp, of her being liquidated.
There is danger that the deprivation of the Romans may be ours also'.
And then he quotes from Jackson Knight's *Cumaean Gates* (1936), 'The
male principle, which is seen in Fascism now, is always fighting the
female principle, which has found its way into Communism, and lost
much of itself as it went.'[32]

The associations of father primarily with country (secondarily with
city) and mother primarily with city (secondarily with country) inform
his poetry but are, as we have seen, reversible. Furthermore, although
London and Wales are the places that most condition his poetry, they do
not inform the tension between country and city in a simple, paradig-
matic way. Antithetical places can be the same place at different times or

even the same time. In *In Parenthesis*, the army (which is a nomadic, largely urban-Cockney tribe) is both dehumanising in its discipline and humane in its fellowship. In *The Anathemata*, late mediaeval London is a place where gratuitous culture and utilitarian civilisation retain some balance. In the poem entitled 'The Sleeping Lord' (written in 1966–7) contemporary Wales is, although still largely rural, a place without value-balance, where the land and sea suffer. Here cultural vitality is gone but may return, as it had in a former time:

> does the vestal flame in virid-hilled Kildare
> renew from secret embers
> the undying fire
> that sinks on the Hill Capitoline? (93)

The poem closes by suggesting a possible return of cultural vitality:

> Does the land wait the sleeping lord
> or is the wasted land
> that very lord who sleeps? (96)

Any reflection in Jones' poetry of his own psychological tensions and split and shifting alliances is important from a reader-response perspective. Parental symbolism powerfully engages readers, often on an unconscious level. Yet even to consider Oedipal tension is danger-ous because it welcomes psychological reductionism by which the poetry is seen merely as a symptom of neurosis. Such a reduction would be as untrue to the poetry as it already has been to his pic-tures.[33] In successful art, private feeling, even when discernible, is always subordinate to cultural syntax and considerations of aesthetic form and meaning.

The city and the country and London and Wales meant a great deal to him personally, but he was not interested, as an artist, in himself. He was no expressionist. Place in his poetry always has symbolic meaning relative to his on-going critical analysis of contemporary Western civilisation. He is true to his conviction that art must be objective, a view he derived largely from Roger Fry and Jacques Maritain in 1919–21. Jones writes in his preface to *The Anathemata*, 'the workman must be dead to himself while engaged upon the work, otherwise we have the sort of "self-expression" which is as undesirable in the painter or the writer as in the carpenter, the cantor, the half-back, or the cook' (12). He was convinced that subjectivity corrupts art, yet he also realised that art originates in strong feelings and that the poet can only write well about what he knows and loves, which, in his Preface to *The Anathemata*, he identifies as place. He asks these questions:

What for us is patient of being 'actually loved and known', where for us is 'this place', where do we seek or find what is 'ours', what *is* available, what *is* valid as material for our effective signs?

Normally we should not have far to seek: the flowers for the muse's garland would be gathered from the ancestral burial-mound . . . It becomes more difficult when the bulldozers have all but obliterated the mounds . . . and when where was this site and where these foci there is *terra informis*.

To what degree, for instance, is it possible for the 'name' to evoke the 'local habitation' long since gone? I do not raise these questions in order to answer them, for I do not know what the answer may be, but I raise them in order to indicate some of the dilemmas which have been present with me all the time.

(24–5)

The difficulty for Jones is that place was changing. For him as for the other great modernists, this changing place was not merely London or Dublin or Britain or Wales but the entire Western world. He overcame the difficulty by writing from experiences of place familiar to him since earliest childhood, but experiences that were also symbolically typical, even – everywhere in the world today – universal.

Great art transcends particularity but remains rooted in it. In art, the universal cannot do without the particular as it can in philosophy or literary theory. (Theory may be so fashionable today because it is the intellectual equivalent of late-civilisational megalopolitan de-particularisation, a flight from the humanly real and significant and the aesthetically particular.) Jones believed that unless the setting or object or basic experience of an art-work is known first-hand by the artist, it will probably not seem true in art. He cared a great deal about form, although he preferred the hyphenated term 'form-content' since, however distinct in theory, form and content can never be separated in experience. Content is a constituent of artistic truth (or falsehood). Artistic truth was not, for Jones, equivalent to realism – he would have shuddered at the thought; it meant the expression of the universal through the particular. Because he was interested in the whole of human experience, he objected to the nominalism of the mediaeval philosopher William of Ockham, which he had discussed with friends in the 1920s and 1930s.[34] Ockham held that the world consisted only of unrelated singularities and that universal conceptions or names had no meaning.[35] (In many respects, nominalism is the mediaeval prototype of late twentieth-century 'deconstruction'.) From about 1925, three years before he began to write poetry, he was committed in his painting to expressing the universal through the particular. For this reason, and although he loved Wales and was very British (as distinct from English), he was no mere nationalist and certainly not, as he has ludicrously been called, a regionalist.[36] Owing partly to his becoming a Catholic in 1921, he was, more than any important native-born English writer, European in intellectual perspective. But in his art – his painting and his poetry – he is not European; of all major modern British poets and painters, Jones is the most richly and deeply British. No writer since Malory has contributed so much so authentically to the Arthurian tradition we call the Matter of Britain – which is, after Christianity, the unifying myth of the Western world. Paradoxically, his being so deeply British makes him so universally human. In 1929 he read with approval these words by Gide: 'By nationalizing itself a literature takes its place and finds its significance in the concert of humanity . . . What more Spanish than Cervantes? more English than Shakespeare? more Italian than Dante? . . . more Russian than Dostoiewsky, and what more universally human than these writers?'[37] In the margin beside this passage, Jones writes these words: 'three bloody cheers'.

CHAPTER 4

'Shut, too, in a tower of words': Dylan Thomas' modernism

John Goodby and Christopher Wigginton

> I never thought that localities meant so much, nor the genius of
> places, nor anything like that. (Dylan Thomas)[1]

In one of the more bizarre asides in 'The Function of Criticism', an
essay which has come to look increasingly radical the more the notion
of a unitary modernism is revised, T. S. Eliot observed that 'the pos-
sessors of the inner voice ride ten in a compartment to a football
match at Swansea, listening to the inner voice which breathes the
eternal message of vanity, fear and lust . . . It is a voice to which, for
convenience, we may give a name: and the name I suggest is Whig-
gery'.[2] The claim is evidence of Eliot's rightward progression in the
1920s, a coincidental seizing on the birthplace of Dylan Thomas as a
location for irredeemable provincialism. For Eliot, having Vetch Field
rather than Little Gidding as a destination is a sure sign of the plebeian 'inner voice'; Swansea equals Dissent, industry, philistinism and
possibly also internal British difference, a would-be insider's put-down
to distract from Eliot's self-fashioning as Anglican, classicist and mon-
archist. Yet the slur cuts both ways, and can equally be said to furnish
a starting-point for a consideration of Thomas' poetry and its relationship to modernist precursors like Eliot himself. In this chapter we shall
argue that while Thomas was, in several ways, the closest of his generation to *The Waste Land* and the essays on the Metaphysicals and
Renaissance dramatists, his work also acts as a form of punishment for
high modernist condescension, embodying as it does the fear expressed in *Sweeney Agonistes* that life is no more than 'birth and copula-
tion and death'. It will, we hope, be shown that this kind of uncertain
and dual relationship with other writers and texts – close yet critical,
derivative yet strikingly original – is a key aspect of Thomas' writing
and its reworking of modernism.

In order to do this we will be looking at the poetry most influenced by modernism, that from the first three collections; *18 Poems* (1934), *Twenty-Five Poems* (1936) and *The Map of Love* (1939). The stress will be on its liminal and hybrid qualities, its negotiations of constructions of Welshness through a Gothicised, even grotesque modernism, set in the context of the New Country reaction against modernist experimentalism and the social crisis of the 1930s. We will end with a brief consideration of the transition between the often gnomic compression of the earlier poetry and the more accessible later style, suggesting some connections between Thomas' use of voice and his continuing resonance within popular culture. In adopting these approaches we are conscious that understanding of the poetry – perhaps more than with any other modern poet of equivalent stature – has been delayed by superannuated critical paradigms. These, largely of a New Critical/Leavisite and/or Freudian vintage, are made more difficult to deal with by their collusion with the enormous quantities of biography, reminiscence and anecdote surrounding the poet, as well as by his position between polarised Welsh national(ist), British and international identities. The result of Thomas' iconic status as the type of self-doomed poet and the assault on it – most notoriously by Amis and Holbrook – has been to make detached critical assessment exceedingly difficult. It has also tended to confine much of the best recent work on Thomas to a wary, if lucid, empiricism.[3]

It is no coincidence that the decline in interest since 1970 or so dates from the rise of critical theory as a major force in the academy, and the reasons for this – to which we return later – have much to do with the anathema, for those influenced by the poststructuralist critique, of 'voice', of literary presence and authority, and an uncritical acceptance of his detractors' characterisation of Thomas' work as late-Romantic. Interestingly, Thomas' critical fortunes resemble those suffered until recently by (post)colonial and Irish literatures, for long the safe havens of those unwilling to come to terms with newer critical approaches. This, in itself, would suggest that he is overdue for the kinds of reading which are now proving so fruitful in these formerly neglected areas. Since the 1970s, in fact, those outside the narrow world of Anglo-Welsh literary studies have charted an unthinking middle course between the acolytes and detractors precisely because they rarely thought seriously about Thomas at all.[4] The difficulties involved in breaking with this approach can be seen in the swiftness with which even now those who begin by appealing for fresh appraisals, such as Neil Corcoran and Alan Bold, descend to the old *ad hominem* clichés.[5] This kind of fudging of the issues is no longer acceptable, we feel; given the centrality of Thomas to 1930s poetry, to the transition from modernism to the Movement in the UK and to the mid 1950s revolt against academicist poetry in the USA, it is high time that one of the century's most discussed poets ceased to be one of its most critically misinterpreted and neglected.

Born in 1914, Dylan Thomas came of age as a poet in the early 1930s, a period of economic turmoil, social radicalism and the supersession of high modernism by new literary styles. Auden's *Poems* (1930), the *New Signatures* (1932) and *New Country* (1933) anthologies edited by Michael Roberts, and collections by poets represented in them – William Empson, Cecil Day Lewis, William Plomer, Stephen Spender – swiftly established a non-experimental, discursive, politically left poetic norm.[6] This response to modernism has been summed up by Spender:

> What we had . . . in common was in part Auden's influence, in part also not so much our relationship to one another as to what had gone before us. The writing of the 1920s had been characterised variously by despair, cynicism, self-conscious aestheticism, and by the prevalence of French influences. Although it was perhaps symptomatic of the political post-war era, it was consciously anti-political . . . Perhaps, after all, the qualities which distinguished us from the writers of the previous decade lay not in ourselves, but in the events to which we reacted. These were unemployment, economic crisis, nascent fascism, approaching war.[7]

Spender's account, perhaps out of tactical necessity, describes a modernism which is the mirror-image of the practice of those under 'Auden's influence'. The result now seems curiously distorted; how could Pound, Wyndham Lewis, Lawrence, 'the writing of the 1920s', have seemed 'consciously anti-political'? For Spender, however, the definition of the political is relatively narrow and sociologistic, and the notion of politics as purely superstructural is revealed in his switch from the internal and subjectivist ('despair') to the external and determinist ('lay not in ourselves'). It is a shift endorsed more recently by historians of modernism. Thus, Malcolm Bradbury and James McFarlane argue that after 1930 'certain elements of Modernism seem to be reallocated, as history increasingly came back in for intellectuals, as, with the loss of purpose and social cohesion, and the accelerating pace of technological change, *modernity was a visible scene open to simple report*' (our emphasis).[8] 'Visible'; 'open'; 'simple'; such qualities were anathema to Thomas who, precociously aware of metropolitan literary developments, rejected them for a closed and complex writing in which formal conservatism was estranged from itself by its modernist content, and modernist form undermined by an organicist pseudo-coherence.

If the New Country poets turned a diagnostic gaze upon society, Thomas deliberately opposed what he saw as their presumptive hyper-rationality. Small wonder, then, that William Empson, discussing *18 Poems*, found them 'very off the current fashion'. Just how 'off' can be seen by comparing Auden's 'Sir, no man's enemy' with the opening verse of 'Light breaks where no sun shines', a poem which helped confirm Thomas' arrival on the London literary scene and was included in his first collection:

> Sir, no man's enemy, forgiving all
> But will his negative inversion, be prodigal:
> Send to us power and light, a sovereign touch
> Curing the intolerable neural itch

> Light breaks where no sun shines;
> Where no sea runs, the waters of the heart
> Push in their tides;
> And, broken ghosts with glow-worms in their heads,
> The things of light
> File through the flesh where no flesh decks the bones.[9]

Although the initial difficulty of Auden's syntax and 'unpoetic' vocabulary reveal modernist influence, after the second line the piled-up opening clauses unravel and the sense of the poem becomes, and remains, accessible. The difficulties posed by 'Light breaks', however, are of a different order, even though it is (by Thomas' early standards) syntactically straightforward. The difficulties, characteristic of his poetry of this period, are many; they include the disconcerting combination of lack of specificity (of time, place, etc.) and lack of abstraction (lack of one usually implies the presence of the other), and the use of the grotesque rather than irony as a mode of critique (this largely stems from the Metaphysical trope of the body as cosmos).[10] Despite the differences in approach, however, the New Country writers were generally impressed by *18 Poems*.

One reason for this (along with the mid 1930s reaction to New Country which Thomas was seen as having initiated) was an intellectual climate heavily influenced by Freudianism and surrealism. Freud, of course, was central to the decade's poetic of demystification; as Robin Skelton has claimed, Freud was read politically, as a champion of individualism and freedom and an honorary socialist. Indeed, any psychoanalytic exposé of human nature was regarded, *per se*, as revolutionary.[11] Thus, in 1936 Cecil Day Lewis could mark the difference between Thomas, Barker, Gascoyne and Clifford Dyment on the one hand, and New Country poetry on the other, but place both within broadly Freudian parameters; in an echo of the politics of Popular Frontism which began in 1934–5, the younger poets were treated as literary allies against a common enemy. If Auden was the gallant lieutenant leading the main body of troops over the top, Thomas was the salt-of-the-earth NCO in charge of a more plebeian team of sappers who would detonate their mines under the ruling class, the id teaming up with the ego to strike against the tyrannical (and increasingly fascist) bourgeois superego.

Yet although Thomas linked his poetry to the general interest in Freudianism, in a questionnaire of 1934 and elsewhere, his avowed distrust of system – embodied in his poetic practice – makes it impossible to read it as programatically psychoanalytic. This is not to say that the work cannot be analysed, of course. Stuart Crehan, in one succinct account, argues that Thomas made 'a Freudian exemplar of himself' and that the poetry arose from a conflict between the rebellious libido and a repressive superego which was an internalisation of paternal authority.[12] To illustrate his point he cites another piece from *18 Poems*, 'The force that through the green fuse drives the flower':

> The force that through the green fuse drives the flower
> Drives my green age; that blasts the roots of trees
> Is my destroyer.
> And I am dumb to tell the crooked rose
> My youth is bent by the same wintry fever.[13]

In this most typical of Thomas' early poems, as Crehan notes, 'the phallic fuse and ejaculatory flower are symbolically repressed by a root-blasting force which turns the speaker's initial energy against itself. As if this were not punishment enough, the speaker's super-ego repeatedly reminds him of his inability to speak ("And I am dumb to tell").' Throughout the poetry, for Crehan, there runs a symbolism of castration which in Freud is associated with birth itself – 'the prototype of all castration' – while the desire to return to the womb 'is a substitute for [the] wish to copulate' and so avoid the castrating father. This reminds us of Thomas' ambivalent attitude toward his own father, encourager of his own 'lovely gift of the gab' but also a brooding presence, at one level the monitory figures, simultaneously terrible and pitiable, of the poems. Yet the dominant tone of the treatment of such material is ambivalence, as Thomas' response to the attacks on 'Light breaks' for its 'obscenity' shows.[14] At this time he discussed his poetry in terms which echo Auden's of the need to 'strip bare' the recesses of the self, but at the same time stressed its reliance on an inassimilable morbidity, and rejected the idea that it should have a therapeutic role.[15] As Tony Conran points out, 'This reluctance to come clean is not a fault of *18 Poems* but a condition of their being.'[16] Nevertheless, the traditional weaknesses of Freudian criticism – a tendency to ignore differences and a slippage from text to author – can be seen at work even here, and in Thomas criticism historically they have tended to acquire exaggerated form. If Crehan is right to view the adoption of a Freudian role as only one among many, the issue of role-playing raised in making oneself an 'exemplar' nevertheless goes beyond psychological structures to issues of social and literary identity. The ambiguity and role-playing ultimately derive from marginally modernist, national and historical locations out of which Thomas manoeuvred his banal psychic material (keen awareness of mortality, adolescent male sexuality) at a critical angle to the *zeitgeist*.

Given their social agendas, the New Country poets were incapable of grasping that Thomas' resistance to their own abstraction and discursiveness was a major part of his point.[17] As a result they relegated the poetry he wrote to an ancillary, subaltern status, a complement to, rather than a critique of, their own. Reviews show that they often regarded Thomas as a hit-or-miss, as well as an impressive, writer. MacNeice, for example, described *18 Poems* as wild and drunken speech, but with the saving grace of rhythm. Spender, less sympathetic, claimed it was 'just poetic stuff with no beginning or end, or intelligent and intelligible control'.[18] Such responses linked Thomas with surrealism, and played a crucial part in the reception of his poetry. Thomas argued that his poems were not automatic writing and therefore not surrealist; the ignorance pleaded in a letter of 1934 is typical: 'But who is this Gascoyne? I saw a geometrical effort of his in one *New Verse*, and also a poem in which he boasted of the ocarina in his belly. Is he much subtler or more absurd than I imagine? It is his sheer incompetence that strikes me more than anything else.'[19]

This kind of response – to protest painstaking craftsmanship – was understandable. Yet both the denial and its narrow definition of surrealism have been accepted too uncritically; Thomas was, after all, an avid reader of the avant-garde *transition*. Moreover, the 'last snapshot of the European intelligentsia', as Walter Benjamin called surrealism, was in fact a complex set of artistic practices which went far beyond voluntarism or associationism, as a glance at the variety of surrealist visual art –

say, Dali's hallucinatory realism and the collage of Ernst's *La Semaine de Bonté* – will reveal. (The claim that surrealism in Freudian terms simply *inverts* passive realism is true up to a point, but overlooks the linkage between the movement and political activism, most strikingly illustrated by André Breton's yoking of radical surrealism to Trotsky's Fourth International.) More important, to the extent that surrealism had affinities with the Metaphysicals' violent yoking together of heterogeneous images (the conceit as a distant cousin of Lautréamont's collision between an umbrella and a sewing machine on a dissecting table) there was a link between surrealist practice and the climate created earlier by Eliot and Grierson. Thomas, an avid reader of Donne, exploited such similarities to forge a semi-surrealised Metaphysical mode, a form of Gothic, from a marginalised and belated Welsh modernism. In this – as with Freudianism – he was pragmatic and ambivalent rather than systematic. 'Altarwise by owl-light' from *Twenty-Five Poems* (1936), most frequently adduced as proof of surrealism, reproduces surrealist effects. Sonnet VI, for example, ends:

> Adam, time's joker, on a witch of cardboard
> Spelt out the seven seas, an evil index,
> The bagpipe-breasted ladies in the deadweed
> Blew out the blood gauze through the wound of manwax. (*CP*, 61)

The point, however, is not that such lines have no 'real' meaning to be unravelled; they do (although that is not the whole point either). It is, rather, that it would be obtuse to deny the calculated appeal here to a sense of the surrealist absurd. Thomas, in other words, guys and mimics the attributes of a metropolitan style where it can be made to coincide with his own tactics of estrangement, but stops short of becoming a surrealist *pur sang* – as, for example, David Gascoyne did. In both embracing and rejecting surrealism he created a provincial simulacrum of surrealism, or what might be called (for want of a better word) surregionalism.

This parodic (dis)engagement was enacted at the high point of surrealism in Britain, the London Surrealist Exhibition of June 1936, when Thomas toured the galleries offering visitors cups of boiled string as he enquired: 'Weak or strong?'[20] His use of surrealism in his work at this time can probably be seen most strikingly in his prose fiction. Again, these works arouse and then exploit readerly expectations; 'The Orchards', for example, is a surrealist parody, a rich elaboration on the nervously dismissive humour of the letter to Spender:

Put a two-coloured ring of two women's hair round the blue world, white and coal-black against the summer-coloured boundaries of sky and grass, four-breasted stems at the poles of the summer sea-ends, eyes in the sea-shells, two fruit trees out of a coal-hill: poor Marlais' morning, turning to evening, spins before you. Under the eyelids, where the inward night drove backwards through the skull's base, into the wide, first world on the far-away eye, two love-trees smouldered like sisters. Have an orchard sprout in the night, an enchanted woman with a spine like a railing burn her hand in the leaves, man-on-fire a mile from a sea have a wind put out your heart.[21]

Thomas, then, cannot be read solely in terms of Freudianism or surrealism; both are period elements he deployed tactically, while the desire to emulate which we might detect in their usage is inseparable from a simultaneous sense of rejection and self-mockery, of centrality and marginality, of purity and heterogeneity. Such disconcertingly *hybrid* conjunctions account for much of the incomprehension, then and now, of the poetry. For as Homi Bhabha has argued in *The Location of Culture*, what disturbs the metropolitan centre most profoundly are those identities seen as sham, those which, in the act of imitating, disturb the fixed and binary categories of identity politics, of them/us, self/other. Thus, '[Hybridity's] threat . . . comes from the prodigious and strategic production of conflictual, fantastic, discriminatory "identity effects" in the play of a power that is elusive because it hides no essence, no "itself"'.[22] The whole tenor of the critical attack on Thomas, we should remember, centres on his alleged *in*authenticity, on the poet as impostor. Crucially for Bhabha, and for a more nuanced understanding of the importance of Thomas' location(s), hybrid writings have to be distinguished from the simple inversion of the binary terms of a relationship; 'Hybridity represents that ambivalent "turn" of the discriminated subject into the terrifying, exorbitant object of paranoid classification – a disturbing questioning of the images and presences of authority . . . [it] is not a third term that resolves the tension between two cultures'.[23]

Most discussions of the relationship between Thomas' work and his Swansea origins relate him in some way to a putatively 'essential' Welsh identity, mirroring precisely those dominant discourses of Englishness they generally purport to displace. Thomas is cast either as the bardic Other of thin-lipped London literati or the Welshman who welshed on his birthright for a mess of BBC pottage. The idea of a hybrid writer – not 'a third term that resolves tension' – confounds polarised views and the process by which they mutually confirm and entrench each other. Bhabha's notion of hybridity derives from the work of the Indian

Subaltern Studies Group, work which emphasises the need to look at postcolonial writing in terms of its subversion of mainstream writing through *mimicry*, what Bhabha also calls 'sly civility', of its location on the boundaries between the provincial and the outright colonial, a location which does not permit a simple ethical response. Subaltern Studies Group members, that is, see traditional nationalist responses to national subordination as totalising, restrictive and ultimately untenable political discourses which are compromised by their tendency to reproduce the repressive, essentialist structures and values of the (ex)colonial/metropolitan centre. In this way they reject opposed positions which are part of the same discourse, each produced within a framework of identity thinking which holds as self-evident the origin of meaning in a unitary self and, by extension (according to the imperatives of liberal ideology), a nation-state. There are, of course, grave dangers of critical aggrandisement here; Wales is not India (although the analogy has been drawn).[24] A closer parallel, however, illustrates the potential for a postcolonial redefinition of some elements of 'Welshness'. Critics in the field of Irish Studies have recently begun to explore the ways in which postcolonialism attempts to fragment and disintegrate the monologism of cultural affiliation and to rethink notions such as mimicry and hybridity 'out of a recognition of the claustrophobic intensity of the relationship between Ireland and Britain'.[25] The distinctiveness of the Welsh situation is not just in its dormancy (this is how traditional nationalism would read it; a 'national spirit' waits to be aroused), but in its even more impacted and compromised nature. In this sense Thomas is – paradoxically – far more 'Welsh' than writers who aspire to an ideal of a pure Welshness – or of Welshness *as* a kind of purity – registering as he does at every level of his poetry the struggle with 'claustrophobic intensity'. It is, we would argue, precisely in the modernism of Thomas that the mark of the onset of a deep historical crisis is found in a form of interstitial writing which confounds simple notions of identity.

Thomas' hybrid qualities can be seen indirectly in the way claims for identifiably Welsh elements in his early poetry have been continuously thwarted by its lack of obvious markers of nationality, despite ingenious attempts to detect the influence of cynghannedd or Welsh speech rhythms presumed to result from *métèque* status.[26] Although a more oblique influence has been detected in his ability to take 'an outsider's advantage of the English language' (somewhat inflated by Walford Davies to a 'delight' in 'revenging' himself on the 'imperial, standardising norms of the English language'), it can scarcely be distinguished from the kinds of linguistic subversion which mark many poets, regardless of origin, and particularly those who write, as Thomas did, in transitional periods. More important is a shifting relationship toward fixed identities perceived as constraints. Thomas' ambivalence toward nationality was expressed not so much in his outright denials ('Land of my fathers – my fathers can keep it') as in the tongue-in-cheek styling of himself as the 'Rimbaud of Cwmdonkin Drive', a *voyant* who felt lost without 'the aspidistra, the provincial drive, the morning cafe [and] the evening pub' of suburbia.[27] His poetic identity, or rather *process*, is precisely this mediation between the bardic and the banal, the balance of *hywll*-inflated rhetoric and literary *lèse-majesté*.[28] Conran has deemed Thomas' national identity 'largely a negative thing – he is not English'; but this itself is a one-sided assessment. In the Machereyan sense the 'negative thing' is also an absence that speaks, and what it speaks of is an initially enabling isolation, a source of self-belief, a calculated philistinism and defensive humour.

But if consideration of Thomas' status forces us to modify our view of the way in which national 'identity' operates, what precisely was his relationship to Welsh modernism? As Gareth Thomas has pointed out, in Thomas' time 'no Anglo-Welsh literary tradition that was in any way comparable to the Anglo-Irish had yet been established'.[29] The Anglo-Irish/Anglo-Welsh comparison is devastating, of course, precisely because Welsh modernism was patchy and disparate even by comparison with the English variety. If modernism in Britain was largely imported – think of James, Conrad, Pound, and Eliot – it was heavily Irish-influenced. Predictably, the Welsh variety has been seen solely in terms of its input to the definition of British (i.e., English) modernism, in the shape of David Jones. Although its anomalousness and belatedness are arguably a sign of writing which deals with the condition of Welshness, concentration on Jones' high modernism (endorsed by Eliot, and publication by Faber) has led critics away from Welsh modernism. This is particularly the case with poets writing in Welsh, but Anglo-Welsh writers have also suffered.

Crucial to an appreciation of Thomas' Welsh modernist context is the work of the fiction writer Caradoc Evans. Evans – to use Frank Kermode's term, a paleo-modernist (that is, a writer modernist in content but not in form) – was author of the pioneering short-story collection *My People* (1915), described as the Welsh equivalent of Joyce's *Dubliners*. It combines anecdotal structure with savage, grotesque realism in its attack on rural Welsh Nonconformism, hypocrisy, greed and cruelty, and made Evans himself 'the most reviled man in Wales'. There is no doubt that Thomas, who visited Evans in 1936, saw him as a literary hero.[30] But Evans is also a literary forerunner in the sense that his tales reverberate with the discourses of Nonconformism; their language is 'simple, often majestic, and suggestive also of parable and myth', while mocking those who use it for blatantly repressive ends.[31] As in Thomas' poetry, religion's musical and rhetorical resources – part of its radical tradition – were exploited, even as the social forms it had capitulated to were critiqued.

Yet as well as belonging to a later generation, very different forces intersected in Thomas than in Evans; his upbringing was freethinking, his surroundings suburban and his literary and political contexts more radical and cosmopolitan (again, this requires qualification; rejecting organised religion, Thomas seems to have opted for a form of Lawrentianism, a faith in the interrelatedness of all things which became more religiose during the 1940s). Again, it would be wrong to see this as a simple split, this time along urban–rural lines. Swansea lies at the westernmost point of English-speaking South Wales, its frontier, liminal situation reinforced by the fact that it also represented the class divide which Thomas' parents had crossed in order to achieve middle-class respectability. In the 1920s the Welsh-speaking farming communities of Carmarthenshire still lay within easy reach of Thomas' home; Swansea was a mainly (but not totally) English-speaking town hemmed around to the north and west by its Welsh-speaking hinterland. Historical change was less equivocal and inflected the treatment of Welsh identity as repression and ambiguity. Not only did the effects of the First World War postdate *My People*, so too did the economic crisis which gripped Wales from the early 1920s. This can be put another way by noting that Thomas' move to London in 1934 was that of an entire Welsh generation. And if Wales was more closely tied to England than any other of the UK's component parts, it was because its economy – lopsided to serve imperial rather than domestic needs – had produced what Gwyn A. Williams has called an 'offshore working class', with its middle-class appendages. It was thus especially vulnerable to the decline of British power; recession bit more deeply and earlier in Wales than anywhere else in Britain.

The Depression pushed the already high unemployment level up to 32 per cent, a figure around which it lingered until the end of the 1930s.

The demographic effects were devastating; over half a million people left Wales in the 1930s, most of them from the South. Though it was one of the more advanced areas of the South Walian economy, 'even Swansea with its poets and musicians . . . fell into a pall of neglect and depression, a collapse of social capital and a dismal legacy in bad housing, ill-health, poor environment'.[32] Thomas' own (dis)location ensured both relative personal comfort and an inescapable awareness of suffering; his political response was a socialism as intense but more diffuse and durable than that of the more overtly Left poets. The general disaster of the times sharpened the differences between a generation of radicalised Anglo-Welsh writers and Welsh-language writers, whose nationalism and rural values were often reinforced by ethnic–linguistic exclusivism, or even flirtations with fascism.[33] As Conran claims, 1930s Anglo-Welsh writers had nowhere to go but London: 'They either stayed in Wales and festered in isolation, or they offered themselves as international or colonial recruits to the London intelligentsia. Nationalism was hardly an option for most of them.'[34]

This is an important point given recent attempts to interpret modernism in nationalist terms. Robert Crawford's *Devolving English Literature*, for example, argues that modernism should be read as a provincial revolution against a complacent Anglocentric literary establishment, and this can clearly be applied in some measure to Thomas. Crawford is certainly on firm ground when he opposes what he calls 'cursory' accounts of modernism which stress its 'cosmopolitanism and internationalism to present it as a facet of "high" metropolitan culture'. Yet the resultant claim that the provincial/demotic on the one hand and cosmopolitanism on the other 'are not opposites; they complement one another' seems to us too neat a reversal, a too-easy overcoming of very real and material differences of class, gender and so on within the nation and modernism as a literary trend. Crawford overlooks the role of bourgeois nationalist culture in submerging the kinds of internal national differences which produce hybrid, mixed, boundary writings (for his argument to work, the desire to integrate within the London literary and social mainstream on the part of writers like Thomas also has to be seen in purely personal terms as an error of judgment).[35] To view modernism chiefly as an outgrowth of a wholly positive nationalist self-assertion, then, is to depoliticise both nationalism and modernism; celebration of national difference erases internal difference and ignores nationalism's reactionary potential. Crawford cannot account for the juxtaposition of 'international' *and* 'colonial', and ultimately settles for the kind of cultural identity politics sketched above, according to which Thomas can only be interpreted as either 'genuinely' Welsh or an inauthentic showman.

What this suggests is that it is the acceptance of the existing terms of the debate about Thomas – authentic or inauthentic, success or failure – which is the truly impermissible critical move. In other words, when Paul Ferris, for example, registers 'fears' that Thomas' poems 'are thick with the affectations of poetry', we would see this as a problem not so much for Thomas' poems as for a narrow and conventional conception of poetry, and modernist poetry in particular.[36] *All* poetry – in its intertextual, parasitic, hybrid practice – is 'thick with the affectations of poetry', and this is not altered by presenting subjective moralising (who defines 'affectation', and on what grounds?) as universally agreed judgments. Modernism itself can be read as literary parody, and it is precisely what constitutes 'affectation' – or what the Russian Formalists would have called 'the literary' – which demands attention in Thomas' work. In this connection an area which immediately suggests itself is the use of grotesque style and the Gothic, elements which can be linked to Thomas' displaced, hybrid location and which have traditionally been seen in more purely Freudian and surrealist guise. Traditionally associated with mixing and impropriety, grotesque style and Gothic have affinities with Evans' black humour and brutal sexuality as well as with larger literary trends. The grotesque played a central role in Welsh modernism, as Conran has argued: 'Modernism in Wales is most at home with the grotesque. It is there that modernism characteristically shows itself, in Saunders Lewis as much as in Caradoc Evans and Dylan Thomas. The nightmare of monstrosity underlies the middle-class rejection of the *buchedd*, the sense of being suffocated by its hypocrisy and narrowness.'[37]

It is in the short stories written before *Portrait of the Artist as a Young Dog* (1940) that the Gothic and grotesque aspects in Thomas are flaunted most extensively. Many of the stories – some collected in *The Map of Love* (1939) – centre on the imaginary Jarvis valley. Jarvis is Evans' Manteg at one remove, Gothicised under the pressures of social crisis and literary displacement, and it provides the setting for a collection of Welsh rural stereotypes; thus, its weather is always lowering, its landscapes charged with apocalyptic threat and repressed sexual energy, its scattered dwellings inhabited by children, murderers, gardeners and vivisectionists, haunted by the Holy Six and other religious fanatics, by witches, visionaries, lunatics, decayed gentry. Despite the critical solemnities pronounced over them, however, the stories have more than a hint of *Cold Comfort Farm* about them, referring as they do to the town of Llarregub ('bugger all' when read backwards), and containing such characters as Sam Rib, Dai Twice and Old Vole. This location, then, is a version rather than a copy of that of Evans, travestying even as it draws on its bleak realism. What applies to the prose applies, yet more variously, to the poetry. Both *18 Poems* and *Twenty-Five Poems* trail their Nonconformist, Gothically inflected properties, and are crammed with – to list a sample – ghosts, vampires, a 'Cadaver' figure, references to Struwwelpeter, tombs, sores, flies, cataracts, carcasses, cancers, 'cypress lads', hanged men, mandrakes, gallows, crosses, worms and maggots. Both books exude a charnel atmosphere of decay and mortality and their libertarian strivings are inextricably linked to the darker aspects they purport to reject, with the first poem of the first collection exploring the idea that the 'boys of summer' are 'in their ruin', always in the process of themselves becoming 'the dark deniers'.

From this it is clear that, far from being 'universal' in its portrayal of adolescent crises of identity, Thomas' extraordinary blend of sex and death is not just of its time and place, but also very lower-middle-class and *male*.[38] The early poems chart not the achievement of stable identity but a realisation of its impossibility – in both national and personal terms – figured in part through gender. In pushing back to pre-natal origins, the speakers of the poems are attempting to reach the point at which they can escape the anxieties of sexual maturity facing Thomas himself. Thus, in 'Before I knocked' (in *18 Poems*), the speaker is without specific gender, both 'brother to Mnetha's daughter / And sister to the fathering worm', existing 'in a molten form' (*CP*, 11). Nevertheless, this is no prelapsarian or ahistorical vision; even before birth suffering cannot be escaped:

> My throat knew thirst before the structure
> Of skin and veins around the well
> Where words and water make a mixture
> Unfailing till the blood runs foul;
> My heart knew love, my belly hunger;
> I smelt the maggot in my stool.   (*CP*, 12)

But if there is a gesture toward the elimination of anxiety, there is also a petit-bourgeois bravado, a desire to exorcise uneasiness by dramatising it. As elsewhere in Thomas' poetry, then, the unborn child is identified with, even as he rebels against, paternal and metaphysical authority. He is Christ – 'You who bow down at cross and altar / Remember me and pity Him / Who . . . doublecrossed my mother's womb' – and Christ is the representative of the father, of the phallocentric authority of the Symbolic Order and the promise of plenitude. He is also, however, the betrayed son ('doublecrossed'), both masculine and feminine, what Thomas called the 'castrated Christ' of official religion, and the attempt to escape anxiety by imagining an ungendered past generates new anxiety in the actuality of the father-dominated present. The anxiety, it might be argued, *is* the poetry; Christ is Logos, the word, the poet-as-hero charting his narcissistic, masturbatory sexual experience in 'My hero bares his nerves' (*18 Poems*). Writing, the means of achieving paternal sanction for the son, and thus the way to sexual experience, breaks down leaving the speaker trapped in a cycle of identity formation through self-abuse. Masturbation and writing both figure as an unnerving absence and as a disquieting plenitude:

> And those poor nerves so wired to the skull
> Ache on the lovelorn paper
> I hug to love with my unruly scrawl
> That utters all love hunger
> And tells the page the empty ill.
> . . .
> He holds the wire from this box of nerves
> Praising the mortal error
> Of death and birth, the two sad knaves of thieves,
> And the hunger's emperor;
> He pulls the chain, the cistern moves.   (*CP*, 14)

Either form of self-authentication disrupts itself (and it is noticeable that the poem begins in the first and ends in the third person). The paper – both writing paper and tissue paper – is 'lovelorn' because it bears the evidence of an absent presence, the unruly scrawl of ink/semen telling the narrator of the deferral of real voice or love as opposed to his auto-affection. In his discussion of Rousseau's *Confessions* in *Of Grammatology*, Derrida comments on the dangers of this process in terms of the 'supplement', that addition which would complete self-presence but which instead reveals its incompletion and lack: '[a] terrifying menace, the supplement has not only the power of procuring an absent presence through its image; procuring it for us by proxy [*procuration*] of the sign, it holds it at a distance and masters it. For this presence is at the same time desired and feared.'[39] Because of its assumption of authority, Thomas' 'baring' of this 'nerve' clearly threatened a more understated, 'English' self-presence, as revealed by a critical language which charged him, on occasion, with sexual immaturity and unmanliness. Typical of this kind of attack is Robert Graves' claim that 'Thomas was nothing more than a Welsh demagogic masturbator who failed to pay his bills.'[40] Interestingly, Graves mirrors here the notorious assaults on Keats' poetry a century before; just as Keats' 'shabby genteel' class origins, for Byron, were linked to masturbatory immaturity in his poetry ('Johnny piss-a-bed Keats'), so Thomas' class and national identity, and through them his poetry, are impugned by Graves.[41]

The value of Gothic to Thomas, then, stemmed from its generic capability for organising disparate stylistic and thematic elements – parodic appropriation, belated modernism, social radicalism, sexual uncertainty and the plenitude/lack of writing – within the outrageous constructedness which is its hallmark. Precisely the excess of Gothic enables it to perform this kind of function; as Fred Botting has pointed out, Gothic is the 'signification of a writing of excess' which shadows the progress of modernity and enlightenment with a dark counter-narrative.[42] In this way it also fulfilled Thomas' career need to subvert New Country hyper-rationality and dogmatism (although not neces-sarily in a merely irrational or ahistorical manner; as Crehan notes, the 'rich polysemy and fluidity' of the early poetry – thematic as well as linguistic – can be seen as an attempt to keep alive the dialectic which had been frozen by Stalinism by the early 1930s, just as it was simultaneously being erased by Hitler).[43] Gothic – like Thomas' work – operates with hybrid states and forms, insisting on the inescapability of the biological bases of existence. In it, as in the poetry generally, 'ambivalence and uncertainty obscure single meaning', while the anxiety over boundary transgression it feeds off was, at the geopolitical level, in line with the 1930s *zeitgeist*.[44] In alluding to a Gothic model – *Frankenstein* – to describe his practice at this time, Thomas implicitly defended such an oblique approach: 'So many modern poets take the living flesh as their object, and, by their clever dissecting, turn it into a carcass. I prefer to take the dead flesh, and, by any positivity of faith that is in me, build up a living flesh from it.'[45]

We are not claiming here, of course, that a Gothic thematics 'explains' Thomas' early work; what we do feel is that it provides a framework for interpreting a series of Welsh and modernist elements in that work, and that it has been overlooked because of the lack of awareness of those writing about Thomas of recent developments in criticism. The basic evidence, however, is clear enough, and possible Gothic influences – Thomas' 'serious' reading, interest in film and taste in pulp fiction – have been known for years.[46] Thomas' devotion to the work of the horror novelist Arthur Machen, for example, has occasionally been mentioned in critical work but not really considered significant.[47] Machen, the author of what has been described as 'the most decadent book in English', *The Hill of Dreams* (1907), 'took up Darwinian anxieties as the basis for terror', mixing among others Huysmans, Pater, *La Queste del Sante Graal* and Sherlock Holmes. In *The Great God Pan* (1894), to take one example, a doctor operates on a young girl to open her 'inner eye' to the existence of Pan. The resulting visionary power eventually drives her mad, and when the 'hell-child' born after her coupling with Pan dies, it passes through all the stages of biological species reversion, ending up as 'primal slime'. Parallels with 'The Lemon' and other works by Thomas might be drawn, but the important link lies in the resemblances between Machen's biological and physical emphases and Thomas' concern with cycles of inter-involved growth, biologic recapitulations and pre-human states of consciousness. It is precisely this kind of influence, of course, which can be used to answer the 'glandular' charge so often levelled against Thomas' work.

This aspect of the work needs to be seen in the light of a powerful modernist influence, besides that of Eliot: D. H. Lawrence. There are many obvious similarities; shared provincial and class outsiderness, Nonconformist background (and personal puritanism) and an emphasis on redemption through the flesh rather than the disembodied intellect. The relationship of both to the dominant metropolitan styles of the day is also similar. Tony Pinkney has argued that Lawrence attacked the classicising 'anti-Wagnerian' modernism of Mansfield, Pound, Joyce, Eliot and Lewis in order to forge an alternative Expressionist, northern-Gothic variety.[48] Lawrence's fiction generally – think of *The Rainbow* or *The Plumed Serpent* – rejects the Hellenism running in English culture from Arnold to Hulme and Eliot 'in which "criticism", "consciousness" and "irony" are cardinal virtues', in favour of the creaturely virtues of a more 'native' tradition deriving from Morris and Ruskin. It is this form of modernism which, in the Lincoln Cathedral pages of *The Rainbow*, is shown as incorporating classicism's 'virtues' within its host of small details rather than expelling them. The point is that only Gothic 'deconstructs the rigid model of inside/outside . . . Its outside is its inside; even the sly stone faces that denounce its incompletion are, after all, part of it. The Gothic contains its own "negation", which thereafter ceases to be its negative pure and simple, and is rather granted a local validity within a more generous system which exceeds it.'[49] The last part of this, it may be, reveals something of the limitations of Thomas as an artist and the major difference between him and Lawrence.[50] Nevertheless he can be seen as developing aspects of Lawrence's 'northern' modernism, the 'sly stone faces' of Lawrence perhaps recalling the 'sly civility' of Bhabha's subaltern and Thomas' own critical face-pulling.

Any discussion of Thomas' relationship to modernism must touch at some point on his use of language. This has consistently been seen as *the* distinguishing feature of his work, and he was well aware of its central, even compulsive nature: 'I use everything and anything to make my poems work . . . puns, portmanteau words, paradox, allusion, paronomasia, paragram, catachresis, slang, assonantal rhymes, vowel rhymes, sprung rhythm.'[51] The 1930s poetry displays not just the systematic foregrounding of the 'device' as a vehicle of estrangement, but also a belief that poetry should work 'out of' words, not 'towards them', recalling the Mallarméan dictum that 'Poems are made of words, not ideas.' At its most extreme, this yields attempts at wholly non-referential poems whose antecedents lie among the Russian 'zaum' poets, the Dadaists and the Gertrude Stein of *Tender Buttons*.[52] One point of such exercises, of course, is to prove that no writing can completely escape meaning-construction at the hands of a sufficiently determined (or self-deluded) reader. Only two of Thomas' poems – 'How Soon the Servant Sun' and 'Now' – go so far, and they show the parodic aspect of his modernism, foreshadowing in their extremism the shift away from it in the poetry of the 1940s. Yet even when not testing limits, Thomas is completely modernist in his insistence on the materiality of language and in the autonomy he grants to words. It was in this connection that he insisted he be read *literally*: his objection to Edith Sitwell's well-intentioned explication of the first sonnet of 'Altarwise by owl-light' was that 'She doesn't take the literal meaning: that a world-devouring ghost-creature bit out the horror of tomorrow from a gentleman's loins . . . This poem is a particular incident in a particular adventure, not a general, elliptical deprecation of this horrible, crazy, speedy life.'[53]

It is worth saying a little here about the implications of modernist practice for Thomas' style, since his 'everything and anything', in its relationship to the constraints of the poetry's conservative form, represents an internalised, imploded, even mimic modernism. The plethora of devices *replicate* the effect of modernist techniques such as collage, creating modernist textual instability and epistemological uncertainty. The parodic element which helps constitute modernist writing is fore-grounded in this poetry. Thus, rhyme schemes and stanza patterns are deployed whose elaborate ingenuity is in excess of any mimetic or structural requirement.[54] Syntax is sabotaged, such that 'normal' gram-mar becomes at least as hard to construe as modernist fragmentariness, usually through the deferral of main verbs by subordinate, but appar-ently independent, clauses. Of the poem which opens 'Hold hard, these ancient minutes in the cuckoo's month, / Under the lank, fourth folly on Glamorgan's hill, / As the green blooms ride upward, to the drive of time' (*CP*, 44), Walford Davies claims that

In these lines we are bound to hear *Hold hard these ancient minutes* as a main clause, even though the commas show that the real main clause is 'Hold hard . . . to the drive of time'. And before we've grasped as much, we will also have heard (as a complete syntactic unit, despite the comma) *As the green blooms ride upward to the drive of time* . . . Similar ghost-effects of syntax occur too often in Thomas to be mere accidents. He seems bent on accommodating them.[55]

And this is a straightforward case: in 'When, like a running grave, time tracks you down' there are no less than *thirty-four* subordinate clauses (some as short as a single word) in an opening sentence that stretches for twenty-five lines over five five-line verses. Not only does this stretch the possibilities of syntax; as with the use of surrealism and Freudianism there is more than a hint of mockery, of an effect analogous to what Bakhtin calls the double voice of parody.

Such procedures raise the issue of narrative briefly considered in the reference to 'Light breaks where no sun shines.' Virtually all of Thomas' poems are organised around a powerful narrative drive, a seemingly irresistible unfolding of event. Narrative is vital because it provides both an armature to which the many devices the poems require can be attached and a pretext for their deployment in the first place. Defending his poetry in 1934 Thomas argued that 'all good modern poetry is bound to be obscure. Remember Eliot: "The chief use of the 'meaning' of a poem, in the ordinary sense, may be to satisfy one habit of the reader, to keep his mind diverted and quiet, while the poem does its work upon him."'[56] 'Meaning', as Thomas also made clear in 'Answers to an Inquiry', refers to narrative; the echo is of 'Tradition and the Individual Talent', in which Eliot likens the phenomenal text of the poem to a bone used to distract a guard-dog by a burglar before he goes about his business, the lived materiality of the poem – as in *The Waste Land* – acting as a cover for, and authentication of, the operations of the ghostly discourse of the mythologies framing it. The narrative of *The Waste Land* is famously discontinuous, yet its very discontinuity produces a metanarrative, aided and abetted by Eliot's knowing annotations. In Thomas' poetry, on the contrary, the local narrative of the poem appears to offer immediate coherence, unity and closure, but is frequently empty, or banal, in the usual sense. That is, the discursive meaning-content is usually straightforward, invariably relating to the interrelatedness of the human and cosmic, the inextricability of processes of decay and growth. When Thomas wrote of the New Country poets that he could 'see the sensitive picking of words, but none of the strong inevitable pulling that makes a poem an event, a happening, an action perhaps, not a still-life or an experience *put down*, placed, regulated' he went only part of the way to explaining the difference between his work and theirs.[57] More to the point is the claim that the drive toward unification (of body, spirit, cosmos, etc.) leads directly to a language use in which the materiality and autonomy of the signifier is a given. Thomas grants images almost the same degree of 'literalness' and autonomy, such that poems are not only *not* sustained by external reference, but that they seem to be generated by the self-evolving dynamic of images, in narratives whose linguistic events frequently exceed any abstractable sense. Thomas' description of his writing process alludes to this: 'I let, perhaps, an image be made emotionally in me and then apply to it what intellectual and critical force I possess – let it breed another, let that image contradict the first, make, of the third image bred out of the other two together, a fourth contradictory image, and let them all, within my own imposed formal limits, conflict.'

This kind of poem is entirely, or almost entirely, interiorised, moving solely amongst irreducibly literal images that 'nevertheless seem to have the kind of air of significance about them that tempts us (unhelpfully) to unpack the poem like a suitcase'.[58] One image 'breed[s] another' in a piece like 'Where once the waters of your face', in which the initial mention of 'waters' is elaborated in a series of *implicit* metaphors; that is, the vehicle (the figurative part of the metaphor) – 'mermen', 'channels', 'wet fruits', 'corals' and so on – is not related back to its tenor (what is actually being referred to) – sexual desire, psychic depths, the amniotic 'waters' of the embryo. This is a narrative that 'just never *had* a real-world equivalent that could stand as referent [ie: as tenor] in the first place'.[59] Narrative advances, but the poem has been turned inside out; or, to use a different image, it is as if we are viewing the back of a tapestry. Paradoxically the high degree of control the poems display is offset by the arbitrary power of individual words and images of their development.

There is a social dimension to this. In Saussurean terms the stress on verbal autonomy weakens the links between signifiers and their socially agreed signifieds, raising linguistic arbitrariness above ostensible message content. According to Saussure all meanings attached to signifiers are arbitrary, since meaning is generated not by homologies between words and things but through the system of differential relationships between words themselves. To enable social discourse to occur, however, the bonds between signifier and signified are habitually agreed to be stable. Yet as Saussure points out, for the individual subject the bond never ceases to be an arbitrary one. The putative stability of social meanings inevitably becomes naturalised, and it is this fossilisation of the signifier–signified bond which Thomas' writing subverts, attacking the repression of our pre-moral delight in words. Put a different way, this could be taken to indicate the operation of the 'semiotic' in Thomas' work, that infantile, pre-gendered, inchoate energy which, according to Julia Kristeva, is repressed by our induction into the symbolic order of social injunctions which marshal signifiers with their signifieds. As Crehan argues, a poem like 'From love's first fever' is about the ways in which, through the process of language acquisition, we are *interpellated* as human subjects, accepting an inherited system of agreed linguistic meanings. Again, the radical implications of Thomas' poetic practice have been overlooked by critics who seek (or fail to find) a social dimension to the poetry precisely because they look for evidence only at the level of overt reference or allusion.

As he used up the poems from his adolescent notebooks, pushing certain aspects of his work to their logical conclusion in *Twenty-Five Poems*, Thomas' poetry began to signal a shift away from modernism in *The Map of Love*. 'After the funeral' is the prime critical exhibit in discussions of this turn, with 'Once it was the colour of saying' usually offered as his renunciation of the early work. In accepting these truisms there is always a danger of missing some important points. For one thing it is the *later*, not the earlier, poetry which is most full of 'the colour of saying'. Thomas – partly due to personal circumstances, partly due to the marginalisation of experimental writing and partly due to the new crisis of impending world war – was trying to write more accessibly by the late 1930s: the poems mentioned date from the year of Munich,

1938, and may be read beside more explicit 'crisis poetry' of the time, such as MacNeice's *Autumn Journal*. One less-frequently noticed consequence is the changed role of the *voice* that such 'accessible' writing implies. What seems purely technical – the fact that the sense of 'When, like a running grave' simply cannot be sustained, in being read aloud, across minefields of devices and multiple clauses – had profound implications for the *kind* of poetry Thomas wrote. Invariably, the decision to give intelligibility a higher priority weakened the Gothic-inflected modernism of the early style, its hybrid and heterogeneous qualities; and, in a number of poems in *The Map of Love*, the advantages and disadvantages of change are thematised and discussed in a self-conscious manner which is new.

One of these is 'How shall my animal', which opens by confronting the issue of expression and repression head on:

> How shall my animal
> Whose wizard shape I trace in the cavernous skull,
> Vessel of abscesses and exultation's shell,
> Endure burial under the spelling wall . . .
> Who should be furious,
> Drunk as a vineyard snail, flailed like an octopus,
> Roaring, crawling   (*CP* 14)

Beginning with a conventional image – of an inexpressible self as an 'inner animal' – the poem enacts rather than discusses the problems of expression which will involve burying it 'under the spelling wall' of speech and writing through a series of quasi-surreal evasions of definition, the 'animal' mutating from snail to octopus (and to lion, turtle, fish and horse). That this is part of a larger literary debate is clear in the third verse, which opens by contrasting Thomas' method with those of New Country poets, the 'Fishermen of mermen' who 'creep and harp on the tide' opposed to those who 'trace out a tentacle' with 'a living skein, / Tongue in the thread, [and] angle the temple-bound / . . . cavepools of spell and bone'. The capture, or 'spelling out' of the beast/animal is its death, although it is suggested (in the link between 'wizard' and the sense of 'spelling' as the casting of spells) that it collaborates in its capture and destruction. Articulated in language it gasps and dies, 'cast high, stunned on gilled stone', although the final lines make it clear that this is an internal death: 'Lie dry, rest robbed, my beast. / You have kicked from a dark den, leaped up the whinnying light, / And dug your grave in my breast.' The acknowledgment of this death – although belied, as usual in

Thomas, by the poem's verbal and syntactic energy – can be interpreted as a recognition of what was lost in the shift to referentiality in *The Map of Love*, making this poem part of Thomas' farewell to modernism.

Can the move away from modernism, finally and briefly, be related to the peculiar evolution of Thomas' critical and popular fortunes? Andreas Huyssen has written of later modernism being defined by a split between the political and the aesthetic avant-gardes; yet as we have seen, with the complicating of unitary modernism, the certainty with which a writer like Thomas would once have been placed in the 'aesthetic' camp now seems presumptuous.[60] Certainly, by broadening definitions of the 'political' in 1930s poetry and stressing the liminal, hybrid and transgressive qualities which Welsh origins imposed on Thomas, it is possible to see his work as problematising this kind of division. Thomas remains a central and awkward fact of the decade; in him modernist difficulty, parodic–bardic persona and suburban Swansea petit-bourgeois produce what might be seen as a Derridean 'supplement' to complete and undermine the standard, 'audenary' histories of 1930s poetry. By 1938 Thomas was externalising elements of his imploded modernism and jettisoning others, shifting his focus from language as the primary area of interest. The more he did this, the more – in an apparent paradox – he was credited with his 'gift of the gab'. He was, of course, not the only example of a modernist who felt that the consensual pressures of war demanded concessions to realism and, ultimately, an inclusive religious vision – to return to our starting-point and 'The Function of Criticism', we need only think of *Four Quartets*. Yet the conservative forms in which Thomas' work was cast meant that, under the circumstances, a personally identifiable and self-authenticating 'voice' was strengthened by such a move, and the 1940s poetry diluted linguistic autonomy, the 'warring', dialectical qualities it had possessed in the 1930s.

The later investment in personal voice – because of the potency of the final years of the career in shaping reception – has been read retrospectively to cover all of Thomas' poetry. It can still be claimed that 'it is not as constructions or as sets of influences that we experience the poems. Their power comes from a unique and resonant voice', and this is a sign of the amount of demystification still required.[61] An assertion like this fends off crude sociological interpretations, but at the expense of evading issues like the importance of parody to modernism, or the role played by phonocentric prejudice in the reception of Thomas' work (phonocentrism being defined as belief in the absolute proximity of voice and being, of voice and the meaning of being, of voice and the ideality of meaning). The problem is the failure to specify what is meant by 'voice'. Performance? Writerly style? Or the more philosophical 'presencing' of the author? In Thomas criticism it tends to be all of these, confusing the massive authority of the readings and personal legend with the poetry's sincerity (an index, for others, of its bogusness). Thomas' own confusion of these aspects was, in one sense, the secret of his success; but it is for just this reason that criticism needs to avoid imprecision. Rather than succumb to the authority of the poet's utterance, or phonocentrism itself, we would stress the need to tackle it both as a barrier to understanding and a key to Thomas' critical fortunes.

This is because on the one hand the voice which, for a superficial form of deconstructionism, betrays Thomas, can itself be seen as an obstacle in the way of its incantational resonance. The materiality of the language of Thomas' poetry and the tangible qualities of his now unfashionable reading style can today be seen as enabling. If his method of reading strengthens the nostalgia for an ineradicable source of meaning anterior to and constitutive of all sign systems, it nevertheless works, in its baroque richness, to present the materiality of the sign, pulling in the other direction against linguistic idealism and 'naturalness', sonorously and grandly excessive of any strict regime of sense. On the other hand, the voice alerts us to the fact that far from obscurity and popularity functioning as opposed terms in Thomas' case, they are actually complementary. Karl Shapiro has written of Thomas' presence performing 'the impossible', creating 'a general audience for a barely understandable poet'.[62] Although this baffles Shapiro, the fact that this occurred in the USA raises the issue of the role of the 'culture industry', as Adorno and Horkheimer dubbed it, and Thomas' importance to nascent counter-cultural trends at the height of the first Cold War; his performances were, as Louis Simpson has pointed out, a catalyst for revolt against the academicised, conservative, New Critical-dominated poetry of the time.[63] It would be wrong, however, to see the idea of Thomas as a father of the Beats or of the Lowell of *Life Studies* as a merely ironic one, for it is at this point his influence passes from the purely literary to become (along with Sylvia Plath, perhaps) that of the type of the doomed contemporary poet. It was precisely his 'obscurity', it might be said – and in a more genuinely ironic way – which *proved* his authenticity to non-initiates, guaranteeing his status in more than a poetic sense as a popular cultural icon (and, later, a cultural icon for pop) long after his death.[64]

CHAPTER 5

'Literally, for this': metonymies of national identity in Edward Thomas, Yeats and Auden

Stan Smith

Poetry, Mr Baldwin has assured us, is essentially a harmless voca-
tion, so long, that is, as the poet shuts out from his vision all that
part of life which might affect the 'harmless' character of his work.
This narrow view of the artist's function is a very modern one.

Ralph Fox, *The Novel and the People* (1937)

Every one of our little fights or attacks was significant, they made
panoramic pictures of the struggle in the people's eyes and lived on
in their minds. Only in our country could the details of an individual fight expand to the generalisations of a pitched battle . . . [T]he
people saw the clash between two mentalities . . . and two philos-
ophies of life; between exploiters and exploited. Even the living
were quickly becoming folklore.   Ernie O'Malley, *On Another Man's
Wound* (1936)

Eleanor Farjeon records an exchange in 1915 with Edward Thomas,
who had just enlisted in the Artists' Rifles:

It might have been next year when we were walking in the country that I asked
him the questions his friends had asked him when he joined up, but I put it
differently. 'Do you know what you are fighting for?' He stopped, and picked
up a pinch of earth. 'Literally, for this'. He crumpled it between finger and
thumb, and let it fall.[1]

Literal it wasn't, of course. Thomas let fall the earth as soon as he'd
made his point; he didn't take it home to set up as a national shrine.
After all, there was plenty more where that came from. But the
metonymy is symptomatic. What that 'pinch' of earth stands in for, in
the first instance, is the 'country' in which they are walking. But this is
only the terminal point of a series of metonymic reductions. For the
'country', by which Farjeon means the countryside, the cultivated
landscape around them, stands in, in turn, for 'the country' as nation

113

state, and, beyond that, a metaphysical and transcendent entity, not subject to rational analysis or empiric demonstration. Thomas himself had published in 1913 a small book called *The Country* which explored precisely this verbal ambiguity, and had distinguished the English countryside from the idea of the British nation state, regretting the loss of 'the small intelligible England of Elizabeth' and the substitution of 'the word Imperialism instead' and the imperial concept of a 'Greater Britain'. In 1915, 'Britain' – a word Thomas avoids except in Celtic and Arthurian contexts – was in its most central dynamics not an agricultural economy but an industrial one, the world's leading producer of coal and steel and heavy manufacturing, and a global banker and trader, the heartland of a political, industrial and commercial empire on which the sun never set, of which the colonial and dependent territories, together with the ex-colonial 'white commonwealth' of Canada, Australia, New Zealand and South Africa, constituted that 'Greater Britain' Thomas dismisses with contempt.

For all his ruralism, Thomas himself was no ostrich with regard to industrialism. One of his most powerful essays, 'Mothers and Sons', in *Rest and Unrest* (1910), for example, describes the tawdry squalor of a South Wales mining village. Yet in conceptualising 'England' it is to a mythical pastoral heartland that he turns, one summed up in the title of his 1909 travel book, *The South Country*: that spread of rural counties which extends from the Kentish Weald in the east through Sussex, Hardy's 'Wessex', into Wiltshire and the Hereford and Gloucestershire border country, and down to Devon and Somerset, though it rarely extends into Cornwall, except in calling up ancient Britons and the Arthurian legacy. Thomas' 'England' can incorporate, at times, 'the lowlands of John Clare's Northamptonshire as they were when the kite still soared over them',[2] and the Warwickshire of Shakespearean pastoral. It certainly does not include the heavy industry of Birmingham or the rest of the industrial Midlands and North. Wordsworth's Lake District, mediated by literary romanticism, is an occasional exception. In his own admission, this South Country is metonymic, a part simultaneously larger and smaller than the whole it represents, standing in for the totality of Englishness, but at the same time no more than a parish pond (not even a Wordsworthian lake):

This is not the South Country which measures about two hundred miles from east to west and fifty from north to south. In some ways it is incomparably larger than any country that was ever mapped, since upon nothing less than the infinite can the spirit disport itself. In other ways it is far smaller – as when a mountain with tracts of sky and cloud and the full moon glass themselves in a pond, a little pond.[3]

Thomas' 'England' is a peculiarly disjunct, decentred terrain. One of his travel books is called *The Heart of England* (1906), but just as this 'heart' is to be sought by quitting London in the opening chapter, 'Leaving Town', so it recedes as he pursues it, lost in the interstices of the landscape. The peripatetic nature of these travel essays comes to embody the very rootlessness of the subject – in both the psychological and political senses of that word – who cannot find his place in the world, for whom homesickness is an ontological condition. *The Heart of England* actually ends in Wales, a terrain which got a volume to itself in Thomas' *Beautiful Wales* (1905), as did *The Isle of Wight* (1911) and *Oxford* (1903), the latter, Thomas' alma mater, the nearest such a decentred rurality comes to a capital. Another book of wayfarings, *The Icknield Way* (1913), follows the prehistoric track from its obscure origins in East Anglia to its obscure destination somewhere near Swindon (though taking this westbound route itself implies an ideological decision about the location of 'the heart of England'). As George Orwell suggests in his reproachful pastiche title of this romanticising, nostalgicist genre, there is no *Road to Wigan Pier* in such writings. The space Thomas' figures inhabit is neither Eliot's cosmopolitan modernist waste land nor the anxious border country of Auden's frontier, a quite different class and generational use of the topographical topos. It is essentially one of nooks and crannies, 'a place of innumerable holes and corners', as Thomas wrote in the essay 'England' on the outbreak of war in 1914. His archetypal Englishman, 'Lob', in the poem of that name, is last seen disappearing down a path that seems to lead nowhere. The innumerable villages in which he might be found are themselves 'Lurking to one side up the paths and lanes, / Seldom well seen except by aeroplanes'.[4] The intrusive, totalising view of the modern world represented by that aeroplane is a perpetual threat to such a culture of evasion and elusiveness.

In *The South Country*, Thomas envisaged 'a history of England written from the point of view of one parish, or town, or great house'.[5] If Edward Thomas is seen as the quintessential poet of Englishness, it is precisely in such selective, skewed and unrepresentative metonymies of nationhood that his potency resides. His landscapes repeatedly offer metonymies of a totality that cannot be grasped. At the heart of such metonymies is dispossession. They offer traces of something which no longer exists, or exists elsewhere – is precisely not here. There is an interesting correlation in his reflection in *Heart of England* on 'the old ballads and folksongs', which shifts, in its final movement, to a sense of larger cultural dispossession. Such songs are 'in themselves epitomes of whole generations, of a whole countryside . . . the quintessence of many lives and passions' which 'lend themselves to infinite interpretations . . . launch us into an unknown . . . They come to us imploring a new lease of life on the sweet earth, and so we come to give them something . . . out of our own hearts, as we do when we find a black hearthstone among the nettles.'[6] The image of partial repossession ('a new lease') turns, at the last moment, into one of dispossession: the people who made these songs are expropriated, and so are audience and readers. All that remains are these 'epitomes', testimonies to a lost inhabitancy, metonymic traces that ratify absence. In the same way, the poem 'A Tale' recovers in imagination the lineaments of a ruined cottage of which now even the walls have disappeared, to be imagined only in memory. All that remains 'to tell the tale' of erstwhile habitation are the 'everlasting flowers / On fragments of blue plates' scattered among the crawling periwinkle (*CP*, 145).

If 'England' exists, it is as a site of dispossession and abandonment. Consider, for example, the much anthologised poem 'Adlestrop', where the train's unwonted stop offers a momentary intuition of oneness with the whole English countryside extending beyond, something which, however, gets 'mistier and mistier' figured by the receding voices of birds singing into the circumferential distances of Oxfordshire and Gloucestershire (*CP* 66). For all the apparent dreamy remoteness of this, Adlestrop was actually on the main line from London to Ledbury, Thomas' likely destination. The train would have been serviced in the railway workshops of Swindon, where his Welsh grandfather and uncle worked, fuelled by coal from the pit villages of South Wales, and made of steel processed there and forged probably in Sheffield. Adlestrop was, in fact, a locus in a vast network of relations that integrated the whole country. This century witnesses the slow acclimatisation of the train in such ruralist writing. It is, for example, a central metonymy of travelling selfhood in Louis MacNeice's thirties poems. There are several scenes set in railway carriages in Thomas' prose, but in the poetry the train is usually seen at a distance, its steam ascending to the heavens, its presence assimilated to the landscape, naturalised. The railway as a real mode of employment, central to Thomas' family history, is expunged. Thomas himself was born in London only because his father had

moved there from South Wales as a senior clerk in the railway service.
Such suppressions are the basis of metonymy, and they fulfil a crucial
ideological function in the construction of national identity. In the poem
'Tears', for example, the poet experiences only a trace, the 'ghosts' of
tears, seeing 'Soldiers in line, young English countrymen' in white tunics
playing 'The British Grenadiers' (*CP*, 23). The music itself is *unheimlich*,
resonant with displaced significances. Though it implies that the soldiers, 'Fair-haired and ruddy, in white tunics' might be Grenadiers, and
therefore, as the name would suggest, combatants, the idea of war is
expunged from the poem (the white uniforms signal non-combatancy),
except in Housmanish innuendo of some possible future fate. The final
location of the poem is a complex tissue of dispossessions, alluding to a
national identity figured only in its absence, invoked metonymically by
the music and the *mise-en-scène*:

> The men, the music piercing that solitude
> And silence, told me truths I had not dreamed,
> And have forgotten since their beauty passed.

There is, here, only the memory of having had an experience, cut off
from past and future ('had not dreamed', 'have forgotten'), leaving an
emptiness at the heart of the event like that in the multiplying negatives
of the poem 'Old Man'. In the end, then, there is a restoration of
'solitude and silence' in the self's felt exclusion from the national
military–patriotic identity the tune proposes. (When I was a child in the
early 1950s at a Church of England primary school, this and similar
songs remained the regular fare of school music classes.) Thomas
himself dissociated his poem from the current jingoistic mood of wartime, writing to Edward Garnett that 'I don't think I could alter "Tears"
to make it marketable. I feel that the correction you want made is only
essential if the whole point is in the British Grenadiers as might be
expected in these times.'[7]

There is, in fact, in Thomas a failure – or a refusal – to participate in
such jingoistic redactions of nationality. In 'August', for example, he
records the 'harmony' created by village and mountains and sky, only to
add, ruefully, 'It was a time when the whole universe strove to speak a
universal speech . . . but, as it seemed, owing to my fault, the effort was
unsuccessful, and I rose hurriedly and left the village behind.'[8] There is a
complex sense of exclusion here. This is a Welsh scene, and, in Wales,
he is an Englishman; in England, a Welshman. He wrote to a friend of
his 'accidentally cockney nativity' in Wandsworth, claiming to feel 'at

home' in Wales; but elsewhere he spoke of finding in an imagined South
Country his true, spiritual locus: 'Yet is this country, though I am mainly
Welsh, a kind of home, as I think it is more than any other to those
modern people who belong nowhere.'[9] Like the gypsies in his *George
Borrow*, such 'modern people' are everywhere 'foreigners but as native as
the birds'.[10] Thomas' 'English words', in the poem 'Words', come not
only 'From Wiltshire and Kent / And Herefordshire, / And the villages
there' but also 'From Wales / Whose nightingales / Have no wings' (*CP*,
95; an allusion to the Welsh choral tradition). This would seem to imply
an unproblematic identification of Welshness and Englishness, and
indeed he records in *The South Country* that his own Welsh family had its
roots across the Severn, moving to Wales in one of those perpetual
migrations that everywhere made up what he calls elsewhere a 'settled
Englishness'. In his poems he can evoke a time even before that, when
'our blackbirds sang no English'. But what persists is, in fact, the
opposite of rootedness: the condition of belonging nowhere.

Such metonymic relations constitute Thomas' characteristic way of
relating to the English landscape, summed up in the vision in *Beautiful
Wales* of 'the power of the calm, vast, and windless evening, of which the
things I saw were as a few shells and anemones at the edge of a great
sea'.[11] That power, represented by the trivial flotsam and jetsam which
are its traces, is withheld, contrasting with the sense of weakness and
powerlessness of the individual. But it is not simply a magical natural
quality; rather it is the epitome of the immense historically accumulated
power of the nation state, a cultural, political, juridical and military
potency.

Thomas' wartime anthology, *This England: An Anthology from her Writers*
(1915), along with his article of the same name, is the original coining of
the phrase (from John O'Gaunt's deathbed soliloquy in *Richard II*)
which was to become axiomatic to the cult of English national identity
in the following decades. Yet Thomas notably distinguishes his collection as culled 'from the work of English writers rather strictly so called',
'excluding professedly patriotic writing . . . never aiming at what a
committee from Great Britain and Ireland might call complete', adding
that 'I wished to make a book as full of English character as an egg is of
meat.'

The corporeality of this image is significant, of the same order as that
handful of dirt. In 'England' Thomas observes that in Walton's *Compleat
Angler*, 'I touched the antiquity and sweetness of England – English
fields, English people, English poetry, all together. You have them all in

one sentence, where the milkwoman, mother of Maudlin the milkmaid, is speaking to Piscator and Venator', promising syllabub and the ballad of 'Chevy Chase'.[12] But what is significant in the latter passage is the way the tactility of the metaphor shifts into pastoral abstraction (the milkmaid is not inappropriately called 'Maudlin'), in a recession from reality to romance which recalls those birds in the misty distances of 'Adlestrop'. 'Some goal / I touched then', Thomas says in the poem, 'I never saw that land before', a goal mysteriously related to 'A language not to be betrayed' which he shares with the birds and the trees (*CP*, 100). But it evaporates as soon as touched. Again, 'one nationality / We had, I and the birds that sang', he claims in 'Home' (*CP*, 128); but for no more than an instant, an intuition of shared experience which dissolves as, Faustlike, he tries to grasp it. In both instances, it is the tangible, touchable immediacy of the physical world around him, as with that peck of dust, which substitutes for the metaphysical 'country' of national and civic identity. It is the birds and the trees that constitute his national community.

In this, Thomas believed he shared something with that disappearing 'peasantry' which for him was the true epitome of Englishness, represented most potently in the figure of 'Lob', but disclosed with phenomenological inwardness in one of the 'patriotic' essays on Englishness in time of war, 'It's a long, long way':

I should like to know what the old soldier meant by 'England', if it was anything more than some sort of a giant with Gloucestershire for its eyes, its beating heart, for everything that raised it above a personification. His was a very little England. The core and vital principle was less still, a few thousand acres of corn, meadow, orchard, and copse, a few farms and cottages; and he laughed heartily over a farmer's artfulness who had hid away some horses wanted by the War Office. If England was against Germany, the parish was against Germany, England, and all the world.[13]

'England' here becomes for each individual simply a projection of self, as Thomas acknowledged in 'England', admitting that 'If England lies like a vast estate calm around you, and you a minor, you may find faults without end. If England seems threatened you feel that in losing her you would lose yourself.'[14] Yet at the same time, in his review of 'War Poetry' in the journal *Poetry and Drama* in December 1914, he dissociates himself from 'The writer of ... patriotic verses', who 'appears to be a man who feels himself always or at the time at one with a class, perhaps the whole nation, or he is a smart fellow who can simulate or exaggerate this sympathy'. For Thomas, England could never be experienced whole, but only in such a metonymic series, a congeries of decentred holes and corners. As he wrote to Gordon Bottomley from his military training camp: 'I furbish up my knowledge of England by finding some place that each man knows & I know & getting him to talk. There isn't a man I don't share some part with.'[15]

Thomas' epitome of the old Gloucestershire soldier, snug in his parish, is the figure of his own social evasiveness, refusing any totalisation of the national culture, but instead seeking refuge in holes and corners hidden from all but the overflying aeroplane. Yet it implies that there is, somewhere else, a displaced totality to all these particular places. In this context, the geometric model Thomas uses on several occasions to define the topography of a decentred nation is instructive. As he writes in 'England': 'I believe that England means something like this to most of us; that all ideas of England are developed, spun out, from such a centre into something large or infinite, solid or aery, according to each man's nature and capacity; that England is a system of vast circumferences circling round the minute neighbouring points of home.'[16]

The identification of the parish of the self with the national ensemble of England is put into the mouth of a fictional character in a failed novel published just before the outbreak of war, *The Happy-Go-Lucky Morgans* (1913). There, in what is portentously distanced as 'Mr Stodham's sermon', Wordsworth is echoed in a favourite Thomas citation, to affirm the importance of 'this England . . . where we have our happiness or not at all', for 'we are limited creatures, not angels, and . . . our immediate surroundings are enough to exercise all our faculties of mind and body'. For all the understated modesty and rhetorical distantiation, Thomas himself seems to embrace the tone of the pulpit in this insistence on the interdependence of subject, subjectivity and nation, mediated once again through the trope of a tangible 'earth':

England made you, and of you is England made. Deny England . . . and you may find yourself some day denying your father and mother . . . [H]aving denied England and your father and mother, you may have to deny your own self, and treat it as nothing, a mere conventional boundary, an artifice, by which you are separated from the universe and its creator. To unite yourself with the universe and its creator, you may be tempted to destroy that boundary of your own body and brain, and die. He is a bold man who hopes to do without earth, England, family, and self.[17]

Mr Stodham's rhetorical inversion lies behind the assertion of 'This is no case of petty right or wrong' that 'The ages made her that made us from the dust: / She is all we know and live by' (*CP*, 165). This poem opens with a rejection of jingoism and 'fat patriot' alike, refusing to hate Germans or 'grow hot / With love of Englishmen, to please newspapers'. But it rises, in its conclusion, to a crescendo of patriotic sentiment which recalls Shakespeare's Henry V before Agincourt. The same source seems to be picked up in the most famous (and subsequently most derided) piece of English nationalist writing to come out of the Great War, Rupert Brooke's sonnet 'The Soldier', a poem which in its central image shares in this national ideology of 'holes and corners'.

Brooke's poem, for all the adulation and subsequent derision it has received, is not a piece of unthinking jingoism. Given Brooke's own Fabian socialism, this is hardly surprising. It is in many ways a perfect adumbration of Louis Althusser's idea of the construction of the (political and experiential) subject. Unlike Thomas, who merely lifts and drops a clod of earth symbolically, Brooke has become one with his country in the most literal sense: his dust *is* 'for ever England', and nothing else can or should be thought ('think only this of me').[18] Yet this English dust occupies 'some corner of a foreign field', not in any act of colonising investment, but as a metonym of a deeper involution in national identity. The foreign field is itself a rich earth (no jingoism here), and the 'richer dust' it conceals is not necessarily richer – though the ambiguity is central to the tone – because it is English, but because it is 'literally', as organic matter, rich compost; but primarily because it is the only trace of a human subject who once breathed and swam and had a home, and is now a kind of ambassador of Englishness abroad.

This subject was constructed both physically and in consciousness by his national culture: 'A dust whom England bore, shaped, made aware / . . . A body of England's', constituted, Althusser would say, by the ideological apparatuses of the nation state which 'Gave, once, her flowers to love, her ways to roam', only to demand everything back, and an end to all that restless roaming. The metaphorical 'heart' then figures the self's inextricability from the constitutive discourses of the national culture, both more and less than the complex once-living consciousness. Now, 'all evil shed away', it is the metonymy of a larger whole, 'A pulse in the eternal mind, no less', which acts as a front, one might say, for the nation. It gives back what it's been given, in an ideology of exchange, reciprocity, in which even laughter is a culturally learnt discourse, not something spontaneous and ahistorical but acquired, and reproduced, 'under an English heaven'. The ultimate return on that investment, the gift the loyal subject receives back in exchange for its allegiance, Thomas had predicted in his poem 'The Signpost'. It was all, 'Literally, for this': 'A mouthful of earth to remedy all / Regrets and wishes shall freely be given' (*CP*, 22).

Amidst all that poking around in holes and corners as the key to Englishness, there is one image in Thomas' writings which almost leads on to a totalisation of national identity. In the essay 'This England' he writes of his moment of uncomprehending commitment when, in the heart of the country, he turned to look at the moon rising in the east, to realise for the first time that the same image hung over the Meuse in France, and over 'those who could see it there' – those 'soldiers in the east afar' of whom he wrote in the poem which picks up and transmutes this prose passage, 'The sun used to shine.' At the same moment, he records, he was 'deluged'

by another thought, or something that overpowered thought. All I can tell is, it seemed to me that either I had never loved England, or I had loved it foolishly, aesthetically, like a slave, not having realized that it was not mine unless I were willing and prepared to die rather than leave it as Belgian women and old men and children had left their country. Something I had omitted. Something, I felt, had to be done before I could look again composedly at English landscape, at the elms and poplars about the houses, at the purple-headed wood-betony with two pairs of dark leaves on a stiff stem, who stood sentinel among the grasses or bracken by hedge-side or wood's-edge. What he stood sentinel for I did not know, any more than what I had got to do.[19]

The overpowering of thought ('deluged' is a significant word) is characteristic of such momentary engulfments of conventional 'parochial' experience, a structure of feeling akin to totemism. Behind the image evoked here is a whole English tradition that takes Thomas back, unconsciously, to the 'small intelligible England of Elizabeth', recalling another English poet, pastoralist and soldier, Sir Philip Sidney, author of *Arcadia* and of a famous invocation to the moon ('With how sad steps, O Moon, thou climbst the skies!'), who also died on a Flanders battlefield. Yet the most striking note remains that final perplexity, recalling the hesitations and bewilderment of a poem such as 'Old Man'.

It's instructive to contrast Thomas' use of the moon here, gesturing toward a collective solidarity and vision, with Yeats' confident deployment of the same traditional poetic motif in such a poem as 'Blood and the Moon' (1928). Yeats' moon forms part of a potent trinity of traditional tropes, together with his Norman tower at Thoor Ballylee and the 'Odour of blood' joined to it in the title. Yeats' metonymies are ferociously totalising, sweeping all before them in the insistence on their emblematic, synecdochic character. Yeats allows no equivocation: this is a 'powerful emblem' which he has masterfully 'set . . . up'. There is no delicate stalking of significance here, but a thunderous, overweaning voice. The tower itself, with a ruined roof, duplicates unequivocally the poet's sense of his own, Ireland's and the age's defective character:

> In mockery I have set
> A powerful emblem up,
> And sing it rhyme upon rhyme
> In mockery of a time
> Half dead at the top.[20]

The self-regarding analogy is with Amphion, the music of whose lyre raised the walls of Thebes without the need for physical labour as, Yeats would like to have believed, his writing helped forge the Irish nation state from inchoate raw materials. This is the obverse of that self-important questioning in 'Man and the Echo' (1939) about responsibility for the violence of the independence struggle and the civil war that followed it. Thebes, of course, was a city notoriously torn by fratricidal civil war (something which adds resonance to Yeats' use of the figure of Oedipus in his later poems). Here, tower, self and nation are all alike constructed not only in material stone but in ideology, the 'bloody, arrogant power' of the race 'Uttering, mastering it', creating a 'powerful emblem' which magically holds together edifice and state.

That the tower is 'Half dead at the top' converts it into a metonymy which expresses, on the one hand, the condition of the subject, Yeats himself, and, on the other, of the state to which he is subject. Yeats is visualising here the traditional cartographic image of Ireland as the poor old woman whose head is the six-county Ulster statelet, with Lough Neagh as the eye: hence 'Half dead at the top' because, as yet, incompletely rebuilt.

Nationhood is not a natural construction. It is essentially a work of artifice, for the nation has to be ideologically 'uttered' to be validated. Yeats imagined that his own 'Easter 1916' was the originary 'uttering', the bloody christening anthem of the Irish state. (The poem is still widely sold in reverential imitation scroll form in many tourist shops in contemporary Ireland, alongside the rebels' declaration of statehood.) He consolidates his bid for a totalising iconography in language of a decidedly statist nature. This uttering is at one and the same time a declaration of independence and oath of allegiance:

I declare this tower is my symbol; I declare
This winding, gyring, spiring treadmill of a stair is my ancestral stair.

But it is also an act of appropriation, claiming to self, tower and state a
retrospective metonymic lineage of great Anglo-Irish figures all of
whom would have been astonished to find themselves in such company:
Goldsmith, Swift, Berkeley and Burke, the latter indeed a sworn opponent of the idea of Irish independence. But it is Burke, who 'proved the
State a tree', who is here explicitly invoked as the founding, ratifying
father of Yeats' idea of Irish nationhood, rejecting the 'mathematical
equality' of British democracy for the 'unconquerable labyrinth' of an
oligarchic Ireland. Further ratification for Yeats' act of ideological
invention is provided by Berkeleyan idealism. By divine appointment,
Berkeley 'proved all things a dream' (all the better to raise city walls with
music, then) – even 'this pragmatical, preposterous pig of a world, its
farrow that so solid seem'. But if such a farrow will 'vanish on an instant
if the mind but change its theme', this is not the effortless act by which
Amphion sang Thebes into existence. Ireland, of course, is traditionally
the old sow that devours her farrow. Nationhood requires the kind of
ethnic cleansing that cleared out most of Yeats' own Anglo-Irish Ascendancy compeers from the ancestral sty.

To cope with this bitter and anfractuous reality, Yeats deploys another metonymic sleight of hand, invoking Swift's 'Saeva Indignatio' to
provide 'The strength that gives our blood and state magnanimity of its
own desire' (Yeats' title has here mutated into a recollection of Shirley's
'The glories of our blood and state'). With remarkable cool, Yeats inserts
a surreptious first person plural into a poem which has, till this point,
been composed of a dissociated 'I' and a series of abstract third persons.
But, in speaking of 'The strength that gives our blood and state magnanimity of its own desire', he carefully avoids starting with the pronoun
'we', which would be to presume upon a collective national subjectivity
yet to be constituted. Rather, he prepares the way by using the possessive adjective 'our' to qualify a supposedly objective 'blood and state',
which then takes on at once an impersonal subjectivity as the 'magnanimity of its own desire' (the possessive adjectives 'its own' again doing
most of the work). Such savage indignation consumes all that it does not
embrace with 'intellectual fire'; out of that burning a collective 'we' can,
eventually, be plucked. In the past seven centuries of this tower, Yeats
proposes, generations of soldiers, assassins, executioners have shed
blood out of 'abstract hatred' or 'blind fear'. But what is original, and

originary, now, is the significance of this new blood-letting: it is a meaningful, a totalising act, not simply one of a potentially endless series of meaningless atrocities. There is 'Odour of blood on the ancestral stair'; and only after that claim to an 'ancestral' lineage has been staked can Yeats speak with pronominal confidence of a 'we, that have shed none', who now '*must* gather there' (my emphasis), compelled by national fervour to that same blood sacrifice out of which all nations are constituted, 'to clamour in frenzy for the moon'.

In the splendour of his emblems Yeats is borne across the difficulty of justifying the violence and uncertainty of this national setting forth. The totalising metonymic compulsion, first uttered in the aggrandising emblems of tower, moon and blood (violence, but also lineage), is finally embodied in a sequence of free-floating pronouns, forging a 'we' out of disparate 'I's, 'he's, 'they's and 'it's, to such an extent that the poem's final question, a pertinent enquiry as to whether nation-building is worth the candle, seems merely rhetorical, easily dispersed by a return to the grand emblems of tradition:

> Is every modern nation like the tower,
> Half dead at the top? No matter what I said,
> For wisdom is the property of the dead,
> A something incompatible with life; and power,
> Like everything that has the stain of blood,
> A property of the living; but no stain
> Can come upon the visage of the moon
> When it has looked in glory from a cloud.

The image of a moon bursting in glory from the clouds is straight from that Shelley invoked early in the poem. But it does not resolve the anguishing about the price paid for nationhood of the previous section – which includes the extirpation of Yeats' own Anglo-Irish Protestant minority. Power, Yeats insists, is a property of the living; and it is here, ironically, that the contrast with Thomas is most evident. For Thomas' peasants, like the poet himself, are essentially passive and powerless, dependants on the landscape they inhabit, work, walk. They are not engaged in building, uttering, mastering nationhood. On the contrary, if they are active at all, it is only in defence of locality, parochiality, the here and now of a pinch of earth and of sundry holes and corners. They, rather than Yeats' Irish, are the truly colonised, for it is their abjection to know no remedy for their powerlessness, indeed, to take satisfaction in their marginality and seclusion. Whereas Yeats' national metonymies all strive toward the condition of music, synthesising conflict, orchestrating discord, creating a unitary, all-encompassing emblem out of disparate materials, Thomas' remain transfixed in their anecdotal particularity, minute neighbouring points of home forever in the margins of the great circumferences they would not dare disturb, in the lost places of the landscape.

Despite what F. R. Leavis called his 'distinctively modern sensibility',[21] Thomas remains essentially *pre*modernist in his decentred, vagrant subjectivity. Yeats, on the other hand, is ferociously modernist in his centralising, totalising compulsion, integrating subject, state and natural and social worlds in a system of vast circumferences circling a single, unifying core. In contrast with both, W. H. Auden's stance is decidedly *post*modernist. If, like Thomas, he prefers the peripheries to the centre, his drive, like Yeats', is toward totalisation. Auden's margins are not corners to hide in but, crucially, frontiers to cross, from beyond which a disdainful subject totalises only to reject, and totalises by rejecting, the national culture which made him what he is.

Auden's 1930s persona makes precisely that choice Mr Stodham had proposed as impossibly bold and autodestructive, denying 'earth, England, family, and self', treating his own subjectivity as no more than 'a mere conventional boundary, an artifice', constructed in subjection. Whereas Thomas' English villages hide from the overflying aeroplane, Auden's characteristic point of vantage on Englishness lies precisely in the panoptic view the aeroplane affords, inviting us to 'Consider this, and in our time, / As the hawk sees it or the helmeted airman'. Yeats' hawk in 'The Second Coming' loses its essential identity by breaking free from its functional relation with the falconer, a metonymy of universal ruin. His Irish Airman foresees his death because he is unable to reconcile the conflicting allegiances of England and Ireland, in a war irrelevant to his true loyalties. But Auden's hawk and airman assume a masterful identity in the very act of denial and renunciation.

The moon in Auden's 1933 poem, 'Out on the lawn', which echoes Thomas' 'The sun used to shine', certainly collectivises its objects, but it does so precisely by reducing everything, persons and things alike, to objects, objectifying diversely experienced subjectivities to the single, homogeneous status of cultural artefacts:

> Now North and South and East and West
> Those I love lie down to rest;
> The moon looks on them all:

> The healers and the brilliant talkers,
> The eccentrics and the silent walkers,
> The dumpy and the tall.[22]

Nationality is denied by a moon that 'climbs the European sky'; so too is the boundary between 'earth, England, family, and self'. These cultural artefacts, including the poet himself, are indistinguishable from the churches, power stations and art galleries on which the moon stares with equal indifference, as 'blankly as an orphan'. That last, transferred epithet indicates a key strategy Auden effected in his 1930s poems, embracing the very disaffiliation Thomas courted and feared, and Yeats stubbornly and ebulliently refused. This moon is 'attentive' only to gravity, looks down with the same indifference on the lucky, leisurely English scene as on the violence done (the echo of 'The sun used to shine' is evident here) 'Where Poland draws her eastern bow'. Whereas Thomas' moon offers a common, communal focus for the eyes of multifarious Englishmen, and Yeats' a ratifying transcendence at once inhuman and familiar, making sense of fratricidal, nation-forging brutality, Auden's moon signifies a wilful renunciation of national identity, a refusal of allegiance and subjection. The synoptic standpoint assumed here is already that dissociated, alienated spectatorial stance evoked in the title of the 1936 volume in which this poem was collected, *Look, Stranger!* By the time of the poem 'Dover' a year later, the subject gazes beyond the nation's geographical, political and linguistic limits, and the full moon over France 'cold and exciting . . . returns the human stare' with a dangerous flattery that invites to the renunciation of all particular allegiances. Overhead, 'The aeroplanes fly in the new European air, / On the edge of that air that makes England of minor importance'. England is not only diminished but relativised by this cold exterior gaze: 'Within these breakwaters English is spoken'; but beyond them lies 'the immense improbable atlas'.[23]

Gravity is a potent analogy for the relation of parts to the whole in a national culture. In Yeats' 'The Second Coming' it is the precondition of custom and ceremony; without it, 'Things fall apart, the centre cannot hold; / Mere anarchy is loosed upon the world'.[24] For Auden, however, gravity is a paradigm of unfreedom, a kind of original sin. In the 'Prologue' to *Look, Stranger!* it is the condition of the fallen apple (in Thomas' 'The sun used to shine', the vulnerable national self is seen as 'an apple wasps had undermined'), in an Audenish yoking of heterogeneity which telescopes Newton's scientific advances and the myth of the

Fall. The poem opens with a vatic vision of England, Shakespeare crossed with Blake, as 'This fortress perched on the edge of the Atlantic scarp, / The mole between all Europe and the exile-crowded sea'.[25] It proceeds to an apparently patriotic appeal which seems to echo Brooke and Thomas, before the image turns back upon and subverts itself:

> make us as Newton was, who in his garden watching
> The apple falling towards England, became aware
> Between himself and her of an eternal tie.

If national identity is like gravity, it cannot be a matter of prayer and supplication: it inhabits the realm of necessity, not freedom. The apple *must* fall toward England. But the poem proceeds to proclaim an end to the national 'dream' of 'uniting the dead into a splendid empire', which is 'already retreating into her [England's] maternal shadow'. It discloses a nation everywhere bereft, its 'impoverished constricting acres' confronting another 'possible dream' which is already steering its unwavering keel through the night, 'out of the Future and into actual History', toward 'the virgin roadsteads of our hearts'. This dream may be cloaked in references to Merlin and Stonehenge, but the key phrase is one associated with Lenin and revolution, in 'its military silence, its surgeon's idea of pain', an association recalled throughout the volume, in, for example, the quotation from Krupskaya's biography of Lenin in 'Our hunting fathers', and finalised in the direct reference of the closing 'Epilogue' to 'the really better world', represented by 'the neat man / To their east who ordered Gorki to be electrified'.[26]

One metonymic strategy of this volume was to become central to Auden's subsequent thinking about nationality. It is indicated in this use of the city of Gorki, renamed after the Russian revolution in honour of its 'bard', Maxim Gorki, to represent the whole of the new Soviet order which stands beyond the frontier, ironically eyeing this fallen bourgeois world. (Lenin described communism as 'soviets plus electricity'.) The technique is articulated in 'Prologue's' quick thumbnail sketches of 'the Lancashire moss', Glamorgan's 'glove-shaped valleys' and Dumbarton's 'furnaces gasping in the impossible air', figuring the three constituent nations of Britain metonymically by the parochial but representative cameos which stand in for them, representative *because* parochial.

'He was silly like us', Auden wrote famously in his elegy for W. B. Yeats, and his silliness resided, in part, in his parochiality, his preoccupation with 'the parish of rich women', in tandem with his nationalism.[27] Auden refused to buy, that is, the grand totalisations of Yeatsian rhetoric, and it was in the quarrel with Yeats' rhetoric that much of his 1930s critique of English national identity was forged. Yeats, he wrote to Stephen Spender in 1964, made him 'whore after lies', substituting the compromising rhetorical flourish for the authenticity of dissection and analysis. Hence Auden's insistence, in the elegy for Yeats, that 'poetry makes nothing happen', in direct response to Yeats' self-regarding anguish, in 'Man and the Echo', about his responsibility for the violence out of which Ireland was reborn: 'Did that play of mine send out / Certain men the English shot?'[28] Auden's own rhetoric had recently been recruited in another cause in which national identity was violently contested in a civil war, in Spain, and the Yeats elegy concludes with what is almost Auden's last word on nationalism: a vision of the separate nations of Europe, each sequestered in its hate, waiting, in the nightmare of the dark, for the war that is about to erupt.

'In Memory of W. B. Yeats' was in fact collected, together with the revised version of the poem 'Spain', in the same section of *Another Time* (1940). This same section also includes his elegies for the exiles Freud (deconstructor of 'the ancient cultures of conceit' and 'the monolith / Of State') and Ernst Toller, the suicidal victim of 'a Europe which took refuge in [his] head . . . too injured to get well'. It proceeds, via a poem about the outbreak of that European civil war, 'September 1, 1939', to conclude with an 'Epithalamion' which, in the face of catastrophe, celebrates a pan-European marriage, calling the whole European cultural and intellectual heritage to witness an alliance which stands, metonymically, for international reconciliation of the 'Hostile kingdoms': 'Superstition overcome / As all national frontiers melt'.[29]

Auden wrote at length about the pitfalls of nationalism in his 1939 prose obituary for Yeats in *Partisan Review*, 'The Public v. the Late Mr William Butler Yeats'. 'Of all the modes of self-evasion open to the well-to-do', says the Public Prosecutor in this imaginary 'trial', 'Nationalism is the easiest and most dishonest. It allows to the unjust all the luxury of righteous indignation against injustice.'[30] Yeats himself, after the Easter Uprising, wrote a 'masterpiece' of duplicity 'which could offend neither the Irish Republican nor the British Army . . . indeed a masterly achievement', while 'In the last poem he wrote, the deceased rejected social justice and reason, and prayed for war', thus aligning himself with 'a certain foreign political movement' (fascism) generally acknowledged to be 'the enemy of mankind'. (The poem referred to is 'Under Ben Bulben', which cites the nationalist John Mitchel's prayer 'Send war in our time, O Lord!')[31]

The Defence Counsel argues against what he calls this 'impassioned oratory', refusing the idea of political correctness as a test of poetic virtue. He demands, rhetorically: 'In an age of rising nationalism, Dante looked back with envy to the Roman Empire. Was this socially progressive?' In 200 years' time, he continues, when our children have made a better world order, 'who but a historian will care a button whether the deceased was right about the Irish Question or wrong about the transmigration of souls?' However, if the question of nationalism is to be addressed, in the present, the Defence is unequivocal. Yeats' reactionary views can be explained 'partly because Ireland compared with the rest of western Europe was economically backward, and the class struggle was less conscious there'. If the Prosecutor has 'sneered at Irish Nationalism' he nevertheless 'knows as well as I that Nationalism is a necessary stage towards Socialism'. But Yeats' greatest achievement, he continues, is to produce a totalising vision beyond both parochiality and nationalism:

The fairies and heroes of the early work were an attempt to find through folk tradition a binding force for society; and the doctrine of Anima Mundi found in the later poems is the same thing in a more developed form, which has left purely local peculiarities behind, in favour of something that the deceased hoped was universal; in other words, he was looking for a world religion. A purely religious solution may be unworkable, but the search for it is, at least, the result of a true perception of social evil.

In all this, Yeats showed 'a continuous evolution towards what one might call the true democratic style', to the 'social virtues of a real democracy' which are 'brotherhood and intelligence'. Yeats' metonymic enquiries, that is, were always directed toward finding the whole symbolically represented in the parts, to creating a balanced relation between centre and peripheries. For Auden, however, this is not something which nationalism can supply, so that Yeats' best moments remain incomplete tokens, partial representations of a true totalisation which only international socialism can bestow.

Look, Stranger! is in many ways Auden's most powerful deconstruction of the British national culture. He complained that Faber chose the title for this second collection of poems without consulting him. In the American edition, he insisted on the title *On this Island*. Both titles come from the opening lines of one of its most famous poems, and both of them, in isolation, metonymically misrepresent what the poem, and the volume, are about. The opening line invites the reader to 'Look, stranger, at this island now', without exclamatory pointing (which excitedly alters the tone of the address), and with 'at' instead of 'on' (an alteration which was to confirm the US title).[32] The poem offers a series of partial views of this island, in line with the cinematic style Auden had acquired from his work with the GPO Film Unit. The poem was indeed originally written for a documentary film about Britain based on a series of visual vignettes. The stranger is invited to stand stable and silent 'here' (following the 'now' of the first line), as if to emphasise the minute neighbourly particularity of the stance. This stranger need not be any kind of specular outsider, a foreigner or, as the titular foregrounding suggests, an alien from some future, better world, bringing news from nowhere to the unenlightened present, but simply a tourist in an unfamiliar place; and the island need not be a metonymic Britain but simply any holiday island: both the Isle of Man and the Isle of Wight have been suggested as locations.

The leaping light 'discovers' all these phenomena for the stranger's delight, but it is unclear what the actual relation is between seer and seen. In the second stanza the stranger is invited to pause at 'the small field's ending'. The emphasis on smallness is important, for if this is a metonymy for Britain, it is only in that Britain is a nation of small things. The national symbolism of an embattled history is certainly invoked in the image of the chalk walls falling to the foam, which 'Oppose the pluck / And knock of the tide', with echoes, in the sucking shingle, of Arnold's 'Dover Beach'. Yet the scene remains a particular, not a totalising one, returning to the gull that lodges on the cliffs for a moment, then in the final stanza pulling back, cinematically, from the particulars to what is ostensibly a whole view, of the ships diverging far off and the clouds sauntering reflectively in the water all summer long. However, the moment of instant perception is not the one that offers totality, for, we are told, 'the full view / Indeed may enter / And move in memory' – but in memory only. Auden does not offer, here, the kind of momentary intuitive unity of subject and nation, part and whole, which left Edward Thomas perplexed and unknowing among the betonies. The invitation to 'look at' or 'look on', that is, is an ambiguous one, playing with the prophetic voice, then shrinking from it into personalised and particularised experience, reining in the self that wants to envisage 'the full view', by reminding it of its own parochial and restricted experience, refusing generalisations while simultaneously implying them.

When Auden lies back and thinks of England, he seems drawn, almost involuntarily, to a kind of Homeric catalogue of places and

events. Thomas' essays on the national reaction to war offered representative cameos up and down the country, from Swindon to Newcastle.
But Thomas remained rooted in the particularity of anecdote, which
sealed off any larger claims to representativeness. Auden's epitomes by
contrast are serial, potentially endless, overflowing with a sense of the
uncontainable totality they evoke, but in the process insisting on their at
times arbitrary representativeness. In this, he combines the appro-
priative megalomania of Yeats with the diffident, self-subverting marginality of Thomas.

Significantly, perhaps, the most sustained instance of this formula is
the long poem of 1940–1 which constitutes his first American volume,
published as *The Double Man* in the United States and *New Year Letter* in
Britain. In American reminiscence, Auden's England becomes an allegorical terrain, not a patch of real earth to be dug and planted, as in
Thomas' 'What matter makes my spade', with its compacting of men
who fought in Marlborough's European campaigns and ancient Britons
buried in the same dense, historically stratified soil. Thomas' 'system of
vast circumferences' here gives way to an endless system of differences
existing primarily as language, discourse. The poem evokes England in
a kind of serial patriotism which betrays the loyalty to each parochial
scene by moving speedily on to the next, subverting each in turn by
turning its alleged biographical resonance into a cheery allegoric token
of something else which is larger and ineffable and precisely, like
Thomas' England, elsewhere. Such camp allegorising identifies Auden
as already postmodern, pulling the carpet from under his own oaths of
allegiance, delighting only in the perpetual circulation of signifiers.
Here, nothing stands stable, but slips and slides under that which it
stands in for, pretends to understand. As he had written in his elegy for
Ernst Toller, 'We are lived by powers we pretend to understand.'
National identity is structured like a language, and

> England to me is my own tongue
> And what I did when I was young.

A fugitive in New York from 'the torn / Old Europe where we both
were born', Auden tells the German refugee Elizabeth Mayer that

> I can but think our talk in terms
> Of images that I have seen,
> And England tells me what we mean.
> Thus, squalid beery *Burton* stands
> For shoddy thinking of all brands;

> The wreck of *Rhondda* for the mess
> We make when for a short success
> We split our symmetry apart,
> Deny the Reason or the Heart;
> *Ye Olde Tudor Teashoppe* for
> The folly of dogmatic law,
> While graceless *Bournemouth* is the sloth
> Of men or beaurocrats [*sic*] or both.[33]

But if these places 'stand for' moral derelictions in the national character, it is no longer clear how Auden himself stands in relation to them,
whether he can't stand them or wouldn't stand for them; whether he
would be prepared, like the contemporary American 'Fugitive' writers,
to take his stand for the values and virtues they betray. Rather the scenes
have taken on a kind of arch and whimsical typicality that puts the
national culture in quaint quotation marks, a kind of touristic terrain
like the 'maps' on souvenir tea-cloths. Similarly, a little later, a whole
history, personal and social, is embodied in the landscape of places he
has known, arbitrarily exploiting merely personal associations to make
vast claims about the human condition. Whether meeting someone
while window-shopping in Paris, bumping through Iceland on a bus,
discussing current affairs with clubwomen over tea, or talking man to
man in Pullman washrooms,

> Whenever I begin to think
> About the human creature we
> Must nurse to sense and decency,
> An English area comes to mind,
> I see the native [*sic*; *sc.* 'nature'] of my kind
> As a locality I love,
> Those limestone moors that stretch from *Brough*
> To *Hexham* and the *Roman Wall*,
> There is my symbol of us all.

But, as he was to record, wistfully, in his post-war poem 'In Praise of
Limestone',

> If it form the one landscape that we the inconstant ones
>   Are consistently homesick for, this is chiefly
> Because it dissolves in water[34]

The dissolving landscape, that is, finally stands in for the dissolute and
inconstant self that is homesick for it, but knows you can't go home
again. Metonymically, it figures only the dispossession of the subject that

lacks it: no use here crumbling a piece of chalk in the hands; nothing to stand up for in that. Considering the differences between English and American cultures, in his Introduction to *The Faber Book of Modern American Verse* in 1956, Auden stumbled on a contrast which explains what is happening to his English locations in *New Year Letter*:

Whatever their doubts and convictions about the purpose and significance of the universe as a whole, Tennyson's Lincolnshire or Hardy's Dorset were places where they felt completely at home, landscapes with faces of their own which a human being could recognize and trust.

But in America, neither the size or condition or climate of the continent encourage such intimacy. It is an unforgettable experience for anyone born on the other side of the Atlantic to take a plane journey by night across the United States. Looking down he will see the lights of some town like a last outpost in a darkness stretching for hours ahead, and realize that, even if there is no longer an actual frontier, this is still a continent only partially settled and developed, where human activity seems a tiny thing in comparison to the magnitude of the earth.[35]

In middle age, a helmeted airman no longer, the stranger looks on a world without frontiers which is, in a sense, all frontier, turning to think of those two representative English and American novels, *Oliver Twist* and *Huckleberry Finn*, 'the heroes of which are both orphans', so different in their relation to the idea of belonging: Oliver, 'his fondest dream, to have a home'; Huck 'announc[ing] his intention to light out by himself for the West'. What is figured here, in epitome, is the postmodern dilemma of identity, of the subject's relation to the place which gave it identity and substance – a dilemma, Auden notes, first expressed by American writers because they first experienced 'the dehumanized nature and the social levelling which a technological civilization was about to make universal'.[36] This, then, for Auden, is the postmodern condition, recognising, in relation to the national culture which made them, like Kafka's allegoric anti-heroes, as *New Year Letter* puts it:

> The Truth where they will be denied
> Permission ever to reside.[37]

CHAPTER 6

Reactions from their burg: Irish modernist poets of the 1930s

Alex Davis

In 1917 A. R. Orage's *New Age* printed a series of three articles by Ezra Pound that, in defence of 'civilisation', targeted 'Provincialism the Enemy'. In the third essay, in the course of arguing that 'a definite start on the Channel Tunnel would be worth many German defeats', Pound attacks the 'sub-sectional criers within [these] Islands', concentrating his scorn on Ireland, principally on the Northern Unionists but without sparing Irish nationalism:

Neither from South Ireland nor from Ulster has anyone spoken on behalf of civilisation, or spoken with any concern for humanity as a whole. And because of this the 'outer world' not only has no sympathy, but is bored, definitely bored sick with the whole Irish business, and in particular with the Ulster dog-in-the-manger. No man with any care for civilisation as a whole can care a damn who taxes a few hucksters in Belfast, or what rhetorical cry about local rights they lift up as a defence against taxes. As for religion, that is a hoax, and a circulation of education would end it. But a nation which protects its bigotry by the propagation of ignorance must pay the cost in one way or another. Provincialism is the enemy.[1]

Pound's article appeared fifteen months after the execution of the leaders of the Easter Rising, repulsion at which significantly changed large sections of the Irish populace's attitude toward the rebellion; and the series as a whole commenced the same month, July 1917, in which, at least in part as a consequence of this change of opinion, Éamon de Valera won a landslide victory on a Sinn Fein ticket in the Co. Clare by-election. Unionist 'hucksters' were beginning to feel as embattled as before the war, with the commencement of which the 1912 Home Rule Bill had been shelved for the duration of hostilities. Such, for Pound, is Irish provincialism: the protestation of 'local rights' and nationalist politics is the enemy of the 'circulation' of civilisation; it marks a regression to a parochial mindset, the erecting of mental as much as geographical boundaries when what is needed are tunnels, both literal and metaphorical, between the peoples of Western Europe.

With the signing of the Anglo-Irish Treaty in 1921, and the creation of the Irish Free State and that of Northern Ireland, Pound's Olympian dismissal of the 'Irish business' would come to be shared by a number of Irish writers, from both sides of the border. Pound's position finds an otherwise unlikely supporter in the period's most heated poetic invective against Ireland in the years between the Treaty and the Second World War or 'the Emergency' as it was dubbed in the South. Those parts of Louis MacNeice's *Autumn Journal* (1939) that address themselves to the North's and South's cultural and economic stagnation unequivocally view Irish provincialism as the enemy.[2] Turning a jaundiced eye firstly on the Free State, MacNeice asks:

> Griffith, Connolly, Collins, where have they brought us?
> Ourselves alone! Let the round tower stand aloof
>   In a world of bursting mortar!
> Let the school-children fumble their sums
>   In a half-dead language;
> Let the censor be busy on the books; pull down the Georgian slums;
>   Let the games be played in Gaelic.[3]

MacNeice's ironic, and exasperated, cry of *Sinn Fein* ('Ourselves alone!' (*sic*)) is succeeded by a cruel picture of the insularity of Irish life in the late 1930s; the effects on children of teaching exclusively through Irish in the national school system, the introduction of censorship, botched housing developments in Dublin – each of these functions as a metonym for Southern Ireland's provincialism. Looking to Northern Ireland, and to Belfast, 'A city built upon mud; / A culture built upon profit', MacNeice draws his reader's attention to the economic slump that quickly succeeded the wartime boom, and which, by the date of his writing, had become an outright recession:

> And the North, where I was a boy,
>   Is still the North, veneered with the grime of Glasgow,
> Thousands of men whom nobody will employ
>   Standing at the corners, coughing.[4]

MacNeice's representation of Ireland in 1938 is, by his own admission in the prefatory note to the poem, an 'over-statement'.[5] Moreover, the dispirited tone of *Autumn Journal* is in line with a number of British acts of 'literary stocktaking', as Peter McDonald terms them,[6] at this date, and registers the Northern Irish poet's re-negotiation of the relationship between poetry and politics in the aftermath of the Munich agreement and the Spanish Civil War. That said, the Ireland of *Autumn Journal* is not unrecognisable as the Ireland of the period: MacNeice's depiction of Irish culture has the same relationship to its referent as the equally exaggerated views expressed in Samuel Beckett's 1934 essay, 'Recent Irish Poetry', which J. C. C. Mays argues 'bears the same relation to reality as an infra-red photograph which obliterates contours'.[7] Beckett's essay, published in the *Bookman* under the pseudonym 'Andrew Belis', turns on an over-sharp distinction between poets influenced by the Revival, whom he dubs 'the younger antiquarians',[8] and poets cognisant of and influenced by continental and Anglo-American modernism. It is an analysis which delineates, in the specific context of Irish poetry, an insularity comparable to that identified in MacNeice's broader diagnosis of Irish cultural and political life. Whereas MacNeice targets the 'round tower' of de Valera's Ireland, Beckett's essay lambastes Yeats' *The Tower* and *The Winding Stair and Other Poems*, and their deleterious effect, as he sees it, on contemporary Irish poetry. Beckett's abrasive essay praises the work of his friends and contemporaries Brian Coffey and Denis Devlin to the extent that they 'evince awareness of the new thing that has happened, or the old thing that has happened again, namely the breakdown of the object, whether current, historical, mythical or spook'.[9] Such awareness constitutes a 'rupture of the lines of communication' as literary conventions become problematic, and thus defines the work of Coffey and Devlin against that of 'our leading twilighters', who include Austin Clarke, Padraic Colum, Monk Gibbon, F. R. Higgins and James Stephens. These poets, according to Beckett, recycle the 'accredited theme[s]' of the Revival; in 'flight from self-awareness' the poetic subject is staged against 'the correct scenery, where the self is either most happily obliterated or else so improved and enlarged that it can be mistaken for part of the *decor*'.[10]

Toward the close of his argument Beckett claims that in the poetry of Coffey and Devlin is 'the nucleus of a living poetic in Ireland'. In 1930 the two poets had published at their own expense a slim volume, containing poems by both authors, in a print-run limited to 350 copies. *Poems* was neither a commercial nor a critical success, and neither author chose to reprint their contributions in any subsequent collection. Though almost entirely forgotten, the volume is of considerable interest in that, alongside Beckett's *Whoroscope*, published in the same year, it signals at the very beginning of the 1930s a highly self-conscious awareness, on the part of a small number of poets in the South of Ireland, of the innovative poetics of European and Anglo-American modernism. The 1930s would see the appearance of a number of collections and pamphlets by these poets: Coffey's *Three Poems* (1933) and *Third Person* (1938), Beckett's *Echo's Bones and Other Precipitates* (1935) and Devlin's *Intercessions* (1937), the latter three volumes published by the Belfast-born George Reavey and his London-based Europa Press. These three poets were not alone in their literary predilections: the slightly older poet, Thomas MacGreevy, author of the first critical monograph on T. S. Eliot, brought out his *Poems* in 1934; while Austin Clarke recalled late in his life a group of poets, including 'Lyle Donaghy, Valentine [*sic*] Iremonger, Donagh MacDonagh [and] Denis Devlin', who 'gathered in the tea-room above the St Stephen's Green Cinema . . . They were all in revolt against the Irish Literary Revival and were enthusiastic followers of T. S. Eliot, whose play, *Murder in the Cathedral* had been performed at U[niversity] C[ollege,] D[ublin] with much success.'[11]

Clarke loftily adds that he 'ventured to suggest to these young poets that they should try to follow Eliot's own example and try to express their reaction from our literary tradition just as he had defined his reaction from his own burg, St Louis', but his advice 'was not heeded'. Clarke revealingly conflates the poet's 'reaction from' a preceding movement in literary history (in the case both of him and of 'these young poets' that of the Literary Revival) with the 'reaction from' his or her 'burg', a term suggesting a broader milieu than the purely literary. Elsewhere, in an essay contemporaneous with his reflections on the 1930s, he again speaks of the influence of Eliot on certain Irish poets, perceiving it as disempowering, arguing that 'ironically enough' Devlin's best-known work is not that in which he wrote 'in the intellectual manner of modern French poets', but an elegy for Michael Collins ('The Tomb of Michael Collins'); and that for MacDonagh success came when he 'turned back to Irish themes' with his verse-comedy *Happy as Larry*.[12] Clarke's remarks are indicative of his open antagonism toward literary modernism, as he understood it, which he berates on several occasions for its lack of location, its placelessness. In a 1929 review of Pound's *Selected Poems*, to take one example among many, he notes 'a spiritual homelessness, a restlessness that goes deeper than free verse, in his work'. Pound has 'refused to settle down at any poetic address, avoided responsibilities, knocked wittily at many doors without waiting for an answer'.[13] In other words, the kind of free 'circulation' of cultural capital Pound argues for in 'Provincialism the Enemy' is, for Clarke, a disabling expropriation from one's burg.

Coffey and Devlin's *Poems* lacks the kind of direct 'poetic address' Clarke demands of poetry to the extent that its contents are coloured by the poetic 'homelessness' attendant upon a high modernist conception of language. Certain of the poems in the collection possess that self-conscious attention to their own medium which is the hallmark of the great modernist artefacts written in the wake of the First World War. It is a self-reflexivity that Charles Bernstein, among others, associates with 'the crisis of representation' manifested in radical modernism, its 'discovery of the entity status of language – not just verbal language but signification systems/processes; thus the working hypothesis about the autonomy of the medium, of the compositional space; the flattening of the Euclidean space of representing and its implicit metaphysics of displacement and reification of objects'.[14] That which Clarke calls 'homelessness' and Bernstein 'displacement' is modernism's expropriation from the Real, and hence from a consensual or normative discourse. Though the work of two practising Catholics, *Poems* is marked by the 'Protestant stylistic contortions, which express a subjectively validated vision', that Christopher Butler sees as 'canonical for Modernism'.[15] One such contorted poem in the collection is Devlin's 'Now', a text which recalls various high modernist depictions of Western civilisation as exhausted, its tradition lacking meaningful contact with an enervated present. 'The Urn of the Occident is filled', says the persona, as over its cultural ashes he ponders the shallowness of modernity:

> Arrogant gathering of sense and movement and passion
> To interpret to men the profoundest soul of a man
> Disgust and tire like a long-drawn out farewell
> The Good no longer enfevers the sons of Plato,
>> *Pure white and azure sky*
> The Hymn to Beauty is no longer chanted
>> *Dull cold and ivory Aphrodite.*[16]

As the poem continues, however, it develops precisely the kind of 'reaction from' the Irish literary tradition that Clarke felt was missing in the poetry discussed in the tea-room over St Stephen's Green Cinema. The text scrutinises the shop-worn tropes of a literary tradition perceived as in a state of terminal decline – 'The Hymn to Beauty', it would appear, having atrophied into a stale lyricism:

> Eternally emerald pastures of Ireland; English lanes winding
>> *One-ery, two-ery.*
> Through smothering blossom; old book shops in Paris;

Ziccary zan
Larks singing in Sussex and Deirdre's now bloodless lips.
Hollow-bone, crack-a-bone.
Vines in Avignon rich-smell charged, and brown men of Connaught.
. . .
Tweedle dum-Twadle dum.
O Bridges, O Belloc, O Blunden, O Chesterton, Yeats; O La Mare![17]

The nursery-rhyme interjections in this passage upbraid recent Irish poetry, that of the Literary Revival and after, as well as mocking the idealised ruralism of the Georgian poets. For an Irish poet of Devlin's generation, drawn toward *symboliste* and surrealist poetry, the Revival's appropriation of Gaelic materials and its celebration of the West of Ireland must have seemed by 1930 poetically anaemic ('Deirdre's now bloodless lips'). Similarly, the urban backgrounds of Devlin and like-minded contemporaries rendered largely irrelevant the depictions of the 'emerald pastures of Ireland' in the work of post-Revival poets such as Higgins and Gibbon. Stressing an essentially pastoral identity to Ireland, the dominant poetry in the period following the Revival might well have appeared as alien to Devlin as that of Blunden or Bridges. 'Now' thus reacts as much to literary representations of the Free State as it reiterates Eliot's gloomy prognosis of the Occident.

Nevertheless, in rejecting the '*Twadle*' of a poetry thronged by the 'brown men of Connaught', Devlin's poem maintains a distance from the European avant-garde, mocking the latter's faith in the emancipatory potential of the revolution of the word:

Let us be Anarchists by all means
How many miles is it
Dethrone the Verb and the Substantive
To Babylon.
. . .
Hail to the Holy Adjective!
Three-score and ten.
What's beauty, truth, life, love, what's me?
Can we get there?
Don't know, don't know, don't know.
By candle-light?
Pull down that gilded rubbish. We
Candle-Light.
In metaphysic, apotheo –
How many miles is it?
– sise Adjective. Hail Sitwell.[18]

The historical avant-garde's desire to 'Pull down that gilded rubbish' was an attempt to realign the aesthetic with lived experience at large, thus destroying its institutional status *as* art.[19] For Devlin, such an anarchic questioning of literary tradition – that made, for instance, by his admired surrealists – is to contribute to the destruction of the Occident, an end to the artist's perennial preoccupation with 'beauty, truth, life, love'. Devlin's wariness *vis-à-vis* the avant-garde at this early stage of his career is indicative of the trajectory of his subsequent poetic career, from the playful appropriations of surrealist devices in *Intercessions* to the New Critical qualities of the poetry he wrote in the 1940s and 1950s, qualities that led to his championing by Allen Tate and Robert Penn Warren.[20] The impasse reached in the early poem is that those poetic absolutes it cannot break with are no longer unproblematic ('*What's* beauty, truth, life, love. . . ?') – even the stability of the lyric subject who would give voice to them is doubtful ('what's me?').

The poem's modernist dilemma should be seen in the immediate context in which it was composed: the 'Now' in which the poem exists is that of Ireland in the immediate aftermath of the Censorship of Publications Act (1929), an act which protected the Irish populace as much from modernist texts as from pornographic materials. In Terence Brown's view, 'An almost Stalinist antagonism to modernism' is evident in much of the press coverage of the cultural life of the 1930s; a rejection of 'surrealism, free verse, symbolism and the modern cinema . . . combined with prudery (the 1930s saw opposition to paintings of nudes being exhibited in the National Gallery in Dublin) and a deep reverence for the Irish past'.[21] Writers who stood opposed to the cultural insularity of this period, including Patrick Kavanagh, Seán Ó Faolain and Frank O'Connor, would develop over the next two decades a largely realist aesthetic in their attempts to demystify the ideology developed by the Irish Ireland movement in the early decades of the century, particularly in the work of D. P. Moran and Daniel Corkery, which would achieve its most infamous formulation in de Valera's St Patrick's Day speech of 1943, with its vision of an Ireland of 'frugal comfort', 'joyous with sounds of industry, the romping of sturdy children, the contests of athletic youths, the laughter of comely maidens'.[22] An indigenous modernist aesthetics is, if not absent, a fitful presence in the literary landscape of Ireland in the inter-war years; with the notable exception of Flann O'Brien, Irish writers drawn to experimental modes of writing gravitated in the early 1930s to London and continental Europe, specifically Paris.

Comparing the contents of the *Dublin Magazine* during the 1930s with those of the *Bell*, edited by Ó Faolain from 1940 to 1946, Anne Fogarty notes the extent to which the former's willingness to include articles on aspects of avant-gardism and modernism gives way in the latter journal to an increasingly embattled tone, the change between the two organs indicative of 'the increasing constriction and oppressiveness of the Irish cultural scene'.[23] The refreshingly cosmopolitan *Ireland To-day*, edited by O'Connor from 1936, published work by Coffey and Devlin among others; but though running to twenty-two issues, it was short-lived, its final number appearing in March 1938. Devlin's 'Now', read in its Irish context of composition and publication, is thus both an oblique commentary on the claustrophobic cultural conditions culminating in the Censorship Act and proleptic of the growing insularity of the decade ahead.[24] (In its magazine publication, it might be noted, the poem's title was 'Decay'.) The poem concludes with the 'Urn of the Occident' waiting for an 'Embalmer' to 'impose resigned hands on [the] rich ashes' of Italy, Spain, Germany, England and France, yet it is less Occidental decay than Ireland's literary scene that arguably informs Devlin's Embalmer's vision of cultural 'desolation': 'The world is sudden a medium grey; and he beholds / . . . / Quick hypnotised, the wooden hobby horses / Roundabout roundabout roundabout round'.[25]

The 'medium grey' of Irish poetry at this date is that which Beckett atomises in 'Recent Irish Poetry'. His critique polemically reiterates Devlin's dismissal in 'Now' of an ossifying Celticism, though the essay refrains from 'disoblig[ing]' either Devlin or Coffey by quoting from their 1930 *Poems*. Rather, Beckett quotes from Devlin's 'Est Prodest', subsequently collected in *Intercessions*, seeing in the poem the 'influences' of 'Corbière, Rimbaud, Laforgue, the *surréalistes* and Mr Eliot, perhaps also . . . those of Mr Pound':[26]

> Phrases twisted through other[,]
> Reasons reasons disproofs
> Phrases lying low
> Proving invalid that reason
> With which I prove its truth
> Identity obscured
> Like the reflections of
> One mirror in another
> Reasons reasons disproofs.[27]

Beckett's choice of quotation foregrounds the 'awareness' in Devlin's poetry of that 'breakdown' of object and subject in many ways characteristic of modernist writing: the poem's intricate attempt to 'prove' the existence of an extra-linguistic deity foundering on the rocks of its own textuality. Yet Beckett's point in quoting these lines is equally a strategic intervention into Irish poetics: in 'evading the bankrupt relationship' of subject and object, Devlin (and Coffey) *also* evades 'the *Gossoons Wunderhorn* of that Irish Romantic Arnim-Brentano combination, Sir Samuel Ferguson and Standish O'Grady',[28] two writers central to the formation of Yeats' cultural nationalism and that of the Literary Revival as a whole. The poem, in Beckett's reading, is thus a 'reaction from' its 'burg' in precisely the manner that Clarke found missing from the work of those Irish poets for whom Eliot rather than Yeats was a formative influence.

It needs to be said that Beckett's Yeats and the 'younger antiquarians' are largely straw men, his depiction of the Revival a burlesque. In particular, the essay's summary dismissal of Clarke's 1929 collection, *Pilgrimage and Other Poems*, is, as I shall argue later, woefully inaccurate. As John P. Harrington has observed, Beckett's 'critique of cut-and-dried Ossianic goods [is] virtually as old as those goods themselves':

By attacking antiquarianism, Beckett did not relinquish his own involvement in local culture. Instead, he joined a dissenting factor of impeccable credentials that has been an important feature of modern Irish literature in all but its crudest revival forms or most exigent aims . . . The immediate obsolescence of the antiquarian goods and endorsement of an awareness of modernity is embedded in discussions of the Irish revival contemporary with it.[29]

Beckett's championing of the experimental poetry of Devlin and Coffey is, from this perspective, a critique of recent Irish culture in line with those made by writers antipathetic toward literary modernism; and in this respect, 'Recent Irish Poetry' stands alongside, rather than against, the subsequent editorials of Ó Faolain in the *Bell*, and prefigures Kavanagh's unflinching *exposé* of the hardships underpinning the 'frugal comfort' of de Valera's Ireland in *The Great Hunger* (1942). Linking such diverse texts is a shared *Ideologiekritik*; distinguishing them is the presence in Beckett, and in Coffey and Devlin, of literary devices adapted from the writings of the preceding generation of high modernists.

David Lloyd sees in Beckett's work the 'reappropriat[ion]' of 'certain modernist procedures from the marginal site of a post-colonial nation, commencing quite programmatically in the 1930s with a rejection of the already ossifying obsession of Irish writers with "antiquarianism", the recurrent reproduction of Celtic material as a thematic of identity'.[30]

For Lloyd, the deployment of 'modernist procedures' enables Beckett to avoid the impasse of nationalism, which, in seeking the authentic identity of the nation's people, nevertheless remains tied to the identitarian thought underpinning European imperialism: 'the nationalist desire to develop the race into authenticity, borrowed already from a universalist ideology, produces the hegemonic conditions for the ultimate perpetuation of imperial domination even after independence is achieved'. Beckett's 'aesthetic of non-identity' dislocates rather than reconciles subject and object; and to this extent can be interpreted as gesturing toward a way of writing that refuses the concepts of authenticity and identity that are, for imperialist and nationalist alike, crucial components of an aesthetic in which literature serves 'to mediate subject and object, to produce reconciliations between individual and totality'.[31] The latter aesthetic is that promulgated by the Irish Irelanders, as in Corkery's emphasis on the *representative* function of a national literature, in which the writer speaks from and to his nation. Beckett's poetry pursues a contrary course to that advocated by Corkery in *Synge and Anglo-Irish Literature* (1931). Its radical modernism, for Lloyd, is a development of the strategies of 'minor literature' as exemplified in the work of the nineteenth-century Irish poet, James Clarence Mangan, whose disjunctive poetry resists incorporation within the canon of romanticism through devices which include the grotesque mixing of registers, in which bathos hilariously undercuts conventional sentiment, the creation of spurious translations, and the deployment of complex personae in the place of a stable lyric subject. Beckett's 'breakdown' of subject and object in 'Recent Irish Poetry' thus replays Mangan's 'recognition of the disintegration of the individual subject of the bourgeois state, questioning the principles of originality and autonomy that underwrite that conception of the subject'[32] – and in so doing repeats Mangan's critique of nationalist poetry's reconciliatory role.

In the light of Lloyd's argument, it becomes possible to see that the plight of the expropriated personae of Beckett's poetry – who prefigure the more famous narrators and characters of the later novellas and the *Trilogy* – is not reducible to existential 'throwness'. That is, the modernist 'homelessness' or 'displacement' experienced by the speakers of Beckett's early poems is conditioned by, and constitutes a reaction from, the Irish Free State. 'Enueg I', collected in *Echo's Bones and Other Precipitates*, opens with a characteristically Beckettian expulsion from a 'home':

Exeo in a spasm
tired of my darling's red sputum
from the Portobello Private Nursing Home
its secret things[33]

The 'secret things' of the Portobello Nursing Home allude, as Lawrence Harvey has established, to the tribulations of the damned behind the gate of Dante's *Inferno*.[34] Ejected from this hell, Beckett's speaker walks along the decrepit banks of the Grand Canal in Dublin, 'trundl[ing] along rapidly now on [his] ruined feet / flush with the livid canal', noting at Parnell Bridge 'a dying barge / carrying a cargo of nails and timber'. The dismal urban scene, the bridge over the canal, the allusion to *Inferno* III – all are reminiscent of Eliot's Dantesque treatment of the 'Unreal City' of London in *The Waste Land*, a text which the poem can be seen in part as rewriting in a Dublin location:

Under the brown fog of a winter dawn,
A crowd flowed over London Bridge, so many,
I had not thought death had undone so many.
Sighs, short and infrequent, were exhaled,
And each man fixed his eyes before his feet.[35]

Eliot's notes to his poem admit the indebtedness of his imagery to Dante, his Londoners likened to the shifting, worthless spirits Dante encounters just inside the gates of Hell. Where Dante beholds these figures with detached contempt, however, Eliot's speaker is part of the crowd, from within which he hails an acquaintance, Stetson: 'You who were with me in the ships at Mylae!'[36] So too, in Beckett's poem the persona would appear to be one of Dante's damned: selfishly 'tired of [his] darling's red sputum', his exit from the 'secret things' behind the gates of the Portobello Private Nursing Home is more of an entrance into a Dublin-based inferno than an escape. In the middle of his journey through the city and its environs the speaker comes across 'a little wearish old man', not Tiresias, but

Democritus,
scuttling along between a crutch and a stick,
his stump caught up horribly, like a claw, under his breech, smoking.[37]

Democritus' theory of atomism, in which reality is the accidental result of the collision of particles or atoms, conditions the poem's narrative of random encounters, including the meeting with the philosopher, whose

further belief that the atoms accrue one to the other in a rotary
movement finds a correspondence in the circular walk made by Beckett's
persona. Democritus provides Beckett with a conception of matter as
atoms in the void, a philosophy that provides a cosmic underpinning to
the poem's emphasis on the chaotic nature of everyday experience.

The speaker's perambulations take him out of the city to which he
returns via a suburbia bristling with literary resonance:

> Next:
> on the hill down from the Fox and Geese into Chapelizod
> a small malevolent goat, exiled on the road,
> remotely pucking the gate of his field;
> the Isolde Stores a great perturbation of sweaty heroes,
> in their Sunday best,
> come hastening down for a pint of nepenthe or moly or half and half
> from watching the hurlers above in Kilmainham.[38]

Lawrence Harvey has noted the allusions to Isolde in both the shop's
name and in Chapelizod (Chapel of Isolde), the poem thus evoking 'the
many exiles of Tristan and Isolde',[39] the persona's alienated state finding
a quirky parallel of sorts in that of the doomed lovers. I would add to this
that the allusion to Isolde once again links the poem to *The Waste Land*, in
the first part of which Eliot quotes from Wagner's *Tristan und Isolde*:
'*Frisch weht der Wind / Der Heimat zu / Mein Irisch Kind / Wo weilist du?*'
('Fresh blows the wind / homeward: / my Irish maid, / where do you
linger?').[40] The longing for the beloved '*Irisch Kind*' by Wagner's sailor is
grotesquely parodied in Beckett's poem, his persona having commenced
his journey by leaving his own consumptive 'darling' or 'Irish child'.
The allusion, via Wagner, to Eliot's poem is reinforced when one recalls
that, shortly after the citation of the sailor's song, Eliot quotes the
dispiriting words sung to the dying Tristan as he awaits the ship carrying
Isolde: '*Oed' und leer das Meer*' ('Deserted and empty is the sea').[41] In
'Enueg I' the female rather than the wandering male is ailing, but this
difference (characteristic of the misogynist streak in Beckett's early
writing) merely overlies the deeper shared preoccupation with wasting
and death, in an urban and suburban environment, one finds in
Beckett's and Eliot's texts.

The reference to Chapelizod in Beckett's enueg also suggests the
presence of Joyce: Chapelizod is the Co. Dublin village in which the
Mullingar Inn of Joyce's *Finnegans Wake* is located, home to Humphrey
Chimpden Earwicker, Anna Livia Plurabelle, Shem the Penman,

Shaun the Post and Issy. And *Work in Progress*, as *Finnegans Wake* was known in the mid 1930s, incorporates a version of the story of Tristan and Isolde (Issy), or 'Trustan with Usolde',[42] in the 'Mamalujo' section, which draws on both Wagner's opera and Joseph Bedier's *Romance of Tristan and Iseult*. Joyce's scene of seduction is also an instance of scopophilia, as the couple are watched by the four senile Mamalujo. In Beckett's poem, there is none of the amorous titillation of the *Wake*'s recasting of the legendary lovers, while the gentle irony of Joyce's episode contrasts sharply with Beckett's sardonic tone: Beckett's Tristans are 'sweaty heroes', downing pints in parodic allusion to the philtre drunk by the original lovers. As if to underscore the difference from the *Wake*'s emphasis on cyclical regeneration, Beckett's enueg portrays the topographical landmark associated with Issy's mother, Anna Livia Plurabelle, as a diseased prostitute: 'Blotches of doomed yellow in the pit of the Liffey; / the fingers of the ladders hooked over the parapet, / soliciting'.[43]

The two intertexts for Beckett's 'Enueg I', *The Waste Land* and *Finnegans Wake*, are useful in determining the poem's response to its historical conjuncture. The struggle for Irish independence is tangentially touched upon in the poem's reference to Kilmainham, in the jail of which Parnell and other prominent Land Leaguers had found themselves in 1881, and which, more recently, had housed members of the IRA. That the boozing Tristans have come from a hurling match at Kilmainham is of a piece with 'The critique of modern Ireland' Harrington observes in Beckett's 1938 novel *Murphy*, which 'directly addresses the subordination of the heroic impulse formulated in the literary revival era and inevitably deflated by the realities of the Free State'.[44] One of the many dimensions to *Finnegans Wake* is Irish history from 1916 to 1923, its preoccupation with resurrection equally an investigation of the Easter Rising and its aftermath, the text concluding with a 'Surrection! Eireweeker to the wohld bludyn world'.[45] Joyce's own critique of narrow nationalist pieties is a constant from the stories of *Dubliners* to the *Wake*'s disparaging references to de Valera, and in this respect Beckett's enueg follows Joyce's disenchantment with Ireland after the Anglo-Irish Treaty, 'The wastobe land, a lottuse land, a luctuous land, Emerald-illuim, the peasant pastured'.[46] Beckett's poem conjoins the *Wake*'s 'wastobe land' and Eliot's waste land: the purgatorial aspects of Joyce's text, as analysed under Joyce's direction in Beckett's essay on *Work in Progress*, 'Dante . . . Bruno . Vico . . Joyce', given the infernal tinge of Eliot's Unreal City.

Thomas MacGreevy's contribution to the same collection of essays in which Beckett's piece on *Work in Progress* appeared also emphasises the connections between Joyce's text and Dante's *Purgatorio*. MacGreevy's connections between Joyce and Dante, however, are more programmatic than Beckett's, his essay succumbing to 'The danger . . . in the neatness of identifications' of which Beckett warns in his own essay on the *Wake*.[47] Thus, in MacGreevy's reading of Joyce, his purgatorial *Work in Progress* follows his *Inferno*, that is, *Ulysses*: 'As Homer sent his Ulysses wandering through an inferno of Greek mythology and Virgil his Aeneas through one of Roman mythology so Dante himself voyaged through the inferno of the mediaeval Christian imagination and so Mr Joyce sent his hero through the inferno of modern subjectivity.'[48] MacGreevy's essay had previously appeared in *transition* 14 (1928); in *transition* 18 appeared his own poem of 'the inferno of modern subjectivity', 'School of . . . Easter Saturday Night (Free State)', retitled as *Crón Tráth na nDéithe* in his *Poems*. *transition* 18 also included a section of *Work in Progress*, but MacGreevy's poem, completed according to Susan Schreibman by 1925/26,[49] clearly owes more to *Ulysses*, at least as MacGreevy understood Joyce's novel. His note to the poem included in *Poems* 'acknowledge[s] the debt, so far as form is concerned, to modern French and Spanish writers of the eclectic school, as also to Mr Joyce and the one or two writers in English who have successfully adapted the technique of *Ulysses* to their own literary purposes'.[50] MacGreevy's adaptation of the 'technique of *Ulysses*' would appear to comport with Eliot's interpretation of the novel in his famous *Dial* review '"Ulysses", Order, and Myth', in which Eliot claims that the Homeric parallels are 'simply a way of controlling, of ordering, of giving a shape and a significance to the immense panorama of futility and anarchy which is contemporary history'.[51] *Crón Tráth na nDéithe*'s elliptical collage of literary and musical allusions attempts to give 'shape' and 'significance' to Ireland in the immediate aftermath of the cease-fire called by Republican forces, the date of which MacGreevy appends to his poem: '*Easter Saturday, 1923*'.[52] In this respect the poem is, as David Pierce argues of the *Wake*, 'a Civil War text';[53] yet it takes its formal and structural cues from *The Waste Land*, to which Eliot's reflections in his piece for the *Dial* better apply than to their ostensible Joycean pretext. In the third section of MacGreevy's poem the persona, travelling through war-damaged Dublin in a cab, passes down O'Connell Street and across O'Connell Bridge:

The king, his inns, behind!
But there's little room for him now.
Poor king's a-cold.

Poor inns o'court
To be all but all of Gandon left!

When the Custom House took fire
Hope slipped off her green petticoat
The Four Courts went up in spasm
Moses felt for Hope

Folge mir Frau
Come up to Valhalla
To *gile na gile*
The brightness of brightness
Towering in the sky
Over Dublin[54]

The allusion to the final act of Wagner's *Das Rhinegold*, where Wotan invites Fricka into the newly built Valhalla, ironically counterpoints the recently created Free State with Wotan's fortress. Indeed, the poem makes this explicit at the end of this section: 'Do not look for a star / Or Valhalla / / Our Siegfried was doped by the Gibichungs.' Yet the parallel also works to set side by side the hypocrisy and deceit that lie behind Wotan's construction of Valhalla in Wagner's opera and the political machinations surrounding the signing of the Anglo-Irish Treaty. The allusion, in its complex suggestiveness, is clearly informed by Eliot's practice in *The Waste Land*, which MacGreevy discusses to good effect, particularly with regard to Wagner, in his *T. S. Eliot: A Study* (1931). MacGreevy's use of Shakespeare in this passage is equally reminiscent of *The Waste Land*, albeit on a less ambitious scale. Taking in the Georgian architecture of Dublin designed by James Gandon, the speaker jumbles Edgar's words in *King Lear* as he sees the King's Inns, which had passed unscathed through the violence of 1916–23. As Susan Schreibman points out, the amusing allusion makes the reader recognise that it is 'poor Tom' MacGreevy who is cold, as his cab rattles through the nightscene.[55] But the reference to a sovereign for whom 'there's little room' in Ireland presumably refers also to George V, in whose armed forces MacGreevy had served from 1917 to 1919, including a stint in the front line at the Somme. For MacGreevy's poem is as much a poem of the First World War as of the Irish Civil War. The war-

battered buildings of this Dublin waste land are perceived by an ex-
combatant (unlike Eliot), a demobbed British soldier, moreover, who
was also an Irish nationalist. Herein lies the crucial difference between
Crón Tráth na nDéithe and *The Waste Land*. On the one hand, the route
traced through Dublin in the poem is a journey through 'the inferno of
modern subjectivity' that MacGreevy found in *Ulysses* and which his
poem structures by means of devices familiar from Eliot's own 1922
work. On the other hand, however, MacGreevy's poem is far more
context-specific, more *localised*, than Eliot's (in which London is somehow interchangeable with other Unreal Cities, 'Jerusalem Athens Alexandria / Vienna London'.)[56] The reason for this difference between the
two works is spelled out in part in MacGreevy's monograph on another
soldier-poet, Richard Aldington, in which he argues that the abstract or
'remote manner' of expression discernible in parts of Eliot as well as in
other modernist writers has its origins in Mallarmé's symbolism. For the
writer who 'went through the war' such abstraction is not an option,
because 'The effect of the war . . . has been to bring their work closer to
objective reality'.[57] MacGreevy is not advocating a return to realism: he
claims that the war 'is so vast and so terrible to look back on' that a
writer like himself or Aldington 'cannot, in the nature of things, fall into
the mere pathetic of, say, Monet or Zola'.[58] As *Crón Tráth na nDéithe*
illustrates, MacGreevy's experiences at the front are inseparable from
his conviction that the empire for which he had fought had betrayed its
promises to Ireland. Earlier in the poem, its organising consciousness
recalls British propaganda urging Irishmen to fight on behalf of other
Catholic nations, as the Dublin cityscape blends with the Western front:

> Wrecks wetly mouldering under rain,
> Everywhere.
> Remember Belgium!
> You cannot pick up the
> Pieces[59]

The poem recurrently conflates the Great War with the Irish Civil
War, as in the damning juxtaposition of the Treaty of Versailles in 'the
Galerie des Glaces' with Irish politics and society after the Anglo-Irish
Treaty, the 'gombeenmen / On blue hills of office'.[60] Forced 'closer to
objective reality' due to the pressure of historical events fully imbricated
with his lived experience, MacGreevy's poetry nevertheless cannot
'return' to a realist conception of language as transparent signification.
His text is conditioned by that 'discovery of the entity status of language'
Charles Bernstein sees in radical modernism, 'the autonomy of the

medium' resulting in an 'implicit metaphysics of displacement and reification of objects' – the Beckettian 'rupture of the lines of communication'. The speaker of *Crón Tráth na nDéithe* is fixated by the object-world glimpsed from beyond his cab, the ruined buildings and the recent events they starkly represent: 'Look! / Look! / Oh, Look! / Look and see!' Yet his sense of 'displacement' is agonisingly apparent in the way in which the Great War has seemingly rendered impossible any totalising comprehension of recent history, the poem playing off his perception of Dublin with memories of the all-too-visible horrors of the trenches: 'Why see? / You that saw!'[61]

MacGreevy's *Crón Tráth na nDéithe* shares with Beckett's 'Enueg I', and the majority of the poems Beckett collected in *Echo's Bones and Other Precipitates*, a sharply delineated sense of place. Beckett's subsequent poetry moves away from such localism, a move paralleled by his shift from English to French. As Patricia Coughlan observes: 'The poems [in French] start to behave differently as to setting: the Dublin and occasionally London settings, topographically laden and often cumbersome, have . . . gone, and in the best of the French poems . . . it is simply not appropriate to speak of setting at all.'[62] Coughlan views this paring away of recognisable settings as enabling; a means of pushing beyond the 'complex hermetic miseries', in Hugh Kenner's words,[63] preserved in the early poems in English. MacGreevy's career as a creative writer, by way of contrast, draws to a close with the publication of *Poems* (with the exception of a small number of exquisite, uncollected later poems). His relative poetic silence after *Poems* is due, presumably, to a tangle of reasons; but among them the discrepancy between his modernist poetics and the cultural priorities in Ireland of *both* post-independence nationalism *and* its critics must surely have played a part. In Terence Brown's words:

it may be that the paucity of an explicit, developed interest in modernism in Ireland in its post-independence phase also has to do with the fact that nationalism itself as a structure of feeling allowed for the expression of what elsewhere became identified with the reactionary cultural politics of the general movement. Irish writers and ideologues could dispense with the formal originality of the Revival's poetics, with its links to, and parallels with, modernist experiment, but could nevertheless indulge themselves, in the midst of general crisis, in conservative ideological accounts of past and present which were elsewhere the basis of modernist sociological and historical expatiation.[64]

There was little house-room for the kind of poetry MacGreevy wrote in a society in which, as Brown further observes, Daniel Corkery's conservative cultural views are the counterpart of those expressed in

Eliot's *Notes Towards the Definition of Culture*. Corkery's sense of culture precludes the kind of experimentation Eliot's allows for; the Irishman's own fiction being formally closer to that of those writers, such as Ó Faolain and O'Connor, antipathetic to Irish Ireland, than to either the products of the Literary Revival or modernist writing elsewhere. In David Lloyd's terminology, Corkery's call for a literature that would reconcile subject and object finds no support in MacGreevy's poetry's disjunction of poetic subject and environment. His poetic of estrangement reflects disillusionment with post-independence Ireland, a disaffection more paralysing than Beckett's because in tension with a nationalism absent from his younger friend's work.

In a 1934 letter to MacGreevy Brian Coffey congratulated him on the appearance of *Poems*, optimistically claiming that 'I think . . . you have, in practice, distinguished between the AngloIrish [*sic*] school of writers and the hypothetical poets of Ireland who are to come after you.'[65] Coffey's postulated 'hypothetical poets' prefigure by just two months Beckett's affirmation of a 'nucleus of a living poetic in Ireland', which included Coffey, in 'Recent Irish Poetry'. The prematurity of Coffey's claim is movingly attested to in the long poem he began to write in the early 1950s in St Louis, *Missouri Sequence*, the first section of which is dedicated to MacGreevy, author of the first book-length study of St Louis' most famous son. MacGreevy functions as a node around which cluster Coffey's reflections on the baleful influence, as Coffey sees it, of Yeats on Irish poetry, and the consequent failure of an indigenous modernist poetry to emerge:

> Dear Tom, in Ireland,
> you have known
> the pain between
> its fruiting and the early dream
> and you will hear me out.[66]

This is not the place for a discussion of the important body of poetry Coffey produced subsequent to the lengthy silence maintained between *Third Person* (1938) and the drafting of *Missouri Sequence*. Of relevance in the present context is the way in which Coffey's poetry of the 1930s follows that of MacGreevy, Beckett and Devlin in turning to Anglo-American and European modernism for models distinct from those of the Literary Revival and later. Coffey had been seriously studying Eliot's poetry, as well as Pound's, from at least the early 1930s, and the effects of this study are most apparent in his *Three Poems*. In contrast to

Beckett's *Echo's Bones*, Devlin's *Intercessions* and MacGreevy's *Crón Tráth na nDéithe*, Coffey's chapbook is swamped by Eliot's influence. The first of the *Three Poems*, 'Exile', owes too much to Eliot's 'Portrait of a Lady':

> 'Flowers become you'.
> Funny to shiver so
> Within me, when my eyes must surely shine
> Deepening my words . . .
> . . .
> But, as you say, I give you tears only
> To enter in your record of the day.[67]

while the second, 'Dead Season', leans heavily on 'The Love Song of J. Alfred Prufrock' and the second part of *The Waste Land*:

> I am tired, tired, tired. I will go home now,
> The train clanking through the greasy fog,
> The train clattering between the tenements,
> I shall ask them to shut that window,
> Smoke, smuts, fog pouring in choking me.
> '*Will you open that window, open that window please*'.
> . . .
> 'Yes. I'd do it again'. 'No you can't, you can't'. . . .
> To sleep. To die. Out on the broad hillside,
> '*Will you open that window, open that window please*'.[68]

Edna Longley is right to say that such poetry does not represent much of an advance on that of Higgins and other poets over-reliant on Yeats: 'Poetic Modernism could not be imported at a stroke by exchanging . . . pastiche Yeats for pastiche Eliot.'[69] But Longley strategically ignores the more complex negotiations with Eliot *and* Joyce in the poetry of Beckett and MacGreevy in this decade, as well as Devlin's wholly successful meshing of Eliot and French surrealism in a poem like 'Est Prodest'. It is equally a mistake on Longley's part to view the 'importation' of modernism as somehow an alternative to the project of Austin Clarke in this period. Longley argues that 'During the 1930s and 1940s . . . [i]t seemed important to break or weaken Anglo-Irish and English literary links infinitely complicated by a shared language. One route to separateness was Austin Clarke's absorption in and of Gaelic poetry. Another was Modernism.'[70] Oddly enough, Longley reiterates Beckett's placing of Clarke among the 'younger antiquarians' in 'Recent Irish Poetry', though without of course Beckett's condemnation of Clarke (one continued in the vicious lampooning of Austin Ticklepenny in *Murphy*).

Clarke's open hostility to Pound is to a notion of modernism as international and therefore 'homeless'; yet his own poetry from the late 1920s should be seen as a provincial modernism that outflanks the obstacles encountered by those poets, like MacGreevy and the young Coffey, whose modernist experiments come to grief at least in part because of the cultural provincialism of the Free State.

Late in life, Clarke would come to qualify his negative opinion of Pound, as is evinced by his poem 'Ezra Pound', from *Old-Fashioned Pilgrimage and Other Poems* (1967). In this text, Clarke recalls 'pooh-pooh[ing] his poems':

> Why should my pen, I thought, dip pity
> In praise for another American poking
> At European curios
> In the backroom of our Serendipity
> Shop, gawky stranger from Idaho,
> Rough rider with stetson, jaunty pose,
> Browning in holster, nudging the elbow
> Of Yeats and T. S. Eliot[71]

Pound's 'spiritual homelessness', however, must be held against his formal restlessness, the results of which, the poem claims, deserve the highest accolades, and this regardless of his war crimes:

> Rhyme, echo the name of Ezra Pound
> Whom the war capitalists impounded.
> For miserable years he pounded
> The wall of modern verse, expounded
> The madness of dollar, franc and pound.
> Forget the theories he propounded,
> But praise the language he compounded.
> The centuries are in that pound.[72]

Clarke's ingenious rhymes turn on the difference between the profits made by the 'war capitalists' who imprisoned Pound and the hard currency of the latter's poetry – 'that pound', the value of which lies in its relation to the 'centuries' of literary tradition, stands in sharp contrast to the empty exchange-relations of capitalism, 'The madness of dollar, franc and pound'.

Clarke's belated tribute to Pound, then, salvages his experiments in literary form not only from his fascist economic and racial 'theories', but also from his poetry's lack of rootedness in a specific, familiar locale, the work of an expropriated 'American poking / At European curios'. It is a generosity that Clarke, in the essays on Irish poetry which he wrote subsequent to *Old-Fashioned Pilgrimage*, did not extend to those Irish poets influenced by Pound as well as Eliot. Clarke sees their work as irredeemably weakened by its failure to attend to place and an indigenous literary tradition; a weakness, moreover, that Clarke believes actually runs counter to their expressed admiration for Eliot, whose poetry creatively reacts against its author's birthplace or 'burg'. In Clarke's late responses to Pound and the Irish poets of the 1930s one can detect in this purportedly anti-modernist writer an awareness of his affinity, at the level of linguistic innovation, with Pound: his antipathy to modernism comes into focus as the product of a narrow identification of literary modernism with an aesthetics indifferent to national and regional boundaries. Yet, as Patrick Crotty has observed, Clarke shares much with the 'modernist localism of William Carlos Williams and Hugh MacDiarmid'.[73] Clarke's cool review of Pound's *Selected Poems* appeared in the same year as his *Pilgrimage and Other Poems*, a volume in which Clarke's appropriation of the sound-patterns of Irish-language poetry can be seen as, on the one hand, groping toward the modernist localism of Williams and MacDiarmid, and, on the other, as a 'poking' at Gaelic 'curios' in a manner not radically dissimilar to the Celticism of the Irish Literary Revival.

PART TWO

An American place

CHAPTER 7

Pound's places

Peter Nicholls

In summer 1912, Pound undertook two walking trips in the South of France. The first, taking in such important troubadour sites as Hautefort and Excideuil, was brought to a halt after two weeks when news reached him in Limoges of Margaret Cravens' suicide. The young woman had been the poet's benefactor, and there were hints too of an attachment from which Pound may have withdrawn. Whatever the facts of the matter, the tragedy made a strong mark on Pound.[1] After spending a desultory June in Paris, he set off once again and in the next three weeks travelled some thousand kilometres of the Midi, half of them on foot. The notebook recording his impressions was intended to provide material for a volume to be called *Gironde*, though dissatisfaction with his prose style and the diversion of energies into other projects left the work unfinished.

The manuscript of *Gironde* has disappeared, but what remains is the series of small notebooks in which Pound recorded his impressions of the troubadour landscape. These have now been edited by Richard Sieburth and provide a fascinating insight into Pound's thinking at this time.[2] One of the aims of the trip was to test his theory that an allegory of military strategy was encoded in Bertran de Born's 'Dompna pois de me no'us chal', in which the reference to idealised ladies in various castles might suggest a hidden map of Bertran's political designs. Pound's interest in this possibility – 'Is it a love poem? Did he sing of war?' – found its most memorable expression in the poem 'Near Perigord', published in 1915. But the interest of the notebooks far exceeds these speculations. For it is here, for the first time, that Pound moves beyond the mystical locations of his early verse to discern the traces of poetic energies in an actual landscape. The transition, though, was a complex one, and the notebooks register Pound's distinct unease about adopting the role of the romantic tourist. His reluctance to travel by 'steam contrivance' (6) rather than on foot reflected a constant if predictable sense of opposition of past and present. Entering Poitiers, for example, he notes that 'The worst side comes first upon you – out of a plain of poplars and flat rivers – a scurry of houses burrowing into cliff, and thus modernity, such forces as damned the soul of Mansard hurl themselves upon one. I was discouraged' (5–6). Yet such 'discouragement' is felt as something to be resisted, since it fosters too easily that sense of anachronism and homesickness which Pound was now trying to expel from his writing – 'going my way amid this ruin and beauty', he remarks, 'it is hard for me at times not to fall into melancholy regarding that it is gone, and this is not the emotion I care to cultivate for I think other poets have done so sufficiently' (22).[3]

To be sure, Pound is keenly responsive to those places on his itinerary which do not bear the impress of modernity, places like Uzerche which 'does nothing that it did not do in the middle ages' (33). Yet, at the same time, he strives for a discipline of attention to this 'land so thick with ghosts' (35) which will be conditioned by the rugged actuality of the roads on which he walks: 'I had set out upon this book with numerous ideas, but the road had cured me of them. There is this difference, I think, between a townsman & a man doing something or going somewhere in the open, namely that the townsman has his head full of abstractions. The man in the open has his mind full of objects – he is, that is to say, relatively happy' (33–4). I say that Pound 'strove' for this kind of perception because the discipline it entailed did not come easily to him. In fact, the notebooks frequently register an uncertainty about the exact nature of his aims in undertaking this sometimes gruelling walk. Noting his 'discouragement' in Poitiers, Pound observes that nonetheless 'There are here quiet gardens but this is not what I came for' (6). Beyond testing his hypothesis about Bertran de Born (the 'numerous ideas', perhaps, with which he had set out), what exactly had Pound come for?

In his Introduction to *A Walking Tour*, Sieburth remarks acutely that:

Nature, dismissed as mere 'scenery', is conspicuously absent from the narrative: Pound's roving eye is only drawn to that already aestheticized (and semiotized) arrangement of place into legible contour which he calls 'landscape' – a field of visual particulars seized not as ineffable totality but as a sequence of detached details whose fragmentation observes the same erotic scenario as the fetishized attributes of Bertran de Born's 'composite lady'.   (xvii)

The notebooks are indeed studded with imagistic perceptions of the landscape, but Pound's reflections on his journey also exhibit a certain

ambivalence about the kind of 'seeing' which characterises the detached gaze of the tourist. So while 'It is on my conscience that I should
go to Gourdon & Roc Amadour', he doesn't visit these places because
'9408 people have been to Rocamadour & 9409 have written brilliant
descriptions of it' (38–9). The 'impressionistic or realistic method' had
provided an escape from 'dogma, generalities, inexact "ideas"', but this
had led in turn to 'a failure to see where description of a thing is worth
while either because it is normal or because it is extreme' (7). These remarks
are made during the visit to Angoulême, where Pound remarks that
'There is a cathedral for connoisseurs, my real objection is to the idea
that one come to "see" or that all travel is to study the phases of
architecture visigothic or otherwise, or that one should tap a certain
cask of emotions in the teeth of every cathedral' (7).[4] Pound's bypassing
of Gourdon and Rocamadour along with his refusal to take the
Baedeker tour of architectural monuments amount to more than simple
snobbism, raising some important questions about the adequacy of
visual description. For he is keenly aware of the power of guidebooks to
shape and control one's perception of place – he had prepared for his
own trip with the aid of Justin Smith's lavishly illustrated two-volume
The Troubadours at Home[5] – and the book he hopes to write is intended to
transcend the merely descriptive. At times his refusal of objective nota-
tion registers a reluctance to confront traces of modernity in the landscape – 'you know how little I want to see the place as it is', he remarks
in his entry on Poitiers (5) – but it is also related to a larger sense that 'I
come to feel rather than to see' (7). Pound acknowledges that it may
seem that 'I make & write of a sheer voyage of sentiment' (7), but in fact
those sites which possess extraordinary historical and visionary density
cannot actually be 'seen' in the simple sense of tourist observation:
'Cahors & Rodez: not that one should see, or sees them, for some
names are so heavy with unreality that we can never find them – not
tho' our senses deceive us' (41).

The most extended meditation on this theme occurs in Pound's entry
on Arles:

There are machines, there are ghosts & corpses of cities, all of them, but no,
Arles is the other sort, the living complex – like Venice, or Verona, or perhaps
Cadiz, even tho I throw in this last as mere venture.

You can not in any real sense *see* such places, you pass & you return, & you
know like fate in the weaving that some time you will come back for good there,
for a time that is, for a liason [*sic*], for this is in the run what it comes to, a
satiation, a flowing out from yourself into the passion & mood of the complex.

Then there are cities that are passionate in their personal hold upon us. You may play the string as you like. It is not the bath of the crowd, it is different, it is the place, the place that made the people, it is seductive as the creative principle is always seductive, it touches or it clings and we go out & through & into it, and are one with it, infused & inflowing.   (64)

In this passage, Pound seems to be trying to connect the perception of place with the motif of visionary metempsychosis which runs through his early verse. In the entry on Beaucaire, for example, further speculations about the role of memory in these experiences leads him to write in similar terms of 'how many persons may flow thru us or flow past us while we are alive', the phrasing here strongly reminiscent of the early poem 'Histrion', where Pound conjures with the thought 'that the souls of all men great / At times pass through us'.[6]

'Place', then, for Pound is a particularly rich and absorbing concept. While it is disclosed through a praxis of visual perception which is keenly attuned to nuance and detail, it is also enmeshed in a network of memories and fantasies. Much as he prizes accurate observation, Pound responds to particularly auratic places as sites of intermingled temporalities. As is suggested in the passage just quoted, the motif of 'return' is, and would continue to be, the emotive principle behind his sense of a 'magic' of place. And it is a kind of double movement that this 'return' entails – the casting back of memory, personal and cultural, to an imagined past, and at the same time a projection forward, as a future return to a place now being visited. Pound's exposure to the troubadour landscape prompted a series of fragmentary reflections on the nature of memory, sometimes, as in the entry on Beaucaire, to the exclusion of any observations about the place being visited (especially notable here, since the distinctive 'slim gray' tower at Beaucaire would only feature later, in Ur-Canto I):[7]

> Certain things happen & continue, they exist in us by a species of recurrence, they fall vividly into our days & nights after they are in one sense over & done with.
>
> And there are other things, often 'more important' often more seemingly vital which pass into a sort of unreality & seem like a dream or fiction.   (68)

This idea of 'unreality' and the related distrust of mere 'seeing' suggests that, for Pound, the genuinely visionary place can only become truly 'real' *after* it has been visited, after it has been absorbed into a mnemonic complex which includes other remembered places and perceptions.

In this respect, Pound's sensitivity to place has more than a little in common with Walter Benjamin's account of 'aura':

What is aura, actually? A strange weave of space and time: the unique appearance or semblance of distance, no matter how close the object may be. While resting on a summer's noon, to trace a range of mountains on the horizon, or a branch that throws its shadow on the observer, until the moment or the hour become part of their appearance – that is what it means to breathe the aura of those mountains, that branch.[8]

To put this passage from Benjamin alongside Pound's thoughts about landscape and memory is to point up the extent to which his imagist commitment to accuracy of detail and to 'objectivity' ran parallel to an intuition that an intense experience of place might have the paradoxical effect of focussing the mind elsewhere. So, for example, Pound had written in 1910 from Sirmione to Margaret Cravens: 'Here I am more or less drowned in beauty, but it isn't the lake, or the hills, or even – almost even the olive trees, but the four red leaves of a poppy that are the *poetry* simply because they go beyond themselves & *mean* Andalucia & the court yard at Cordova.'[9] Here Pound seeks to avoid the seductiveness of the lake's beauty – the idea of being 'drowned' in it might seem to predict the passive 'floating bodies' of the lotophagoi in Canto xx – and fixes instead on an object which has the suggestive power to transport the mind elsewhere. Once again, he wants to distinguish between 'place' as something static, which might be felt to 'contain' and perhaps immobilise the mind, and those features of it which in signifying something 'beyond themselves' instigate that affective movement which, for Pound, characterises the imagination. Critics have, arguably, been too ready to accept Pound's programmatic valuation of the 'concrete' above the 'abstract', for in some respects the famous axiom that 'the natural object is always the *adequate* symbol' might properly be rewritten with the emphasis placed on 'symbol' rather than on 'adequate'.[10]

I have spent some time with Pound's travel notebooks because they give an idea of the complexity of the transition between his early verse and what we tend to think of as the inaugural phase of modernism proper as that is represented by Imagism and Vorticism. Too often this transition is described as a move away from the derivative and nostalgic moods of the early poems to the more clearly instigative and future-oriented poetics of modernism. Yet the role of nostalgia in Pound's poetics cannot be specified so simply. The sensuous Platonism of the

early visionary poems was something he was never able fully to re-
nounce, even though later he sometimes sought to resist its appeal.
From the beginning he was drawn to the Platonic notion of learning as
'recollection' (*anamnesis*) and it was that specialised sense of memory
which led to his fascination with Richard St Victor's idea that 'by
naming over all the most beautiful things we know we may draw back
upon the mind some vestige of the heavenly splendor'.[11] The same
fantasy lay behind his other conjectures that 'the poetic fact pre-exists'
and that the music of poetry enacts 'the sensation of the soul in ascent'.[12]
Poetry may thus make good an initial loss, restoring some vestigial
perception of an original wholeness and identity.

Here we may recall one of Charles Olson's comments in his account
of his visits to St Elizabeth's: 'I don't think it has been sufficiently
observed, if it has been observed, how much [Pound's work] is a
structure of mnemonics raised on a reed, nostalgia.'[13] Olson is thinking
primarily of Pound's habit of collecting good anecdotes, but the insight
obviously has wider relevance, especially since the function of ecstatic
perception in the early poems is strongly marked by a sense of potential
home-coming (*nostos*), a return which will later supply the residual
Odyssean structure of *The Cantos*. Yet the importance of nostalgia as a
structure of feeling in the poem can also be seen at the local level where,
as poet Robert Duncan has noted, it conditions particular forms of
measure:

That one image may recall another, finding depth in the resounding, is the
secret of rime and measure. The time of a poem is felt as a recognition of return
in vowel tone and in consonant formations, of pattern in sequence of syllables,
in stress and in pitch of a melody, of images and meanings. It resembles the time
of a dream, for it is highly organized along lines of association and impulses of
contrast towards the structure of the whole. The same impulse of dream or
poem is to provide a ground for some form beyond what we know, for feeling
'*greater than reality*'.[14]

Implicit in Duncan's response to these recurring rhythmic signatures
and phrasal parallelisms in *The Cantos* is the notion that nostalgia, the
'recognition of return', has a momentum and power of organisation
which is at once retrospective and proleptic. It is, in other words, a
desire which underwrites a certain form of narrative, with the immanent
sense of this 'recognition' intimating movements back and forth across
the poem. Just as there is no present moment that does not contain
traces of past and future, so there is no auratic place that does not

resonate with echoes of others. Even in the notebooks of his walking tour, for example, when Pound is actually standing in the landscape of which he writes there is a strong pull to create what Sieburth calls 'a kaleidoscopic montage of topographical features' (xvii), with allusions to the 'Chinese background' (48) and to the 'Sky jap pink & grey' (50) which predict the much later, more daring view of 'Mt Taishan' from the detention camp at Pisa.

In *The Cantos*, this syncretism is the mark of the visionary moment, where the specific markers of place can be sublated so as to secure a landscape which is typical rather than particular. To borrow a distinction from Michel de Certeau, we might say that place yields to space in these lyrically heightened passages of the poem. For de Certeau, 'place' refers to 'a determination through objects that are ultimately reducible to the *being-there* of something dead, the law of a "place"', while 'space' denotes 'a determination through *operations* which, when they are attributed to a stone, tree, or human being, specify "spaces" by the actions of historical *subjects* (a movement always seems to condition the production of a space and to associate it with a history)'.[15] In de Certeau's account, the experience of 'place' has about it a certain inarticulacy and secrecy: 'Places are fragmentary and inward-turning histories, pasts that others are not allowed to read, accumulated times that can be unfolded but like stories held in reserve, remaining in an enigmatic state, symbolizations encysted in the pain or pleasure of the body. "I feel good here"' (108).

This account of place certainly seems to resonate with Pound's response to Sirmione, especially in de Certeau's contrasting conception of space as bound up with a temporal and historical 'movement'. Interestingly, de Certeau also connects 'place' with 'seeing': description oscillates between the terms of an alternative – either *seeing* (the knowledge of an order of places) or *going* (spatialising actions); either it presents a *tableau* ('there are . . .'.), or it organises *movements* ('you enter, you go across, you turn . . .'). De Certeau develops what he calls a 'pedestrian rhetoric' – literally, a rhetoric of walking – for which turns and detours are comparable to stylistic figures and turns of phrase. Without pressing too far the analogy with de Certeau, one can see that the notion of the mind 'travelling' underlies many of the perceptual frames of *The Cantos*. To avoid a merely contemplative 'seeing' of places which relegates them to a subjective memory of an immobile past, emphasis is placed on what is perceived while the perceiver is in motion. In contrast to place, space is exilic, requiring an openness to the contingent and unexpected. So one of Pound's principal models for *The Cantos* is the Odyssean voyage which is narrated 'not as you would find it if you had a geography book and a map, but as it would be in a "periplum", that is, as a coasting sailor would find it'.[16] In *The Cantos*, this movement is both a spatial and a temporal one – landscape is not simply seen in passing, but is caught up into the dynamic complex of memory and imagination: 'certain men move in phantasmagoria; the images of their gods, whole countrysides, stretches of hill land and forest, travel with them'.[17]

This idea of an imaginary space informs Pound's early speculations about a particular visionary 'psychology' which he traced from the troubadour songs through to the mysticism of the Italian *trecento* poets. It is given definitive expression in the well-known evocation in his essay on Cavalcanti of

the radiant world where one thought cuts through another with clean edge, a world of moving energies '*mezzo oscuro rade*', '*risplende in sè perpetuale effecto*', magnetisms that take form, that are seen, or that border the visible, the matter of Dante's *paradiso*, the glass under water, the form that seems a form seen in a mirror, these realities perceptible to the sense, interacting.[18]

The 'radiant world' is 'clean', 'without hell-obsession' (153), preserving 'some proportion between the fine thing held in the mind, and the inferior thing ready for instant consumption' (151). In its subtle dialectic between passion and intellect, between the thing seen and the mental image,[19] Cavalcanti's great canzone, 'Donna mi prega', supplies a precise scholastic vocabulary with which to define this mental topology: 'The "formato locho" is the tract or locus marked out in the "possibile intelletto"' (188). When we turn to *A Draft of XXX Cantos*, we can see how Pound attempted to create such a 'tract or locus' in his own long poem. This first sequence is coloured throughout by his experience of the landscapes of Italy and Provence, but it is constantly overlaid by allusions to a composite, mythological landscape which reduce the specificity of particular places.[20] The dominant effect is of things refracted through another medium – like 'the glass under water, the form that seems a form seen in a mirror', the divinities which animate this landscape are perceived at one remove, partially dissolved in an ambient medium of air and water. The metamorphoses of Canto II, for example, reveal 'Beasts like shadows in glass' (II/8), 'the coral face under wave-tinge' (II/9), and 'glass wave over Tyro' (II/10), while other Cantos conjure with 'the faceted air' (XX/92), 'The leaves cut on the air' (XXI/99), and 'The trees melted in air' (XXIX/146). The effect is somewhat akin to what Michel Foucault terms the 'virtual space' of the mirror: 'it makes this place that I occupy at the moment when I look at myself in the glass at once absolutely real, connected with all the space that surrounds it, and absolutely unreal, since in order to be perceived it has to pass through this virtual point which is over there'.[21] Before long, this landscape becomes familiar, with its flashes of colour, 'the stair of gray stone / the passage clean-squared in granite' (xvi/69), the 'hills under light' (xvii/77) and its hovering, suspended presences – 'as of waves taking form' (xxiii/109) and 'the palace [that] hangs there in the dawn' (xxv/117). Duncan's sense of a motif of 'return' which is felt in tone and stress is everywhere in evidence, as Pound quickly establishes particular rhythms of disclosure. Canto ii, in fact, provides many of the key signatures which would haunt the work as a whole. Pound's description of rhythmic constructions as 'cut[ting] a shape in time'[22] nicely expresses the intention here, as spondaic compounds ('pad-foot', 'lynx-purr', and so on) combine with an incantatory use of the present tense to produce a space in which the mind can free itself from the dense particularity of the historical materials which press upon it. Objects are presented but in a curious movement of distantiation are somehow withheld, situated 'over there', in Foucault's phrase – 'Nor bird-cry, nor any noise of wave moving, / Nor splash of porpoise, nor any noise of wave moving' (xvii/76) – and in one of Pound's favourite locutions, we have the 'Sand as of malachite' (but not of malachite), 'the turf clear as on hills under light' (xvii/77) and 'Sound: as of the nightingale too far off to be heard' (xx/90). Strong deictic markers – 'there', 'now' – insist on the presentness of the moment even as the details of the landscape are partially withdrawn – 'the light now, not of the sun' (xvii/76), and so on.

But in what sense can we regard these quiet, 'clean-squared' landscapes as 'locations of modernism'? Much that we find here has, in fact, a decadent lushness:

> The columns crystal, with peacocks cut in the capitals,
> The soft pad of beasts dragging the cars;
> Cars, slow, without creak   (xx/95)

In passages such as these there is an awkward tension between form and content, the sculptural motif which is meant to register an 'ethical' commitment to verbal and rhythmic precision sitting uneasily with the Pre-Raphaelite 'softness' of Pound's mythological decor.[23] The remoteness of such panoramas indicates how easily the visionary measure can slip back into a simple nostalgia which has no connection with the poem's forward movement. The difficulty here is more than a technical or stylistic one since the 'return' which these privileged landscapes are intended to articulate is to a mythological world which expresses some kind of collective memory. Pound's later, deliberately anachronistic description of *The Cantos* as 'the tale of the tribe'[24] gestures toward something fundamentally different from the contemporary historical sense, with its focus on sequence and progress. In its splicing together of mythological and historical materials, *The Cantos* seeks to surmount the modern split between history as a public expression of the life of the nation, on the one hand, and memory as something purely private, on the other.

In elaborating a distinction of this kind, the French historian Pierre Nora observes that modernity 'has substituted for a memory entwined in the intimacy of a collective heritage the ephemeral film of current events'.[25] There is, on the one hand, that primitive form of 'real memory' which was 'unself-conscious, commanding, all-powerful, spontaneously actualizing, a memory without a past that ceaselessly reinvents tradition, linking the history of its ancestors to the undifferentiated time of heroes, origins, and myth – and on the other hand, our memory, nothing more in fact than sifted and sorted historical traces'. We are witness to the 'conquest and eradication of memory by history', says Nora, hence our construction of what he calls 'lieux de mémoire' – 'Museums, archives, cemeteries, festivals, anniversaries, treaties, depositions, monuments, sanctuaries, fraternal orders' (12) – institutions which provide 'protected enclaves' of the past in an era in which these nostalgic 'rituals of a society without ritual' are constantly threatened by the historical sensibility. Such sites of memory offer residual expressions of historical continuity at a time when historical consciousness is increasingly occupied with a sense of its own discontinuity with the past. We have gone, says Nora,

from the idea of a visible past to an invisible one; from a solid and steady past to our fractured past; from a history sought in the continuity of memory to a memory cast in the discontinuity of history. We speak no longer of 'origins' but of 'births'. Given to us as radically other, the past has become a world apart. Ironically, modern memory reveals itself most genuinely when it shows how far we have come away from it. (17)

Nora's account of memory and history is particularly suggestive in light of some of the main tensions in Pound's developing epic. The attempt to re-invoke a 'live tradition' in the face of modernity's 'accelerated grimace' and its expressive vehicle, the 'prose kinema',[26] is obvious enough, but what is more interesting is the constant pressure imposed on the compensatory 'lieux de mémoire' by the 'intellectual and secular' forces of history. One way of understanding the visionary locations of *The Cantos* might be to see them as attempts to reintegrate history and memory, to reactivate the sacred and affective components which modern history seeks to erase.[27] Without such spaces, 'history' is always about to dissolve into 'two gross of broken statues' or 'a few thousand battered books', as Pound observes in *Hugh Selwyn Mauberley*.[28] When place is elevated to space and when time acquires some kind of imma-nent unity a certain continuity might be won back – nature might become again the world in which people act and work, rather than the metaphorical backdrop of Western lyricism,[29] and history might be absorbed back into memory, thus conflating public and private worlds. That, at any rate, might be one way of characterising Pound's ambition in the early Cantos, though, as I have suggested, the visionary landscape too often becomes a 'protected enclave' which is valued for its 'quiet-ness' and remoteness from the turmoil of 'history'. Two actual places, however, offer more dialectical possibilities: the Tempio built by Sigis-mundo Malatesta in Rimini, and the city of Venice. Cantos VIII–XI offer what was to be Pound's most detailed investigation of one particular place, though what is particularly striking is that the Tempio remains a kind of virtual presence here.[30] Given Pound's intense response to this building and to the works it contains, it is initially surprising that the poem seems to resist the temptation to any visual evocation. Instead, emphasis is placed on the turmoil of activity from which the Tempio emerges, on the complex of alliances and negotiations which surround its construction. There is little trace here of the heightened, visionary measure; indeed, the rhythm articulates a prosaic, historical world of sequence and repetition:

> And we beat the papishes and fought
> them back through the tents
> And he came up to the dyke again
> And fought through the dyke-gate
> And it went on from dawn to sunset
> And we broke them and took their baggage   (XI/48)

For all Pound's fascination with the Tempio as a kind of 'pagan' monument to Sigismundo's mistress Isotta, the lyric implications of the building – 'a song caught in the stone'[31] – are only developed obliquely, with the most forceful phrases registering the willed act of construction: 'He, Sigismundo, *templum aedificavit*' (VIII/32), 'And he began building the TEMPIO' (IX/35). It is as if Pound is reluctant to allow the Tempio to compose itself as an object for the contemplative gaze, and even in a rare moment when we are promised a visual glimpse of the building the focus shifts sinuously to another site:

> The filigree hiding the gothic,
>   with a touch of rhetoric in the whole
> And the old sarcophagi,
>   such as lie, smothered in grass, by San Vitale.   (IX/41)

The handling of Venice as a visionary location is rather different. In two Cantos – XVII and XXV – historical Venice is embedded in rich fantasies of organic and inorganic order. In XVII, the evocation of Diana brings back a familiar landscape and cadence:

> The green slope, with white hounds
>   leaping about her;
> And thence down to the creek's mouth, until evening,
> Flat water before me   (XVII/76)

In the lines that follow, the Ovidian landscape is conjoined with that of Venice:

> and the trees growing in water,
> Marble trunks out of stillness,
> On past the palazzi,
>   in the stillness,
> The light now, not of the sun.

In the remainder of the Canto, which Pound described as 'a sort of paradiso terrestre',[32] the vision moves smoothly between the space already familiar from Canto II ('the cave salt-white, and glare-purple') and

> the forest of marble,
> the stone trees – out of water –
> the arbours of stone –
> marble leaf, over leaf,
> silver, steel over steel   (78)

The imagery here expresses ancient fantasies about the organic life of stone and its power to conjoin natural and human energies. Pound probably absorbed such motifs from Ruskin's talk of 'marble foam', the 'marble foliage', and 'the forest branches turned to marble' in *The Stones of Venice*.[33] The theme received further development in the work of Pound's friend Adrian Stokes who responded with similar intensity to the conjunction of nature and artifice in the stonework of Venice: 'if in fantasy the stone of Venice appear as the waves' petrifaction, then Venetian glass, compost of Venetian sand and water, expresses the taut curvature of the cold under-sea, the slow, oppressed yet brittle curves of dimly translucent water'.[34] For Stokes, as for Pound in these Cantos, Venice embodies 'An image of living process as an order in space [which] depends entirely upon the medium of clear light which is yet not dazzling'.[35] Stokes' account of Venice is remarkably similar to Pound's earlier description of it as a 'living complex'.[36] For both men, the city encapsulates the dual movements of life and death, of symbolisation and actuality: 'There, the lives of generations have made exteriors, acceptable between sky and water, marbles inhabited by emotion, feelings turned to marble.'[37]

In Canto xxv, Pound focusses more closely on these 'generations', amassing historical detail about the Palace of the Doges, which is intercut by a passage which returns us to the lagoon as it has been evoked in xvii:

> Which is to say: they built out over the arches
> and the palace hangs there in the dawn, the mist,
> in that dimness,
> or as one rows in from past the murazzi (117)

Here fantasy is interwoven with fact, the palace which seems to hang 'there in the dawn' now given documentary foundations. The ways in which we come to 'see' Venice are thus multiple, as traces of its construction in history combine with a remembered measure which draws the city into the imagination's 'tract or locus'. Reaching the final Cantos of this first sequence, Pound's sighting of 'Beauty on an ass-cart' outside Perugia returns us once more to this composite landscape, the compressed allusions to Venice (now unnamed) signalling at once the curve of reminiscence and an encoded celebration of creativity which propels the poem forward:

> Eyes brown topaz,
> Brookwater over brown sand,
> The white hounds on the slope,
> Glide of water, lights and the prore,
> Silver beaks out of night,

Stone, bough over bough,
      lamps fluid in water,
Pine by the black trunk of its shadow
And on hill black trunks of the shadow
The trees melted in air.   (xxix/145–6)

In the next two sequences of Cantos (xxxi–xli (1934) and xlii–li (1937)), the privileged sites make only intermittent appearances. Pound's attention here is focussed on instances of creative activity and on the usurious forces against which it has to struggle for expression. Events now take precedence over sites,[38] and when a visionary space is opened it is deliberately figured as a domain of action rather than of contemplation. So the erotic 'beat of the measure' in Canto xxxix ('From star up to the half-dark / From half-dark to half-dark') emerges from the encounter of the 'hard-boiled' Odysseus with temptress Circe,[39] and Canto xlvii connects his 'sail[ing] after knowledge' (236) with the practical wisdom of Hesiod's *Works and Days* ('Begin thy plowing / When the pleiades go down to their rest' (237)). With Canto xlix, the landscape of ancient China further simplifies the rhythm of work which gives these spaces 'the light of the doer' (li/251):

Sun up; work
sundown; to rest
dig well and drink of the water
dig field; eat of the grain
Imperial power is? and to us what is it?   (xlix/245)

As he moves into Cantos lii–lxxi, however, Pound begins an extensive study of the vicissitudes of imperial power in China, basing the first part of the sequence on J. A. M. de Moyriac de Mailla's *Histoire Générale de la Chine* (1777–85). Something fundamentally different begins to take place at this point in the poem. Pound's dependence on his Enlightenment source roots the China Cantos in a movement of decline and fall across a massively extended period of time. There is, as I have noted elsewhere, an abstracted, 'spatial' feeling for history here, as particular actions and events are absorbed into a generalised rhythm of recurrence and endurance.[40] Various references to Mussolini's economic policies suggest a deep-lying parallel to be drawn between China and the Italian state, a parallel which Pound attempts to induce by an attention to both nations as agrarian economies. Here the Chinese land mass has an insistently ideological function as a figure for national unity. As Homi Bhabha remarks in another context: 'the political unity of the nation consists in a continual displacement of the anxiety of its irredeemably plural modern space – representing the nation's modern territoriality is turned into the archaic, atavistic temporality of Traditionalism. The difference of space returns as the Sameness of time, turning Territory into Tradition, turning the People into One.'[41]

The imaginary place which is 'China' in these Cantos represents Pound's deep desire for political unity and for a common identity grounded in tradition. This world is, indeed, a 'protected enclave', in Nora's sense; in fact the repeated acts by which it is secured against the incursions of 'others' – 'the taozers and hochang' (312) who seemingly pose a persistent threat to Confucian order – form one of the main narrative motifs of the sequence. 'Place', at this point, allegorises political investment, and the movement of 'return' can only be to a lost past which no amount of allusions to contemporary Italy or invective against 'taozers' can reanimate. There is no movement 'elsewhere', no desire to forge new meanings; instead the mind is immobilised by this monolithic history, driven down a narrow ideological groove from which the only relief is the relentless motion of linear chronology. Nor does Pound's rapid collaging of *The Works of John Adams* in the next group of Cantos release us from the pedagogical straitjacket. Here we are more frequently within the world of the particular and the detail of the private life, but so closely is Pound's text bound to that of his source that no alternative space is offered unless it be that of the rather inappropriately abstract expression of law alluded to in the closing quotation from Cleanthes' hymn to Zeus ('Zeus aye ruling all things, founder of the inborn qualities of nature' (LXXI/421)).

If the China and Adams Cantos effected (in Nora's sense) a radical separation of history from memory, then the collapse of Mussolini's regime and Pound's subsequent internment in the detention camp at Pisa suddenly compelled the poem in a new direction. Cut off from any kind of archive, memory and imagination offered the only liberation from the place of his confinement. '[I]n sight of Mt Taishan @ Pisa', Pound's mind travelled restlessly through remembered landscapes and cities, the name of a place often sufficient to reanimate distant experiences. Here we find a developed dialectic between 'place' and 'space' as the poem attempts to salvage what it can from the wreckage of European history. Certain locations are like de Certeau's 'places', 'fragmentary and inward-turning histories' whose full significance is available only to private memory ('Sirdar, Bouiller and Les Lilas'

(447)), while others are imaginary spaces of exhilaration and momentary freedom:

> Serenely in the crystal jet
> as the bright ball that the fountain tosses
> (Verlaine) as diamond clearness
> How soft the wind under Taishan
> where the sea is remembered
> out of hell, the pit
> out of the dust and glare evil
> Zephyrus / Apeliota
> This liquid is certainly a
> property of the mind   (463)

Here the fountains of Verlaine's 'Clair de Lune' are coupled with the remembered motion of the sea to lift the poet from the 'hell' in which he finds himself, the 'dust' and 'glare evil' recalling with an ironic inflection the more literary 'hell' of the early Cantos. This movement of waters is 'a / property of the mind', 'an element / in the mind's make-up / est agens and functions / dust to a fountain pan otherwise'. The image of 'the rose in the steel dust' – 'the *forma*, the concept [which] rises from the death', as Pound had earlier described it in *Guide To Kulchur*[42] – transfigures the dust of mortality, allowing the mind to move even though the poet sees himself as one who has 'passed over Lethe'.

The Pisan Cantos represent, in this sense, an extraordinary effort of will as Pound endeavours to memorialise a world now irreparably damaged. Anxiety about what might remain (the Tempio, he believed, had been 'destroyed' by Allied bombing (473))[43] was matched by a steady conviction that 'nothing matters but the quality / of the affection / . . . that has carved the trace in the mind' (471). In the detention camp at Pisa, Pound managed to produce the fullest realisation of his intuition that the rhythms of memory might transform place into space: here the oppressive detail of the death cells and 'the ideogram of the guard roosts' (442) were coupled with a minute perception of natural phenomena which led in turn to a Confucian recognition of the total 'process' of nature. In the extremity of his situation, the landscape of captivity was somehow redeemed, purged of its brutal materiality:

> Plura diafana
> Heliads lift the mist from the young willows
> there is no base seen under Taishan
> but the brightness of 'udor ύδωρ
> the poplar tips float in brightness
> only the stockade posts stand   (LXXXIII/544–5)

Yet the remarkable lightness and buoyancy of much of the writing in the Pisan sequence, coupled with its moments of wit and affection, were much harder to sustain after Pound began his long incarceration at St Elizabeth's hospital. In the first of the visionary landscapes of *Section: Rock-Drill*, for example, the familiar ascending rhythms attempt an exit from 'Erebus, the deep-lying' (xc/620), 'Out of heaviness where no mind moves at all' (xc/621). The Canto develops through a complex mesh of allusions to images and rhythms from earlier parts of the poem: the lights taken down to the sea, the 'water jets from the rock', 'the stone taking form in the air', the 'furry assemblage', and so on. Yet where the earlier landscapes had yielded open spaces and 'new sky' (xvi/69), the overall effect of this Canto is one of a procession of interiors, of private places where the self is mirrored back to the self. There is the 'hill's fold', the narrow beach, the space of the Tempio, the room at Poitiers – a sequence of enclosures whose encompassing security allows a poetic ascent which rhymes with the 'rise and fall' of the waves and with the 'semina motuum' (seeds of motion) whose place in the 'process' is elided with a coded reference to Hitler, 'furious from perception'. This Canto reminds us that for all the pathos of weakness and fragility, 'Trees die & the dream remains', and as we move to xci the narcissistic framing of this utopian moment is reaffirmed in an imagery of reciprocal gazes: 'from the green deep / he saw it, / in the green deep of an eye' (xci/625), and so on. What the poet now seeks is 'the protection of crystal', a state of absolute clarity and purity in which self and object are one, mutually regarding and mutually sustaining.

This turning inward runs parallel to Pound's growing attraction to ancient feudal economies. In the Confucian Cantos xcviii and xcix, where he draws on *The Sacred Edict* of K'ang Hsi,[44] space dwindles to an extreme localism of place: 'Earth and water dye the wind in your valley' (703), 'Establish the homestead' (718), 'One village in order' (723) and so on. There is a persistent desire for homecoming, for a return to origin, 'with Chou rite at the root of it' (722). 'The plan is in nature / rooted' (723), and the social order is likewise organic and eternal: 'The State is corporate / as with pulse in its body' (721); 'The whole tribe is from one man's body' (722). This landscape exists in what Mikhail Bakhtin calls 'folkloric' time, not in history. This is the time of the idyll, in which, notes Bakhtin, we find:

an organic fastening-down, a grafting of life and its events to a place, to a familiar territory with all its nooks and crannies, its familiar mountains, valleys, fields, rivers and forests, and one's own home . . . This little spatial world is limited and sufficient unto itself, not linked in any intrinsic way with other places, with the rest of the world.[45]

In Cantos xcvii and xcix, this narrowing of focus is complemented by the crackerbarrel tone of Pound's translation: 'And if your kids don't study, that's your fault . . . Dress'em in folderols / and feed'em with dainties, / In the end they will sell out the homestead' (719). This irascible moralism largely disappears in the final moments of his long poem, however, as Pound discovers another, even more remote landscape, that of the Na-khi kingdom of Southwest China. His interest in this little-known people and their exotic mountainous landscape was triggered by his discovery in 1956 of Peter Goullart's *Forgotten Kingdom* and the works of the principal authority on the Na-khi, Joseph Rock.[46] Here, indeed, in 'Rock's world that he saved us for memory / a thin trace in high air' (cxiii/800) was a place 'sufficient unto itself'. As the final sequence of Pound's poem folded more closely about itself, so this land of forests and peaks offered an enchanted 'homeland', a place (in Goullart's words) 'shut off from the world by its great mountains' (259). Pound's way of using these materials tells us a lot about his final conception of a paradisal end to *The Cantos* mainly on account of his lack of interest in many of the themes explored by Goullart and Rock. Pound is responsive, of course, to the tragic loss of much of Rock's archive in a submarine attack, but there is little sense of the disappearing Na-khi culture which he 'saved us for memory' – little sense, that is, of its exposure to modernity and of the waning of its religious memory.[47] In contrast to Goullart and Rock, Pound is not really concerned with the people who inhabit this landscape, with the different tribes of the region, some of which are 'helpless and declining'. Even more striking, Goullart's mission during his nine-year stay in Likiang was to set up industrial cooperative societies 'to help poor craftsmen',[48] and one might have expected Pound, with his enduring attraction to forms of guild organisation, to have focussed on this. In the closing stage of the poem, however, it is primarily to the landscape of the Na-khi kingdom that Pound is drawn, not only because of the minutely detailed account which Rock supplies, but also because it functions (in John Peck's phrase) as 'the symbolic landscape of a ceremonial stage'.[49] Not only is this world of 'snow, rain, artemisia / also dew, oak and the juniper' (cx/792) cut off from the outside, it is also a kind of liminal place, suspended between life and death. So in the opening of Canto cx, we move from the 'quiet' Basilica of Torcello and the 'wave exultant' of the

Venetian lagoon, to the Na-khi 'wind sway' rites used to expiate the spirits of lovers who have committed ritual suicide.[50] The image of 'mountain lakes in the dawn', associated here with the 'lake waves' of Garda, creates another composite landscape of stillness and reflection. These are now places of rest, at once 'exultant' and elegiac, where the mind is freed momentarily from the burdens of self-hood and 'history'. Recalling de Certeau's distinction between place and space, we might conclude that 'being there' is now enough, allowing release from those exilic spaces of action which Pound had sought to create in the earlier parts of the poem. Yet these pre-historic tableaux have their own encoded history, and not least for us, as readers now who cannot but see them as the symbolic close of one great arc of modernism. For a postmodern culture which prizes (at least philosophically) tropes of exile and nomadism, which sees the poet as, in Maurice Blanchot's words, 'a wanderer, the one always astray, the one to whom the stability of presence is not granted and who is deprived of a true abode',[51] for such a culture the beauty of Pound's homecoming carries a cost which always remains to be paid.

CHAPTER 8

Wallace Stevens and America

Lee M. Jenkins

In the *Prologue* to his *Kora in Hell: Improvisations*, William Carlos Williams intimates a kinship of sorts with Wallace Stevens as the other American modernist poet who 'stayed at home' and chose not to 'run to London' as Pound and Eliot had done.[1] Yet, in terms of an American *locale* as a poetic, Stevens and Williams more often emerge as sparring partners than as partners. Stevens' poem of 1945, 'Description without Place', where 'the theory of description matters most' and where 'It is a world of words to the end of it, / In which nothing solid is its solid self' was greeted with indignation by Williams, who had argued as early as 1921 that 'If Americans are to be blessed with important work it will be through intelligent, informed contact with the locality which alone can infuse it with reality', and who had gone on to argue in 1925 in his *In the American Grain* that America has seldom been realised as a place, but more often as an ideal or myth, as a description without, or independent of, place.[2]

Stevens, for his part, may have been parodying Williams' brand of cultural localism back in the twenties, in his poem 'Anecdote of Men by the Thousand' from *Harmonium*, where 'The soul, he said, is composed / Of the external world' and where 'There are men of a province / Who are that province' and

> There are men whose words
> Are as natural sounds
> Of their places
> As the cackle of toucans
> In the place of toucans.   (*CP* 51)[3]

It may be possible to identify an early and a late 'regionalism' in Stevens' *Collected Poems*, but Stevens' response to Florida in his first book, *Harmonium*, suggests that the relationship with region is sometimes a troubled one. The Florida tropics (which Stevens visited on business

178

trips) can offer a heady mix of fertility and artistic creativity, as in the poem 'Nomad Exquisite', Stevens' local, Floridian, version of the modernist primitive, where

> the immense dew of Florida
> Brings forth
> The big-finned palm
> And green vine angering for life

eliciting 'hymn and hymn / From the beholder' (*CP* 95). And 'The Comedian as the Letter C' ends, as Shakespearean comedy ends, in marriage and in the celebration of fertility, when Crispin's voyages are over and he 'Dwelt in the land' (*CP* 40).

But there is a darker version, too, of the earthy sensuality of *Harmonium*. In poems like 'Infanta Marina', 'Two Figures in Dense Violet Night' and 'O Florida, Venereal Soil', the poet displaces his sexuality onto the external Floridian scene, asking his companion to 'Be the voice of night and Florida in my ear' and figuring Florida as a seductress, a 'Donna, donna, dark' when 'Lasciviously as the wind, / You come tormenting, / Insatiable' (*CP* 86, 48). Florida-as-woman is at once desirable and predatory: for Stevens, the romance with region has illicit, 'venereal' undertones – and as such offers a contrast with the way Williams unfolds his cultural localism as sexual parable in the second issue of *Contact*, the little magazine designed to emphasise the relationship between words and the locality which *breeds* them. Here, Williams figures America as a beautiful young virgin ripe for insemination by the poet, while Europe is a syphilitic old hag whom the American poet must spurn in order to survive.[4] Yvor Winters has argued that in 'The Comedian as the Letter C', 'Stevens appears to have slipped . . . into the Whitmanian form of the romantic error common enough in our literature, but current especially in Stevens' generation and espoused in particular by Stevens' friend William Carlos Williams: the fallacy that the poet achieves salvation by being, in some way, intensely of and expressive of his country'.[5] That Stevens dabbled with ideas of region is evident from the subsection titles – *In the Northwest, In the South* – that he gives to the poems in the early sequence 'Primordia', first published in 1917 in the little magazine aptly named *Soil*. And yet Stevens' distance from Williams' cultural localism is enforced if we read 'The Comedian as the Letter C' as a pessimistic work – there is the 'regional' *fallacy* as opposed to felicitousness of Stevens' Comedian, Crispin, who overturns the 'Nota' on which his poem, 'The Comedian as the Letter C', begins –

Nota: man is the intelligence of his soil,

– to read, later:

Nota: his soil is man's intelligence.

'That's better', remarks Stevens' dry narrative voice. Crispin's 'Idea of a Colony', however, revisits the palpable absurdities of 'Anecdote of Men by the Thousand' – as when Crispin 'made a singular collation. Thus: / The natives of the rain are rainy men' and when the 'premises' on which Crispin propounds his colony provide that 'The man in Georgia waking among pines / Should be pine-spokesman' – the logical extension of which is that 'The melon should have apposite ritual' (*CP* 36, 37, 38, 39).

Recent versions of Stevens proposed by his critics attempt to reverse the paradigm that Stevens is solely the poet of the abstract, and argue instead that he is also a poet who is acutely attuned to the world in which he lives and to the events which have shaped that world. In his Introduction to the special 'Stevens and Politics' issue of the *Wallace Stevens Journal*, the guest editor, A. Walton Litz, notes that 'The remarkable thing' about this issue of the journal 'is that one cannot conceive of its having been formed ten or even five years ago'. What is formed here, Litz explains, is 'an exploration of the "other" Stevens, the poet who lived in the real world and was profoundly affected by the most traumatic public events of his life: two World Wars separated by the Great Depression'. The essays which follow Litz's apology for a 'new historicism' in Stevens-studies are united, both implicitly and explicitly, in their rejection of Marjorie Perloff's analysis of Stevens' 'Notes Toward a Supreme Fiction' (1942) as 'fearful and evasive', a poem – and by suggestion an oeuvre – which is 'designed to convince both poet and reader that, despite the daily headlines and radio bulletins, the real action takes place in the country of metaphor'.[6]

The contributors to the 'Stevens and Politics' issue of the *Wallace Stevens Journal* are right to assert that there *is* a linkage between Stevens and the wider world. Yet at the same time Perloff is surely right in suggesting that the relationship between Stevens and America – especially in the early 1940s – is a problematic one; and it is problematic not least, I would suggest, because of the mythology Stevens constructs in many of his poems and prose essays from this period around the figure called the 'hero' or 'major man', a figure in which the imagination is bound up with mastery and the supervention of the will, a figure which, within an otherwise compendious body of secondary literature on Stevens, has received surprisingly – and perhaps suspiciously – little attention.

Presaging the appearance of this 'figure of capable imagination', Stevens' poetry from the 1930s to the 1940s involves a severe self-attenuation of the qualities of his first book. Although it has its darker register too, *Harmonium* is a poetry of colour, of comedy, of sex; but these qualities disappear as if by *fiat* in Stevens' later work. Perhaps because the *Harmonium*-poet was dubbed effete, an aesthete and dandy, Stevens stopped writing poetry between 1924 and 1930; and his poems of the 1930s, returning to Stevens' adolescent desire to be one of the 'man-poets', make a bid for the authority involved in his early association between 'Poetry' and 'Manhood'.[7] This association between poetry and manhood is prefigured, although it is for the most part latent, in *Harmonium* – becoming manifest in, for example, the boisterous sun-men of the seventh stanza of 'Sunday Morning'. Active where the woman of the poem is passive, these men are the precursors of the 'capable', masterful figures of Stevens' later poetry (*CP* 69–70).[8]

Part of Stevens' new project for poetry-as-manhood is the attenuation of the Floridian belongings of *Harmonium*. The 1936 'Farewell to Florida', a poem of disturbing sexual repression, signals a sea-change in Stevens, an attack on the female South. In the *Collected Poems*, 'Farewell to Florida' is strategically placed to open Stevens' second book, *Ideas of Order*, and thus demands to be read as a deliberate proclamation, a reply to *Harmonium*, with its uncompromising statement that 'The past is dead':

> To stand here on the deck in the dark and say
> Farewell and to know that that land is forever gone
> And that she will not follow in any word
> Or look, nor ever again in thought, except
> That I loved her once . . . Farewell. Go on, high ship.   (*CP* 118)

The rejection of the 'venereal soil' of Florida here takes the terms of the rejection of a lover; but if Stevens has in mind not only the northward journey of the Old English (and Pound's) Seafarer but also Aeneas sailing away from Dido and her Carthage, the hatreds and bitternesses that seem to be involved in his poem are foreign to the ancient model:

> I hated the weathery yawl from which the pools
> Disclosed the sea floor and the wilderness
> Of waving weeds. I hated the vivid blooms   (*CP* 118)

The destination sought by Stevens' poem-ship is at once resolutely masculine and 'leafless': sterile. We are introduced into the world of 'these men', an exclusively male environment which is produced in explicit opposition to the fecund, female qualities of *Harmonium*. The poem's drive to overstatement and its masochistic edge – 'carry me / To the cold' – suggest that the poet too urgently wants his reader to believe that the aesthetic of *Harmonium* was aberrant, and that he is now 'return[ing] to the violent mind' which is his proper poetic habitat. The destination the poet now seeks – 'My North' – is less clearly defined than his rejection of Florida and the South. Indeed, Stevens' 'North' is climate rather than geography, a climate of *thought* as well as of weather, the 'sullen' and 'turbulent' climate of the 1930s.

In more general terms, Stevens' poetry after *Harmonium* until the late poetry of the 1950s involves a shift from the world outside to the world of the poem, a shift from a localised poetic to descriptions without places. Florida *does* recur in *Ideas of Order* – in 'The Idea of Order at Key West', for instance – but here *place*, as the title of that poem suggests, is secondary to *idea*, and there is a significant change of emphasis in Stevens' conception of the imagination. Contrast, for instance, 'The Idea of Order at Key West' with 'Anecdote of the Jar', from *Harmonium*, a satirical exploration of the relation between an imposition of order and the world outside, where the imagination, in its desire to marshal the 'slovenly' wilderness, is bound up with mastery. This 'Anecdote' can be read as a cautionary tale which warns of the sterility – 'It did not give of bird or bush' – attendant upon thorough-going 'dominion'. In contrast, in the later 'Key West' poem, 'The lights in the fishing boats at anchor' 'Mastered the night and portioned out the sea', acting as an analogue for 'The maker's rage to order words of the sea'. *The Man with the Blue Guitar* (1937) stresses this change in emphasis: the would-be exuberance of the blue guitarist who 'held the world upon his nose' masks an unsettling and at times even a manic rage to mastery which we do not find in *Harmonium* (*CP* 76, 130, 178).

The 'hero' or later the 'major man' makes his entrance in Stevens' next book, *Parts of a World* (1942). This is a book of antagonisms between two radically different kinds of poetry, and the principal themes and tensions are contained in its title – parts and whole, parts and world.[9] Some of the poems in *Parts of a World* have a vocabulary of desire, of relativism, of *parts* of a world. Other poems, the 'hero' poems, embrace synthesis. The metaphors associated with Stevens' 'hero' figure are metaphors of autotelism, of self-sufficiency – and by implication, given their American context, of isolationism.

Tension between parts and whole is, for the Stevens of the late thirties and early forties, both the explicit subject of a number of poems and, in a more general overview, the persistent anxiety of the poetry. In poems of relativism in *Parts of a World*, like 'On the Road Home', we are told that 'There is no such thing as the truth' and that 'Words are not forms of a single word.' Here Stevens comes down firmly against synecdoche,[10] maintaining instead a relativism which, the poem proposes, is productive – it is after saying that there is no single 'Truth' that 'the tree, at night, began to change, // Smoking through green and smoking blue'. Imaginative transformation of this kind would presumably not be available in a 'Truth' (*CP* 203). And in the poem 'Landscape with Boat' Stevens exposes the fallacious thinking of the 'he' who

> never supposed
> That he might be the truth, himself, or *part* of it,
> That the things that he rejected might be *part*
> And the irregular turquoise, *part* . . .
> . . . and all these things together,
> *Parts*, and more things, *parts*. (*CP* 242, my emphases)

A sceptical poetry of relativism in *Parts of a World*, a poetry of *parts* which resist synthesis into a greater whole, a poetry which resists closure and which acknowledges that the mind can never be satisfied, is uneasily juxtaposed with a poetry which welcomes closure and synthesis and unity, and which celebrates centres, spheres, self-sufficient *worlds*. The poet is trapped, perhaps, in a vicious hermeneutic circle in which the parts can't explain the whole and vice versa. 'Man and Bottle' shows Stevens on the brink of the 'central' poetry of the 'hero', casting about for an idiom appropriate to war, for a poetic which,

> to find what will suffice,
> Destroys romantic tenements
> Of rose and ice
>
> In the land of war. (*CP* 238)

'Man and Bottle' has to 'persuade that war is *part of itself*, / A manner of thinking' (*CP* 239, my emphases).

If war is part of itself, then the *poem* assumes the status of a combatant, and can claim that poetry is a destructive force. Stevens' poem with the title 'Poetry is a Destructive Force' also claims that poetry is a decreative force:

> That's what misery is,
> Nothing to have at heart.
> It is to have or nothing. (*CP* 192)

The syntax here recalls that of Stevens' early poem of decreation, 'The Snow Man', where 'One must have a mind of winter' to behold the 'Nothing that is not there and the nothing that is' (*CP* 10). Like 'Man and Bottle', where 'The mind is the great poem of winter', 'Poetry is a Destructive Force' uses decreation as a synonym for destruction, allowing the poet to imply a wider world scene and thus lending his poem a platform, a strength, in the midst of 'misery' – Stevens tells us that this lionised poetry 'can kill a man'.

'Man and Bottle' raises the question of priorities: war is *part* of itself, part of poetry. Poetry, then, is already a whole; and must be persuaded that war is part of that whole: and yet the poem is also described as 'A man at the centre of men', as a capable fighting man 'In the land of war'. 'Man and Bottle' fights, but it also fights shy, of testing its claims. The poem wants *both* to emphasise its own, 'whole' status, to which war stands as a *part, and* to suggest, like the *Coda* to 'Notes Toward a Supreme Fiction', an analogy between the poem and war which empowers the poem, 'A manner of thinking, a mode / Of destroying' (*CP* 239).

The *Coda* to 'Notes Toward a Supreme Fiction' tells its addressee, 'Soldier', that the *poet's* war is 'a war that never ends' (*CP* 407). Although the poet's war is privileged, in its endlessness, over the soldier's war, the *Coda* does propose an analogy between the two. In 'Man and Bottle' Stevens does not propose an equality between poetry and war, but relegates war to 'part' in persuading that 'war is part of itself, / A manner of thinking'. Harold Bloom, writing about Stevens' poetry of this period, insists that this is poetry in which world war is 'only a trope'.[11] But Stevens wants it both ways – the analogies he makes between poetry and war *do* lessen the significance of the war, and render war as 'only a trope', but these warlike analogies also *empower* Stevens' poetry, enabling Stevens to claim that poetry, and not war, is the supreme 'martial art'.

'Of Modern Poetry' is a companion 'poem of the mind in the act of finding / What will suffice'. The poem reserves for itself a processual character – 'The poem of the mind *in the act of finding*' – *and* posits a significant role for itself in the sphere of action: 'It has to think about war / And it has to find what will suffice' (*CP* 240). 'Man and Bottle' and 'Of Modern Poetry' were first published, together, in 1940, under the title 'Two Theoretic Poems'. Both poems want to retain their declared 'theoretical' status *and* assume a 'central' role in the world of events and world war.

The unequivocal idiom of the 'hero' in *Parts of a World* is articulated most forcefully in a triad of poems, in 'Montrachet-le-Jardin', 'Examination of the Hero in a Time of War' and in the poem I will focus upon here, 'Asides on the Oboe'.

The opening gambit of 'Asides on the Oboe' is a rejection of relativism:

> The prologues are over, It is a question, now,
> Of final belief. So, say that final belief
> Must be in a fiction. It is time to choose.   (*CP* 250)

Stevens' tone here moves between playful irony and a felt urgency. Against the improvised music suggested by the poem's title, and against the ironic play in the announcement that 'The prologues are over' in these opening lines which, prefacing the poem, themselves act as a 'prologue' of sorts, is the urgency of the 'now', and the insistence that 'It is time to choose.'

It may be 'time to choose', but what is the nature of the choice Stevens demands that we make? For America in 1940, when the poem was written, the 'choice' was clear – intervene in the war in Europe or isolate. For Stevens, the 'choice' seems, rather, to be between the relativism of preliminary manoeuvres or 'prologues', and what he calls 'final belief'. This 'final belief', Stevens tells us, 'Must be in a fiction'. This is Stevens' version of William James' 'will to believe', the concept that belief is a psychological imperative – so what we happen to believe *in* is less important than the prerequisite of belief in itself. Stevens elaborates on his statement that 'final belief / Must be in a fiction' in a 1942 letter, where he says that 'If one no longer believes in God (as truth), it is not possible merely to disbelieve; it becomes necessary to believe in something else . . . one's final belief must be in a fiction.'[12]

The poem which follows the three introductory lines of 'Asides on the Oboe' produces the fictive 'hero' in whom, according to Stevens, it is necessary to believe, the 'hero' or 'central man' who, in his totalising nature, closes off the subversive possibilities of irony latent in the poem's 'prologue'.[13]

The poem proper begins with a survey of what Stevens calls 'obsolete fiction[s]'. The 'metal heroes that time granulates' are the statues of great men which Stevens repeatedly brings into his poems only to dismiss with asperity and consign to the 'dump' of the world's jaded images. In contrast to these corroded 'metal heroes' is 'The philosophers' man' who 'alone still walks in dew'. The 'hero', in our introduction to him here, courts tautology – he is 'alone still' the sole surviving viable fiction. The word 'still' is repeated three times in this opening stanza, and on each occasion the word combines a sense of stillness, a sense of an almost beatific 'peace', with the unique character of this 'hero' who *still* stands as belief, who endures.

Stevens goes on to describe the 'impossible possible' nature of his 'hero'. He is 'the man of glass', brittle, 'Who in a million diamonds sums us up'. The glass-like fragility of the 'hero' is offset by his totalising centrality. Describing the 'hero' Stevens is carried away on a wave of hyperbole: big claims about the 'hero' follow one fast upon another, until we may wonder if the 'hero' is eventually more a defensive than a consummate conception. The 'hero' is

> The *central* man, the human *globe*, responsive
> As a mirror with a voice, the man of glass,
> Who in a million diamonds *sums us up*. (*CP* 250, my emphases)

The 'hero' figure which recurs in Stevens' poetry from the forties has its own privileged vocabulary – keywords or groups of related words are repeatedly used to describe him. Stevens' 'heroic' lexicon of opalescence, purity, the crystalline and transparency in 'Asides on the Oboe' – words like 'dew', 'milky', 'immaculate', 'naked', 'mirror', 'man of glass', 'diamond' and 'transparence' – recurs in other of Stevens' 'hero' poems. In everyday usage, something transparent is something we can see through or something that is easily understood, obvious, evident; and accordingly it may be that Stevens' 'glass man' is less fragile than he is indicative of an absence of hidden motives – the 'glass man' is unshadowed, frank, a sort of Visible Man, from the ethical equivalent of an anatomy textbook. In Stevens' 'hero' poetry, however, 'transparence' and related words are abstracted from normal usage and transferred into the idiom of the 'hero'. Taken together, Stevens' 'hero' poems form a self-referring system or private mythology, in which each individual 'hero' poem refracts light only on the other 'hero' poems, mirroring the special vocabulary associated with the 'hero'. In 'Examination of the Hero in a Time of War', the 'hero' is once again described in terms of crystals and centrality:

> A thousand crystals' chiming voices,
> Like the shiddow-shaddow of lights revolving
> To momentary ones, are blended,
> In hymns, through iridescent changes,
> Of the apprehending of the hero.

These hymns are like a stubborn brightness
Approaching in the dark approaches
Of time and place, becoming certain,
The organic centre of responses,
Naked of hindrance, a thousand crystals.
To meditate the highest man, not
The highest supposed in him and over,
Creates, in the blissfuller perceptions,
What unisons create in music.   (*CP* 279–80)

The crystalline imagery in 'Asides on the Oboe' describes the already achieved perfection of the 'diamond globe'. In this canto from 'Examination of the Hero in a Time of War', the same imagery charts a synthesising, 'blending' movement from parts to whole, from the many to the one. The crystal voices are 'blended' in 'hymns' and 'becoming certain', the crystals form 'The organic centre of responses', in a culmination of the numinous idiom of the 'hero'. As in 'Asides on the Oboe', the hero-language and the synthesising action of the 'hero' are compared with music, with the identity of pitch, the complete agreement, of 'unisons'.

In the second stanza of 'Asides on the Oboe' though, Stevens seems to want to set his 'hero' in some kind of wider 'folk' tradition – now Stevens presents the 'hero' as a pedlar who arrives in the summer to sell his wares. The 'hero'

> sets this peddler's pie and cries in summer,
> The glass man, cold and numbered, dewily cries,
> 'Thou art not August unless I make thee so.'   (*CP* 251)

In 'Montrachet-le-Jardin', too, Stevens would place his 'hero' poetry in the tradition of 'the earliest poems of the world' – a tradition which guarantees primal, original power. These 'earliest poems' lead to a hero's progress into a fairytale land:

> Since in the hero-land to which we go,
> A little nearer by each multitude,
> To which we come as into bezeled plain,
>
> The poison in the blood will have been purged,
> An inner miracle and sun-sacrament   (*CP* 262)

The folksy pedlar-hero of 'Asides on the Oboe' is also 'The glass man, cold and numbered': he is diaphanous and distant, he is 'numbered' in that he is metered, prosodic, the creature of poetry; he is 'numbered' in the sense of being designated or singled out from the mass; and, of course, it may be that his days are numbered. The 'hero' here is described by the word 'dewily', so he is related to the natural world – and yet he also has sway over it. This portentous 'numbered' man is given a single line of direct speech – 'Thou art not August unless I make thee so.' Stevens claims for his 'hero' an earthy authenticity, where the 'hero' is related to the seasons – he 'cries in summer', the proper season for the hero in 'Examination of the Hero in a Time of War', too – and yet Stevens also conceives of the 'hero' in terms of an assertive and imperious version of the high romantic imagination, which *prescribes* the seasons – 'Thou art not August unless I make thee so.'

In 'Montrachet-le-Jardin', we are told that

> it is a question of
> The naked man, the naked man as last
> And tallest hero and plus gaudiest vir.   (*CP* 262)

'Montrachet-le-Jardin' joins with the 'final belief' of 'Asides on the Oboe' in presenting the 'hero' as unsurpassable, consummate. Yet, as well as stressing his incommensurability, Stevens also asks us to accept the 'hero' as 'plus gaudiest vir' – as, in 'Asides on the Oboe', he wants his 'hero' to be both 'glass man' and pedlar. But in 'Montrachet-le-Jardin', the exuberance is strained and overplayed, and so (if Stevens is not being ironic about the concept of heroism, as some of his critics would no doubt protest) the *vif* which Stevens presumably intends to express in his French epithet falls flat. In the ninth canto of 'Examination of the Hero in a Time of War', the 'hero'

> seems
> To stand taller than a person stands, has
> A wider brow, large and less human
> Eyes and bruted ears: the man-like body
> Of a primitive. He walks with a defter
> And lither stride. His arms are heavy
> And his breast is greatness.   (*CP* 277)

As in the 'tallest' 'hero' of 'Montrachet-le-Jardin', it is sheer physical size that is stressed here: 'taller', 'wider', 'large', 'bruted', 'heavy', 'greatness'. The aggrandised 'hero' is perhaps an example of how, according to Stevens, the vast scale of world war 'affects the scale of one's thinking and constitutes a participating in the heroic'.[14] In the later 'major man' poem, 'Chocorua to its Neighbor', the talking mountain describes the 'major man' – 'How singular he was as man, how large, / If nothing more than that, for the moment, large' (*CP* 302).

In its final stanzas, 'Asides on the Oboe' abandons the present tense and turns to a form of historical narrative. The words 'One year' which introduce the last sections of the poem place the 'hero' in time, although not in a specific time or year. The present urgency of the poem's opening – the 'now' and the 'It is time to choose' – is modulated at the end of the poem – the crisis of this 'One year' is safely in the past:

> One year, death and war prevented the jasmine scent
> And the jasmine islands were bloody martyrdoms.
> How was it then with the central man? (*CP* 251)

These lines appear to take us outside the world of the poem, to ask, what was the effect on the 'central man' or 'hero' of this external event of war? But all Stevens tells us is what we already know – that the 'hero' is consummate, that he is 'the sum' – Stevens asks 'Did we / Find peace?' only to answer 'We found the sum of men.' The word 'peace', which is associated with the 'hero' earlier in the poem, takes on a new resonance with the reference here to 'war'. Yet the war, in which the 'hero' suffers, is finally unable to intrude on his diamond globe. War is seen as an enabling rather than a divisive force, insofar as its effect is that 'we and the diamond globe at last were one.' It's not enough to be 'partly one', Stevens says near the end of the poem – and at the end, the relativism of 'parts' is entirely done away with. Instead of 'parts', we have the autotelic 'world' of the 'hero', 'The glass man, without external reference'.

The poem, too, is finally 'without external reference': there is no reference to a world beyond the 'globe' of the 'hero'. The diamond-studded 'hero' of 'Asides on the Oboe' is the 'impossible possible' projection of the imagination, a self-contained and pristine man of glass who remains unsullied by external events and by war. Similarly, in 'Examination of the Hero in a Time of War', we are told that while others 'secrete within them / Too many references', the 'hero' would 'Destroy all references' (*CP* 279).

'Asides on the Oboe' ostensibly *addresses* the external event of the war, yet the poem works to *subsume* the world and the war into its own autotelic 'world'. Both the globe-like 'hero' and the sealed poetic world he represents act as bulwarks against an external world which is viewed as a threat to the self-contained world of the poem. And yet Stevens' very fascination with heroes and major men suggests something much more pro-active and actively warlike. Stevens constructs a private mythology around his 'hero' – but one which, because of the time of its production and the wider wartime resonance of 'heroism', also gestures toward a public relevance.

Wallace Stevens' modern relevance is itself something of a battleground. Since the 1940s, Stevens' poetry – especially the poetry he wrote *in* the forties – has been appropriated by almost every new movement in literary criticism and theory, with each new critical school seizing on Stevens as the poet who more than any other proves tractable to the theory and practice of that particular school. Stevens has been co-opted by New Critics and Formalists, *and* he has been championed as a poet whose language anticipates the language of deconstruction.[15]

In the 1940s, Stevens wrote poems with titles like 'Martial Cadenza' and 'Examination of the Hero in a Time of War' – and yet between the critical factions there is a general consensus that Stevens' poetry of this period is a 'pure' poetry, a poetry which has no truck with the actual world. Helen Vendler, for instance, makes no reference at all to the Second World War in her extended Formalist reading of 'Examination of the Hero in a Time of War'; and for the American deconstructionists, Stevens' wartime poetry is all provisional and open-ended word play.[16] Yet, as 'Asides on the Oboe' and other of the 'hero' poems show, a very different idiom can also be found in the Stevens of the early forties, where the poet's 'notes toward', his provisional vocabulary, is countered by his 'supreme fiction', his desire for a heroic, unified and self-enclosed poetic 'world'. Stevens may have been attracted, intellectually, to relativism and to the provisional, but temperamentally he was drawn to unity, to closure, to the sealed world of the poem where the poet himself calls all the shots.

The 'hero' makes Stevens' poetry of the forties more problematic than many of his exegetes are prepared to acknowledge; and, as I have said, there has been surprisingly little critical analysis of the 'hero' or 'major man'. This may be one example of his critics taking Stevens too much on his own terms: and the terms laid down for the 'hero' are 'no external reference'.

An exception to this rule of thumb is Alan Filreis, who, in his *Wallace Stevens and the Actual World*, concentrates on Stevens' work *circa* the Second World War, and *does* attempt to link Stevens with the actualities of the world in the period under discussion, by reading the poetry and prose of 1939–41 as 'a form of isolationism' and 'a readiness to withdraw into the basic fact of American distance'.[17] So, for Filreis, who is one of the foremost apologists for a 'new historicism' in Stevens-studies, Stevens' refusal of 'external reference' *is* referential precisely because it has to do with that refusal of external reference found in American isolationist thinking. This is a circular argument; where Filreis is much more convincing is in his contextualisation of Stevens in relation to the New Criticism, and the relationship between the rhetoric of the New Criticism and that of American isolationism – as John Fekete points out, 'the cultural politics of the New Criticism are linked with the political culture of the period'.[18] The differing critical appropriations of Stevens' poetry have already been mentioned, but in the early forties, Stevens' reputation was in the making, and depended to a considerable extent on the lionisation of his work by New Critics like R. P. Blackmur, John Crowe Ransom and Allen Tate.[19] A poem like 'Asides on the Oboe', which champions at a thematic level organic form and unity and which refuses 'external reference', intersected perfectly with the pedagogical mores of the New Critics themselves. As Filreis points out, the New Critical credo of aesthetic detachment found its political corollary in isolationism. But, as Filreis again notes, in the run-up to American involvement in the Second World War, the New Critical idiom was itself fighting for survival: the New Nationalist movement spearheaded by Archibald MacLeish insisted that it was unpatriotic to focus on the mere *structure* of a poem – instead the poetic and critical imagination had to be devoted to American national unity and to the pending American war effort. Tate, a Southerner, mocked the call for national unity; but, as Filreis shows, the New Criticism also proved adept at tactical manoeuvring, taking over for its own purposes highly politicised catchwords like 'unity' to argue that a *poem* is a unity, a world in itself. Where MacLeish argued that America must intervene in world events, a New Critic like Ransom argued that the world was to be found in the 'world's body' of the *poem*.[20]

The sealed globe and hostility to external reference of a poem like Stevens' 'Asides on the Oboe' were not only tractable to New Critical interpretation, but appeared to endorse the isolationist ideology of many of the New Critics themselves.[21] In his 1941 public lecture 'The Noble Rider and the Sound of Words', Stevens' response to the wider world is again embattled and defensive – he talks, for instance, of the need for poetry to evade or to resist 'the pressure of reality'. As Filreis notes, Stevens' alignment with the New Criticism seemed to be signed and sealed when this lecture was published in 1942 in a collection edited and introduced – with a strong dose of New Critical and isolationist rubric – by Allen Tate.[22]

But Stevens' own position was not identical with the isolationist position adopted by Tate and others. For a start, as an insurance executive with the Hartford Accident and Indemnity Company,

Stevens knew that American involvement in the war would be good for business. And Stevens' poetry from 1939 to 1942 displays a tension *between* attraction to the autotelic world of the poem and desire for engagement, for intervention, in the wider world. Such a tension between detachment and engagement was already nascent in Stevens' poetry of the thirties, as the curious statement Stevens added to the dust jacket of his *Ideas of Order* shows: 'The book is essentially a book of pure poetry. I believe that, in any society, the poet should be the exponent of the imagination of that society . . . particularly in life at present'.[23] References to society and to the 'present' condition of America sit uneasily alongside the reference to 'pure poetry'. Stevens' 'fudge' didn't work, though, and his poems of the thirties were savagely attacked by Marxist critics for their lack of social and political engagement.[24]

At the beginning of his 'Asides on the Oboe', Stevens tells us that 'It is time to choose.' But in terms of the debate between isolation and intervention in America, Stevens doesn't choose. The autotelic, non-referential 'world' of the 'hero' replicates New Critical tenets and can be read as a poetic endorsement of American isolationism; and yet his frequent recourse to the 'hero' suggests that Stevens is also powerfully attracted by the power-by-proxy offered by his 'major men' and other poetic progeny.

Where Filreis attempts to historicise the Stevens of the early forties, Vendler takes a different, ahistorical, approach, when she argues that, in the 'hero', Stevens 'hankers after . . . the masculine common life'.[25] The fifth canto of 'Examination of the Hero in a Time of War' does propose the 'common man' as 'hero' – 'The common man is the common hero. / The common hero is the hero' (*CP* 275) – and Vendler suggests that 'The hero . . . is the source of Stevens' new preoccupation with the common language and its common forms; and the framing of a poetry out of the speech of the million presents him with a linguistic problem analogous to the creation of a hero from the common soldier.'[26] Yet the 'hero' poems qualify again and again any aspiration they may voice to be in contact with the 'common' and with 'common language'. And in 'Examination of the Hero' 'common fortune' – which follows the proposition of the 'common hero' – isn't given much of a chance: the first example of 'common fortune' the poet chooses is 'the entrails / Of a cat', something belonging on the dump, and Stevens concludes this canto of the poem in a pun on 'common-places' (*CP* 275). The poem in *Parts of a World* with the title 'The Common Life' is a pen-and-ink drawing in which 'The men have no shadows / And the women have only one side' (*CP* 221). And the 'hero' poetry isn't simply a desire on Stevens' part to be in touch with fighting men, as Vendler suggests – 'Asides on the Oboe' is cocooning in its refusal of 'external reference', and its 'hero', like the 'plus gaudiest vir' of 'Montrachet-le-Jardin', is hardly involved in straightforward soldiery, if in soldiery at all.

But if the 'hero' fits uneasily with the 'common' in Vendler's phrase the 'masculine common life', her use of the word 'masculine' should nevertheless be underscored. The 'hero' has an emphatically male prerogative. Stevens' 'heroic' imagination involves a disrelishing of female for male apparent in his poetry after *Harmonium* and made explicit in *Parts of a World* in the poem called 'Mrs Alfred Uruguay'. The woman of the poem's title, known only by her husband's name, voices a desire for nakedness which the poet mocks – because she is a woman, she cannot share in the naked exuberance of the 'ring of men' in 'Sunday Morning', and her 'sayings' are, like those of the woman of 'Sunday Morning', over-ridden, here quite literally, by the masculine noble rider, the 'figure of capable imagination' – aka the 'hero' (*CP* 248). In the poem 'Life on a Battleship', included in the first edition of *Parts of a World* but subsequently (and wisely) excluded by Stevens from the *Collected Poems*, we are told that 'On *The Masculine* one asserts and fires the guns.' This is the virile imagination of mastery prefigured in 'Farewell to Florida', another poem with a ship and an all-male crew.[27]

Stevens' hostility to 'external reference' makes it tempting to try perversely to find references, analogues and contexts for his 'hero'. A genealogy of sorts of the 'capable' figure can of course be traced to Nietzsche and to Emerson[28] – but with caveats. In 1942 Stevens claimed that he had not read Nietzsche since he was a young man, but subsequently went to considerable trouble to order a 20–25 volume edition of Nietzsche's works.[29] Yet it is risky to force a comparison – Stevens' 'hero' isn't disruptive like Nietzsche's Zarathustra, but is a synthesiser, is leisured, self-regarding, where Zarathustra is strenuous, combative, communicative. Where Nietzsche maintains a relativistic scepticism, Stevens' 'hero', without relativism, sums us up. *Nietzscheanism*, rather than Nietzsche, might offer a more profitable analogue for Stevens' 'hero' poems: in his essay 'English Writers and Nietzsche', Patrick Bridgwater examines 'the cult of hardness' which 'looms large in British Nietzscheanism', and quotes Edwin Muir's confession that 'although I did not know it, my Nietzscheanism was . . . a "compensation". I could not face my life as it was and so I took refuge in the fantasy of the Superman.'[30] Stevens' 'hero', similarly, is generated out of a psychological imperative, at least as much as from a historical or national context.

Even so, the promotion in Stevens' poetry in the era of Hitler and Mussolini of a masterful and totalising figure is surely troubling, the more so in the light of Stevens' own – seldom cited – political opinions, like that voiced in a 1935 letter about Mussolini's invasion of Ethiopia. Stevens remarks in this letter that 'I am pro-Mussolini, personally', and he goes on to add the rider that 'The Italians have as much right to take Ethiopia from the coons as the coons had to take it from the boa-constrictors.'[31]

In later letters, Stevens is more guarded – he asks, in 1940, apropos of his poem *Owl's Clover*: 'If the future . . . also comes to nothing, sha'n't we be looking round for some one superhuman, to put us together again, some prodigy capable of measuring sun and moon, some one who, if he is to dictate our fates, had better be inhuman, so that we shall know that he is without any of our weaknesses and cannot fail?'[32]

One of the first reviews of *Parts of a World* is Hi Simon's 1942 notice 'The Humanism of Wallace Stevens'. As its title suggests, Simon's review argues that in the 'hero', Stevens elaborates a new and distinctive kind of humanism. It was to Simons that Stevens had written his 1940 letter about the 'superhuman' 'prodigy' who is to 'dictate our fates' – and recalling this letter in his review of *Parts of a World*, Simons has difficulty in persuading himself that 'humanism' is, after all, an accurate description of Stevens' 'hero'-project: 'When this figure, or its proto-type, first appeared [in *Owl's Clover*], as a "super-animal" to "dictate our fates" . . . he bore some suspicion of resemblance to a sort of fuehrer. Things in the present collection like "Life on a Battleship" don't quite clear him of it.'

Simons goes on to declare that 'the definitive characterization' of the 'hero' is to be found in other poems in *Parts of a World*, where the 'hero' 'personifies those capacities for noble living and thinking in which the average man transcends himself'.[33] But one has the feeling that Simons is reluctant to engage too closely with his 'suspicion' about the 'hero' – and how, in 1942 when his review was written, can Simons confidently separate the Captain of 'Life on a Battleship', in whom Stevens isn't quite cleared of the charge of promoting a 'fuehrer' figure, from the other manifestations of the 'hero' in *Parts of a World*? The 'hero' in canto xv of 'Examination of the Hero in a Time of War' is, like the 'prodigy' of Stevens' 1940 letter to Simons, a totaliser, 'capable of measuring sun and moon', whose function is precisely 'to put us together again'.

The attraction to demagoguery, or at least to hero-worship here, recurs in the 'hero' poems Stevens is also writing at this time, where the 'hero' isn't Mussolini, but a heroic surrogate for the poet himself. The 'hero' is a personal projection which is fielded as an historical necessity. Like the Jungian archetype, the 'hero' is produced in 'extreme situations', like that of world war, and, again like the archetype, the 'hero' is presented as a facet of a mythopoeic imagination; but, if the 'hero' is presented in terms of the archetype, he should perhaps be read in terms of the persona. Stevens' 'hero' poetry may be an examination of the 'hero' as a 'capable' persona for the poet, rather than anything more actively participant. Like Hemingway, who once punched him on the nose at Key West, Stevens seems to have desperately needed to believe something about his own powers; he needed to deploy, if only in his imagination, his phalanx of major men and heroes – a need heightened by the prospect of a wartime world of fighting men. Stevens dreaded being seen as a 'minor man' and his 'hero' can be seen as a psychological defence mechanism transferred into an aesthetic.[34]

Stevens' 'hero' is a mythological bulwark against the encroaches of a turbulent world, a peaceful and self-protective globe in himself – and yet the 'hero' is also military and martial. Canto xv of 'Examination of the Hero in a Time of War' describes the curiously contradictory 'pastimes' of the 'hero' – the 'hero' is aggrandised and active, he is 'Man-sun, man-moon, man-earth, man-ocean', and 'the hero is his nation, / In him made one', but the 'hero' is also more quietly self-contained, when 'he studies the paper / On the wall, the lemons on the table' (*CP* 280, 279). In his double aspect, Stevens' 'hero' offers less an insight into the relationship between Wallace Stevens and American national politics, than a psychological insight into Stevens himself, an insight which queries as much as it endorses the designation of the Stevens of the forties as the great poet of the abstract.

Stevens' *Collected Poems* is less the seamless whole that his critics often propose than a book of ruptures, and his late poems reconsider the conjunction of imagination and mastery – and the personification of this pairing in the 'hero' or 'major man' – which we find in Stevens' poetry from the late thirties and early forties. The poem 'Imago' from the 1950 collection *The Auroras of Autumn* involves a modulation from 'major' to 'medium man', a diminishment of the major figure which is also suggested in other poems from this collection: 'Angel Surrounded by Paysans' and 'A Primitive Like an Orb'. A number of the poems in *The Rock*, the last section of Stevens' *Collected Poems*, can be read as palinodes, although they are palinodes which lack the apparent candour of, for instance, Yeats' late retractions (with the proviso that Yeats' late candour may itself be another mask) – Stevens' 'new knowledge of reality' (*CP* 534) is still hemmed about by 'the intricate evasions of as' (*CP* 486). Yet Stevens tells us that the poems of *The Rock* are 'Not one of the masculine myths we used to make' (*CP* 518): in 'The Plain Sense of Things', the poet admits that 'A fantastic effort has failed' (*CP* 502) and in the poem 'The Rock' he ventures a 'queer' – and refreshing – 'assertion of humanity' (*CP* 525). In 'Lebensweisheitspielerei', we are given a sense of a diminished world, of 'a dwindled sphere', where the power of the sun is 'Weaker and weaker', but where, in compensation, 'Each person completely touches us / With what he is' (*CP* 504). This is not to suggest, as Kermode suggests, that Stevens' late poems are entirely taken up with 'fortuities of earth that solace us and make a world': the savage earth-mother, 'Madame La Fleurie', hardly conforms to Kermode's interpretation of the late Stevens according to a stoic Heideggerian *dasein* – Madame waits to devour the poet who must 'bring all that he saw into the earth' (*CP* 507). *The Rock* is, rather, a sceptical and revisionary coda to his oeuvre, which stands as a fascinating testament to *doubt* at the end of Stevens' life.[35]

And yet the poetry Stevens writes at the end of his career is also, often, a late efflorescence of moments of extraordinary elegiac beauty, in which the poet does not need to arrogate powers to himself. The most remarkable of the late poems are an evocation of what 'Local Objects' calls 'that serene'.[36] The 1954 poem 'Dinner Bell in the Woods' suggests that the life of the imagination, while it may be tempting, is also ill-favoured – 'He was facing phantasma when the bell rang. / The picnic of children came running then'. The poet is, as it were, saved by the bell, and the poem's concluding line tells us that he remains 'outside the door of phantasma', that he remains in the world. The world of the imagination which, with the spectral suggestion in 'phantasma', is now seen as something insubstantial and even unhealthy, is dispelled by the corporeal and wholesome world of children, as 'substance' replaces 'the leaner being' of fictions (*CP* 434).

> The smaller ones
> Came tinkling on the grass to the table
> Where the fattest women belled the glass.[37]

In suggesting an emergence from the sealed world of the poem, *The Rock* and a number of Stevens' other, unpublished, late poems also attempt a rapprochement with Stevens' own American region, Connecticut. The theme of the local supersedes the theme of the hero. In 'The River of Rivers in Connecticut', from *The Rock*, the weight of the mythological river of death, Stygia, is countered by the topographical reassurance of local place names – Farmington and Haddam. This poem, like the later and uncollected 'A mythology reflects its region . . .' involves the 'folk-lore / Of each of the senses', reflected in a 'local abstraction'. 'A mythology reflects its region . . .' produces the 'he in the substance of his region' who is more yeoman than 'hero' (*CP* 533).[38]

Late Stevens doesn't suggest a final reconciliation with Williams' cultural localism so much as a reconciliation with, and a progression from, the ambivalent 'regional' poetic of *Harmonium*. It is germane here to point to Stevens' 1948 essay 'John Crowe Ransom: Tennessean', where a distinction is made, in terms of *place*, between a poet's early and his late poems: 'One turns with something like ferocity toward a land that one loves, to which one is really and essentially native . . . This is a vital affair, not an affair of the heart (as it may be in one's first poems), but an affair of the whole being (as in one's last poems), a fundamental affair of life, or, rather, an affair of fundamental life.'[39]

Relationship with place is now figured in terms of the 'whole being', an involvement which is different in kind from Stevens' earlier, defensive, versions of poetic self-sufficiency. When, in 1955, Stevens recorded a piece for the Voice of America's 'This Is America' series, his script, entitled 'Connecticut Composed', indicates that the troubled relationship with nation, in the poetry of the early forties, has mellowed, in Stevens' later thought, into a more congenial relationship with his own *locale*. In his 'Connecticut Composed', Stevens insists that 'the nature of the land is part of . . . ourselves'; he talks of 'coming home to the American self in the sort of place in which it was formed. Going back to Connecticut is a return to an origin.'[40]

If Stevens' late poems signal an emergence from the closed worlds of his earlier phase, these poems also indicate a break with that strain of high modernism which privileges the autotelic artwork. This might, in turn, suggest some of the directions – like confessionalism and a renewed attention to the local, American *place* – which American poetry will take after Stevens, in the *post*modernity of the later fifties and sixties. The 'confessional' aspect of Stevens' late work may arise from the general climate of the fifties, with the onset of the Cold War and the rise of individualism, or may be more specific to the psychological trajectory of Stevens' *Collected Poems*: but, if the late poems do not, in any definitive sense, *foreground* trends in American poetry *after* Stevens, then it is legitimate, at least, to re-read Stevens' late work in the contexts of confessionalism and localism.[41] The defensive quality of Stevens' poetics of the forties suggests a problematic relationship with the world outside the world of the poem, and with America as nation; at the very end of his career, it seems that Stevens *can* speak less equivocally as the 'Voice of America' when he speaks of his own American region.

CHAPTER 9

Locating the lyric: Marianne Moore, Elizabeth Bishop and the Second World War

Fiona Green

In his 1936 essay 'The Irrational Element in Poetry' Wallace Stevens writes, 'we are preoccupied with events, even when we do not observe them closely'.[1] The poet's relation to external events, proximate and remote, preoccupied Stevens in the years leading up to and beyond America's entry into the Second World War. For American civilians, especially before Pearl Harbor, the location of the war seemed irreducibly distant. This chapter is about how that distance intervenes and is negotiated in American poetry in the period when the United States is moving toward intervention in Europe. Although the argument takes some of its bearings from Stevens' thinking, the primary focus of attention is the work of Marianne Moore and Elizabeth Bishop.[2] It has become customary for readings of Moore and Bishop to array the two poets sequentially, to distinguish Bishop as the postmodern heir to Moore's modernism; my project is rather different in that it investigates their simultaneous adjustments to impending hostilities.[3] The crucial difference between them for this purpose has to do with spatial rather than temporal coordinates. According to my argument, the 'violence without'[4] that calls for poetic modification varies in pressure according to each poet's location within the United States, so that local as well as national conditions give shape and materials to the poetry that emerges.

This chapter, then, is in part concerned with the effect of geographical location on the development of American poetry in wartime. But my interest in space and location has another, and ultimately more significant aspect. I want to consider the displacement of historical meanings (especially wartime meanings) onto objects and processes that attempt to master space – to traverse, measure or occupy it. These objects and technologies – the radio, the postal system and the procedures of cartography – are seen as manifestations of the wartime environment in which Moore's and Bishop's poetics develop.

In the late 1930s and early 1940s Marianne Moore was living in

Brooklyn, Elizabeth Bishop in Key West. Bishop, famously itinerant, travelled in this period to Europe and Mexico, and also shuttled from Florida to New York at regular intervals. Marianne Moore, meanwhile, stayed put in the Brooklyn apartment that she – also famously – shared with her mother. In her ambivalent memoir, 'Efforts of Affection', Bishop recalls that the atmosphere of the Moores' apartment 'was of course "old-fashioned", but even more, otherworldly – as if one were living in a diving bell from a different world, let down through the crass atmosphere of the twentieth century'.[5] Moore corroborates the evidence that her preferred habitat was a refuge with its own climate, remembering Brooklyn as having 'an atmosphere of privacy', and sustaining 'an air of leisure'.[6] Bishop's Key West, by contrast, was an environment of public activity and work. No longer the Stevensian Florida of imaginative plenty, nor a place of vacation and retreat, increasing US naval activity at Key West situated this previously isolated location at the verge of a gathering storm.[7]

It is Wallace Stevens who provides the most iterated formulations of the modernist poem under 'the pressure of reality'.[8] American modernism's response to a war of which it cannot claim to have direct experience is often thought of in relation to Stevens, and as bearing on the status and workings of the lyric. For example, the detachment conventionally associated with lyric poetry has recently been read as a product of, or at least analogous to, American isolationism, with Pearl Harbor motivating, or coinciding with, a shift to an interventionist practice.[9] To see how such thinking might be fine-tuned to pick up on Moore's and Bishop's poetry, we need first to give some schematic outline to the lyric itself.

The lyric voice pours forth unhindered, the marks of place and time finding no purchase on its immaculate surface. What allows the lyric to live this frictionless life is that it's insubstantial, and it is this lack of substance that safeguards it from historical vicissitudes. If one conception of lyric purity is as a kind of emptiness, there is a second blueprint that imagines the lyric as full – but full only of *itself*. Such an ideal was nurtured in the mid-century environment of American New Criticism: the New Critics imagine the lyric as cutting a substantive geometric figure, they think of it as having an architecture that, by a miraculous feat of internal tensions, manages to hold itself aloft.[10] Somehow this New Critical lyric maintains its shape and integrity without the buttress of external referents. Elizabeth Bishop's 'Imaginary Iceberg' could stand in for this paradigm: it 'cuts its facets from within', its arrested crystalline geometry 'self-made'.[11] In neither of these schemes – whether the lyric is thought of as intangible or as substantial – does it engage with its environment: it is not born of, and has no bearing on, the material world. In certain phases of history this kind of detachment seems improper: like Bishop's iceberg, the lyric floats sublimely unaware of the wreckage that lies around it, and it may even be charged with having caused that wreckage by its intransitive quietism.

There is yet another perspective, however, in which lyric detachment is regarded as a measure not of evasion, but of resistance: Stevens saw it that way in 1936. Anticipating his famous wartime formula whereby 'the imagination press[es] back against the pressure of reality', he writes 'the greater the pressure of the contemporaneous, the greater the resistance. Resistance is the opposite of escape'.[12] In this view the lyric is produced by the encounter of internal and external forces; rather than creating a private, aestheticised space, its holding back from public discourse reads as a decisive response, one that constitutes an alternative integrity. On this line of thought, detachment, withdrawal from current conditions, is not merely the deferral, but also the prerequisite, of changing those conditions.

Marianne Moore is not readily classifiable as a lyric poet. Her insistent use of quotations, for example, makes for the polyphony that is characteristic of her best-known work, and her preference for observations of observations is also at odds with the immediacy claimed for the lyric. The indirections, ironies and seeing at second hand that typified her early poetry, though, proved inadequate in the face of world war, and in the 1940s a single unmediated voice began to emerge, in the monologic lyricism of such poems as 'What Are Years?' and the exclamatory rhetoric of her most anthologised war poem, 'In Distrust of Merits'. The problem with these lyrics, many of Moore's critics have found, is that they do not properly engage with the events they try to address.[13] 'In Distrust of Merits', for example, claims 'there never was a war that was / not inward' and it is this interiorising of external events, coupled with the poem's rhetoric of transcendence (it ends 'Beauty is everlasting / and dust is for a time') that casts it as an instance of lyrical escape.[14]

This chapter goes on to look at some less familiar poems that Moore wrote in the late thirties and early forties, which were eventually published in her 1941 collection *What Are Years*. These poems, produced inside the 'diving bell' of the Brooklyn apartment (a microcosm of neutral America) gesture toward a lyric that is both susceptible and resistant to historical forces. Unlike the New Critical poem, the lyric Moore invents is made of materials – paper, for example – whose value and availability tend to fluctuate. The immunity of the lyric voice is likewise open to risk: Moore presents it as the mechanised voice of wartime radio, and in this guise it may fall prey to enlistment in the service of propaganda.

While Moore's poetry, already established, was modified by the approach of war, Elizabeth Bishop's poetic was just taking shape. Her first book, *North & South*, was published in 1946. Concerned that 'none of the poems deal directly with the war' and that this would leave her 'open to reproach', she asked her publisher to include a disclaimer 'to the effect that most of the poems had been written, or begun at least, before 1941'.[15] There is, in fact, one poem in that collection – 'Roosters' – which contains explicit references to war. Before turning to that poem I shall argue that events in Europe bear indirectly on Bishop's early poetry, and that they do so by adjusting her perspective on territory. I approach Bishop's writing of the 1940s via her Floridian mappings of the thirties, and my suggestion is that shifting territorial claims in Europe and in Key West intrude on her conception of lyric space. Having looked at the resistant lyric of Moore's Brooklyn, and moved South to Bishop's territory in Florida, I turn to the relationship between the two poets. As well as exerting head-on pressure on Moore's and Bishop's poetry, the war makes a kind of side impact on transactions between them. It does so by impressing itself onto the mail.

Three poems that were included in Moore's collection *What Are Years* (1941) were first published a year earlier in the *Kenyon Review*: the lyric that shares the collection's title is flanked by 'Four Quartz Crystal Clocks' and 'A Glass Ribbed Nest' (later retitled 'The Paper Nautilus'). Both the larger historical context and the local publishing environment of this group of poems are significant. Roosevelt's increasingly success-ful attempts to revise neutrality legislation – the repeal of the arms embargo in October 1939 for example – were widely seen as definitive moves toward involvement in what was, to the isolationist faction until April 1940, a 'phony war'. Recently established by John Crowe Ran-som, the *Kenyon Review* adopted an isolationist posture, which Ransom thought of as a form of non-alignment.[16] Moore's poem 'What Are Years?' seems ideally suited to this context. The poem's central figure, a wave trapped in a chasm that 'in its surrendering / finds its continu-ing', makes for containment and equilibrium. This lyric's formal con-tainments (its refrain-like structure) and its impacted oxymorons ('res-olute doubt', etc.) harbour a captive bird 'grown taller as he sings', until the closing paradox 'This is mortality, / this is eternity' seals the poem *against* history, against the catastrophic years that are interrogated, but implicitly dismissed, in the rhetorical question of its title.[17]

If this lyric reads as a model of transcendent non-alignment, the poems that accompany it are less definitively suspended: 'Four Quartz Crystal Clocks' doubts the viability of poetry immune to changes in pressure, and 'A Glass Ribbed Nest', as we will see later, is exposed to the wartime machinations of the mail. The origin of 'Four Quartz Crystal Clocks' is well known: Moore's 1939 telephone bill included a flyer from Bell Telephone containing an advertising blurb about 'the world's exactest clocks', the quartz crystals that regulate the time signal. Again, these 'worksless clocks' that 'tell / time intervals to other clocks' while themselves secured in a 'time vault' dispense their influence from a safely neutral position. If the external atmosphere were allowed to infiltrate their sealed space,

> a quartz prism when
> the temperature changes, feels
> the change and that the then
> electrified alternate edges
> oppositely charged, threaten
> careful timing;[18]

In the naturalised form of a temperature change, the war would make its buffered impact on local conditions, interfering, amongst other things, with syllabic timing.[19]

The quartz crystal that is protected from these temperature fluctuations is associated with lyric inertness: the quasi-organic structure of quartz suggests inward refraction and self-sufficiency.[20] But there is a second source for this poem that Moore reveals in the notes appended to the poem in *What Are Years*, and it's this that exposes the enclosed impartiality of her crystals to the outside air:

> Checked by a comparator with Arlington,
> they punctualize the 'radio,
> cinéma', and 'presse', – a group the
> Giraudoux truth-bureau
> of hoped-for accuracy has termed
> 'instruments of truth'. We know –
> as Jean Giraudoux says
>
> certain Arabs have not heard – that Napoleon
> is dead;

Moore's note to this section reads: 'Jean Giraudoux: "Appeler à l'aide d'un camouflage ces instruments fait pour lat [*sic*] vérité qui sont la radio, le cinéma, la presse?"' "J'ai traversé voila un an des pays arabes où l'On [*sic*] ignorait encore que Napoleon était mort". *Une allocation readiodiffuseé [sic] de M. Giraudoux aux Françaises à propos de Sainte Catherine*; the *Figaro*, November, 1939.'[21]

Moore's incorporation of this fragment of newspaper finds a parallel in Stevens' thinking. Stevens warns that if the artist places himself in an aesthetic vacuum, any external pressure will cause its collapse. To resist that pressure, he writes, 'the painter may establish himself on a guitar, a copy of *Figaro* and a dish of melons'.[22] Stevens is arguing that the artist must ballast his space with 'the contemporaneous', and this is the procedure Moore has followed: alongside her protected quartz prisms she places a scrap of newspaper – and not just any newspaper, but the *Figaro* itself. But whereas the synthetic cubist might have included this fragment of worldly stuff for its quiddity alone, Moore also reads of contemporary issues within it.

The novelist and playwright Jean Giraudoux, who had recently been appointed Commissaire Général à l'Information, made his radio broadcast on 26 November 1939, and the transcript from which Moore quotes was published in the next day's *Figaro*. His topic was the susceptibility of the radio to enlistment in the 'propaganda war' being waged by Germany. 'In an era of slow news' before the advent of long-distance mass communication, he says, 'people really confronted each other'. Direct confrontation, however, is no longer possible: the news is mediated. As a consequence, warfare has become not 'a struggle between good and evil', but 'a sort of race, or competition between advertisers'. Germany is currently winning that race: 'she equipped the world so that no one, even in the depths of Tibet, could shy away from the news that she transmitted. Only a year ago I travelled across Arab countries *where they still did not know that Napoleon was dead*, but there was not a single move of Hitler's that they didn't know about instantly.'[23] Giraudoux goes on to ask how France should resist such an enemy: 'now that at the front in a battle of terrible realism, in hand to hand combat, the real Germany and the real France confront each other, should we create an invented France to combat this imaginary Germany? *enlist in the service of camouflage the radio, cinema and press*, instruments that were made for truth?'

Giraudoux ends by rejecting both the 'terrible realism' of direct encounter and the option of entering the propaganda war. In a conclusion oddly reminiscent of Stevens, he recommends that his listeners turn instead to those who give space to the 'mother of nations and great peoples, the imagination', for, he claims, 'we are in an era when you need imagination to see reality'.

The radio presents special problems for theories of speech and writing. Though as a vocal medium it seems to promise presence, this is a voice whose origin is absent. Thus the radio might be said to stand at a mid point between the transparent verifiability of the spoken utterance and the errors and slippages to which writing is traditionally considered prone – as Moore puts it in 'The Pangolin', man is the 'writing- / master' who 'writes errror with four / r's'.[24] And the mechanically transmitted voice has something further in common with writing: it is capable of occupying space. Giraudoux warns that the mass-mediated voice can do the expansionist work of belligerent nationalism by ensuring that its *news* penetrates and settles in the most distant geographical locations. By comparison with German expansion the French imperial phase looks innocent, because, without the help of radio technology, there were parts that news of its fortunes could not reach ('certain Arabs have not heard – that Napoleon / is dead').[25]

Of course, there is a certain irony about this radio transmission: Giraudoux's speech relies on the very instrument that he claims is least trustworthy. Moreover, the fragment Moore quotes is one step further removed from its vocal origin: the *transcript* of a radio broadcast, a piece of writing, it is even more liable to error. The rest of her poem plays with the puns and slippages that breed when speech is repeated in writing: although 'repetition [. . .] / should be synonymous with accuracy', writing exposes differences that speech would conceal, those seen but not heard, for example, in 'the bell-boy with the buoy-ball'. The essential point here is that the very inclusion of the *Figaro* fragment in Moore's time-vault poem undermines the promise of transparency that is contained and protected there. To ballast her lyric, to make it proof against external pressure, she must also endanger it, exposing its inviolable voice to the infections of writing.

The news that reaches the American poet over the airwaves may be untrustworthy, distorted by its fickle medium. What happens to the radio in wartime – its cooptation for propaganda purposes – might also imperil the lyric's intransitive voice. Moore, who had for some time felt isolationism to be unconscionable, acknowledges the impossibility of neutrality in respect to both the news she receives and the poetry she produces. Staying in one place and operating as a receiver and transmitter, the radio stands for the compromised lyric she wanted to write.

The poem ends by calling up another mechanised voice, the speaking clock:

> And as
>
> Meridian 7 one-two
> one-two gives, each fifteenth second
>   in the same voice, the new
> data – 'The time will be' so and so –
> you realize that 'when you
>   hear the signal', you'll be
>
>
> hearing Jupiter or jour pater, the day god –
>   the salvaged son of Father Time –
> telling the cannibal Chronos
>   (eater of his proxime,
> new born progeny) that punctual-
>   ity is not now a crime.

The voice salvaged from time would serve well as a definition of lyric poetry, and the final verdict here rehabilitates the lyric by exploiting the dual sense of 'punctuality'. These lines conflate the ideas of the lyric as a 'punctual spot' (having neither duration nor magnitude), with another, more customary sense of punctuality, that is, being in precisely the right place at the right time.[26] Here, then, is a prescription for a *localised* lyric – and of course the word 'punctual- / ity', itself fractured over two lines, is vulnerable to its particular spatial environment.[27]

Elizabeth Bishop spent New Year's Eve 1935 alone. At midnight, so she told Frani Blough, she dialled the speaking clock: 'I had a curiosity as to what Meridian 7–1212 would have to say so I called up. Without even a flicker in her voice, she said, "When you hear the signal, the time will be twelve o'clock". Bzzz. "When you hear", etc. So that's what mechanization does.'[28] At this moment, curiously pre-emptive of Moore's 1940 poem, the time is told by an unwavering mechanised voice on which the particular hour makes for no inflection. This incident punctuated a solitary evening in which Bishop was preoccupied with geographical space: she had spent New Year's Eve looking at a glassed map of the North Atlantic and writing a poem.[29] That poem 'The Map', which was chosen for the opening of *North & South*, transforms an aerial view of a coastline into a cartographic artefact, a schematised design in which print coexists with landscape:

The names of seashore towns run out to sea,
the names of cities cross the neighbouring mountains
– the printer here experiencing the same excitement
as when emotion too far exceeds its cause.[30]

The poem ends with a line that has since been read as Bishop's signature statement: 'more delicate than the historians' are the map-makers' colors'. Bishop's map-makers apparently trace the lines of physical, rather than political, geography. Unlike historians, these cartographers do not 'assign' colours to countries, but simply record the contours and boundaries present in the natural landscape. This sense of impartiality underwrites another assumption in the poem's closing lines: that an aerial perspective is a neutral one. From a bird's-eye view, Bishop claims, 'topography displays no favorites; North's as near as West'. In 1935, then, both the voice that marks time and the lines that demarcate space claim immunity from the pressures of the historical moment.

There is one shape that troubles the otherwise tranquil landscape of 'The Map': that of 'Norway's hare' which 'runs South in agitation'. It was an aerial photograph of Norway that would compel Bishop to write her militarised 1940 poem 'Roosters', and by that time the presumed innocence of the aerial perspective had been severely jeopardised. The intervening stage in this process of growing distrust is glimpsed in Bishop's 'Florida' (1939). Here the landscape is not unassailable: from the air the ground is 'dotted as if bombarded', marked by the impact of 'cannon balls' and 'shells'. Florida also bears other traces of past violence:

> arranged as on a gray rag of rotted calico,
> the buried Indian Princess's skirt;
> with these the monotonous, endless, sagging coast-line
> is delicately ornamented.[31]

The buried remnant of calico recalls the violent seizure of territory entailed in the formation and expansion of the United States.[32] The alligator cry which comes at the end of the poem from 'the throat of the Indian Princess' is heard not as a timeless exclamation, but as issuing from a punctual moment of colonial rapacity. Above this troubled landscape,

> Thirty or more buzzards are drifting down, down, down,
> over something they have spotted in the swamp[33]

In this poem, then, the bird's-eye view reveals the residual violence that marks the state of Florida as annexed territory. But more than that, Bishop's predatory birds suggest that it's the aerial perspective *itself* that is intent on capturing what it has spotted from above: adopting such a perspective must be understood not merely as a means of recording the process of territorial expansion, but also as instrumental in that process.

Although the disclaimer in *North & South* (most of the poems were written before 1942) suggests that the war need not enter American poems until America has entered the war, events in Europe had begun by 1939 to make claims on the poetry Bishop was writing in Key West. Germany's annexation of European territory, I am suggesting, prompted her to adjust her own conception of occupied space, and to mistrust the expansionist tendencies of the elevated cartographic eye. As we have seen, warfare finds its way into her 1939 view of Florida, and implicates the aerial perspective adopted there. Germany's annexation of Scandinavia in April 1940, when 'Norway's hare' could no longer outrun German expansion, forced Bishop to make these adjustments explicit.

'Roosters' is the only poem in *North & South* that refers directly to the war. Bishop wrote to Marianne Moore, 'in the first part [of 'Roosters'] I was thinking of Key West, and also of those aerial views of dismal little towns in Finland and Norway, when the Germans took over, and their atmosphere of poverty'.[34] It seems from this letter that Bishop is mapping the aerial view of occupied Scandinavia onto her own position in Key West. Her Floridian buzzards are now replaced by roosters:

> over our churches
> where the tin rooster perches
> over our little wooden Northern houses,
>
> making sallies
> from all the muddy alleys,
> marking out maps like Rand McNally's:
>
> glass-headed pins,
> oil-golds and copper greens,
> anthracite blues, alazarins,
>
> each one an active
> displacement in perspective;
> each screaming, 'this is where I live!'[35]

The roosters' cries mark out the extent of Germany's territorial claim, as Bishop's letter goes on to explain: 'about the "glass-headed pins": I felt the roosters to be placed here and there (by their various crowings) like the pins that point out war projects on a map'. In this poem, bird song becomes, much like the wartime radio broadcast, an accessory to military manoeuvres.

Germany's annexation of European territory turned out to have a particular impact on Bishop's Key West. In the build up to American intervention, the navy's requisition of buildings threatened to make her homeless. Leaving Key West for Mexico in 1942 Bishop writes, 'It is impossible to live here any longer. The Navy takes over and tears down and eats up one or two blocks of beautiful little houses for dinner every day. Probably [Bishop and Crane's] house on White Street will go too.'[36]

European invasions both cause and prefigure the navy's consumption of Bishop's own domain in Key West, and her proximity to this increased naval activity, especially after Pearl Harbor, made her feel that Key West was 'no place to be unless one is of some use'.[37] In 1943, having returned from Mexico, she found brief employment as a war worker, and her job brought to an uneasy focus the problems she was encountering as a poet. The glass that had protected her maps now served a different function: the labour board set her to work in a naval optical shop. Wallace Stevens writes that war is constituted of 'fact on such a scale that the mere consciousness of it affects the scale of one's thinking'.[38] As we'll see, changes of scale have a devastating impact on Bishop once the map-maker takes cognisance of the historian: her long letter to Moore about her experience in the optical shop illustrates the debilitating changes of scale that result when conceptions of space and distance are perceived in relation to contemporary events.

Bishop's job meant she 'could spend a lot of time – had to – watching everything through magnificent optical instruments of every kind'. It lasted only five days – she had to give it up because 'the eyestrain made [her] seasick'. Nevertheless the work made for a sense of contact with current events: 'it was the only way of finding out what *is* going on in Key West now, seeing the inside of the navy yard and all the ships'. Bishop was intrigued and frustrated by her co-workers:

I was infinitely impressed with the patience of those men *fiddling* day after day with those delicate, maddening little instruments. I don't think I could do it, even if it hadn't made me sick. And their lack of imagination would get more and more depressing – not one of them had any idea of the *theory* of the thing, *why* the prisms go this way or that way, or what 'collimate' and 'optical center' really mean, etc.[39]

Much could be read in this letter about Bishop's deflating the overt masculinity of her colleagues – perhaps she could not do their job because she had no 'maddening little instrument' to fiddle with – but that's another story.[40] What interests us here is the myopia Bishop diagnoses, but which she claims not to have suffered: despite (or because of) their work with instruments that enhance sight, these men are themselves short-sighted, unable to see the bigger picture for their obsessive interest in tiny details.[41] Bishop, by contrast, claims to see things in a larger perspective, which encompasses not only the theory of optics, but also the war in which the navy's instruments are to be used. Much as the bird's-eye view in 'Roosters' was thoroughly compromised by its complicity with military expansion, this enlarged sense of scale proves disorientating, makes Bishop seasick, and renders her incapable of doing her job either as a poet or as an optical worker: 'I want so badly to get something good done to show you', she writes to Moore, 'I don't know what the obstacles are or why I don't really take up lens grinding.'

Bishop's letter finally turns to her own and her correspondent's situations: 'You speak of being "handicapped by solitude", but to me you seem the very height of society. It is terribly lonely here and I find myself growing stupider and stupider and more like a hermit every day.' Frustrated by the distance that intervenes between herself and the war, and simultaneously incapacitated by the lenses that might bring it closer, Bishop struggles to collapse the distance between herself and Moore, to restore the intimacy of face-to-face speech: 'this [letter] is too long', she writes, 'but I want to *talk*'.

If the radio (a single voice) works as one analogue of the lyric poem in wartime, the letter (a sealed utterance) would serve well as another. The contents of personal correspondence, though they rely on the mail, should be impervious to its machinations. Barring accidents, letters are private, immune to and unchanged in transit. Just as the imagined reader of the lyric pays no attention to its packaging (even though its dissemination depends on the mechanisms of print culture) so the eager recipient of the letter does not dwell on the size and colour of the envelope, nor on exactly how the letter has fared in its encounter with the post office. However, post office markings were made *legible* in wartime: my contention is that the surface of the lyric is likewise imprinted with national imperatives.

The principal channel of communication between Marianne Moore and Elizabeth Bishop was the mail, and it was with the approach of war that their close relationship reached its crisis point. The poem that caused their disagreement (Bishop's 'Roosters') and the one that anticipates Bishop's withdrawal from Moore's sphere of influence (Moore's 'A Glass Ribbed Nest') were produced and modified in postal transactions. The mail provides the local environment for these exchanges, and it in turn mediates the larger international context: in this way world events are imprinted, via the post office, onto transactions between the two poets.

To illustrate this process, and before turning to the epistolary traffic between Moore and Bishop, I want to look at a poem *about* letters. Moore published 'Walking-Sticks and Paperweights and Watermarks' in *Poetry* in 1936. Five years later it was included, with significant revisions, in *What Are Years.*[42] In those revisions we can trace Moore's developing perspective on the approaching war. The progress of the poem from 1936 to 1941 is toward valuing collective action over personal expression. In its later, wartime version, the poem begins and ends with assertions of unity: the legs of the triskelion symbol 'run in unison' at its opening, while a juniper tree 'objectifies welded divisiveness' at its close. A wax seal depicting a pelican that wounds its breast to feed its young serves in this version as an emblem of self-loss standing for the sacrifice of the individual voice to a 'community of throats', the voice of the nation.

This emphasis on collective action is impressed by the transatlantic mail. The central section of 'Walking-Sticks' is about paper, watermarks and, crucially for this argument, postmarks. The 1936 version reads:

> The paper-mould's similarly
>
> once unsolid waspnest-blue, snow-
> white, or seashell-gray rags, seen through, show
>   sheepcotes, turkey-
> mills, acorns, and anvils. 'Stones grow',
> then stop, and so
>   do gardens. 'Plants grow and live; men
> grow and live and think'. *Utilizey la poste
> aerienne*, trade will follow
>   the telephone. The post's jerky
>
> cancellings ink the stamp, relet-
> tering stiltedly, as a puppet-
>   acrobat walks
> about with high steps on his net,

> an alphabet
> of words and animals where the
> wire-embedded watermark's more integral
> expressiveness had first set
> its alabaster effigy.

The watermark reads here as the translucent imprint of personal expression: 'integral' to the paper, it reveals the mark of its maker. The postmark (known as a 'cancellation' or 'obliterator') is thought of as a crude public writing that obscures the more delicate mark of the individual voice. As war approaches, however, Moore's scale of values alters: clarity more than integrity is increasingly her predilection,[43] so she transfers her allegiance from the interior of the paper to the exterior of the envelope, to the postmark that is now visibly harnessed to the machinery of state:

> 'Airmail is quick.' 'Save rags, bones, metals.' Hopes
> are harvest when deeds follow
> words postmarked 'Dig for victory.'
>
> Postmark behests are clearer than
> the water marks beneath, – than ox, swan,
> crane, or dolphin,
> than eastern, open, jewelled, Span-
> ish, Umbrian
> crown, – as symbols of endurance.

Nostalgia for unmediated 'integral expressiveness' is by 1941 overwritten by 'symbols of endurance', and whereas in 1936 the components of paper-making ('seashell-gray rags') were cohesive and plentiful, in this wartime version the production of paper is no longer a matter for complacency; paper shortages compel the post office to impress on the envelope, and on its recipient, the imperative '*Save* rags.'[44]

The cancellations Moore selects in this version of the poem were stamped by the British GPO. Having consistently rejected proposals to rent out the postmark space for advertising slogans, the post office relented in 1917, introducing the first slogan postmark to boost the sale of war bonds. After the First World War advertising remained permissible so long as it was confined to matters relevant to postal services or highlighting national events.[45] Thus the sealed letter acquires the mark of its environment during its sojourn in the mail. Likewise, I suggest, the historical circumstances of the lyric begin to stamp themselves on its exterior, and those contingent marks, which conduce to collective action and thrift, cancel out the personal expenditure of the lyric itself.

Moore and Bishop's relationship reached a turning point in 1940, when Bishop refused to accept Moore's revisions of her poem 'Roosters'.[46] I want now to return to the third of Moore's *Kenyon Review* poems, 'A Glass Ribbed Nest'. This poem narrates the period of tension in Moore's relationship with Elizabeth Bishop, and, more importantly, it locates that personal crisis in the context of international upheaval. In 1937 Moore had received a gift in the mail, a paper nautilus shell.[47] 'A Glass Ribbed Nest' is about this 'perishable souvenir':

> the intensively
> watched eggs coming from
> the shell, free it when they are freed, –
> leaving its wasp-nest flaws
> of white on white, and close-
>
> laid Ionic chiton-folds
> like the lines in the mane of
> a Parthenon horse [48]

This poem is frequently read as offering a feminised version of Bloomian influence, one that emphasises nurture rather than conflict: the 'intensively watched' younger poet makes a bid for independence which, in turn, grants freedom to the elder.[49] My point is that the larger historical context is also legible in its language – its casting those who write for profit as 'mercenaries', and its rendering maternal love as a 'fortress'. The empty carapace takes the shape of Moore's emergent lyric, absorbing the impact of war, and converting its injuries into 'wasp-nest flaws'. And Moore also seems in this poem to have obeyed the postmark's behest to save paper: her 'wasp-nest flaws' are in fact recycled from 'Jerónymo's House', a poem Bishop had sent her in the post:

> My house, my fairy
> palace, is
> of perishable
> clapboards with
> three rooms in all,
> my gray wasps' nest
> of chewed-up paper
> glued with spit. [50]

The 'perishable' materials of Bishop's 'wasps' nest' are chewed up and re-confected as Moore's 'perishable souvenir'.[51] This moment of

exchange brings us back to Bishop's own work. Disabled by the enlarged scales and shifting perspectives of war, and increasingly sceptical
of the expansionist tendencies of aerial maps, Bishop salvages a smaller
space for the lyric voice in Jerónymo's paper house.[52] That structure,
which contains, among other things, a radio, is temporary:

> When I move
> I take these things,
>   not much more, from
> my shelter from
>   the hurricane.

A delimited, rather than an expansive locale, Jerónymo's house is itself
easily displaced. It provides refuge from Floridian hurricanes and from
the figurative storm of warfare, but its provisional materials cannot give
permanent or impermeable shelter.[53] As Bishop's own Key West home
seemed liable to be overrun by the US naval operation, her lyric voice is
also poised ready to vacate its accustomed recess.

In his review of *North & South* Randall Jarrell wrote: 'all [Bishop's]
poems have written underneath, *I have seen it*'.[54] In the late 1930s and
early 1940s neither Moore nor Bishop had a clear view of the events they
felt ought to preoccupy them most. Both poets found ways of compensating for the blind side of their location, modifying the shape and
materials of their poetry at the behest of local conditions. Although
Bishop's decision was to leave out of her work events that she could not
claim to have observed directly, the pressure of those events is nonetheless perceptible: the enlarged sense of wartime space is answered by a
narrowing of scope in her lyrics, and by their claims only to temporary
life. For Marianne Moore the effect of remoteness on a poetic much
prized for its close and accurate observations was also potentially disabling. Her remedial gesture in *What Are Years* was to open out a violable
lyric voice. Bishop praised Moore's poetry in the 1940s for its 'wonderful
alone quality', and for its seeming 'suspended-in-air'. [55] The poetry I've
been looking at, however, speaks neither of solitude nor of suspension.
Moore's poems are freighted with contemporary substance, so that *this*
lyric voice can work not as a retreat from, but in concert with, public
media.

CHAPTER 10

'In the published city': the New York School of Poets

Geoff Ward

As with Isms, the designation 'School' tends to signify that a retrospective and ultimately academic exercise in mapping an aspect of culture is under way. Just as no artist or poet has (to my knowledge, anyway) leapt forward to proclaim their postmodernism, waiting instead to have it thrust upon them by cultural cartographers, so there comes a familiar moment of ritual disavowal in the narrative of a movement, group or School when its members back away from the implications of tutelage and uniformity. In the case of the New York School of Poets, external circumstances have also played an important role. In a melancholy irony, one turning point in the evolution of the group came with the death of a key member, Frank O'Hara (1926–66), and another came in 1976, when John Ashbery (1927–) won a trio of prestigious literary awards including the Pulitzer Prize for *Self-Portrait in a Convex Mirror* and so vacated the coterie for the canon. Academically speaking, Ashbery was sprung by Harold Bloom, whose allegedly deconstructionist though basically Freudian theory of the 'anxiety of influence' was about to reach its own peak of academic influence. Bloom's model for poetry was rooted in the figure of the poet as a battling individualist, locked in conscious or unconscious combat with powerful precursors whose work had to be internalised before it could be superseded. The concept of any group, coterie or movement of poets was therefore troubling to this essentially patrilineal psychodrama of tradition and the individual talent.

Bloom had to prise his man free from the New York School, whose chief members aside from Ashbery and Frank O'Hara were James Schuyler (1923–91) and Kenneth Koch (1925–). In one sense this posed little difficulty, in that, although the group appeared to underline its collective identity by gesturing back to a relationship with the New York School of Painting, that gesture was as imbued with irony and even comedy as many of the poems are. The generation of Abstract Expressionist painters, pre-eminently Jackson Pollock, Mark Rothko and the late Willem de Kooning, had proved to be the most commercially successful avant-garde of all time, while retaining their romantic New York loft credentials. The Poets of the New York School (note the different emphasis) was a phrase used by John Bernard Myers to mark his sense of an emergent generation of writers he wished to publish in a series of pamphlets bearing the name of his gallery, Tibor de Nagy. These publications appeared sporadically between 1952 and the time of O'Hara's death, and included the latter's *Love Poems (Tentative Title)*. In Myers' view 'It was particularly appropriate in the case of all these new poets that they should find their first publisher in an art gallery director because all of them, in one way or another, were intimately bound with the aesthetics, the people, the politics, the social life and the concerns of the New York art world'.[1] Despite these shared 'concerns', the paintings costing thousands of dollars sold to an eager and an international public, but Myers was often reduced to giving the pamphlets away.

It may seem therefore that the label 'School' comes unstuck as a result of pressures from both within and without: from the divergence of individual lives and careers, from the ways in which the academy has (rightly or wrongly) valued certain poets over others, and because of a historical difficulty attached to the cultural and market valuation of painting over poetry. However, in reviewing the New York School of Poets the apparently more simple and yet more slippery question, to which the remainder of this chapter is devoted, concerns the 'New York' lettering on the label. The island of Manhattan does provide not only the context but the explicit subject of many poems by Frank O'Hara, for whom it was 'greater than the Rocky Mountains' ('Walking'), and who is chided by the sun in one famous poem: 'I know you love Manhattan, but / you ought to look up more often'.[2] James Schuyler wrote regularly about the old, as well as the new, New York. Ashbery by contrast refers to it only rarely, despite spending much of his time in the same block he has lived in for over thirty years. Perhaps to pause over the name of any particular city is immediately to see it divide into sub-sets such as the city as geographical topic, or as visionary *topos* (cf. San Francisco); as backdrop, springboard or convenience; as lover, drug, murderer, home, political condensation, the new Nature or a simulacra-circuit. The editors of the 1970 collection *An Anthology of New York Poets* were as chary about the 'New York' as about the 'School' bit:

Perhaps we do protest too much, but this is to prepare ourselves for the gruesome possibility of the 'New York School of Poets' label, one which has been spewed forth from time to time by some reviewers, critics and writers either sustained by provincial jealousy or the bent to translate everything into a manageable textbookese. Very few of the poets in this anthology were born in New York City, but many of them live here . . . New York has remained for all of them a fulcrum they continue to use in order to get as much leverage as possible in literature, a city where they met and continued their lives together, whether they came from Cleveland or Newark or Cincinnati or Providence or Tulsa. And although the New York tag is an alarmingly useless one, it does remind one that many of these poets met in schools, at Harvard, Columbia, NYU or the New School, sometimes as undergraduates taught by Delmore Schwartz or in poetry workshops taught by Kenneth Koch, Bill Berkson or Frank O'Hara. The crisscrossing of friendships is surprising and inspiring. [3]

The inspiration and crisscrossing of friendships forms the theme of many poems by O'Hara, and of key poems by Schuyler such as 'This Dark Apartment' and 'Dining Out with Doug and Frank' which are also set in Manhattan. Meanwhile New York retained for these writers and their followers its traditional role as 'a fulcrum' used 'in order to get as much leverage as possible in literature' (which, for an unknown gay poet working in the 1950s in the shadow of the famous painters, was precious little).

New York has been a literary centre since the time when Philip Freneau wrote his most celebrated lyrics, and *The Federalist*, arguably the first American literary classic, urged ratification of the Constitution. By the 1840s, when Whitman wrote of himself as 'manhattanese' and Poe in the *Broadway Journal* lamented the rise of progress and the brownstone, New York was the nation's literary capitol. Melville, James, Wharton, Dreiser, Dos Passos, Mencken, Wolfe, Crane and then the other Crane, all lived there. John Steinbeck marvelled at staying within walking distance of the otherwise cosmically disconnected loci where Walt Whitman sweated editorials, Ernest Hemingway punched Max Eastman on the nose and Rudolph Valentino lay in state. As with the writers, many of the publishing houses begun in the nineteenth century retained their grip in the twentieth: Doubleday; E. P. Dutton; G. P. Putnam; Charles Scribner's Sons. Alfred A. Knopf, who had published Mencken, Nathan and Cather, would publish *The Collected Poems of Frank O'Hara* after his death. Over the decades groupings as distinct as the Harlem Renaissance, the St Marks Poetry Project and Nuyorican writing bear witness to the islands within Manhattan. Consequently when John Ashbery ends his epic *Flow Chart* (1991) with an apparent gesture toward Hart Crane ('It's open: the bridge, that way') we must read those lines in the context of the poem's opening 'in the published city', a multi-dimensional context where a postmodern sense of New York City as a mosaic of signifiers to be both composed and interpreted daily by its inhabitants merges with a more traditional sense of the city as a fulcrum for gaining leverage on literature:

> Still in the published city but not yet
> overtaken by a new form of despair, I ask
> the diagram: is it the foretaste of pain
> it might easily be? Or an emptiness
> so sudden it leaves the girders
> whanging in the absence of wind,
> the sky milk-blue and astringent? We know life is so busy,
> but a larger activity shrouds it, and this is something
> we can never feel, except occasionally, in small signs
> put up to warn us and as soon expunged.[4]

As is the case so often in Ashbery's writing, tone and imagery are interestingly at variance; while the tone is melancholy, imploring, faintly elegiac but without a fixed subject for its elegy, the images replace each other at speed, and notwithstanding the 'emptiness' and 'absence' this published city is the counterpart of New York as reflected in the convex mirror of an earlier long poem, 'alive with filiations, shuttlings'.[5] The city is unlike Breton and Aragon's Paris as adventure-playground, nor does it resemble either the hallucinations of Lorca in *Poet in New York* or the 'Unreal city' of Eliot's *Waste Land*, where London, Baudelaire's Paris, 'Jerusalem Athens Alexandria' are equally likely to shimmer and vanish in a superimposition directing the reader's attention away from yet finally toward Eliot's own fraught psyche. Ashbery's city is both less and more like the New York any of us might know. Less, for even in – in fact, precisely in its cold pockets of emptiness – this is a romantic *topos*. The sudden bareness of the girders against the equally bare sky resembles many moments in Ashbery's poetry: 'It was as though I'd been left with the empty street / a few seconds after the bus pulled out. A dollop of afternoon wind.'[6]

In a different way it recalls all those moments in Wordsworth's *Prelude*, or the opening of Shelley's *Julian and Maddalo* in the foreboding and emptiness of the shoreline, where bareness is ambiguous, suggesting both the stripping away of inessentials as a prelude to understanding, and a loss of things in the outer world with which the mind can identify and so console itself. There is a poetic continuity with the nineteenth century which may be more important ultimately than the links or disjunction between contemporary writing and the period of high modernism. The peppering of *Flow Chart* with bits and bobs from Swinburne and Thomas Lovell Beddoes has been much remarked, but the affinity with a consciousness-centred romanticism runs deeper than those gestures. And yet Ashbery's published city still does recall not only romantic landscapes but the scene anyone might have to negotiate emerging from the subway into Times Square or hailing/dodging a yellow cab. '[L]ife is so busy' in the published city that not all of what could be seen can be seen, and not all of what is seen dare be interpreted. Instead we relegate the bulk of the city to an unfelt 'larger activity' that we know is there but that we don't have to deal with, except in the form of its daily punctuation marks, the 'small signs / put up to warn us and as soon expunged'. To attempt to comprehend New York in its conjectural entirety would be to court madness as much as would the opposite vision of bareness, that, in severing humans from what they see, separates us ultimately from each other, from ourselves, and from the continuity of successive moments which, delusory or not, makes life make sense. Dismissing both these poles of perception as inhuman, we have to get the city onto a human scale if we are going to perceive and get about in it at all.

In a theoretical work, *The Secular Grail: Paradigms of Perception* (1993), the Canadian poet Christopher Dewdney writes of a neurological condition, visual agnosia, that leaves its victims unable to recognise everyday objects: 'It is a dysfunctional state, and yet to truly understand the world perhaps it is necessary to achieve intentional visual agnosia. This is because our categorical and nominative consciousness stands between us and a primal apprehension of reality.'[7] Such an intuition, that the ultimately real might stand independently of what anyone conceives it to be, is relevant to the epiphanic moments (or near misses) that recur in Ashbery's poetry, and is one that recurs in North American philosophy, from William James and C. S. Peirce to the present. If we do have to learn an intentional visual agnosia then that would be nowhere more true than in the city, where not to select drastically from the potential perceptual field would be to risk danger. Earlier in *The Secular Grail* in a section entitled with conscious ambiguity 'City States', Dewdney writes as follows: 'Cities are fictional environments. They are ambient identities that, in terms of variety from one city to the next, have recognizable "looks" that their citizens wear as cosmetic name tags. Allegiance to city comes before allegiance to country. One's city is a familial membership.'[8]

The notion that one's city is a familial membership will be explored shortly in relation to the poetry of Frank O'Hara. Remaining for a

moment with Ashbery, it may be that in offering a fictional environment, his poems mimic the city beyond them that remains in a subtle
way their subject. By Dewdney's lights, Ashbery can be read as depicting only rarely a New York to which his ambient poems nevertheless
behave analogously. Like ambient music, which resists crescendo,
finale, resolution in favour of a sonic environment which the listener
can dip into or, by intentional aural agnosia, censor out at will, Ashbery's poetry (so often compared to music, not least by himself) may
operate as a published city while referring to Manhattan spaces only
infrequently.

It will be objected that there are less ingenious explanations for the
relative sparsity of metropolitan imagery in his work. For one thing, it is
often held that, for all the surface bizarrerie of poems entitled 'Daffy
Duck in Hollywood' (not to mention 'Fuckin' Sarcophagi' or 'Yes, Dr
Grenzmer. How May I Be of Assistance to You? What! You Say the
Patient Has Escaped?'), Ashbery's interest lies not in spatial detail but in
temporal extension. It is also true that this poet grew up, not in the city
at all, but on a farm in Rochester, New York State. The poet's topography is, as Bonnie Costello writes, 'a complex one, shaped not only by
rivers, mountains, trees, islands, capes, peninsulas, storms and clouds
but by many a farm and field of grain, barren plains, lakes and ruined
cities. I cannot undertake here an iconography of Ashbery's landscapes,
which anyway keep changing; pastoral, sublime, suburban, bureau-
cratic.'[9] It is true that ambitions of scale in Ashbery's work are not
merely visible in the length of particular works. It may be, however, that
by jumping with a certain ironic universality from the village hall to the
tides in the Bay of Fundy he is reminding us that we all stand on shaky
ground. This is a poetry of scepticism rather than of surveying, its
images illustrative of that mood of pseudo-analytical reverie which is as
much the basis of his work as anything, signalling blockage by recourse
to landscape images as frequently as forward movement, as in the
closing lines of one of his finest poems, 'Grand Galop': 'But now we are
at Cape Fear and the overland trail / Is impassable, and a dense curtain
of mist hangs over the sea.'[10] And while a title such as *The Double Dream of
Spring* (1970) seems to gesture toward what used to be thought of as the
natural world, it in fact quotes the title of a painting by the proto-
Surrealist, De Chirico.

It might be helpful at this point to recall the Knickerbockers.
'Knickerbocker' is an old nickname for New Yorker, and was adopted
around the 1820s by a group including Fenimore Cooper and William

Cullen Bryant, who sought the development of a national literature. The heavy reliance placed by these New York writers on rivers, mountains, prairies and so forth was bound up with political issues of national pride. The oblique but definite patriotism of poems by Ashbery such as 'Pyrography' suggests a lingering relationship, once again with nineteenth-century literature, which is hedged about but not wholly defined by irony. Ashbery's work argues that the poetry of the published city may illustrate itself using all that the dictionary holds, without ever truly leaving its location.

Literature is a family affair. The outdated image of writing within Western culture as an act of solitary self-communing is called into question not only by the large number of blood and marriage ties across the canon: the Sidney family, the Wordsworth brother and sister, the married Shelleys (and Mary's parents), the Brontë sisters, the various Rossettis and so on. Prominent in the weekend press as I write this are articles on the Amises, *père et fils*, and on the publication of *Birthday Letters*, poems by Ted Hughes about his first wife, Sylvia Plath. Recent research on non-canonical literature, for example drama and other writing by women in the English Renaissance, only reinforces the centrality of family as collaborators or backers, as audience and addressees. Where authors have not addressed their family explicitly, they have done so in ways that remain encrypted or displaced within the text, and where their own family has been rejected or is not implied by that text, they have gone out and sought another one, be it inside or outside literature. All Shakespeare's plays are about families. All nineteenth- and twentieth-century coteries and avant-garde groups are familial. Some – the Jena Circle, the Pisan Circle – literally involve close relatives, but all literary movements and groupings are family circles, entailing the possibility of corruption, competition, incest or sibling rivalry, as much as, say, proud parenting. In one sense pushed too far, Harold Bloom's theory of the self-made but secretly sharing writer did not go far enough, tethered as it was to a Freudian 'family romance' that, like all Freud's fictions, argues for the fatedness of human affairs. In literary-familial activity, as distinct from the biological family tree or the analyst's fern-clogged waiting room, roles can be reversed or change from year to year, text to text, sentence to sentence.

Although it offers a wealth of information, the recent biography of Frank O'Hara is somewhat florid in the telling, and no more so than in its handling of family matters.[11] Salient questions no doubt remain to be raised concerning the poet and his biological family, but as with most homosexual writers, the really important family is the one he met after moving to the city. Such groupings are among the locations of modernism. References to his sexuality in O'Hara's poetry tend to be glancing or coded, understandably so in those pre-Stonewall days. There were other reasons to try to turn the closeted nature of the coterie to advantage so as to make the best of a constrained situation. James Schuyler wrote on painting, John Ashbery has been an art critic all his professional life, and Frank O'Hara at the time of his death was an associate curator at the Museum of Modern Art in New York. Organising important circulating exhibitions, frequently of Abstract Expressionist art, and writing the first monograph on Jackson Pollock, he was noticeably interested in blurring the distinctions between friendship, academic criticism and a body of poetry that among other things offers the most detailed representation of an artistic milieu in the Western canon. Yet where his painter friends and mentors made the covers of *Time* and *Life*, the poetry failed to sell. When we add to this O'Hara's carelessness about his manuscripts, his evident contentment with the role of poet's (and painter's) poet, and his famous dithering over what to send to publishers, it is clear that when it came to poetry, Frank O'Hara had to keep it in the family.

It is highly probable that while some of these pressures were forced on him by historical and other circumstances, an intentional agnosia made him more or less blind to publication in his lifetime precisely so that *The Collected Poems of Frank O'Hara* could emerge as they did, posthumously. Across such an acreage of print, O'Hara's 'familial membership' of his city, to borrow Dewdney's phrase, can be fully stressed among as well as in individual poems. Some readers, for example Helen Vendler, like the poetry but feel they have to put up with the name dropping and gossipy allusions that make the work such an artistic soap opera cum latter-day *Lives of the Poets*: 'Tedious though the in-group references (to Bill and Kenneth and Janice and Edwin and Vincent and so on) can be, they are genuinely invoked to make the real precious, an experiment that is at least worth trying.'[12] This view would ultimately, and not unreasonably, locate O'Hara in a genealogy that would include both Carlos Williams and the *omnium gatherum* tendency of American verse after Whitman; however, it misses the aspects of O'Hara's practice that bear on his immediate, New York 'family'. Take the poem 'Adieu to Norman, Bon Jour to Joan and Jean-Paul', which scales new heights or depths of name-dropping from its title on. To work out that the title refers to Norman Bluhm, Joan Mitchell and Jean-Paul Riopelle opens the door to interpretation in one way, while potentially tying the poem down in another. While O'Hara wants to celebrate individual identity and achievement, he also wants to be free, 'like a bird / flying over Paris et ses environs', ditto his New York environs, so as to hold together in graceful movement ('balayeur des artistes') what would otherwise ossify in stasis. After line 22, the poem runs as follows:

> I wish I were reeling around Paris
> instead of reeling around New York
> I wish I weren't reeling at all
> it is Spring the ice has melted the Ricard is being poured
> we are all happy and young and toothless
> it is the same as old age
> the only thing to do is simply continue
> is that simple
> yes, it is simple because it is the only thing to do
> can you do it
> yes, you can because it is the only thing to do
> blue light over the Bois de Boulogne it continues
> the Seine continues
> the Louvre stays open it continues it hardly closes at all
> the Bar Américain continues to be French
> de Gaulle continues to be Algerian as does Camus
> Shirley Goldfarb continues to be Shirley Goldfarb
> and Jane Hazan continues to be Jane Freilicher (I think!)
> and Irving Sandler continues to be the balayeur des artistes
> and so do I (sometimes I think I'm 'in love' with painting)
> and surely the Piscine Deligny continues to have water in it
> and the Flore continues to have tables and newspapers and people
>   under them
> and surely we shall not continue to be unhappy
> we shall be happy
> but we shall continue to be ourselves everything continues to be possible
> Rene Char, Pierre Reverdy, Samuel Beckett it is possible isn't it
> I love Reverdy for saying yes, though I don't believe it   (*CP* 328)

Like another fine though very different poem, 'Sleeping on the Wing', 'Adieu . . .' was knocked out in response to a direct challenge to O'Hara's skills as an improviser, and an athletic banging at the keys is part of its appeal. But as usual with the poems of this period (1959), doubts underlie the excitement of the surface which, once glimpsed, spill shadows everywhere. This dark side is not the unconscious of the poem talking but rather its gravitational pull back into what is, as distinct from what the poet would like to be the case. O'Hara's is frequently a poetry

of the idealised family, names – Reverdy! Char! – chanted as talismans
against boredom and mortality, less famous ones – Joe! Kenneth! –
thrown in optimistically so that they too may be lifted to the gallery of
heroes. This is less a poetry of the real, to return to Helen Vendler's
doubt, than a poetry of the ideal working through an acknowledgment
of the real. The *New York Times* review of the *Collected Poems* came closer
in noting that 'If we put up with the sterile chatter and maudlin
benedictions, it is because we recognize with O'Hara that in play we
sometimes impersonate our better selves and, replenishing the sources
of our feelings, momentarily defeat passing time.'[13]

There are at least three versions of identity in play here. One is fixed;
for example, Samuel Beckett (the style of whose novel *The Unnamable* is
parodied in this poem) is a highly deliberate choice, comic ironically by
virtue of Beckett's tragic reminders of pain that puncture Reverdyan
romanticism. Identity is simultaneously open and token; Allen, Peter,
Joe, Kenneth, Shirley *et al.* are named, but it doesn't entirely matter who
they are: we all have friends like Joe. Thirdly and most subtly, identity is
presented as having to shift out of kilter in order to continue to be itself,
so that the painter Jane Freilicher has to become Jane Hazan, through
marriage, in order to continue. More darkly, General de Gaulle has to
'be Algerian' in order to keep being de Gaulle, in 1959.

Meanwhile it seems that Joe, in order to be himself, is not coming to
Kenneth's, though he is coming to lunch with Norman:

> I suspect he is making a distinction
> well, who isn't

These are the most important lines in the poem, which frequently
argues against them. It wants and does not want an unmediated,
celebratory oneness of human endeavour; 'making a distinction' is both
a curse and yet remains an impersonation of our better selves. O'Hara
and his generation wrote in the wake of Williams' assertion that anything is a fit subject for poetry, and many of their efforts were bent on
the non-judgmental inclusion of the hitherto excluded. At the same
time, O'Hara writes as a man of taste, a dandy, a critic, a curator, and so
many of the poems are Art Chronicles, to adopt the title of his selected
essays, that entail rigorous distinctions. This also may be said to be
characteristic of the New York literary family as it conjoins the radical
and the critical, much as, forty years before, the city had been the base
simultaneously for the Harlem Renaissance, John Reed's and other
writings on the Russian Revolution, imported journals of literary mod-

ernism such as the *Dial* and the *Little Review*, and Algonquin Round Table productions such as the *Smart Set*.

Three weeks prior to typing his adieu to Norman Bluhm, O'Hara composed another valediction, 'The Day Lady Died', which would in time become his most anthologised poem, and the recipient of most critical attention. 'The Day Lady Died' is overtly about the death of 'Lady Day', the jazz singer Billie Holiday, but also about the death of one of the Frank O'Haras, and the immanent disconnectedness that makes any day seen clearly a day of the dead. His great poem 'In Memory of My Feelings' had spoken of the necessary murder of sundry selves, so as to 'save the serpent in their midst' that the poet identifies with poetry (*CP* 257). Those little deaths were played out against images of national and world history in ways deriving (in so far as they derive from anywhere) from literary modernism. 'The Day Lady Died' speaks of a point of transition in cultural history that spells the demise of the modernist O'Hara. The poem calls for its narrative to be reread in the light of its ending, and so is given in its entirety:

It is 12.20 in New York a Friday
three days after Bastille day, yes
it is 1959 and I go get a shoeshine
because I will get off the 4.19 in Easthampton
at 7.15 and then go straight to dinner
and I don't know the people who will feed me

I walk up the muggy street beginning to sun
and have a hamburger and a malted and buy
an ugly NEW WORLD WRITING to see what the poets
in Ghana are doing these days
                    I go on to the bank
and Miss Stillwagon (first name Linda I once heard)
doesn't even look up my balance for once in her life
and in the GOLDEN GRIFFIN I get a little Verlaine
for Patsy with drawings by Bonnard although I do
think of Hesiod, trans. Richmond Lattimore or
Brendan Behan's new play or *Le Balcon* or *Les Nègres*
of Genet, but I don't, I stick with Verlaine
after practically going to sleep with quandariness

and for Mike I just stroll into the PARK LANE
Liquor Store and ask for a bottle of Strega and
then I go back where I came from to 6th Avenue
and the tobacconist in the Ziegfeld Theatre and
casually ask for a carton of Gauloises and a carton

of Picayunes, and a NEW YORK POST with her face on it
and I am sweating a lot by now and thinking of
leaning on the john door in the 5 SPOT
while she whispered a song along the keyboard
to Mal Waldron and everyone and I stopped breathing   (CP 325)

Although 'The Day Lady Died' is certainly one of what O'Hara called
his 'I do this, I do that' poems, almost all the published criticisms of the
elegy get hung up on this, and so misunderstand the relationship between
the diaristic minutiae of the first twenty-six lines and the arrival of the
poem's ostensive subject only in the final quatrain. Just as Helen Vendler
wanted to explain away her dislike of the familial 'name dropping' by
situating 'Adieu . . .' in a tradition of Williamsian realism, so Neal Bowers
virtually repeats her point in his rationalisation of the 'seemingly uncon-
nected activities' making up the bulk of the poem: 'Death is one of many
random things that could punctuate and focus the seemingly unconnec-
ted activities of an otherwise typical day, making everything from a
shoeshine to a bottle of Strega purchased in a liquor store glow with its
own brilliant significance.'[14] Meanwhile Paul Carroll virtually quotes
William Carlos Williams by stating that 'anything, literally, can exist in a
poem . . . in whatever way the poet chooses . . . without moral or aesthetic
significance . . .'; and concludes that the poem 'is about the common but
sobering feeling that life continues on its bumbling way despite the tragic
death of an important artist or some loved one. Trains for Easthampton
still depart at 4.19.'[15] We know that O'Hara did write the poem on the
day of Billie Holiday's death (like so many of his poems, during the lunch
hour), and that he did take the 4.19 from the old Penn Station to East
Hampton, and that he read the poem aloud that evening to painter Mike
(Goldberg) and writer Patsy (Southgate) at their home, after the dinner
out mentioned in line 6 was cancelled. Immediacy, as must by now be
evident, is important in O'Hara. Or rather, virtual or apparent immediacy, because although the poem is written in the present tense, it depicts
events in the immediate past, which are therefore remembered, and
because remembered, are necessarily reconstructed, selected in preference to rival details, doubtless angled.

    In the poem's closing lines, is it 'I', Billie Holiday's accompanist Mal
Waldron, or 'Mal Waldron and everyone and I' who 'stopped breathing', captivated by her performance? Whichever way the lines are taken
they remain ironic, given that it is she who has now quite literally
stopped breathing. Despite its moments of browsing and sleepy quandariness, the whole poem seems out of breath, rushed, dashing to make

connections between times, trains, people, presents. Yet the discon-
nections are secondary to the very powerfully, familially connected ideas
and metaphors that structure the poem and undermine the reductive
standard argument that O'Hara is a fifties–sixties radical constantly
declaiming his right to bung anything in a poem and call it art. Look at
the French connection: Bastille day, Verlaine, Bonnard, Genet's *Le
Balcon* and *Les Nègres*, Gauloises, Picayunes; then those of negritude:
shoeshine (quite probably), Ghana, *Les Nègres* again, Mal Waldron, Billie
Holiday; and finally the illicit or dangerous juxtaposed with the Bohemian, there throughout (Brendan Behan, for example) but all coming
together in the remembered image of Billie Holiday singing at a point
(though this is not made explicit in the poem) when, hounded by the
police and FBI over drugs, she was banned from living or working in
New York City. The cherished memory of hearing her sing is literally
the memory of a crime. The evening recalled by O'Hara was one when
Mal Waldron accompanied a reading by Kenneth Koch, and Billie
Holiday was persuaded out of the audience to sing, as Koch recalls,
'with her voice almost gone, just like a whisper'.[16] These connections are
reinforced by the associations of the Hamptons, which take O'Hara out
of New York only to recall more members of the family. East Hampton
was a writers' and artists' colony or weekend escape, as it had been for
the Abstract Expressionist painters, and before them the immigrant
European Surrealists such as Max Ernst and André Breton. The poem
insists at one and the same time on disconnectedness, on death breaking
through at random, but also on lines of solidarity, of familial connection
to do with art, dissidence and racial or sexual difference from the
dominant groups in society.

Like all elegies, it is about its author more than its avowed subject,
and the identification between the *chanteuse* singing against the law, and
the homosexual poet whose gayness is outlawed, must be close. An air of
foreboding hangs over the whole poem, and it is important to read the
ending as cool, as being in fact a moment frozen in time, as well as a
warm outpouring. Leaning on the door, O'Hara is stilled in his own
proleptic snapshot of the ways in which he would be pictured in time to
come. The self that dies in this poem is the one standing in an arche-
typally 1950s art-milieu, the Five Spot, where John Coltrane had played
with Thelonious Monk and so forth. But jazz would run into trouble
(i.e., pop music) in the 1960s. The self that survives in this poem is Frank
O'Hara the *shopper*. A lyric poet and lyrical consumer in the era
just prior to late capitalism, this figure looks back in his languorous

quandariness to the Bohemian *flâneur*, checking out the arcades, and forward to the *fin-de-siècle* poet who can order *The Collected Poems of Frank O'Hara* from www.amazon.com without leaving her desk. The ending of the poem is an extension of self-awareness, breathtaking in its ambition. When art turns into culture it is preserved; that is to say, perpetuated in one sense, killed in another. The day Lady Day died is also the day on which that process began, and O'Hara writes warmly so as to reverse it, restoring through memory her art to a cultural icon. To have done that would be achievement enough, but to be able at the same time so coolly to detach himself and see himself written into history from a perspective he would not live to occupy, is something else again. But then as his friend and collaborator Arnold Weinstein put it to me, Frank O'Hara is more alive dead than most people are when they're alive.

The poetry of Frank O'Hara stands in two senses at the city limits. In Battery Park City, the new extension (via a landfill site) to Manhattan's southern tip, lines from his poem 'Meditations in an Emergency' are sculpted alongside Whitman's in the railings on which one leans looking out over the Hudson toward the Statue of Liberty. In another sense, O'Hara's written city is both the culmination and the end of the modernist city that builds, in the work of Eliot, Crane and Williams, on the foundations laid by Whitman. O'Hara, like no other poet before or since, is perfectly at home in his city, and makes the reader want to be there, in some way to inhabit New York through its better self, the poem. It is this very quality of welcome and advertisement that concludes the modernist tradition of urban alienation, with its residual romanticism going back to *Les Fleurs du Mal*, and that ushers in the postmodern period of consumerism and the saturation of the city by culture. His writing also bears out Christopher Dewdney's proposition that 'one's city is a familial membership'. The apparent exclusivity of O'Hara's name-dropping becomes in truth a new inclusiveness, as the persons in his poems become representative and analogous, the family growing beyond the constriction and furrowed brow of the 'School' concept to take in lines of affiliation that are identifiably Bohemian in a 1950s tradition, but which look forward to a more contemporary sensitivity to questions of – for example – race and gender.

The locations of John Ashbery's poetry are the most wide-ranging since his one-time mentor Auden, Pound or indeed Browning, poets he recalls in terms of prolificity and scale as well as variety of spatial reference. His is frequently a comic poetry (and if anything is shared by these New York poets it is wit) and this gives a distinctive inflection to the modernist echoes that also recur in his work. The tones of Eliot, Stevens and Rilke are as present in his recent as in his early poetry, but play second fiddle to a warmth and hospitable comedy which is as nearly a philosophy as anything in their work, but which accepts the reader on a more equal and democratic footing. In 'Grand Galop' we are led to 'a worn, round stone tower' that could be a Chapel Perilous or Childe Roland's journey's end, but the windows have been boarded up with old licence plates and a sign reads 'Van Camp's Pork and Beans'.[17] If something is debunked here, it is so in a spirit that brings us back to a shared world and asks us not to dismiss its supposed trivia too hastily. Ashbery does not write about, but from and inside, the location of New York and a consciousness identified with the city, though as intrepid in ranging beyond its images as the nineteenth-century New Yorkers (and others), whose work his poetry is happy to acknowledge.

Other writers from this circle tend to shuttle between Ashbery and O'Hara in offering more reference to the literal New York than the first, and less than the second. James Schuyler, a poet whose virtually lifelong reclusiveness kept him from the acclaim his work is beginning to receive, writes as precisely about the city as he does about Vermont or his favourite subject, roses. This poem comes from the 1970s:

> *Back*
>
> from the Frick. The weather
> cruel as Henry Clay himself.
> Who put that collection together?
> Duveen? I forget. It was nice
> to see the masterpieces again,
> covered with the strikers' blood.
> What's with art anyway, that
> we give it such precedence?
> I love the paintings, that's for sure.
> What I really loved today
> was New York, its streets and
> men selling flowers and hot dogs
> in them. Mysterious town houses,
> the gritty wind. I used to live
> around here but it's changed some.
> Why? That was only thirty years ago.[18]

As New York rose in the economic firmament, it grew galleries and museums, such as the one named after Henry Clay Frick and stocked by dealers such as Joseph Duveen, intent on importing as much physical evidence of the Italian Renaissance as new money could buy. Later, covert funding by the State Department would float the Museum of Modern Art as cultural flagship in a time of Cold War, thereby giving Frank O'Hara a career. We give art 'precedence', Schuyler's lyric implies, because thriving in the muck and the 'gritty wind' of cities and circumstance, its flowering attention possesses the mysterious ability to include locations larger than itself and hold them open to inspection, a process that discloses not only the dark ironies of history but the warmer light of consciousness, reflecting on '[w]hat I really loved today'.

CHAPTER 11

Modernism deferred: Langston Hughes, Harlem and jazz montage

Peter Brooker

On 15 January 1926, Langston Hughes read first at the Washington Playhouse, then in Baltimore, and at the end of the month at a venue in Claremont Avenue near Columbia University in New York from his newly published first volume of poetry, *The Weary Blues*.[1] The volume was published by Alfred A. Knopf in a striking red, black and yellow wrapper. It carried a drawing of an angular blues pianist on its front by the Mexican caricaturist Miguel Covarrubias and an introduction by the white author, Harlem impresario, friend to Hughes and others of the 'Negro Renaissance', Carl Van Vechten. Vechten had been instrumental in securing the publication of Hughes' book with Knopf and had hosted a party in Hughes' honour in November 1925. His own controversial novel *Nigger Heaven* was also to appear later in 1926.

The reading in Washington was presided over by Alain Locke, Professor of Philosophy at Howard University in Washington and editor the previous year of the special issue of the *Survey Graphic* on black arts and culture and of the celebrated collection *The New Negro: An Interpretation* based upon it.[2] This had announced the arrival of a 'new group psychology' and 'collective effort, in race co-operation' and a social project led by 'the more advanced and representative classes' to reclaim the inspiration and advantages of American democracy.[3] 'The Negro mind', wrote Locke, 'reaches out as yet to nothing but American wants, American ideals.'[4] Locke's emphasis upon the signs of cultural renewal, the evidence of this in the pages of the collection in work by poets, fiction writers, illustrators and essayists on the spirituals, jazz, Africanism and the uniqueness of Harlem made *The New Negro* the symbolic representative text of what came to be called the Harlem Renaissance.

Some of the excitement of this new cultural identity for American blacks must have been in the air at the time of Hughes' reading, but so too undoubtedly were some of the tensions and friction comprising this formation. Many of the familiar positions and cross-currents of the

231

Renaissance move across the face of this moment and it is this dynamic, conflictual, intra- and interracial composition of the Renaissance as a whole that I mean to draw attention to. In itself, this evening in January 1926 stretched back, in a still modestly defined period, to the composition of the title poem 'The Weary Blues' in 1920 and pulled a crowded set of events and experiences forward into itself: amongst them the experience of Hughes' first published poems, notably 'The Negro Speaks of Rivers'; his final break with his father in Mexico; his travels to Africa and Europe; his first meetings with Locke and Countee Cullen, with W. E. B. Du Bois, Jessie Fauset, Blanche Knopf and others, at Harlem parties and literary events; his 'discovery' as a new young Negro poet by Vachel Lindsay at the Wardman Park Hotel in November 1925; and his recent decision to attend Lincoln, a black university, when his contemporaries pressured him to return to Columbia or apply to Harvard.

In one emerging antagonism, Van Vechten had suggested the title of Hughes' volume but this had disappointed Hughes' fellow poet Countee Cullen as catering to whites 'who want us to do only Negro things'[5] and who wondered in reviewing the volume whether blues made for poetry at all.[6] Cullen who was 'in certain ways Hughes' exact opposite'[7] preferred traditional European stanzaic forms and diction to folk forms and idioms. Like Du Bois, eminent editor of *Crisis* magazine and leader of the NAACP (National Association for the Advancement of Colored People), Cullen felt the new Negro must show the race's best artistic and intellectual side. Du Bois' opinion appeared in his offended reviews of Van Vechten's *Nigger Heaven* and of *Home to Harlem*, the uninhibited novel of the lives, loves and music of Harlem blacks by the Jamaican-born Claude McKay, whose example and contribution as associate editor of the socialist journal the *Liberator* had much impressed Hughes.[8]

There were, that is to say, profoundly conflicting views on the proper sources and definition of 'art' circulating at the very outset of the movement. These differences were compounded by the relation of black intellectuals and writers to white friends, supporters and patrons, of whom Van Vechten was one. Patronage was common but, not surprisingly, often thought to risk personal and artistic integrity and a loss of 'race pride'. Much of this thinking was targeted at Van Vechten who it was later felt had distorted Hughes' work; a charge refuted by Hughes who had, for his part, spoken out in defence of *Nigger Heaven*. They remained lifelong friends, whereas Van Vechten's friendships with Cullen and with Locke evidently cooled. One factor was that all three men were homosexual, though Van Vechten and Cullen both married. Hughes' sexuality remains mysterious, but it is clear he was propositioned by both Cullen and Locke. Locke had met him in Paris to ask for a contribution to the *Survey Graphic* and both men had travelled to Italy before separating there. On his return Hughes was affronted by Cullen's advances. This personal history of affection, ardour, misunderstanding also preceded the publication of Hughes' volume and was no doubt a further undertow on 1814 North St as Hughes read his verse.

The moment of Hughes' arrival as a poet of the Negro Renaissance with his first published volume was a moment therefore of genuine common purpose but also of less evident internal differences, upon key matters of race, art and sexuality. As such, I suggest, it provides a picture of the complex configurations of this cultural formation as a whole. There are three factors, either immediately or more distantly active in these months in 1925 and 1926, which filtered out into Hughes' work and the identity of the 'Renaissance' which I want to expand upon. The first is the major site of this formation in Harlem; the second, the role of the blues and jazz in developing a racialised black aesthetic and identity; and the third the meanings given (and which we might give) in this specifically located context and history to modernism.

One of the most striking facts about the young Hughes is the extent of his travels – in one way anticipating his prolific output across genres as one of the first self-declared professional black writers. Before *The Weary Blues* in 1926 when he was twenty-four, he had lived in Cleveland, Mexico and Washington, sailed as cabin boy on a six-month trip to West Africa, sailed twice to Holland, lived, worked and hustled in Paris and Italy.[9] Harlem was hailed in *The New Negro* as the 'race capital', 'a city within a city' and Hughes had felt its affirmative impact on first arriving for his abortive period of study at Columbia in 1921. In *The Big Sea* he writes in what was a common trope in writings of the period, of arriving at the subway of 135th Street in 1921: 'Hundreds of coloured people! . . . I went up the steps and out into the bright September sunlight. Harlem! I stood there, dropped my bags, took a deep breath and felt happy again.'[10] However, Hughes did not reside for any length of time in Harlem until later years. After reading in New York in January 1926, for example, he returned immediately on the night train to Washington where his mother was living. Either side of this date in the twenties, when he was not travelling outside the United States, he lived as a student at Lincoln University in Philadelphia and later in New Jersey, coming into Harlem for the weekends. Here – judging from the accounts in *The Big Sea* – he joined a round of literary and social gatherings, readings, shows, 'parties and parties'[11] in which he sometimes felt out of place and disenchanted by the bourgeois airs of the proceedings.

For Hughes, therefore, Harlem was a vibrant centre, 'a radiant node or cluster' in the language of European Imagism; a vortex, even, 'through which ideas were constantly rushing', and through which he himself moved, in an irregular pattern of departure and return. Just as James Weldon Johnson wished to define the area as neither colony nor ghetto but 'a city within a city',[12] so too for Hughes, as for a figure like McKay who opted for self-exile in Paris, it was a centre within a broader geo-social and artistic network, whose energies travelled back and forth along the lines of force of their lives and work. Hughes' connections with other places and peoples, including artists and writers, consorts with the view of the diasporic nature of the Renaissance, elaborated especially by James de Jongh in his *Vicious Modernism*. This was clear from the outset, however, in the recognition in *The New Negro* of the mixed West-Indian and Afro-American identities of Harlem blacks; in the connection with Europe, and especially Paris, of intellectuals like Du Bois and Locke and of jazz entertainers and celebrities like Paul Robeson and Josephine Baker.

Harlem was therefore the dynamic hub in a dispersed 'travelling' culture: at once a definite place on the map, where artists and residents discovered an enriching cultural community, 'a paradise of my own people' as Claude McKay had put it on his arrival in 1914,[13] but whose symbolic value was felt beyond itself and beyond this immediate sense of a utopian belongingness. We need to recall too how these meanings and connections radiated outwards from an evolving rather than fixed physical locale, how the place on the grid map of Manhattan dramatically changed its literal shape as well as its economic and cultural identity over these two or more decades. In the 1900s blacks lived in the Tenderloin district of lower Manhattan. By 1910, with the migration to the North from the rural South, New York's black population had increased from a few hundred to 5,000. It was at this point that blacks began to move North within the city into Harlem, first into rented accommodation, then as a house-owning bourgeoisie into what Kellner calls the 'beige colony' of the first block West of Fifth Avenue.[14] Whites resisted and then deserted the neighbourhood and house prices dropped. In the early 1920s black Harlem comprised six blocks between 125th and 131st Sts, bounded by the overcrowded crime- and poverty-stricken tenements of Fifth Avenue to the East and the luxury middle-class apartments of Eighth Avenue and Sugar Hill to the West. To the North, from 145th St, the less than two square miles of 'Coogans Bluff' was also black and contained some 200,000 residents. Lenox Avenue was a line of pool halls, cabarets and dives with some restaurants and theatres. The show piece, however, was 'Black Broadway' on Seventh Avenue from 127th to 134th Sts: a fanfare of churches, theatres, business-es, restaurants, speakeasies. Seventh Avenue, writes Kellner, 'was thriv-ing and well groomed and active all day, and from five in the afternoon until after midnight it was brilliant and glamorous and exciting'.[15]

This is the Harlem James Weldon Johnson described in *The New Negro*, expanded now to 'twenty five solid blocks' North of 125th St;[16] an 'inner city' of fine, well-priced housing and economic independence, booming entertainment and active artistic cultural life. Even so, *The New Negro* omitted to describe the poverty and discrimination originally reported in the *Survey Graphic*, and other writers – Wallace Thurman, Hughes and McKay, for example – were in their turn to represent even the Harlem of the heyday of the Renaissance differently. By the end of the decade Harlem was sliding into the recession and the further dramatic decline into the ghetto of the 1930s described by Gilbert Osofsky.

In the twenties, Harlem, we might say, 'jes grew', but, as above, this dynamism brought with it both an intensely felt collective unity and a complex pattern of social and racial differentiation. By the mid-twenties Harlem was unquestionably black. Its population numbered 175,000 black residents and in the most densely populated areas around Lenox and Fifth Avenue it supported 233 residents per acre, compared with 133 per acre in Manhattan. Most were employed as manual labourers or in menial, servicing or domestic work. Many were destitute and trapped in crowded, crime- and vice-ridden tenements without the mobility of the elite blacks of the literary and artistic intelligentsia.[17] Like whites the latter came and went; though, once again, on different terms and even at different times of day. There were 120 entertainment spots in the ten-block area off Lenox Avenue, 25 or so along 'Jungle Alley' along 133rd St,[18] but, as is well known, some were for mixed audiences and some, notably the Cotton Club, were for whites only. Rent parties for blacks took place in Harlem, other kinds of parties downtown.

A revealing illustration of these kinds of differences, involving Hughes, occurred, casually enough so it would seem, on an occasion in May 1925. Charles S. Johnson hosted an impressive banquet to an-nounce the winners of a poetry competition run by *Opportunity* magazine in a Fifth Avenue restaurant near 24th St in downtown Manhattan. Here, writes Rampersad, was 'the greatest gathering of black and white literati ever assembled in one room'.[19] Hughes won first prize for the poem 'The Weary Blues' and after the banquet accepted Van Vechten's invitation to meet him and some others 'for a night on the town' in Harlem at the Manhattan Casino and then the Bamville Club. Musicians from the Cotton Club were going on to the more egalitarian Bamville where blacks and whites danced in mixed couples.

Evidently, Harlem – in its internally differently coded sites and protocols – was for whites a place of spectacle: an exotic 'marginal zone'[20] or 'erotic utopia'[21] where whites could explore their late-night darker selves. Van Vechten, whom Hughes visited the next day with his manuscript of poems, lived downtown on West 55th St. Here Hughes often stayed or attended Van Vechten's celebrated parties. Another guest and herself a party-giver *extraordinaire* was the black heiress A'Leila Walker. She had asked Wallace Thurman to secure her an autographed copy of Hughes' *Weary Blues* in January 1926 and decorated a wall of the elaborate 'Dark Tower' tea room at her mansion on 126th St with a section of the title poem. Harlem too had its wealthy black middle class.

The 'city within a city' was itself internally coded, therefore, as a residential area (for poor, working-class blacks) and entertainment centre (for middle-class blacks and whites): intimately connected to the white and black world of Manhattan and beyond. Emerging technologies and modes of production reinforced this social and spatial hybridity. The offices of the important journals and white-owned publishing industries, for example, were in Manhattan and the NAACP and National Urban League had been established there since the 1910s. It was this materially based cultural apparatus of (in Harlem) theatres, clubs, fugitive magazines, the important meeting place of the 135th St branch of the New York Public Library, and (in Manhattan) of patrons, publishers and related organisations which supported the Renaissance writers and brought them to public attention. And it was this development which at the same time distinguished Harlem from Washington where Hughes first read *The Weary Blues*. Harlem was more 'modern' than Washington because New York was more modern, in its technologies, communications and more egalitarian culture: a locus for the publication of ideas of the modern 'New Negro' and in the NAACP and National Urban League a centre for reform and organised resistance to racial injustice.

Within the larger modernising metropolis Harlem was more of a magnet, a 'Mecca' in the sub-title of the special number of the *Survey Graphic*, than an enclave. It drew peoples and ideas toward it but also expanded and exhaled in ways that re-shaped and patterned the developing city in a series of indentations and cross-hatched lines of communication. The picture emerges of a stratified and permeable heteropolis, experienced simultaneously as an autonomous but dependent, and in significant ways subordinate community within the metropolis. As such, the dynamic physical site of Harlem itself expressed the very 'twoness' of the American Negro as famously described by W. E. B. Du Bois; embodying in its spatial relations the paradox and hope of being at once black and American. In James Weldon Johnson's description, in what turns out to be an unintended but telling echo of aesthetic modernism, Harlem was 'a large scale laboratory experiment in the race problem'.[22]

In January 1926 at the Washington reading, once more, Hughes had planned a jazz performance for the interval. His chosen musician was from the slum area of Seventh Avenue. Alain Locke had however stepped in and hired a performer who could provide more polite jazz.[23] The incident clearly reveals how differences of class and artistic sensibility helped determine the public image and consumption of the new Negro art. That this should be expressed through music is especially significant. Hughes had already decided on an aesthetic which drew upon African American and 'folk' sources, but folk art and music, most conspicuously, had an ambiguous status for Renaissance intellectuals and supporters. Locke, like Du Bois, looked more to the spirituals for this folk source, the 'kernel' indeed for Locke of black folk song, praised for its 'universality', intricacy and 'tragic profundity'.[24] As such, spirituals promised to stand not only as the 'classic folk expression' of the Negro but as 'America's folk song'.[25] His thoughts were accompanied in *The New Negro* by an essay on jazz by J. A. Rogers. Hutchinson and Gilroy have stressed Rogers' case for the democratising influence of jazz but this view in his essay is combined with much else which echoes contradictorily through his own and others' arguments.[26]

This tension surfaces especially in Rogers' view of 'the jazz spirit' as 'being primitive'.[27] In one set of associations where 'being primitive' is equated with 'frankness and sincerity' and 'naturalness', it can be extrapolated as 'a leveller [which] makes for democracy'. On the other hand, where the spontaneity and 'physical basis' of jazz's primitivism is responsible for 'its present vices and vulgarizations, its sex informalities, its morally anarchic spirit', it stands in need of musical refinement and cultivation. This is provided, says Rogers, by 'white orchestras of the type of the Paul Whiteman and Vincent Lopez organizations that are now demonstrating the finer possibilities of jazz music' and in the flattering adoption of American Negro jazz in 'serious modernistic music' notably by French composers. What in one sentence is 'vulgarization' becomes 'primitive new vigor' in another. Rogers ends with a call 'to lift and divert it into nobler channels'[28] – a sentiment and mission echoed, without the tensions of his essay, in the evolutionary schema proposed later by Locke, by which the crudities of Chicago's 'hot jazz' are put through the sieve of the more melodic 'sweet jazz' of New York to produce the third, elevated category of the 'jazz classics' of the big orchestras and the 'symphonic' or 'classical jazz' of Paris. Though Negro, Locke comments, jazz is 'fortunately . . . human enough to be universal in appeal and expressiveness'.[29]

Locke was wary of commercialisation and, for all his evident cultural elitism, positively acknowledged the technical expertise of jazz performers. Others like Countee Cullen would ignore the folk source altogether. Reviewing *The Weary Blues*, Cullen questioned whether blues or jazz poetry should be admitted to 'that select and austere circle of high literary expression which we call poetry'.[30] He wished, he said, repeatedly, to be 'a poet, not a Negro poet'.[31] His theme was taken up by George Schuyler and Hughes replied to both positions in his famous essay 'The Negro Artist and the Racial Mountain' in June 1926. Here he hit out at 'the smug Negro middle class' dogged by the subconscious whisper that 'white is best'.[32] Instead he turns to the 'common people' and to jazz, 'their child', an 'inherent expression of Negro life in America' and 'the tom-tom of revolt against weariness in a white world'.[33]

Hughes' riposte to Cullen and Schuyler served as a manifesto of 'American Negro' poetry; a call to re-articulate blackness in a white America – at the risk of offending either (or both) whites or blacks. Two contemporary incidents suggested how fraught this enterprise was, however. Van Vechten had hailed jazz as 'the only indigenous American music of true distinction',[34] and as part of his researches into its black roots had consulted Hughes on the blues for an article in *Vanity Fair*. After reading in Washington, Hughes met Bessie Smith at Baltimore and asked her opinion of Van Vechten's essay. She was dismissive and saw the blues as a means to making money, not art. If Hughes meant to be in touch with this black blues sensibility he was not, any more than he shared Van Vechten's innocent new enthusiasm and taste

for light jazz. As an 'American Negro' poet he was positioned somewhere between and to the side of both raw blues singer and white
essayist, while in quite another world from most American Negro
leaders.

At the heart of differences on the new Negro, therefore, there were
problematic constructions of folk art, the blues and jazz: the culture of
'the black folk' or 'masses' who artists and intellectuals sought to represent and direct. The ambiguities were such that spirituals or blues or
jazz could be either esteemed as a positive and authentic cultural
expression or rejected as a demeaning presentation of racial identity.
The uncomprehending 'coloured near-intellectuals' of Hughes' essay
tended to view spirituals, pre-eminently, and the blues, less comfortably,
in primitivist or essentialist terms as expressions of an Africanist or
Southern rural folk culture, and to see jazz as the degraded culture of
modern urban blacks. For those seeking uplift, jazz was too evidently
tainted with inartistic and untutored performance, with an unabashed
display of sexuality and with juke joints, drink and prostitution: in short
with 'low' parts of the city, mind and body. But jazz too was constructed
in divergent ways. The dives and cabarets arguably comprised the core
of Harlem's symbolism, the compound 'chronotope' of its identity in
space and time, and the jazz performed there echoed Harlem's ambiguities: at once in Rogers' terms 'a joyous revolt', the 'release of all the
suppressed emotions'[35] and the scene of vice, vulgarity and anarchy.

What Renaissance leaders feared was that 'jazz abandon', in Rogers'
coinage,[36] confirmed the worst stereotypes of the Negro to white voyeurs
and cultural arbitrators, and thus to themselves; hence the arguments
for its necessary refinement and the defence of its diluted and European
'classical' forms. On the other hand, 'the primitive' was esteemed for
being precisely this. Both Hughes and Zora Neale Hurston were on this
count recruited by the immensely rich white patron Mrs Charlotte
(Rufus Osgood) Mason to recover the lost African essence of the American Negro. From 1928 she financed Hughes at college, on his travels and
in his New Jersey lodgings. The experience was to prove traumatic and
the relationship broke down (with some conniving by both Hurston and
Locke) over the issue precisely of 'being primitive'. In Hughes' own,
evidently selective and compressed account in *The Big Sea*,[37] Mrs Mason
had objected to the poem 'Advertisement for the Waldorf Astoria'
which exposed how the new hotel exacerbated discrepancies between
the poor blacks of Harlem and the vast wealth of whites on Park
Avenue. He sat silently while she told him how he had failed himself and

her. It came down, he reflected later, 'to the old impasse between white and Negro'.[38] But if this was the governing division, it carried with it manifest differences of social class, competing notions of the primitive black and artistic creativity, and the personal psychological needs on both sides: of the young brown man, estranged from his family, and the dowager patron who insisted on being called 'godmother'. The involvement of Hurston and Locke, throughout, and more distantly of Van Vechten in the final squabbles and separation in this episode, confirm how these general issues were woven once more into the fabric of gendered, sexual and professional relationships between friends and collaborators. The cultural and artistic movement we unify under the name of the 'Harlem Renaissance' proved once more to be a mutable formation showing all the marks, on these different levels of personality and idea, of divergent and common endeavour, of support and rivalry, and of unequal power.

The traumatic break with Mrs Mason in 1930 was a break with a sentimentalised version of Hughes' own project and the accompanying appeal to an essentialised blackness. 'I did not feel the rhythms of the primitive surging through me', he wrote, 'I was only an American Negro – who had loved the surface of Africa and the rhythms of Africa – but I was not Africa. I was Chicago and Kansas City and Broadway and Harlem.'[39] He emerged with the socially grounded sense of black cultural identity of the 'Negro Mountain' essay and his own class-based allegiance confirmed. It was out of this, I believe, paradoxically as the Renaissance neared its end, that Hughes came to produce an urban-based populist modernism.

The thirties underlined Hughes' allegiance to black proletarian experience and cultural forms, now more emphatically expressed in favour of jazz rather than blues. J. A. Rogers had equated jazz with Americanism: it 'ranks with the movie and the dollar as a foremost exponent of modern Americanism', it had absorbed 'that tremendous spirit of go, the nervousness, lack of conventionality . . . of the American, white or black, as compared with the more rigid formal nature of the Englishman or German'.[40] For their part Europeans, and the German avant-garde, in particular, welcomed jazz and America as joint symbols of the machine age.[41] The black jazz entertainer and America were admired as discordant emblems of an exotic otherness and frenetic modernity combined: a fevered collision of the primitive and the new world. Meanwhile, the vocabulary of 'newness' and 'renaissance' which percolated through the decade, the association of jazz particularly with urban life and with the developing technologies of transport (conveying musicians on an emerging 'circuit' from city to city and continent to continent), of radio, recording and promotion, only confirmed this metaphorical association with progress and social modernity.[42]

But if Harlem and the new Negro and jazz were 'modern' was the latter also 'modernist'? The answer I think is that the jazz of the 1920s was new but evolutionary rather than revolutionary, that its sexual aura was an affront to middle-class respectability in the way that some European modernisms were, but that for all the differences of colour and commercialism between, say, the Fletcher Henderson and Paul Whiteman bands, it was primarily a dance music and, unlike those modernisms, a broadly social, popular art. A 'modernist' jazz appeared, I believe, in the 1940s and 1950s, well after the generally recognised period of the Renaissance, and along with it the most conspicuous and sustained examples of modernist 'jazz poetry' by Hughes, in the sequences *Montage of a Dream Deferred* (1951) and *Ask your Mama* (1961). I want to discuss the first poem in these terms below. Much depends in this, of course, on how we conceive of modernism. At its least controversial this implies a marked degree of formal experimentation within the terms of a given medium. Modernist art comes therefore to claim a self-regarding autonomy – in a way that jazz and swing bands did not. More depends, however, on how this internal innovation addresses the newness of social modernity, on how it is received in this society, on its ideological inflection by class, gender and ethnicity and on its relation to popular culture. The terms of debate in the present instance on the construction of modernism in relation to black writing and culture are most usefully mapped in the positions taken by Houston Baker and George Hutchinson, both of which bear interestingly on Hughes' poem. I want to consider these first.

In *Modernism and the Harlem Renaissance*, Baker directly challenges the hegemony of the Anglo-American-Irish canon of literary modernism. In place of its limited ideas of 'civilisation' and supporting critical categories, he proposes a '"renaissancism" in Afro-American expressive culture as a whole'[43] stretching across the longer modern period of the 1880s to the 1930s. He views this black tradition as exercising either a 'mastery of form' or 'deformation of mastery': discursive strategies by which African-American culture has assimilated and remobilised dominant white discourse in the interests of a 'quintessential' Afro-American spirit or racial 'genius'.[44] Hutchinson, rightly, critiques the binarism of Baker's model and the essentialist notion of black identity it invites. He

stresses instead the 'diverse interracial and interethnic cultural resources' impinging upon and in tension with a conviction of the 'cultural
wealth of black America'.[45] However, this is in the end itself unper-
suasive. Firstly, because the description of an 'intercultural matrix' and
of '*kinship*' across 'ostensibly opposite racial traditions'[46] risks flattening
out what are artistic, social and racialised inequalities, and, secondly,
because while he speaks of 'American modernism' and of 'African
American modernism', Hutchinson does not define these sufficiently in
aesthetic or formal terms.[47] Modernism abuts in his study upon the
leading 'problematic of cultural nationality' and is composed of tendencies in pragmatist philosophy, anthropology and democratic theory
which he tends to assume were an active part of the thinking of the
participants.[48] No doubt he avoids a definition of aesthetic modernism
because this has been corralled by advocates of European high modernism. The result, however, is that this domain of artistic activity is
surrendered rather than reoccupied.

In fact, the kind of description one wants throughout is less a formalist
definition than an account of the terms and criteria by which and when
'high modernism' was established as a settled orthodoxy. What this
would make clear is that, excepting Graves and Riding's *Survey of
Modernist Poetry* in 1927, definitions of modernism, as such, did not
appear until American critics of the 1950s began to ruminate on the
passing of this paradigm.[49] 'Modernism' was therefore a retrospective
construction which did not exist in the mind of its participants in the
same terms as it did for its conservers. It was only at this later point also
that alternative modernisms and 'post modernism' began to come into
view. Baker's 'renaissancism' of 1987 refutes this already waning model
and the limitations of its historical as much as racialised perspective. In
reconfiguring black writing and arts of the earlier twentieth century (and
thus beyond this era) he is in effect refuting the criticism of the mid-
century. Though this critical orthodoxy is his opponent, he tends, like
Hutchinson, to ignore it; and by the same token to ignore the literature
it construed this way.

If we have this historicised cultural construction of modernisms in
mind, the idea of 'renaissancism' and an emphasis upon an interethnic
intertextuality both become appropriate to Hughes. Hughes had
modelled his verse upon American, populist or democratic examples,
both black and white: namely, Walt Whitman, Carl Sandburg and
Claude McKay. In *Montage of a Dream Deferred* the resources of this

tradition were joined with jazz idioms and structure under the organising concept of 'montage' drawn from the vocabulary of European film
and painting. Hughes had entitled a poem 'Montage' in *One-Way Ticket*
(1948) and might have been influenced by the explicitly montaged
composition of John Dos Passos' *USA* (1938). Rampersad reports anyway that Hughes felt that montage was 'the crucial medium of the
twentieth century' and that this coincided with his awareness of the
transformation in jazz by Dizzy Gillespie, Thelonius Monk and other
musicians producing bop and bebop.[50] This was the modernist moment
of jazz composition, when New York became known as 'the jazz capital'
rather than 'race capital' of the world and a moment too when leading
black musicians, notably Miles Davis at the end of the forties, began to
play with white musicians such as Gerry Mulligan, Gil Evans and
Kenny Baker.

Hughes' intentions are clear in the original prefatory note to the
sequence of poems:

In terms of current Afro-American popular music and the sources from which
it has progressed – jazz, ragtime, swing, blues, boogie-woogie, and be-bop – this
poem on contemporary Harlem, like be-bop is marked by conflicting changes,
sudden nuances, sharp and impudent interjections, broken rhythms, and passages sometimes in the manner of the jam session, sometimes the popular song,
punctuated by riffs, runs, breaks, and disc-tortions of the music of a community
in transition.[51]

Montage consequently tracks this community through the psycho-
geography of Harlem locales (Lenox, Minton's, Small's, The Harlem
Branch Y), following life on the street and in time through the passage
from morning to night in an echo of the twilight areas and stark
contrasts between black and white. The poem's social content, vernacular idiom and jazz form are unmistakable. As a poem of sound and
speech, its jazz riffs, trills, neologisms ('combinate', 'trickeration') and
the occasional blues refrain punctuate a sequence of often juxtaposed
'conversationing' voices – of children, women and men expressing
resignation, defiant self-affirmation, cynicism, and the humour of laugh-
ing back 'in all the wrong places'.[52]

These voices speak of the embedded inequalities of this world ('I
know I can't be president'), of its racism and discrimination and the
relative safety of Harlem ('Not a Movie'); the passing equivalence of
white and black (at 'Subway Rush Hour', 'mingled so close . . . so near

no room for fear') and most profoundly of their persistent, complex, reluctant interdependence ('a part of you, instructor. / You are white – / Yet a part of me, as I am part of you / That's American'; 'Theme for English B'). So the poem moves in a zig-zag of single notes, asides and solos against the emotional drumbeat ('Harlem's Heartbeat')[53] of the dream and the dream deferred which rumbles underneath, breaks the surface, and runs the poem to its cumulative end in a jam session of its structuring motifs, themes and phrasing.

We can think with some justice of the poem as being at once 'dialogic', in the full sense of combining consensual and dissident voices in Bakhtin's use of this term, and as a 'jazz poem' which matches the rhythms, harmonies and dissonance of jazz performance.[54] One of the best descriptions of jazz so conceived remains Ralph Ellison's – who felt he had played a role in introducing Hughes to bop and to whom, with Fanny Ellison, 'Montage' was dedicated. Ellison wrote of jazz, with bebop and Charlie Parker in mind, as a dialogic and combative art in which each improvised solo flight springs from a challenge with other musicians; 'each true jazz moment' he saw as 'a definition of identity: as individual, as member of a collectivity and as a link in the chain of tradition'.[55]

Ellison's account closely echoes the general description of modernism offered above and by Harvey.[56] Jazz is 'modernist' by virtue of its internal formal experiment and bebop answers especially to this definition. We can go beyond this, however, if we read into relations between the innovative solo, group dynamics and tradition of jazz, the tensions between the individual and the social mass marking social modernity. Indeed, Nanry's account of jazz and modernity suggests just such a homology between jazz composition and the relation of the individual to the social collective in the new modern city. Jazz, and bebop in particular, comes to model the 'disjunction and uprootedness' experienced by city dwellers and their enforced, 'often painful' search for 'commonality'.[57]

We might want to distinguish between the weaker or stronger, more exploratory and questioning forms that either jazz or jazz poetry can take along these lines. In which case we would need to think in terms of a critical transformation rather than a reflexive homology between artistic and social forms. Any judgment of Hughes' Montage in these terms must take account of its internal form, as above, and social content, but also of its critical purpose and the relation between this 'modernist' jazz poem by a black poet and the prevailing modernist orthodoxy.

The 'boogie-woogie rumble' of the dream runs underneath, is passed on to become common knowledge ('ain't you heard?'); an acquired rhythm shaping a shared consciousness that recognises this deferral as its own experience. The poem's vignettes present strategies for survival and sociality (to 'Dig and Be Dug / In Return');[58] seizing the times which interrupt this rhythm and bring a sunny Sunday (when 'Harlem has its / washed-and-ironed-and-cleaned-best out') or money or love: the lucky break in lives ruled by chance. Sometimes these are stories of individuals, often of couples or of the community who realise a moment of joy and oneness in song or dance or in a street parade. Toward its close, the poem extends its sympathies toward other ethnicities, to Jews and Hispanics in Harlem and (though barely) to whites downtown ('Likewise', 'Good Morning', 'Comment on Curb').

The sense of community here is splintered and unequal but these groups are felt, if fleetingly, to experience a common frustration of their desires. The poem asks 'What happens to a dream deferred? Does it dry up, fester, sag, *Or does it explode?*'[59] The poem warns, therefore, of unrest and riot, such as had occurred in Harlem in the 1930s, but there is no sense that this would be mobilised through any organised social agency. Here, evidently, the poem stumbles. As an expression of collective frustration it seeks a collective solution. This was provided in the poem's first appearance in the credo of America's political character and destiny embodied in the poem 'Freedom Train'. However, this was removed from the sequence by Hughes for the *Selected Poems* of 1959. What remains of the *'Dream within a dream'* of American democracy is a fantasy of jitterbugging, singing unity in Harlem ('Projection') and of its two-tone 'gold and brown' wrapped in 'dancing sound' ('College Formal', 'Renaissance Casino', 'Island'). The change withdraws the earlier belief in the inevitability of the American way but does not abandon the ideal of democracy. The resulting tension, we might say, embodies its eventual structure of feeling, an unresolved duet of black in white, white in black ('a part of me, as I am a part of you').

We might argue too that this tension – felt in the registration of a fragmented, expectant consciousness and an uneasy, because willed and rhetorical, conviction in a renewed cultural and ideological unity – is characteristic of many 'classic' modernist poems. I do not want to suggest that Hughes' *Montage* is finally or fundamentally like *The Waste Land* or the *Cantos*. It shares a topology or problematic with these and other modernist texts, a structure of aspiration and failure to achieve coherence, but there is much too that it does not share; in its sources, its social complaint and democratic sympathies. It is odd perhaps too to think of a modernist poem being produced in 1951. If it is this, it would seem to confirm Baker's argument that black writing renews itself outside the confines of the orthodox Anglo-Irish/American paradigm. The point, however, once more, is that 'canonic' modernism was constructed after the event and that white culture is also (of course) engaged in a process of renewal and consolidation; indeed, that both cultures were involved at this moment, as earlier, in the process of cultural re-definition.

What makes this clear is the appearance in the early 1950s of Ellison's 'modernist' *Invisible Man* and Melvin B. Tolson's 'high modernist' 'E & O.E' and *Libretto for the Republic of Liberia*, a work Rampersad describes as 'the most hyper-European, unpopulist poem ever penned by a black writer'.[60] Both writers offer versions of 'black modernism' which contrast significantly with Hughes' work, as was clear at the time. I want to comment briefly on the example of Tolson. His highly allusive fifteen-page 'E & O.E' appeared with footnotes in *Poetry* magazine (which had had a long association with literary modernism). It was championed there by Karl Shapiro who had earlier rejected poems by Hughes. The same number also ran an essay by William Carlos Williams damning Carl Sandburg, one of Hughes' major inspirations. Tolson's *Libretto* was hailed by the *New York Times* as the equal of Eliot's *Waste Land*, Crane's *The Bridge* and Williams' *Paterson*. Allen Tate praised Tolson as the first Negro poet to have 'assimilated completely the full poetic language of his time and by implication the language of the Anglo-American poetic tradition'.[61] Tolson had succeeded in producing an erudite and inaccessible modernism for a minority and in producing himself as a latter day version of Countee Cullen who wanted to be 'a poet, not a Negro poet'. The assumption in such an aim is that poetry is above race and ethnicity; that it is 'colourless'. But this apparent invisibility is the very power which whiteness as a received and unseen norm possesses.[62] Had Tolson, though a black poet, produced a 'white modernism' for the admirers of T. S. Eliot, or in Baker's terms performed a 'deformation of mastery', re-appropriating hegemonic modernism for the purposes of black culture? The reception of the poem would suggest the first.

What, to put this matter in other terms, seemed to be at issue at this moment was a prevailing cultural 'taste': a compound of the power of the critic, a now 'modernist' tradition, and an aesthetic which esteemed complexity, seriousness and artistic dedication and dismissed simplicity, commercialism and the use of 'folk' idioms. Hughes was accused of all of the latter, but this 'taste' will not break into white versus black. If Tolson succumbed to the example of Eliot, Ellison committed himself to a serious dedication to art and distanced himself from Hughes on that count. Likewise, the jazz of the 1940s and 1950s sought to create a taste for complexity so as to outrun the white business industry and the standardised black and white jazz of the previous era and so establish itself as a black avant-garde art form. Hughes aimed in *Montage* to negotiate between this experimentalism and a common black experience in the name of a future for the American Negro. Such were the terms of his 'populist modernism'.

We may be able to recognise finally, however, that in the 1990s these quarrels over definition are behind us. Raymond Williams suggests that we can make the necessary move beyond the fixities of modernism (and postmodernism) by thinking of how we make 'a modern *future* in which community may be imagined again'.[63] Hughes' 'populist modernism' was generally, and in the terms of one of the poems of *Montage*, a 'Projection', oriented, in its directness, whimsy and unresolved complexities, toward the future – as Williams' remarks are and as the work of Walt Whitman, Hughes' consistent inspiration, also was. To be modern, black and American – this in the end was the deferred common dream of a future democracy upon which Hughes improvised.

Notes

LOCATING MODERNISMS: AN OVERVIEW

1 Peter Nicholls, *Modernisms: A Literary Guide* (London: Macmillan, 1995), p. vii. Other significant reconsiderations of modernism include Raymond Williams' *The Politics of Modernism: Against the New Conformists*, ed. Tony Pinkney (London: Verso, 1989) and its exploration of the tensions between modernist avant-gardes in terms of political praxis. Marjorie Perloff takes a different, twin-track approach in *The Poetics of Indeterminacy: Rimbaud to Cage*, 2nd edn (Evanston: Northwestern University Press, 1983), where she discriminates between a poetics of modernism which follows the symbolist tradition and the anti-symbolist poetics of what Perloff calls 'indeterminacy'. In her later *The Dance of the Intellect: Studies in the Poetry of the Pound Tradition* (Cambridge University Press, 1985), Perloff acknowledges that this dichotomy is perhaps too neat, yet the signature piece in *Dance*, the essay 'Pound/Stevens: whose era?' again proposes a bifurcated modernism, a polarity between Pound as purveyor of indeterminacy and Stevens as the inheritor of symbolist modes of signification.

2 Charles Bernstein, *A Poetics* (Cambridge, Mass: Harvard University Press, 1992), pp. 93, 94.

3 Peter Brooker, *New York Fictions: Modernity, Postmodernism, The New Modern* (Harlow: Longman, 1996), p. 8.

4 Malcolm Bradbury and James McFarlane (eds.), *Modernism* (Harmondsworth: Penguin, 1976), p. 95.

5 Even Ezra Pound, that most 'international' of modernist poets could, in Canto 82, rue that 'ignorance of locality' which, according to Pearce, means that 'men do not know themselves in terms of the very places which give them their culture': Ezra Pound, *The Cantos* (London: Faber and Faber, 1975), p. 525; Roy Harvey Pearce, *The Continuity of American Poetry*, 2nd edn (Middletown: Wesleyan University Press, 1987), p. 86.

6 Georges Hugnet, in 'The Dada Spirit in Painting', argues that, during the First World War, 'Dada's internationalism was an element in its subversiveness'; yet in his 'En Avant Dada: A History of Dadaism', Richard Huelsenbeck discusses the rise of German Expressionism as a 'national achievement' and makes it clear that, in his opinion, German Dada ought to address

German concerns, concerns which Huelsenbeck explicitly opposes to those of Tristan Tzara and other Dadaists: Robert Motherwell (ed.), *The Dada Painters and Poets*, 2nd edn (Cambridge, Mass.: The Belknap Press of Harvard University Press, 1981), pp. 131, 39–40, 41.

7 As Brooker suggests, we need to find 'some passage between the simplified, *papier mâché* Scylla and Charybdis so often labelled modernism and post-modernism'. Using the term 'the new modern' in place of 'postmodernism', Brooker says that 'the "new modern" cannot in my reckoning come simply and dramatically "after" (in the sense that the prefix "post" is often understood) but only from "within" the modern': Brooker, *New York Fictions*, pp. 131, 15. From a philosophical and sociological perspective Albrecht Wellmer argues for 'a conception of modernity which is wider than that of many postmodernists', basing his claim that we have not reached 'the end of modernity' on the thesis that 'the critique of modernity has been part of the modern spirit since its very inception': 'If there is something new in postmodernism, it is not the radical critique of modernity, but the redirection of this critique . . . [P]ostmodernism at its best might be seen as a self-critical – a sceptical, ironic, but nevertheless unrelenting – form of modernism; a modernism beyond utopianism, scientism and foundationalism; in short a post*metaphysical* modernism': Albrecht Wellmer, *The Persistence of Modernity*, trans. David Midgley (Oxford: Polity, 1991), p. vii.

8 Terry Eagleton, *Heathcliff and the Great Hunger: Studies in Irish Culture* (London: Verso, 1995), p. 285.

9 Marjorie Perloff, *The Futurist Moment: Avant-Garde, Avant Guerre, and the Language of Rupture* (University of Chicago Press, 1986), p. 36.

10 J. C. C. Mays, 'Geoliterature', *Poetry Ireland Review* 43/44 (1994), 76; David Jordan (ed.), *Regionalism Reconsidered* (New York: Garland, 1994); Francesco Lorrigio, 'Regionalism and Theory', in Jordan, *Regionalism Reconsidered*, p. 3. See Robert Penn Warren's warning that 'If regionalism is to mean anything at all, it must not be . . . another fad, another facet of our eclecticism' in the light of, for instance, Jerome Rothenberg's 'ethno-poetics', where the Library of Congress Cataloguing-in-Publication data for his *A Seneca Journal* is 'Seneca Indians – Poetry'; see, tangentially, Rothenberg's argument that the 'personal presence', the artist as performer, 'is an instance . . . of localization, of a growing concern with particular and local definitions; for what . . . can be more local than the person?' in comparison with Philip Fisher's claim that 'The regionalism of our own times is a regionalism of race and gender'; and see the anthology *A Geography of Poets*, described by Edward Field (its editor) as 'the most significant development in American poetry since the emergence of the Beats and the New York School of the 50s': Robert Penn Warren, 'Some Don'ts For Literary Regionalists', *American Review* 8 (1936), 148; Jerome Rothenberg, *A Seneca Journal* (New York: New Directions, 1978); Jerome Rothenberg, 'New Models, New Visions: Some Notes Toward a Poetics of Performance', in *The Norton Anthology of Postmodern American Poetry* (New York: Norton, 1994),

p. 643; Philip Fisher (ed.), *The New American Studies* (Berkeley: University of California Press, 1991), p. xii; Edward Field (ed.), *A Geography of Poets* (New York: Bantam, 1979); Field's remarks are cited in William E. Mallory and Paul Simpson-Housley (eds.), *Geography and Literature* (Syracuse University Press, 1987), p. 13.

11 Warren, 'Some Don'ts', p. 143; see Wendell Berry, 'Writer and Region', *Hudson Review* 60 (1987), 15–30.

12 Michael Kowalewski, 'Bioregional Perspectives in American Literature', in Jordan, *Regionalism Reconsidered*, p. 35; Lorrigio, in Jordan, *Regionalism Reconsidered*, p. 4.

13 'I take SPACE to be the central fact to man born in America': Charles Olson, *Call Me Ishmael* (1947) (Baltimore: Johns Hopkins University Press, 1997), p. 11.

14 Robert Crawford, *Devolving English Literature* (Oxford University Press, 1992), pp. 217, 218–19.

15 'Through the local Olson seeks his alternative "universal"': Graham Clarke, 'The Poet as Archaeologist: Charles Olson's Letters of Origin', in F. W. Butterfield (ed.), *Modern American Poetry:* (London: Vision Press, 1984), p. 168.

16 See Alan Bold (ed.), *The Thistle Rises: An Anthology of Poetry and Prose by Hugh MacDiarmid* (London: Hamish Hamilton, 1984), p. 254.

17 Hugh MacDiarmid, *The Complete Poems of Hugh MacDiarmid*, 2 vols. (Harmondsworth: Penguin, 1985), vol. I, p. 423; David Jones, *The Anathemata* (1952) (London: Faber and Faber, 1972), p. 69.

18 Quoted in David Harvey, *The Condition of Postmodernity* (Oxford: Basil Blackwell, 1989), p. 25.

19 Tony Conran, *Frontiers in Anglo-Welsh Poetry* (Cardiff: University of Wales Press, 1997), p. 109.

20 Drew Milne, 'David Jones: A Charter for Philistines', in Iain Sinclair (ed.), *Conductors of Chaos* (London: Picador, 1996), p. 262.

21 Donald Westling, '"Easier to Die Than to Remember": A Bakhtinian Reading of Basil Bunting', *Sharp Study and Long Toil: Basil Bunting Special Issue, Durham University Journal Special Supplement*, ed. Richard Caddel (1995), 93.

22 Charles Olson, *The Maximus Poems*, ed. George F. Butterick (Berkeley: University of California Press, 1983), p. 104.

23 See Malcolm Bradbury, 'A Generation Lost and Found', in *Dangerous Pilgrimages* (London: Secker and Warburg, 1995), pp. 295–358.

24 Malcolm Cowley, *Exile's Return* (1934) (Harmondsworth: Penguin, 1994), p. 206, p. 9; Georg Lukacs, quoted in Jordan, *Regionalism Reconsidered*, p. 24; George Steiner, quoted in Mallory and Simpson-Housley, *Geography and Literature*, p. 4; Leslie Fiedler, *Love and Death in the American Novel* (1960) (Harmondsworth: Penguin, 1984), p. 355.

25 See James Hoopes, *Van Wyck Brooks* (Amherst: University of Massachusetts Press, 1977); H. L. Mencken, *Prejudices*, ed. James T. Farrell (New York: Vintage, 1958).

26 Alain Locke (ed.), *The New Negro* (1925), rpt in Paul Lauter *et al.* (eds.), *The Heath Anthology of American Literature*, 2nd edn, 2 vols. (Lexington, Mass.: Heath, 1994), vol. II, pp. 1587–8. For an extended discussion of links between the Irish Literary Revival and the Harlem Renaissance, see Tracy Mishkin, *The Harlem and Irish Renaissances* (Gainesville: University Press of Florida, 1998).

27 Van Wyck Brooks, quoted in Arthur Frank Wertheim, *The New York Little Renaissance* (New York University Press, 1976), p. 175.

28 John Burt, *Robert Penn Warren and American Idealism* (New Haven: Yale University Press, 1988), p. 11.

29 Ralph Maud, *What Does Not Change: The Significance of Charles Olson's 'The Kingfishers'* (Madison and Teaneck: Fairleigh Dickinson University Press, 1998), p. 22.

30 Crawford, *Devolving English Literature*, p. 227. Eliot's poetics would hold sway in English poetry until the advent of 'Movement' poets like Philip Larkin (born in 1922, the year of the publication of *The Waste Land*) who argued for the recovery of an essential 'Englishness' in English poetry, the implication being that modernist poetics lead to obfuscation not only of the text but also of national identity. William Carlos Williams also attacked *The Waste Land* and defined his own project of American cultural localism in contradistinction to Eliot, prefiguring Charles Olson's critique of Eliot in his poem 'The Kingfishers'. Williams described Eliot's poem as a disaster which set American poetry back by twenty years by returning it 'to the classroom just at the moment when I felt that we were on the point of an escape to matters much closer to the essence of a new art form itself – rooted in the locality which should give it fruit'. Williams, who had said of Eliot in 1939, 'I distrust that bastard more than any writer I know in the world today', also likened the effect of *The Waste Land* to the dropping of the atom bomb: *The Autobiography of William Carlos Williams* (New York: Directions, 1951), p. 174; *William Carlos Williams and James Laughlin: Selected Letters* (New York: Norton, 1989), p. 40.

31 Harold Rosenberg supports the idea of a transnational metropolitan modernism, stating that, with Paris as 'the International of culture', a 'cultural Klondike', 'A whole epoch in the history of art had come into being without regard to national values.' Rosenberg insists that 'Because Paris was the opposite of the national in art, the art of every nation increased through Paris. No folk lost its integrity there; on the contrary, artists of every region renewed by this magnanimous milieu discovered in the depths of themselves what was most alive in the communities from which they had come': Harold Rosenberg, 'The Fall of Paris', in *The Tradition of the New* (New York: Da Capo Press, 1960), pp. 210, 212. Raymond Williams argues that in the modernist era, 'the new metropolitan cities . . . offered themselves as transnational capitals of an art without frontiers', but points out that modernism is 'strongly characterized by its internal diversity': in relation to the metropolis, this diversity ranges 'from the Futurist affirmation of the city to Eliot's pessimistic recoil': Williams, *The Politics of Modernism*, pp. 34, 43.

32 Cowley, *Exile's Return*, p. 47.

33 Locke, *The New Negro*, p. 1587.
34 David Jones' own wasted land is, in his *In Parenthesis*, context-specific, the
   no-man's land of the First World War. Oswald Spengler, *The Decline of the
   West* (London: George Allen and Unwin, 1926), pp. 98, 99; David Jones,
   'The Wall', in *The Sleeping Lord and Other Fragments* (London: Faber and Faber,
   1974), p. 13; Alain Locke, quoted in Ann Douglas, *Terrible Honesty: Mongrel
   Manhattan in the 1920s* (London: Picador, 1996), p. 310. Robert Crawford's
   argument for the synthesis of cosmopolitanism and provincialism in modernism, mentioned above, problematises the dichotomy proposed by Spengler. Compare Spengler's nightmarish 'world-city' and Jones' verdict on the
   modern city with John Crowe Ransom's comment that 'A capital of the
   world would be an intolerable city', and compare Jones' geographically
   specific modernist 'megalopolis' with John Cage's postmodern diagnosis
   that 'Outside the bankrupt cities we live in Megalopolis which has no
   geographical limits': John Crowe Ransom, 'The Aesthetic of Regionalism',
   American Review 2 (1934), 299; John Cage, Preface to 'Lecture on the
   Weather', in *Empty Words: Writings '73–'78* (London: Marion Boyars), p. 5.
35 Langston Hughes, 'Likewise', in *Montage of a Dream Deferred*, in *Selected Poems
   of Langston Hughes* (New York: Knopf, 1959), pp. 266–7; T. S. Eliot, *The
   Complete Poems and Plays of T. S. Eliot* (London: Faber and Faber, 1969), p. 62.
36 Contemporary readers of *The Waste Land* like Wyndham Lewis and Clive
   Bell did see Eliot's poem as a form of jazz – 'O O O O that Shakespeherian
   Rag' – and the observation has been made that Eliot's hometown, St Louis,
   has a rich jazz and blues heritage. As Steven Helmling has pointed out,
   although he knew the work of the Harlem Renaissance poets, the black
   American novelist Ralph Ellison wanted to become a writer on reading
   Eliot's *The Waste Land* – Ellison says of Eliot's poem, 'Somehow its rhythms
   were often closer to jazz than were those of the Negro poets, and . . . its
   range of allusion was as mixed and varied as that of Louis Armstrong':
   Steven Helmling, 'T. S. Eliot and Ralph Ellison: Insiders, Outsiders, and
   Cultural Authority', *Southern Review* 25:4 (1989), 842.
37 See Douglas, *Terrible Honesty*, p. 82.
38 Helmling argues that Ralph Ellison's reading of *The Waste Land* did not
   prompt him 'to entertain any "illusion of disillusion" or any effort to "learn
   from a style of despair"'. No, Ellison says the poem inspired in him a kind of
   hope'. Helmling adds that 'Ellison is one of the few who read the poem as an
   apocalypse, not as a holocaust': Helmling, 'T. S. Eliot and Ralph Ellison', p.
   843.
39 Robert Crawford, 'A Drunk Man Looks at The Waste Land', *Scottish Literary
   Journal* 14:2 (1987), 69.
40 One might think about *The Great Gatsby* in relation to other 'modernisms',
   too – as, for instance, a prose version of *The Waste Land*. Fitzgerald's
   counterpart to Eliot's lament for the decline of belief in the modern
   wasteland is the Valley of Ashes, on which the face of Dr Eckleberg looks
   down from an advertising billboard with his sightless eyes, a blind simulac-

rum of god presiding over an ashen and barren world. Fitzgerald's version of a wasteland extends to the glittering world of the rich, too – when Daisy Fay Buchanan asks 'What'll we do with ourselves this afternoon? . . . and the day after that, and the next thirty years?' she echoes Eliot's woman who speaks in 'A Game of Chess': 'What shall I do now? What shall I do? / . . . What shall we do tomorrow? / What shall we ever do?': Carl Van Vechten, *Nigger Heaven* (1926) (New York: Harper Bros., 1971); F. Scott Fitzgerald, *The Great Gatsby* (1926) (Harmondsworth: Penguin, 1950), pp. 75, 124; T. S. Eliot, *Complete Poems and Plays*, p. 65.

41 Quoted in Douglas, *Terrible Honesty*, p. 303. Claude McKay, while acknowledging that 'Some jeer at Harlem as the capital of clowns whose fame rests upon cults and cabarets', insists that 'Harlem is more than the Negro capital of the nation. It is the Negro capital of the world': *Harlem: Negro Metropolis* (1940) (New York: Harcourt Brace Jovanovich, 1968), p. 15, p. 16. Powell argues that Harlem should be seen both as location and as metaphor, as 'a modern, racial motif that transcended a specific black place or black people', 'a metaphoric racial landscape', both 'Mecca and Metaphor': Richard J. Powell, *Black Art and Culture in the 20th Century* (London: Thames and Hudson, 1997), pp. 53, 54, 50.

42 Houston Baker, *Modernism and the Harlem Renaissance* (University of Chicago Press, 1987), pp. 72, 74, 106, 86–7, 101.

43 Eliot Weinberger, 'American Poetry since 1950: A Very Brief History', *Poetry Ireland Review* 43/44 (1994), 51.

44 As Brooker notes, too often the Harlem Renaissance is 'at best regarded as an appendage to American modernism and judged by its standards': *New York Fictions*, p. 175.

45 As the editors of *The Heath Anthology of American Literature* point out, the Harlem Renaissance should be seen as 'one of the United States's "modernisms"': Lauter *et al.*, *The Heath Anthology of American Literature*, p. 1582.

46 Douglas, *Terrible Honesty*, pp. 5, 82, 86, 98.

47 Quoted in Douglas, *Terrible Honesty*, p. 332.

48 Faith Berry (ed.), *Uncollected Writings of Langston Hughes* (New York: Citadel Press, 1992), p. 23.

49 Quoted in Douglas, *Terrible Honesty*, p. 282.

50 Cowley, *Exile's Return*, pp. 236–7.

51 Lauter, *et al.*, *The Heath Anthology of American Literature*, p. 1580.

52 The final words of Van Wyck Brooks' manifesto for the creative reconstruction of a national American literary tradition are 'a national culture'. 'On Creating a Usable Past', *Dial* (11 April 1918), 337–41.

53 Donald Davidson, *Still Rebels, Still Yankees and Other Essays* (Baton Rouge: Louisiana State University Press, 1972), pp. 271, 277; Jordan, *Regionalism Reconsidered*, pp. xii, xv.

54 Davidson, *Still Rebels*, p. 276; Ransom, 'The Aesthetic of Regionalism', 308, 303; Donald Davidson, *The Attack on Leviathan* (Gloucester, Mass.: Peter Smith, 1962), p. 99.

55 Donald Davidson argues that the thirties – the period of the Southern Agrarian movement – saw 'the redefinition of national consciousness in sectional or regional terms': the Depression of the thirties is, for Davidson, the sign or seal of the failure of twenties cosmopolitanism, the time when expatriate American writers were driven home, and when many of their little magazines closed, opening up space for regional magazines like *Southern Review*: Davidson, *The Attack on Leviathan*, p. 81. John Crowe Ransom, writing in 1934, makes a similar point when he argues that 'Regionalism is not exactly the prevalent economy today . . . Yet, just now, by reason of the crash of our non-regional economy, it tends to have its revival': Ransom, 'The Aesthetic of Regionalism', 294. As Nicholas J. Entrikin observes, 'The concept of provincialism as a positive ideal in American thought is most often associated with the philosophy of Josiah Royce, who prescribed it as an antidote to the pathologies of modernity.' Royce described the inhabitants of the modern city as 'citizens of the world, who have no local attachments': Nicholas J. Entrikin, *The Betweenness of Place* (Baltimore: Johns Hopkins University Press, 1991), p. 69.

56 See Bram Dijkstra, *The Hieroglyphics of a New Speech: Cubism, Stieglitz, and the Early Poetry of William Carlos Williams* (Princeton University Press, 1969), p. 116. David Bennett, 'Defining the "American" Difference: Cultural Nationalism and the Modernist Poetics of William Carlos Williams', *Southern Review* 20:3 (1987), 272, 273, 275. Dijkstra makes a similar point when he suggests that for Williams, a return to American origins was identical with a return to the basis of nature – the object: Dijkstra, *Hieroglyphics*, p. 123.

57 Bennett, 'Defining the "American" Difference', 271, 274.

58 See David Lloyd, *Nationalism and Minor Literature: James Clarence Mangan and the Emergence of Irish Cultural Nationalism* (Berkeley: University of California Press, 1987), and *Anomalous States: Irish Writing and the Post-Colonial Moment* (Dublin: Lilliput, 1993).

59 On the apocalyptic history encoded in *The Secret Rose* as arranged in 1897, see Phillip L. Marcus, *Yeats and the Beginning of the Irish Renaissance*, 2nd edn (Syracuse University Press, 1987), pp. 49–50. For the relationship between Gyles' cover-design for and Yeats' text of *The Secret Rose*, see W. B. Yeats, *The Secret Rose, Stories by W. B. Yeats: A Variorum Edition*, ed. Warwick Gould, Phillip L. Marcus and Michael J. Sidnell, 2nd edn (London: Macmillan, 1992), pp. 272–8.

60 See John Wilson Foster, 'Irish Modernism', in his *Colonial Consequences: Essays in Irish Literature and Culture* (Dublin: Lilliput, 1991), pp. 44–59.

61 Seamus Deane, Headnote to 'Poetry 1890–1930', in *The Field Day Anthology of Irish Writing*, 3 vols. (Derry: Field Day Publications, 1991), vol. II, p. 720.

62 On this topic, see G. J. Watson, *Irish Identity and the Literary Revival*, 2nd edn (Washington D.C.: Catholic University of America Press, 1994), pp. 26–34.

63 W. B. Yeats, 'William Allingham 1824–1889' (1891), in *Prefaces and Introductions*, ed. William H. O'Donnell (London: Macmillan, 1989), p. 69. Yeats makes related observations in his 1891 review of Allingham's collected poems; see John P. Frayne (ed.), *Uncollected Prose by W. B. Yeats*, 2 vols.

(London: Macmillan, 1970), vol. I, pp. 208–12.

64 Yeats, *The Secret Rose*, p. 234.

65 Yeats, *Prefaces and Introductions*, p. 70.

66 Harvey, *The Condition of Postmodernity*, pp. 24–5.

67 See Thomas MacGreevy, 'The Catholic Element in *Work in Progress*', in Samuel Beckett *et al.*, *Our Exagmination Round His Factification for Incamination of Work in Progress* (Paris: Shakespeare and Company, 1929), pp. 19–27.

68 See Samuel Beckett, *Disjecta: Miscellaneous Writings and a Dramatic Fragment*, ed. Ruby Cohn (London: John Calder, 1983), pp. 70–6.

69 See W. J. McCormack, *From Burke to Beckett: Ascendancy, Tradition and Betrayal in Literary History* (Cork University Press, 1994), pp. 224–56.

70 See Lawrence Harvey, *Samuel Beckett: Poet and Critic* (Princeton University Press, 1970), pp. 124–53.

71 Perry Anderson, 'Modernity and Revolution', in Gary Nelson and Lawrence Grossberg (eds.), *Marxism and the Interpretation of Culture* (London: Macmillan, 1988), pp. 322, 324–5.

72 Ibid., pp. 325–6.

73 Ibid., p. 326.

74 Alex Callinicos, *Against Postmodernism: A Marxist Critique* (Oxford: Polity, 1989), p. 43.

75 Fredric Jameson, *Modernism and Imperialism* (Derry: Field Day, 1988), p. 14; and see also Terry Eagleton, *Exiles and Emigrés* (New York: Shocken, 1970).

76 Christopher Butler, *Early Modernism: Literature, Music and Painting in Europe 1900–1916* (Oxford University Press, 1994), p. 230; and see Hugh Kenner, *The Pound Era* (Berkeley: University of California Press, 1971), p. 238: 'Vorticism denoted first of all the Great *London* Vortex. The Future has no locale, an Image or a Cube may turn up in anyone's pocket, but any Vortex is somewhere on the map. And this was the English, not the French or the Russian, version of abstract art.'

77 Wyndham Lewis (ed.), *Blast I* (Santa Barbara: Black Sparrow, 1981), p. 20.

78 Quoted in Michael L. Levenson, *A Genealogy of Modernism: A Study of English Literary Doctrine 1908–1922* (Cambridge University Press, 1984), p. 136.

79 Nicholls, *Modernisms*, p. 173.

80 Ezra Pound, *Pavannes & Divigations* (New York: New Directions, 1958), pp. 146, 147.

I MACDIARMID IN MONTROSE

The author would like to thank the staff of Montrose Public Library, Angus Archives, the William Lamb Sculpture Studio, Montrose Museum and Art Gallery, and the Library of the University of St Andrews for assistance in researching this article.

1 Hugh MacDiarmid, 'The Angus Burghs' (1954) in Alan Bold (ed.), *The Thistle Rises: An Anthology of Poetry and Prose by Hugh MacDiarmid* (London: Hamish Hamilton, 1984), p. 220.

2 See, for instance, Robert Crawford, 'A Drunk Man Looks at The Waste

Land', *Scottish Literary Journal* (1987), 62–78, and *Identifying Poets: Self and Territory in Twentieth-Century Poetry* (Edinburgh University Press, 1993), pp. 42–63; C. M. Grieve, 'Wallace Stevens, *Harmonium*' (1924), and 'Scotland and Belgium' (1922), rpt in Angus Calder, Glen Murray and Alan Riach (eds.), *The Raucle Tongue, Hitherto Uncollected Prose*, 3 vols. (Manchester: Carcanet, 1996–7), vol. I, pp. 178–81, 29.

3 See, for example, W. N. Herbert, *To Circumjack MacDiarmid* (Oxford: Clarendon Press, 1992).

4 Seamus Heaney, 'Interview' (1980), in Nancy Gish (ed.), *Hugh MacDiarmid: Man and Poet* (Edinburgh University Press, 1992), pp. 64–5.

5 Hugh MacDiarmid, 'Literary Angus and the Mearns' (1933), in Calder, Murray and Riach, *The Raucle Tongue*, vol. II, p. 389; Hugh MacDiarmid, 'Montrose', in *Complete Poems*, ed. Michael Grieve and W. R. Aitken, 2 vols. (London: Martin Brian and O'Keeffe, 1978), vol. II, p. 1407; poems in advertisements for this butcher appeared in the *Montrose Review* throughout the 1920s; Andrew Carnegie, *Address at the Unveiling of a Statue to Burns Erected by the Citizens of Montrose* (Dunfermline: Romanes, 1912).

6 Alan Bold (ed.), *The Letters of Hugh MacDiarmid* (London: Hamish Hamilton, 1984), p. 38.

7 Ibid., p. 37; Hugh MacDiarmid, *Lucky Poet* (1943) (rpt London: Cape, 1972), p. 178.

8 C. M. Grieve (ed.), *Northern Numbers* (Edinburgh and London: T. N. Foulis, 1920), p. 4.

9 Bold, *Letters*, p. 37.

10 C. M. Grieve, *Annals of the Five Senses* (1923) (rpt Edinburgh: Polygon, 1983), p. 97.

11 Bold, *Letters*, pp. 32–3.

12 'Burgh of St Andrews, Lammas Market, Partial Closing of Market Street', *St Andrews Citizen*, 9 August 1919, 1.

13 Robert Burns, *Poems and Songs*, ed. James Kinsley (Oxford University Press, 1969), p. 9.

14 'St Andrews Lammas Market', *St Andrews Citizen*, 16 August 1919, 2.

15 Burns, *Poems and Songs*, p. 443 (this is the third line of the poem).

16 Calder, Murray and Riach, *The Raucle Tongue*, vol. I, pp. 18–19.

17 Edward Moore [Edwin Muir], *We Moderns: Enigmas and Guesses* (London: Allen and Unwin, 1918), pp. 15 and 68.

18 Moore, *We Moderns*, pp. 128–9.

19 This is now in St Andrews University Library.

20 Robert Crawford, *Devolving English Literature* (Oxford: Clarendon Press, 1992); see chapter 5 ('Modernism as Provincialism').

21 See especially Nancy K. Gish, *Hugh MacDiarmid: The Man and his Work* (London: Macmillan, 1984), chapter 6; Laurence Graham and Brian Smith (eds.), *MacDiarmid in Shetland* (Lerwick: Shetland Library, 1992).

22 I am grateful to Ms Fiona Scharlau of Angus Archives, Montrose, for this local information, and for letting me see an unpublished paper by Trevor

W. Johns, 'MacDiarmid the Montrosian', which details some of MacDiarmid's contributions to local life; Bold, *The Thistle Rises*, p. 288.

23 Calder, Murray and Riach, *The Raucle Tongue*, vol. 1, p. 45.

24 Christopher Murray Grieve, 'Montrose Municipal Election', *Montrose Review*, 3 November 1922, 4.

25 'A Local Poetess and Novelist', *Montrose Review*, 2 January 1920, 5. Unless otherwise indicated, all the articles cited from the *Montrose Review* are unsigned.

26 'ILP', *Montrose Review*, 5 March 1920, 5.

27 'ILP', *Montrose Review*, 12 March 1920, 5.

28 See Tom Valentine, *Old Montrose* (Ochiltree, Ayrshire: Stenlake Publishing, 1997), pp. 32 and 37.

29 'Round the Town', *Montrose Review*, 19 March 1920, 5; see also, for example, '"Prohibition Experiences", how a Scotsman saw the law in operation', *Montrose Review*, 4 January 1924, 6.

30 Willa Muir, *Belonging: A Memoir* (London: Hogarth Press, 1974), p. 116.

31 'Book Reviews, A Green Grass Widow', *Montrose Review*, 20 May 1921, 7; praise of the 'old gentlewomen' of 'Dean Ramsay' in this piece is repeated in Calder, Murray and Riach, *The Raucle Tongue*, vol. 1, p. 47.

32 'Foreword' to Grieve, *Northern Numbers* (1920), 9.

33 B. L., 'The World of Books, A Literary Causerie', *Montrose Review*, 3 June 1921, 6.

34 Ibid.

35 'New All-Scottish weekly', *Montrose Review*, 4 May 1923, 5; 'Buy "The Scottish Nation"' (advertisement), *Montrose Review*, 13 July 1923, 3; the cover of the *Scottish Nation* for 19 June 1923 presents 16 Links Avenue as 'The Scottish Poetry Bookshop'; 'The Evolution of Scottish Nationalism', *Montrose Review*, 6 July 1923, 2.

36 'The Evolution of Scottish Nationalism', *Montrose Review*, 6 July 1923, 2.

37 'The Library Problem', *Montrose Review*, 17 June 1921, 7.

38 'New Books', *Montrose Review*, 11 November 1921, 3; 'Montrose Poems', *Montrose Review*, 2 December 1921, 7.

39 'Is "Braid Scots" dead?' *Montrose Review*, 16 December 1921, 6.

40 Ibid.

41 C. M. Grieve, 'Home Rule for Scotland' (letter), *Montrose Review*, 20 January 1922, 5; 'Round the Town', *Montrose Review*, 27 January 1922, 5.

42 'Town's Employees' Wages and Holidays', *Montrose Review*, 21 July 1922, 5; 'Ferryden: Notes and Notions', *Montrose Review*, 28 July 1922, 4; 'No More War Demonstrations in Ferryden', *Montrose Review*, 4 August 1922, 4; Calder, Murray and Riach, *The Raucle Tongue*, vol. 1, p. 46.

43 Bold, *The Thistle Rises*, p. 288.

44 Hugh MacDiarmid, 'Nisbet, an Interlude in Post War Glasgow' (1922), rpt. in Bold, *The Thistle Rises*, p. 326, p. 321, p. 324, p. 325.

45 See note 2 above.

46 MacDiarmid, *Lucky Poet*, p. 16.

47 'Directory of Burns Clubs and Scottish Societies', *Burns Chronicle* 23 (1923), 223.

48 Burns, *Poems and Songs*, p. 107.

49 Thomas Amos, 'Minutes of the Annual Conference of the Burns Federation, Council Chambers, Birmingham, 2nd September 1922', *Burns Chronicle* 23 (1923), 181.

50 'Burns' Conference at Birmingham, Montrose Delegate's Speech', *Montrose Review*, 8 September 1922, 6.

51 MacDiarmid, *Complete Poems*, vol. II, p. 1224.

52 'At Birmingham', *Scottish Chapbook* (1922), 43.

53 Alan Bold, *Hugh MacDiarmid* (London: John Murray, 1988), p. 137.

54 Seamus Heaney, 'Burns' Art Speech', in Robert Crawford (ed.), *Robert Burns and Cultural Authority* (Edinburgh University Press, 1997), pp. 216–33.

55 MacDiarmid, *Complete Poems*, vol. II, p. 1219.

56 Burns, *Poems and Songs*, pp. 444–5.

57 MacDiarmid, *Complete Poems*, vol. I, p. 18.

58 Hugh MacDiarmid, *Selected Prose*, ed. Alan Riach (Manchester: Carcanet, 1992), p. 22 ('A Theory of Scots Letters').

59 Thomas Amos, 'Secretary's Annual Report', *Burns Chronicle* 24 (1925), 152.

60 Bold, *MacDiarmid*, p. 159.

61 John Buchan, Preface to Hugh MacDiarmid, *Sangschaw* (Edinburgh: Blackwood, 1925), p. x.

62 MacDiarmid, *Complete Poems*, vol. I, p. 36.

63 Alan Riach, 'MacDiarmid's Burns', in Crawford, *Robert Burns and Cultural Authority*, p. 202.

64 Calder, Murray and Riach, *The Raucle Tongue*, vol. I, p. 186.

65 See such periodic articles as 'Burns' North Country Forbears', *Montrose Review*, 19 May 1922, 6 and 'When Burns was in Montrose', *Montrose Review*, 25 January 1924, 7.

66 Hugh MacDiarmid, 'Jock o' Arnha' (1923), rpt in Calder, Murray and Riach, *The Raucle Tongue*, vol. I, p. 108.

67 Ibid., p. 107.

68 'George Beattie, Author of "John o' Arnha"', Montrose poet's centenary, movement to restore his grave', *Montrose Review*, 21 September 1923, 7; 'Literary Angus and the Mearns', in Calder, Murray and Riach, *The Raucle Tongue*, vol. II, p. 389.

69 Reprinted in Bold, *The Thistle Rises*, p. 331.

70 'Round the Town', *Montrose Review*, 5 January 1923, 5.

71 Hugh MacDiarmid, *Complete Poems*, vol. I, p. 27.

72 C. M. Grieve, 'Montrose Parliamentary Society' (letter), *Montrose Review*, 11 January 1924, 7; 'In Brief' and 'The Next Debate', *Montrose Review*, 1 February 1924, 4.

73 'Montrose Parliamentary Debating Society', *Montrose Review*, 15 February 1924, 5.

74 'Too Many Beggars in Montrose', *Montrose Review*, 15 February 1924, 6.

75 'The Convention of Burghs, Montrose Delegates' Speeches', *Montrose Review*, 4 April 1924, 6.
76 Information from Ms Fiona Scharlau, Angus Archives, Montrose.
77 'Folk-song Recital', *Montrose Review*, 4 April 1924, 7.
78 MacDiarmid, *Selected Prose*, 38.
79 'Indian Journalist on Nationalist Question', *Montrose Review*, 16 May 1924, 7; 'Secretary of State for Scotland in Montrose', *Montrose Review*, 26 September 1924, 6.
80 Elgin W. Mellown, *Bibliography of the Writings of Edwin Muir* (University of Alabama Press, 1970), p. 15.
81 'Alexander McGill' [C. M. Grieve], 'Towards a Scottish Renaissance', *Scottish Educational Journal*, 16 (1925), 66; Hugh MacDiarmid, *Contemporary Scottish Studies*, ed. Alan Riach (Manchester: Carcanet, 1995), p. 93 and p. 100 (in the original article in *Scottish Educational Journal*, 4 September 1925, 31, the word 'will' is italicised; I have retained these italics, omitted in the Carcanet reprint).
82 Willa Muir, *Belonging*, p. 116.
83 Edwin Muir, *Selected Prose*, ed. George Mackay Brown, (London: John Murray, 1987), p. 19 ('A Note on the Scottish Ballads' (1924)).
84 Edwin Muir, *Selected Letters*, ed. P. H. Butter (London: Hogarth Press, 1974), p. 41.
85 'The Montrose Players', *Montrose Review*, 5 February 1926, 5.
86 Muir, *Selected Letters*, p. 53; MacDiarmid, *Contemporary Scottish Studies*, pp. 95, 171–2, and 289–97.
87 'A Rising Forfarshire Artist', *Montrose Review*, 1 May 1925, 4; *William Lamb Sculpture Studio Catalogue* (Angus Council Cultural Services, n.d.), pp. 8–9 and 17.
88 Patrick Elliott, *Edward Baird, 1904–1949* (Edinburgh: National Galleries of Scotland, 1992), pp. 9 and 21; Bold, *The Thistle Rises*, p. 222.
89 Bold, *The Thistle Rises*, pp. 220–1.
90 Robert Crawford, '"The glow-worm's 96 per cent efficiency": Hugh MacDiarmid's Poetry of Knowledge', *Proceedings of the British Academy* 87 (1995), 169–87.
91 David Murison, 'The Language Problem in Hugh MacDiarmid's Work', and Kenneth Buthlay, 'The Scotched Snake', in P. H. Scott and A. C. Davis (eds.), *The Age of MacDiarmid: Essays on Hugh MacDiarmid and his Influence on Contemporary Scotland* (Edinburgh: Mainstream, 1980), pp. 83–100 and 122–57; Herbert, *To Circumjack MacDiarmid*.
92 Bold, *The Thistle Rises*, p. 288.
93 On MacDiarmid attending local Burns suppers see Johns' 'MacDiarmid the Montrosian'; MacDiarmid's selection of work by Burns, *Robert Burns, 1759–1796* was published in London by Benn in 1926 in the Augustan Books of Poetry series; Kenneth Buthlay in his annotated edition of *A Drunk Man Looks at the Thistle* (Edinburgh: Scottish Academic Press, 1987) tracks the continuing use of Burns throughout the poem in his notes.

94 MacDiarmid, *Complete Poems*, vol. 1, p. 88.
95 John, 1: 46 (Authorised Version).
96 Burns, *Poems and Songs*, p. 602.

2 BUNTING AND WELSH

1 Richard Caddel, 'Acknowledged Land: A Biography of "They Say Etna" and a Debate between Bunting and Pound', in Richard Taylor and Claus Melchior (eds.), *Ezra Pound and Europe* (Amsterdam: Rodopi, 1993), pp. 69–77.
2 Nennius, *British History*, ed. and trans. John Morris (London: Phillimore, 1980), p. 37.
3 Aneirin, *Y Gododdin: Britain's Oldest Heroic Poem*, ed. and trans. A. O. H. Jarman (Llandysul: Gomer Press, 1988), p. 69.
4 Dinogad's smock is pied, pied –
Made it out of marten hide.
Whit, whit, whistle along,
Eight slaves with you sing the song.

When your dad went to hunt,
Spear on his shoulder, cudgel in hand,
He called his quick dogs, 'Giff, you wretch,
Gaff, catch her, catch her, fetch, fetch!'

From a coracle he'd spear
Fish as a lion strikes a deer.
When your dad went to the crag
He brought down roebuck, boar and stag,
Speckled grouse from the mountain tall,
Fish from Derwent waterfall.

Whatever your dad found with his spear,
Boar or wild cat, fox or deer,
Unless it flew, would never get clear.
  Translated by Tony Conran, *Welsh Verse* (Bridgend: Poetry Wales Press, 1986), p. 117.
5 Brian Swan, 'Basil Bunting of Northumberland', *St Andrews Review* 4:2 (1977), 33–41.
6 Basil Bunting, 'Out Loud', *Listener* 94 (1975), 274.
7 Jonathan Williams, 'Basil Bunting: An Interview', *Conjunctions* 5 (1983), 75–87.
8 Basil Bunting, *Complete Poems*, ed. Richard Caddel (Oxford University Press, 1994), p. 57.
9 Sean Figgis and Andrew McAllister, 'Basil Bunting: The Last Interview', *Bête Noire* 2/3 (1987), 22–50.
10 William Barnes, *The Dorset Poet*, ed. Chris Wrigley (Wimborne: Dovecote Press, 1988), p. 143.
11 Papers in the Zukofsky Archive in the Harry Ransom Humanities Research Center, University of Texas at Austin. I am indebted to Peter Makin for this information, and much else in this chapter.

12 Basil Bunting, letter to Ezra Pound, reproduced with the permission of the Beinecke Rare Book and Manuscript Library, Yale University.
13 Bunting, *Complete Poems*, p. 109.
14 Meic Stephens (ed.), *Oxford Companion to the Literature of Wales* (Oxford University Press, 1986), pp. 114–15. For an invaluable summary of the development of Welsh verse forms, see Conran, *Welsh Verse*, pp. 310–39.
15 G. G. Evans, letter to the author, March 1992.
16 G. G. Evans, 'Basil Bunting – Summer 1942', *Stand* (1992), 68–70.
17 Basil Bunting, letter to Louis Zukofsky, reproduced with the permission of the Harry Ransom Humanities Research Center, University of Texas at Austin.
18 Basil Bunting, 'Thumps' (lecture given at Newcastle University in 1969), in Richard Caddel (ed.), *Sharp Study and Long Toil: Basil Bunting Durham University Journal Special Supplement* (1995), 18–26.
19 John T. Koch, 'The Cynfeirdd Poetry and the Language of the Sixth Century', in Brynley F. Roberts (ed.), *Early Welsh Poetry: Studies in the Book of Aneirin* (Aberystwyth: University of Wales Press, 1988), pp. 17–41.
20 Ibid., p.21.
21 Ifor Williams (ed.), *Canu Taliesin* (Caerdydd: Gwasg Prifisgol Cymru, 1977), p. 2.
22 Koch, 'The Cynfeirdd Poetry', p. 22.
23 Peter Quartermain, *Basil Bunting: Poet of the North* (Durham: Basil Bunting Poetry Archive, 1990), p. 17.
24 Jenny Rowland, *Early Welsh Saga Poetry* (Cambridge: Brewer, 1990), p. 351.
25 Ifor Williams, *Canu Taliesin*, p. 12.
26 Bunting, *Complete Poems*, p. 60.
27 Ibid., p. 126.
28 Richard Caddel and Anthony Flowers, *Basil Bunting: A Northern Life* (City of Newcastle-upon-Tyne Libraries, 1997), p. 58.

3 ANTITHESIS OF PLACE IN THE POETRY AND LIFE OF DAVID JONES

1 The important expositions of Jones' cultural theory are 'Art and Sacrament', in Harman Grisewood (ed.), *Epoch and Artist* (London: Faber and Faber, 1956), pp. 143–79; and 'Use and Sign', in Harman Grisewood (ed.), *The Dying Gaul* (London: Faber and Faber, 1987), pp. 177–85.
2 Adam Thorpe, 'Distressed Perspectives', *Poetry Review* 86 (1996), 56.
3 David Jones, *In Parenthesis* (London: Faber and Faber, 1937), p. 24. Subsequent page references appear parenthetically in the text.
4 The historic prototype of this attack was that on Mametz Wood on 10–11 July 1916, in which the poet participated, but he does not mention the name of the wood in the poem 'so as not to tie it [the assault] down to a particular action' (David Jones, letter to René Hague, 14 June 1970).
5 W. H. Auden, *A Certain World* (New York: Viking, 1970), p. 373.
6 David Jones, *The Anathemata* (London: Faber and Faber, 1952), p. 89.

Subsequent references appear parenthetically in the text.

7 In *The Anathemata*, after being raped by Mars so that she will give birth to 'the Roman people', Ilis says, "'T's a great robbery / – is empire' (p. 88). She (with David Jones) is endorsing St Augustine's definition of empire as robbery.

8 Elizabeth Ward, *David Jones Mythmaker* (Manchester University Press, 1983), pp. 107–19.

9 Ibid., p. 211.

10 Jonathan Miles, *Eric Gill and David Jones at Capel-y-ffin* (Bridgend: Seren, 1992), p. 92.

11 David Jones, letter to Mr Rates, draft, n.d.; David Jones, ms. draft, n.d. [*c.* 1970]. I am grateful to the trustees of the estate of David Jones for permission to use and quote from his unpublished letters. In this and subsequent endnotes to paragraphs of biographical material, a single note includes all the references used in the paragraph, listed in the order of their use.

12 David Jones in conversation with Tony and Pat Stoneburner, written record, 26 May 1969, 30 July 1969; M. A. Fletcher, Librarian, London Transport Museum, letter to author, 26 May 1988; David Jones, letter to Tony Stoneburner, 30 July 1969; David Jones, taped interview by Peter Orr, early 1970s.

13 David Jones, *The Sleeping Lord and Other Fragments* (London: Faber and Faber, 1974), pp. 67–8. Subsequent references appear parenthetically in the text.

14 See Jones' essay 'The Dying Gaul', in the posthumous collection of his essays, *The Dying Gaul*, pp. 50–8.

15 Petra Tegetmeier, remembering visiting Brockley in 1924, interviewed by author, 12 June 1986, 18 June 1988.

16 Stella Wright, interviewed by author, 26 June 1986; David Jones, letter to Harman Grisewood, 14 November 1970; David Jones in conversation with Tony and Pat Stoneburner, written record, 5 May 1966; David Jones, letter to Tony Stoneburner, 15 May 1970.

17 David Jones, letter to René Hague, 4 September 1974; David Jones in conversation with author, 9 September 1972; David Jones, letter to René Hague, 27 September 1974; Philip Hagreen, letter to author, 26 January 1986; David Jones, letter to Saunders Lewis, 9 April 1970.

18 David Jones, letter to Frank Morley, unposted, January 1953; David Jones, letter to René Hague, 4 September 1974; David Jones, letter to W. H. Auden, 24 February 1954.

19 David Jones, letter draft fragment, n.d.; David Jones in conversation with the author, 9 September 1972.

20 David Jones, biographical note for the British Council, n.d. [*c.* 1971]; David Jones, letter to Harman Grisewood, 12 December 1966; David Jones, letter to Maurice Percival, October 1967; David Jones, letter to René Hague, fragment, n.d.

21 Ernest Hawkins, interviewed by author, 15 June 1988; David Jones in conversation with author, 9 September 1972; *In Parenthesis*, pp. 112–13; David Jones, letter to Tony Stoneburner, 5 August 1969; David Jones, letter

to Helen Sutherland, 14 May 1943.

22 Diana Macartney-Filgate, letter to author, 24 January 1991; Ernest Hawkins, interviewed by author, 15 June 1988.

23 David Jones, letter to Tony Stoneburner, 30 August 1963.

24 David Jones, 'A Letter from David Jones', *Poetry Wales* 8 (1972), 8–9.

25 Jones, 'A Letter from David Jones', 8–9.

26 Tony Hyne, interviewed by author, June 1985; David Jones, letter to Vernon Watkins, 5 April 1962; David Jones, letter to Molly O'Neill, 7 January 1971; David Jones, letter to Saunders Lewis, December 1967; David Jones, letter to Tony Hyne, 18 May 1972.

27 Tony Hyne, interviewed by author, June 1985; David Jones, letter to Vernon Watkins, 5 April 1962; David Jones, letter to Molly O'Neill, 7 January 1971; David Jones, letter to Saunders Lewis, December 1967; David Jones, letter to Tony Hyne, 18 May 1972; Richard Baddeley, *The Borough of Conwyn Handbook* (Borough of Conwyn, n.d.), p. 63; David Jones to René Hague, 'Note on the draft of Kensington Mass' (typescript, n.d.); David Jones, letter to Gwladys Toser, 26 December 1948.

28 David Jones, letter to Peter Levi, 29 January 1965.

29 Harman Grisewood, interviewed by author, August 1983; David Jones, letter to Valerie Wynne-Williams, unposted, 5 April 1962.

30 David Jones, letter to Harman Grisewood, 16 October 1952.

31 David Jones in conversation with author, 9 September 1972.

32 David Jones, 'The Myth of Arthur', in Harman Grisewood, *Epoch and Artist*, pp. 240–1.

33 Miles and Shiel frequently reduces aesthetic phenomena to psychological evidence. See Derek Shiel and Jonathan Miles, *The Maker Unmade* (Bridgend: Seren, 1995).

34 Jones discussed nominalism with Eric Gill in 1924–7 and subsequently with a group of Catholic intellectuals that included Tom Burns, Harman Grisewood, Bernard Wall, Fr Martin D'Arcy, Christopher Dawson and E. I. Watkin.

35 Harman Grisewood, interviewed by author, 23 June 1986.

36 M. L. Rosenthal and Sally M. Gall, *The Modern Poetic Sequence* (Oxford University Press, 1983), p. 10, p. 306.

37 Quoted in Jacques Maritain, *The Philosophy of Art*, trans. John O'Connor (Ditchling: St Dominic's Press, 1921), p. 112.

4 'SHUT, TOO, IN A TOWER OF WORDS': DYLAN THOMAS' MODERNISM

1 Letter to Daniel Jones, August 1935, in Paul Ferris (ed.), *Dylan Thomas: The Collected Letters* (London: Paladin, 1987), p. 197.

2 T. S. Eliot, 'The Function of Criticism', in *Selected Essays* (London: Faber and Faber, 1932), p. 27, p. 29. Terry Eagleton has glossed Eliot's 'Whiggism' in an English context as 'protestantism, liberalism, Romanticism, humanism'. Welsh Dissent, socialism and 'Celtic' emotionalism can be taken to

represent extreme versions of these categories: Terry Eagleton, *Criticism and Ideology* (London: Verso, 1986), p. 147.

3 David Holbrook's attack on Thomas is contained in *Llaregub Revisited: Dylan Thomas and the State of Modern Poetry* (1962) and *Dylan Thomas and the Code of Night* (1972); Kingsley Amis' distaste was expressed frequently and volubly from the 1950s to the 1990s.

4 'Anglo-Welsh', like 'Anglo-Irish', is a critical category which implies not so much a hyphenated culture as a hierarchy of faithfulness to some putative national essence, taken as embodied in the Welsh language.

5 Thus, Neil Corcoran's discussion of Thomas observes that Thomas is 'overdue for a contemporary Bakhtinian reassessment' but fails to provide it. Recognising Thomas as the 'focal point for the anti-Auden disaffection', Corcoran nevertheless discusses him in Auden-derived, even Movement terms ('poetic tact, decorum, responsibility . . . superior discrimination and scruple'), while the early poems are said frequently to defeat 'rational analysis' and to suffer from 'mesmerised and self-obsessed narcissism' and 'glandular compulsiveness'. The glib phrase-making of this betrays its own kind of narcissism, not to mention a certain kind of complacent 'English-ness': *English Poetry Since 1940* (London: Longman, 1993), pp. 41–7.

6 The term 'New Country' is used hereafter to refer to the house style of the Auden-influenced 1930s poets.

7 Stephen Spender, *World Within World* (London: Readers' Union, 1953), p. 119.

8 Malcolm Bradbury and James McFarlane (eds.), *Modernism* (Harmonds-worth: Penguin, 1976), pp. 51–2.

9 W. H. Auden, *Selected Poems*, ed. Edward Mendelson (London: Faber and Faber, 1979), p. 7; Dylan Thomas, *Selected Poems*, ed. Walford Davies (London: Dent, 1993). Further page references to this edition are given parenthetically in the text as *SP*.

10 See Thomas' letter to Pamela Hansford Johnson, early November 1933: 'I fail to see how the emphasising of the body can, in any way, be regarded as hideous. The greatest description I know of our "earthiness" is to be found in John Donne's Devotions, where he describes a man as earth of the earth, his body earth, his hair a wild shrub growing out of the land. All thoughts and actions emanate from the body. Therefore the description of a thought or action – however abstruse it may be – can be beaten home by bringing it onto a physical level. Every idea, intuitive or intellectual, can be imaged and translated in terms of the body, its flesh, skin, blood, sinews, veins, glands, organs, cells, or senses': Ferris, *Collected Letters*, p. 39.

11 Robin Skelton, *Poetry of the Thirties* (Harmondsworth: Penguin, 1971), pp. 30–1.

12 Stuart Crehan, 'The Lips of Time', in Alan Bold (ed.), *Dylan Thomas: Craft or Sullen Art* (London: Vision Press, 1990), pp. 54–6. Crehan's is one of the very best recent discussions of Thomas' poetry; our indebtedness to it is general as well as for specific points.

13 Dylan Thomas, *Collected Poems*, ed. Walford Davies and Ralph Maud (London: Dent, 1989), p. 13. Further references to this edition are given parenthetically in the text as *CP*.

14 After publication in the *Listener*, there were complaints about the poem. In a letter to Pamela Hansford Johnson of March 1934, Thomas revelled in the fact that his poetry had been 'banned' by the BBC. Referring to the verse beginning 'Nor fenced, nor staked, the gushers of the sky', he commented 'The little smut-hounds thought I was writing a copulatory anthem. In reality, of course, it was a metaphysical image of rain & grief . . . all my denials of obscenity were disregarded.' The 'of course' is disingenuous; the second verse of the poem uses sexual (Freudian) imagery. Ferris, *Collected Letters*, p. 108.

15 Thomas' answer to the question 'Have you been influenced by Freud and how do you regard him?' in a questionnaire of the time runs: 'Yes. Whatever is hidden should be made naked. To be stripped of darkness is to be stripped clean, to strip darkness off is to make clean. Poetry, recording the stripping of the individual darkness, must inevitably cast light upon what has been hidden for too long . . . Benefiting by the sight of the light and the knowledge of the hidden nakedness, poetry must drag further into the clean nakedness of light even more of the hidden causes than Freud could realise.' This response – for the consumption of a public – can be compared with, *inter alia*, a private defence of the parodically grotesque and Gothic elements of his work in a letter to Pamela Hansford Johnson of 9 May 1934: 'Tell him [Victor Neuburg] I write of worms and corruption because I like worms and corruption. Tell him I believe in the fundamental wickedness and worthlessness of man, and of the rot in life. Tell him I am all for cancers. And tell him, too, that I loathe poetry. I'd prefer to be an anatomist or the keeper of a morgue any day. Tell him I live exclusively on toenails and tumours. I sleep in a coffin, too, and a wormy shroud is my summer suit': Andrew Sinclair, *No Man More Magical* (New York: Rinehart & Winston, 1975), pp. 219–20; Ferris, *Collected Letters*, p. 134.

16 Tony Conran, *Frontiers in Anglo-Welsh Poetry* (Cardiff: University of Wales Press, 1997), p. 128.

17 Thomas' argument in a review of Spender's *Vienna* of 1934 is a typically shrewd Metaphysical-influenced qualification of Poe's argument for the lyrical as the essence of true poetry: 'There is more than poetry in poems, in that much of the most considerable poem is unpoetical or anti-poetical, is dependent on the wit that discovers occult resemblances in things apparently unlike or upon the intellectual consciousness of the necessity for a social conscience. In a poem, however, the poetry must come first; what negates or acts against the poem must be subjugated to the poetry which is essentially indifferent to whatever philosophy, political passion or gang-belief it embraces . . . As a poem, *Vienna* leaves much to be desired; in the first place it leaves poetry to be desired': Walford Davies, *Dylan Thomas* (Cardiff: University of Wales Press, 1990), p. 9.

18 Rebutting Spender's claims, Thomas protested his conscious and pains-taking craftsmanship: 'My poems are formed; they are not turned on like a tap at all, they are "watertight compartments" . . . Much of the obscurity is due to rigorous compression, the last thing they do is flow; they are much rather hewn': Letter to Henry Treece, 16 May 1938, in Ferris, *Collected Letters*, p. 298.

19 Ferris, *Collected Letters*, p. 105.

20 The exhibition was opened by a green-haired André Breton and his wife, and one of the keynote lectures was delivered (inaudibly) by a diving-suit-clad Salvador Dali, who almost asphyxiated when his helmet became stuck. Other highlights included Paul Eluard's and Herbert Read's lecture on 'Art and the Unconscious' (delivered as they swayed insecurely on the edge of a sofa) and a young woman who wandered the halls carrying a prosthetic leg decorated with roses in one hand and a raw pork chop in the other.

21 Dylan Thomas, *Collected Stories*, ed. Walford Davies (London: Dent, 1993).

22 Homi K. Bhabha, *The Location of Culture* (London: Routledge, 1994), p. 90.

23 Ibid., p.113.

24 See Tony Conran: 'Anglo-Welsh poetry differs from other poetry in the English language . . . it has in its background a different civilisation – it is like English poetry written by Irishmen or Indians.' Quoted by Ned Thomas, 'Constructing a Critical Space', in Nigel Jenkins (ed.), *Thirteen Ways of Looking at Tony Conran* (Cardiff: Welsh Union of Writers, 1995), p. 103. It is not the difference of Welsh from English writing that is questionable here, so much as the suggestion of a more distinct, less impacted difference than actually exists through reference to traditions far less compatible with English.

25 As in Colin Graham, '"Liminal Spaces": Post-Colonial Theories and Irish Culture', *Irish Review*, 16 (1994), 29–43.

26 For more details see John Ackerman, 'The Welsh Background', in C. B. Cox (ed.), *Dylan Thomas* (Englewood Cliffs, N.J.: Holt, Rinehart, Winston, 1972), pp. 25–44. For a spirited counter-argument, see Roland Mathias' 'Lord Cutglass, Twenty Years After', in Dannie Abse (ed.), *Poetry Dimension 2* (London: Abacus, 1974), p. 84.

27 Letter to Vernon Watkins, 20 April 1936. Ferris, *Collected Letters*, p. 222.

28 The function of Thomas' debunking of other writers partly betrays the anti-intellectualism which Walford Davies argues 'cannot be divorced from his very Welshness, his provincialism, or the surprisingly young age out of which most of the poems came'. See Davies' Introduction to *SP*, p. xviii.

29 Gareth Thomas, 'A Freak User of Words', in Bold, *Dylan Thomas*, p. 66.

30 Ferris, *Collected Letters*, p. 172.

31 Caradoc Evans, *My People*, ed. John Harris (Bridgend: Seren Books, 1997), p. 10.

32 Gwyn A. Williams, *When Was Wales?* (Harmondsworth: Penguin, 1991), p. 253. In the town, 28,000 of a total population of less than 200,000 were registered out of work by the early 1930s.

33 Williams, *When Was Wales?* pp. 280–6.
34 Conran, *Frontiers in Anglo-Welsh Poetry*, p. 111.
35 Robert Crawford, *Devolving English Literature* (Oxford University Press, 1992), pp. 218–19. Again, recent work on Irish writing provides something of a corrective; a critique of Crawford which matches our own is made by Peter McDonald, who notes the 'useful warning' sounded in his book, but also the contradictions involved in desiring that a new identity-discourse of nationalism arise from the old one (of Englishness concealed by 'Britishness'): 'A complacent Englishness is no more subverted by (say) a complacent Scottishness than it is by the strident assertion of Irish identity; it is much more likely, in fact, to be reinforced by such pre-programmed systems of declaration': *Mistaken Identities: Poetry and Northern Ireland* (Oxford: Clarendon Press, 1997), pp. 193–4.
36 Paul Ferris, *Dylan Thomas* (Harmondsworth: Penguin, 1977), p. 53.
37 Conran, *Frontiers in Anglo-Welsh Poetry*, p. 113.
38 See Walford Davies, *Dylan Thomas*, p. 21: 'No doubt the sexual assertiveness bespoke a universal condition: one of Thomas' achievements was to make adolescence itself articulate.'
39 Jacques Derrida, *Of Grammatology*, trans. Gayatri Chakravorty Spivak (Baltimore: The Johns Hopkins University Press, 1976), p. 155.
40 Bold, *Dylan Thomas*, p. 92.
41 Marjorie Levinson maintains that it was precisely those 'sensual' and improper aspects of his style – his very 'badness' and excess – which were foregrounded in his most significant poetry. This is a typical outsider strategy which has its similarities with Thomas' own poetic practice of the 1930s: *Keats' Life of Allegory: The Origins of a Style* (Oxford: Blackwell, 1988).
42 Fred Botting, *Gothic* (London: Routledge, 1996), p. 3.
43 Similarly, the charge that Thomas avoids social reality fails to stand up to scrutiny, given the poetry's pervasive thematics of modernity. 'Our eunuch dreams', for example, has film as a governing metaphor, while 'I, in my intricate image' visualises the 'land' as a 'wax disc', and lightning as its 'stylus'. Contemporary events crop up consistently, while the First World War offered itself as a source of imagery partly because 1914 was the year of Thomas' birth, and thus fused personal origins and those of a murderously disintegrative modernity. The case for the effect of the First World War on Thomas and its presence in his poetry is made most thoroughly by James A. Davies in '"A Mental Militarist": Dylan Thomas and the Great War', in *Welsh Writing in English: A Yearbook of Critical Essays*, vol. II (Cardiff: University of Wales Press, 1996), pp. 62–81. Favourite words, such as 'drill' and 'gear', carry associations with machinery: the common claim that 'organic' imagery dominates the early poems is a good example of critical expectation overriding evidence; what Thomas *does* do is yoke together organic and inorganic terms. A very small sample from *18 Poems* would include 'the cemented skin', 'chemic blood', 'the seaweeds' iron', 'the milky acid on each hinge', 'lever from the limes / Ghostly propellors', 'nerves so wired to the

skull', 'your face / Spun to my screws'. To note this is not to deny the concern with the mutuality of growth and decay, but to insist on the dialectical relationship between the two terms.

44 Botting, *Gothic*, p. 3.

45 Ferris, *Collected Letters*, pp. 72–3.

46 His early reading included Blake, Thomas Lovell Beddoes' *Death's Jest-Book*, and Swinburne (the verse in the short story 'The Fight' echoes 'Faustine'), as well as the Gothic qualities of the Elizabethan, Jacobean and Metaphysical writers advocated by Eliot and Grierson. It is perhaps worth noting, given that Thomas was an avid filmgoer, that Boris Karloff's definitive performance in *The Mummy* appeared at the time of the Notebook poems, in 1932. Mummies (usually associated with the passing of time) appear in several early poems. Ancient Egyptian designs and motifs, following the discovery of Tutankhamun's tomb in 1924, were also a major component in the Art Deco style of the late 1920s and early 1930s.

47 For Machen's now little-known work, 'the best in the rather sticky field of genre work which took up Darwinian anxieties as a basis for terror', see David Punter, *The Literature of Terror: A History of Gothic Fictions from 1765 to the Present Day*, vol. II, *The Modern Gothic* (London: Longman, 1996), pp. 22–5. See also Davies, *Dylan Thomas*, p. 55, who notes that Thomas used material from Machen's 1922 *Autobiography* in *Under Milk Wood*.

48 Tony Pinkney, *D. H. Lawrence* (London: Harvester Wheatsheaf, 1990). See especially chapter 2, 'Northernness and Modernism'.

49 Ibid., p. 73.

50 '[A]s in Lawrence's case [sexual assertiveness] also had something to do with a specific culture, in which Bible-based fears of the Apocalypse enjoined retreat into social "respectability". It never drove Thomas, as it did Lawrence, to the exploration of a consistent compensating philosophy, but it certainly decided the emphasis of his protest': Walford Davies, *Dylan Thomas*, p. 21.

51 Sinclair, *No Man More Magical*, p. 232.

52 Davies and Maud comment: 'One might think of "Now" as the poem in which Thomas pays his greatest attention to words in themselves, paying such fanatical attention to them in the way that they weight a line that referential meaning is ultimately lost in the presentational': *CP* 201.

53 Ferris, *Collected Letters*, p. 301.

54 'I, in my intricate image' is in three sections of six 6-line stanzas (108 lines), each of which contains four end-rhyme variations on 'I' or 'is', with the 2 other lines linked by a different rhyme. 'I see the boys of summer' follows an 11–7–10–8–8–10 syllabic pattern through nine stanzas with only one lapse.

55 Walford Davies, *Dylan Thomas* (Milton Keynes: Open University Press, 1986), p. 105.

56 Ferris, *Collected Letters*, p. 97.

57 Ibid., p. 278.

58 Walford Davies, *Dylan Thomas* (1986), p. 111.

59 Ibid., p. 114.

60 See Andreas Huyssen, *After the Great Divide: Modernism, Mass Culture and Post-Modernism* (Bloomington: Indiana University Press, 1986).
61 *SP* xxxvi–xxxvii.
62 Cox, *Thomas*, p. 179.
63 Louis Simpson, *A Revolution in Taste* (New York: Macmillan, 1978), pp. 3–42.
64 Thomas is one of the very few examples of a 'high' art poet lending his name to a rock star – Bob Dylan (another example is Paul Verlaine / Tom Verlaine) – and his image to the cover of a seminal pop album, The Beatles' *Sergeant Pepper* (1967).

5 'LITERALLY, FOR THIS': METONYMIES OF NATIONAL IDENTITY IN EDWARD THOMAS, YEATS AND AUDEN

1 Eleanor Farjeon, *Edward Thomas: The Last Four Years* (London: Oxford University Press, 1958), p. 154.
2 Edward Thomas, *Feminine Influences on the Poets* (London: Martin Secker, 1910), p. 234.
3 Edward Thomas, *The South Country* (London: J. M. Dent, 1909), p. 10.
4 Edward Thomas, *Collected Poems* (London: Faber and Faber, 1965), p. 54. Subsequent page references to this edition are given parenthetically in the text as *CP*.
5 Thomas, *The South Country*, p. 153.
6 Edward Thomas, *The Heart of England* (London: J. M. Dent, 1906), pp. 226–7.
7 The letter is quoted in Garnett's Introduction to Thomas' *Selected Poems* (Newtown: The Gregynog Press, 1927), p. viii.
8 Edward Thomas, *Beautiful Wales* (London: A. and C. Black, 1905), pp. 176–7.
9 Thomas, *The South Country*, p. 7.
10 Edward Thomas, *George Borrow* (London: Chapman and Hall, 1912), p. 237.
11 Thomas, *Beautiful Wales*, pp. 185–6.
12 Edward Thomas, *The Last Sheaf* (London: Jonathan Cape, 1928), p. 109.
13 Ibid., p. 136.
14 Ibid., p. 91.
15 R. George Thomas (ed.), *Letters from Edward Thomas to George Bottomley* (London: Oxford University Press, 1968), p. 259.
16 Thomas, *The Last Sheaf*, p. 111.
17 Edward Thomas, *The Happy-Go-Lucky Morgans* (London: Duckworth, 1913), pp. 220–2.
18 Geoffrey Keynes (ed.), *The Poetical Works of Rupert Brooke* (London: Faber and Faber, 1946), p. 23.
19 Thomas, *The Last Sheaf*, p. 221.
20 W. B. Yeats, *The Variorum Edition of the Poems of W. B. Yeats*, ed. Peter Allt and Russell K. Alspach (London: Macmillan, 1957), p. 480.
21 F. R. Leavis, *New Bearings in English Poetry* (London: Chatto and Windus, 1932), p. 69.

22 W. H. Auden, *Look, Stranger!* (London: Faber and Faber, 1936), p. 14. This volume was published in the United States as *On This Island* (New York: Random House, 1937).

23 W. H. Auden, *Another Time* (London: Faber and Faber, 1940), p. 59.

24 Yeats, *Variorum Edition*, p. 402.

25 Auden, *Look, Stranger!* p. 11.

26 Ibid., p. 67.

27 Auden, *Another Time*, p. 110.

28 Yeats, *Variorum Edition*, p. 632.

29 Auden, *Another Time*, pp. 116–20, 8, 111, 9, 122.

30 W. H. Auden, 'The Public v. the Late Mr. William Butler Yeats', *The English Auden: Poems, Essays & Dramatic Writings, 1927–1939*, ed. Edward Mendelson (London: Faber and Faber, 1977), pp. 389–93.

31 Yeats, *Variorum Edition*, p. 638.

32 Auden, *Look, Stranger!* p. 19.

33 W. H. Auden, *New Year Letter* (London: Faber and Faber, 1941), p. 54. This volume was published in the United States as *The Double Man* (New York: Random House, 1941).

34 W. H. Auden, *Nones* (London: Faber and Faber, 1952), pp. 11–13.

35 W. H. Auden (ed.), *The Faber Book of Modern American Verse* (London: Faber and Faber, 1956), p. 12.

36 Ibid., pp. 14, 20.

37 Auden, *New Year Letter*, p. 70.

6 REACTIONS FROM THEIR BURG: IRISH MODERNIST POETS OF THE 1930S

1 Ezra Pound, *Selected Prose 1909–1965*, ed. William Cookson (New York: New Directions, 1973), pp. 201, 202.

2 MacNeice's reiterated distaste for Pound is manifest in, for instance, his 1935 essay 'Poetry To-day': 'For very many years [Pound] has been repeating, rather hysterically, that he is an expert and a specialist; but he has specialized his poems into museum pieces': Alan Heuser (ed.), *Selected Literary Criticism of Louis MacNeice* (Oxford University Press, 1987), p. 17.

3 Louis MacNeice, *Collected Poems*, ed. E. R. Dodds (London: Faber and Faber, 1966), p. 133.

4 Ibid., p. 133.

5 Ibid., p. 101.

6 Peter McDonald, 'Believing in the Thirties', in Keith Williams and Steven Matthews (eds.), *Rewriting the Thirties: Modernism and After* (London: Longman, 1997), p. 71.

7 J. C. C. Mays, Introduction to Denis Devlin, *Collected Poems*, ed. J. C. C. Mays (Dublin: Dedalus, 1989), p. 26.

8 Samuel Beckett, *Disjecta: Miscellaneous Writings and a Dramatic Fragment*, ed. Ruby Cohn (London: John Calder, 1983), p. 74.

9 Ibid., p. 70.
10 Ibid., p. 71.
11 Austin Clarke, *Reviews and Essays of Austin Clarke*, ed. Gregory A. Schirmer (Gerrards Cross: Colin Smythe, 1995), p. 175.
12 Ibid., p. 166.
13 Ibid., p. 181.
14 Charles Bernstein, *A Poetics* (Cambridge, Mass.: Harvard University Press, 1992), p. 200.
15 Christopher Butler, *Early Modernism: Literature, Music and Painting in Europe 1900–1916* (Oxford University Press, 1994), p. 14.
16 Devlin, *Collected Poems*, p. 103.
17 Ibid., pp. 103–4.
18 Ibid., p. 104.
19 This is the definition of the historical avant-garde advanced by Bürger: 'with the historical avant-garde movements, the social subsystem that is art enters the stage of self-criticism. Dadaism, the most radical movement within the European avant-garde, no longer criticizes schools that preceded it, but criticizes art as an institution, and the course its development took in bourgeois society': Peter Bürger, *Theory of the Avant-Garde*, trans. Michael Shaw (Minneapolis: University of Minnesota Press, 1984), p. 22.
20 See Tate and Warren's Preface to their edition of Devlin's *Selected Poems*: 'Devlin was one of the pioneers of the international poetic English which now prevails on both sides of the Atlantic': Allen Tate and Robert Penn Warren, Preface to Denis Devlin, *Selected Poems* (New York: Holt, Rinehart and Winston, 1963), p. 14.
21 Terence Brown, *Ireland: A Social and Cultural History 1922–1985* (London: Fontana, 1985), p. 147.
22 Quoted in Brown, *Ireland*, p. 146.
23 Anne Fogarty, 'Gender, Irish Modernism and the Poetry of Denis Devlin', in Patricia Coughlan and Alex Davis (eds.), *Modernism and Ireland: The Poetry of the 1930s* (Cork University Press, 1995), p. 214.
24 The fate of two iconoclastic Irish journals in the 1920s prefigures that of *Ireland To-day*. *To-morrow*, the two numbers of which appeared in 1924, published Yeats' 'Leda and the Swan' and Lennox Robinson's short story 'The Madonna of Slieve Dunne', the sexual politics of both texts, which centre on rape, prompting a Catholic backlash. Instrumental in the publication of the short-lived *To-morrow* was Beckett's friend A. J. Levanthal, whose journal the *Klaxon*, the single issue of which appeared in 1923, adopted the tone and look of avant-garde magazines elsewhere, and included Levanthal's long review of *Ulysses* and an essay by MacGreevy on Picasso and the Irish modernist painter Mainie Jellett. On the *Klaxon* see Tim Armstrong, 'Muting the Klaxon: Poetry, History and Irish Modernism', in Coughlan and Davis (eds.), *Modernism and Ireland*, pp. 43–74.
25 Devlin, *Collected Poems*, p. 105.
26 Beckett, *Disjecta*, p. 75.

27 Ibid., p. 76; punctuation added from Devlin, *Collected Poems*, p. 83.
28 Beckett, *Disjecta*, p. 76. Beckett's delightful phrase '*Gossoons Wunderhorn*' is ably glossed by J. C. C. Mays as 'A play on words involving the Anglo-Irish word *gossoon* (lackey or servant-boy) and *Das Knaben Wunderhorn* (1806–8), a collection of German folk songs by Arnim and Brentano': J. C. C. Mays, Headnote to 'Samuel Beckett', in *The Field Day Anthology of Irish Writing*, 3 vols. (Derry: Field Day, 1991), vol. III, p. 248.
29 John P. Harrington, *The Irish Beckett* (Syracuse University Press, 1991), p. 33.
30 David Lloyd, *Anomalous States: Irish Writing and the Post-Colonial Moment* (Dublin: Lilliput, 1993), p. 56.
31 Ibid., pp. 54, 42.
32 David Lloyd, *Nationalism and Minor Literature: James Clarence Mangan and the Emergence of Irish Cultural Nationalism* (Berkeley: University of California Press, 1987), pp. 24–5.
33 Samuel Beckett, *Collected Poems 1930–1978* (London: John Calder, 1984), p. 10.
34 See *Inferno* III.21; see Lawrence Harvey, *Samuel Beckett: Poet and Critic* (Princeton University Press, 1970), pp. 98–9.
35 T. S. Eliot, *The Complete Poems and Plays of T. S. Eliot* (London: Faber and Faber, 1969), p. 62.
36 Ibid.
37 Beckett, *Collected Poems*, p. 11.
38 Ibid., p. 12.
39 Harvey, *Samuel Beckett*, p. 135.
40 Eliot, *Complete Poems and Plays*, pp. 61–2.
41 Ibid., p. 62.
42 James Joyce, *Finnegans Wake*, 3rd edn. (Faber and Faber, 1960), p. 383.
43 Beckett, *Collected Poems*, p. 12.
44 Harrington, *The Irish Beckett*, p. 87.
45 Joyce, *Finnegans Wake*, p. 593. For a concise reading of the political context of the *Wake*, see David Pierce, 'The Politics of *Finnegans Wake*', in Patrick A. McCarthy (ed.), *Critical Essays on James Joyce's Finnegans Wake* (Boston: G. K. Hall, 1992), pp. 243–57.
46 Joyce, *Finnegans Wake*, p. 62.
47 Beckett, *Disjecta*, p. 19.
48 Thomas MacGreevy, 'The Catholic Element in *Work in Progress*', in Samuel Beckett *et al.*, *Our Exagmination Round His Factification for Incamination of Work in Progress* (London: Faber and Faber, 1961), p. 123.
49 For Schreibman's dating of the poem, see *Collected Poems of Thomas MacGreevy*, ed. Susan Schreibman (Dublin and Washington: Anna Livia Press / The Catholic University of America Press, 1991), p. 107.
50 Ibid., p. 57.
51 T. S. Eliot, *Selected Prose of T. S. Eliot*, ed. Frank Kermode (London: Faber and Faber, 1975), p. 177.
52 MacGreevy, *Collected Poems*, p. 24.

53 Pierce, 'The Politics of *Finnegans Wake*', p. 246.
54 MacGreevy, *Collected Poems*, p. 19.
55 See Schreibman's note in MacGreevy, *Collected Poems*, p. 115.
56 Eliot, *Complete Poems and Plays*, p. 73.
57 Thomas MacGreevy, *Richard Aldington: An Englishman* (London: Chatto and Windus, 1931), pp. 31, 32.
58 Ibid., p. 32.
59 MacGreevy, *Collected Poems*, p. 15.
60 Ibid., p. 16.
61 Ibid., p. 17.
62 Patricia Coughlan, '"The Poetry is Another Pair of Sleeves": Beckett, Ireland and Modernist Lyric Poetry', in Coughlan and Davis, *Modernism and Ireland*, p. 196.
63 Hugh Kenner, *A Reader's Guide to Samuel Beckett* (Syracuse University Press, 1996), p. 42.
64 Terence Brown, 'Ireland, Modernism and the 1930s', in Coughlan and Davis, *Modernism and Ireland*, pp. 38–9.
65 Brian Coffey, letter to Thomas MacGreevy, 14 May 1934, Thomas MacGreevy Papers, Trinity College Dublin.
66 Brian Coffey, *Poems and Versions 1929–1990* (Dublin: Dedalus, 1991), p. 70.
67 Ibid., p. 14.
68 Ibid., p. 17.
69 Edna Longley, *The Living Stream: Literature and Revisionism in Ireland* (Newcastle: Bloodaxe, 1994), p. 203.
70 Ibid., p. 202.
71 Austin Clarke, *Collected Poems* (Dublin and Oxford: Dolmen / Oxford University Press, 1974), p. 364.
72 Ibid., p. 365. Brian Fallon notes Clarke's close study of Pound in the 1950s and recalls being 'present once when he discussed the *Cantos* at length with a fellow poet': Brian Fallon, *An Age of Innocence: Irish Culture 1930–1960* (Dublin: Gill and Macmillan, 1998), p. 283.
73 Patrick Crotty (ed.), *Modern Irish Poetry: An Anthology* (Belfast: Blackstaff, 1995), p. 13.

7 POUND'S PLACES

1 See Omar Pound and A. Walton Litz (eds.), *Ezra Pound and Dorothy Shakespear, Their Letters: 1909–1914* (London: Faber and Faber, 1984), pp. 108–19.
2 Ezra Pound, *A Walking Tour in Southern France: Ezra Pound among the Troubadours*, ed. Richard Sieburth (New York: New Directions, 1992). Subsequent references are given parenthetically in the text.
3 On the themes of anachronism and exile in Pound's early work, see Peter Nicholls, *Modernisms: A Literary Guide* (London: Macmillan, 1995), pp. 167–9.
4 Pound's lack of interest in the cathedral is especially notable in view of his

remarks in the later 'Cavalcanti', in *Literary Essays of Ezra Pound*, ed. T. S. Eliot (London: Faber and Faber, 1954), p. 151, on 'the niggly Angoulême, the architectural ornament of bigotry, superstition, and mess'.

5 Justin Smith, *The Troubadours at Home: Their Lives and Personalities*, 2 vols. (New York: G. P. Putnam, 1899).

6 *Collected Early Poems of Ezra Pound*, ed. Michael John King (London: Faber and Faber, 1977), p. 71.

7 'Three Cantos. 1', *Poetry*, 10:3 (1917), 114: 'Beaucaire's slim gray / leaps from the stubby base of Altaforte.'

8 Walter Benjamin, *One Way Street and Other Writings*, trans. Edmund Jephcott and Kingsley Shorter (London: NLB, 1979), p. 250.

9 Omar Pound and Robert Spoo (eds.), *Ezra Pound and Margaret Cravens: A Tragic Friendship 1910–1912* (Durham and London: Duke University Press, 1988), p. 27.

10 *Literary Essays of Ezra Pound*, p. 5. See Daniel Tiffany, *Radio Corpse: Imagism and the Cryptaesthetic of Ezra Pound* (Cambridge, Mass.: Harvard University Press 1995), p. 27: 'Pound's conception of the Image neglects the "real" and even actively seeks to sever itself from the empirical object.' See also Peter Nicholls, *Ezra Pound: Politics, Economics and Writing* (London: Macmillan, 1984), pp. 8–10.

11 Ezra Pound, *The Spirit of Romance* (New York: New Directions, 1968), p. 96.

12 *Literary Essays of Ezra Pound*, p. 54; letter to Viola Baxter Jordan (24 October 1907), in *Paideuma* 1:1 (1972), 109.

13 Catherine Seelye (ed.), *Charles Olson and Ezra Pound* (New York: New Directions, 1975), p. 98.

14 Robert Duncan, 'The H. D. Book: Chapter 4', *Tri-Quarterly* 12 (1968), 82.

15 Michel de Certeau, *The Practice of Everyday Life*, trans. Steven Randall (Berkeley: University of California Press, 1984), p. 118. Further references are given parenthetically in the text.

16 Ezra Pound, *ABC of Reading* (London: Faber and Faber, 1951), pp. 43–4. See also Cantos LXXIV/461, LXXVII/480, LXXXII/541, XCV/659, CVII/771, in Ezra Pound, *The Cantos* (London: Faber and Faber, 1994). Further page references are given parenthetically in the text.

17 Ezra Pound, 'A List of Books', *Little Review* 4:11 (1918), 54–8. For Pound's use of the word 'phantasmagoria', see Ian F. A. Bell, 'The Phantasmagoria of *Hugh Selwyn Mauberley*', *Paideuma* 5:3 (1976), 361–85.

18 *Literary Essays of Ezra Pound*, p. 154. Further references are given parenthetically in the text.

19 '"Veduta forma" must, however, be extrinsic and perceived, if we are to leave any shred of verbal meaning in any term whatsoever': ibid., p. 188.

20 On the idea of a composite landscape, see also John Peck, 'Landscape as Ceremony in the Later *Cantos*', *Agenda* 9:2/3 (1971), 26–69. Also relevant is Donald Davie, 'Landscape as Poetic Focus', *Southern Review* 4 (1968), 685–91.

21 Michel Foucault, 'Of Other Spaces', *Diacritics* (1986), 24.

22 *The Selected Letters of Ezra Pound*, ed. D. D. Paige (London: Faber and Faber,

1971), p. 254.

23 The passage in its entirety (94–5) places strong stress on 'c' sounds to emphasise rhythmic 'cutting': for example, 'The road, back and away, till cut along the face of the rock, / And the cliff folds in like a curtain, / The road cut in under the rock / Square groove in the cliff's face, as chiostri, / The columns crystal . . .', etc.

24 Ezra Pound, *Guide to Kulchur* (1938) (London: Peter Owen, 1966), p. 194.

25 Pierre Nora, 'Between Memory and History: *Les Lieux de Mémoire*', *Representations* 26 (1989), 7–8. Further references are given parenthetically in the text.

26 Ezra Pound, *Hugh Selwyn Mauberley (Life and Contacts)*, in *Collected Shorter Poems* (London: Faber and Faber, 1968), p. 206.

27 See Nora, 'Between Memory and History', p. 9: 'Memory installs remembrance within the sacred; history, always prosaic, releases it again . . . Memory takes root in the concrete, in spaces, gestures, images, and objects; history binds itself strictly to temporal continuities, to progressions and to relations between things.'

28 Pound, *Hugh Selwyn Mauberley*, p. 208.

29 See M. M. Bakhtin, *The Dialogic Imagination*, ed. Michael Holquist, trans. Caryl Emerson and Michael Holquist (Austin: University of Texas Press, 1981), p. 217: 'When the immanent unity of time disintegrated, when individual life-sequences were separated out, lives in which the gross realities of communal life had become merely petty private matters; when collective labor and the struggle with nature had ceased to be the only arena for man's encounter with nature and the world – then nature itself ceased to be a living participant in the events of life. Then nature became, by and large, a "setting for action", its backdrop; it was turned into landscape, it was fragmented into metaphors and comparisons serving to sublimate individual and private affairs and adventures not connected in any real or intrinsic way with nature itself.'

30 For a meticulous account of Pound's extensive researches for these Cantos, see Lawrence S. Rainey, *Ezra Pound and the Monument of Culture: Text, History, and the Malatesta Cantos* (University of Chicago Press, 1991).

31 Quoted in ibid., p. 184. Rainey argues convincingly that Pound's view of the Tempio was a 'late Romantic one' (p. 224) and that he overlooked interpretations which conflicted with his own preferences (the reading of the entwined letters 'S' and 'I' as representing Sigismundo and Isotta was one such case).

32 Quoted from an unpublished letter in Carroll F. Terrell, *A Companion to The Cantos of Ezra Pound* (Berkeley: University of California Press, 1993), p. 73.

33 John Ruskin, *The Stones of Venice*, in *The Complete Works of John Ruskin*, ed. E. T. Cook and Alexander Wedderburn, 39 vols. (London: George Allen, 1903–12), vol. x, pp. 82–3. Donald Davie, *Ezra Pound: The Poet as Sculptor* (London: Routledge, 1965), p. 129, observes that 'Where "marble" appears, or "stone", it is a sign of resurgence and renewed hope', and Tony Tanner, *Venice Desired* (Oxford: Blackwell, 1992), p. 306, remarks that 'the intimate

conjunction of the organic with the inorganic or mineral is often radiantly positive in Pound'. For a detailed discussion of Pound's likely debt to Ruskin here, see Catarina Ricciardi, *EIKONΣ: Ezra Pound e il Rinascimento* (Naples: Liguori, 1991), pp. 227–67.

34 Adrian Stokes, *Stones of Rimini* (1934) (New York: Schocken Books, 1969), p. 20.

35 Adrian Stokes, *The Quattrocento: A Different Conception of the Italian Renaissance* (1932) (New York: Schocken Books, 1968), p. 13. The rejection of 'dazzling' light parallels Pound's light 'not of the sun'. Compare also Ruskin, *Modern Painters*, in *Complete Works*, vol. III, p. 74: 'the utmost possible sense of beauty is conveyed by a feebly translucent, smooth but not lustrous surface of white and pale warm red, subdued by the most pure and delicate grays, as in the finer portions of the human frame'.

36 Pound, *A Walking Tour*, p. 64.

37 Stokes, *Stones of Rimini*, pp. 16–17. See Stokes, *The Quattrocento*, p.14: 'the marbles may afford you an image of living process, one that is complete because therein is employed the perfect objectivity that petrification or death alone can give'.

38 See Nora, 'Between Memory and History', p. 22: 'Memory attaches itself to sites, whereas history attaches itself to events.'

39 Pound, *ABC of Reading*, p. 44: 'You can't tuck Odysseus away with Virgil's Aeneas. Odysseus is emphatically "the wise guy", the downy, the hard-boiled Odysseus.' Note the more colloquial tone of the Canto.

40 See Nicholls, *Ezra Pound: Politics, Economics and Writing*, pp. 112–25.

41 Homi Bhabha, *The Location of Culture* (London: Routledge, 1994), p. 149.

42 Pound, *Guide to Kulchur*, pp. 151–2.

43 Allied bombings in late 1943 and early 1944 destroyed most of the Tempio's roof and all of its apse. See Rainey, *Ezra Pound and the Monument of Culture*, pp. 209–12.

44 *The Sacred Edict of K'ang Hsi*, trans. F. W. Baller, 2nd edn (Shanghai, 1907). For detailed studies of Pound's use of this text, see Carroll F. Terrell, 'The Sacred Edict of K'ang Hsi', *Paideuma* 2:1 (1973), 69–112; David Gordon, 'The Sacred Edict', *Paideuma* 3:2 (1974), 169–90, and 'More on The Sacred Edict', *Paideuma* 4:1 (1975), 121–70.

45 Bakhtin, *The Dialogic Imagination*, p. 225.

46 Peter Goullart, *Forgotten Kingdom* (1955) (London: Readers Union, 1957); Joseph F. Rock, *The Ancient Na-khi Kingdom of Southwest China*, 2 vols., Harvard-Yenching Institute Monograph Series (Cambridge, Mass.: Harvard-Yenching Institute, 1974). For the date of Pound's reading, see Carroll F. Terrell, 'The Na-khi Documents, I: The Landscape of Paradise', *Paideuma* 3:1 (1974), 94. Pound alludes to 'Rock on Na Khi / and lively *Forgotten Kingdom* by Goullart' in a letter of 29 May 1957 to John Theobald; see Donald Pearce and Herbert Schneidau (eds.), *Pound/Theobald: Letters* (Redding Ridge, Conn.: Black Swan Books, 1984), p. 27. See also Peck, 'Landscape as Ceremony in the Later *Cantos*'; and Jamila Ismail, '"News of

the Universe": ²Muan ¹Bpö and *The Cantos'*, *Agenda* 9:2/3 (1971), 70–87.
47 Goullart's *Forgotten Kingdom* ends (pp. 251–9) with the 'liberation' of Likiang by the Communists.
48 Ibid., pp. 48, 78.
49 Peck, 'Landscape as Ceremony', 68. Peck also gives a helpful synopsis of the use made of Rock's work in these late Cantos: 'after the preliminary notes on ²Muan ¹Bpö in Canto 98, the parts of "Rock's world" sort out into military struggle and funeral rites (Canto 101), the suicide night-world of Canto 110 (invoking several Noh plays, even *Takasago*, and constructing both motif and exorcism with their assistance), and finally in Canto 112, the Heaven-sacrifice-as-landscape, giving us the final rite together with a counterpart to the Noh stage itself'.
50 For an extended account of this passage, see Peter Nicholls, '"To Unscrew the Inscrutable": Myth as Fiction and Belief in Ezra Pound's *Cantos'*, in Michael Bell and Peter Poellner (eds.), *Modernism and Mythopoeia: The Problem of Grounding in Early Twentieth-Century Literature* (Amsterdam: Rodopi, 1999), pp. 149–52.
51 Maurice Blanchot, *The Space of Literature*, trans. Ann Smock (Lincoln, Nebr., and London: University of Nebraska Press, 1982), p. 237. See also Philippe Lacoue-Labarthe, 'In the Name of . . . ', in Simon Sparks (ed.), *Retreating the Political: Philippe Lacoue-Labarthe and Jean-Luc Nancy* (London: Routledge, 1997), for a discussion of *Heimlichkeit* and *Unheimlichkeit* in Heidegger. The motifs of 'homeland', 'dwelling', etc., in the late Heidegger exhibit 'a certain propensity . . . towards idyllic inanity' (p. 60) which contrasts with the earlier work's attention to the 'un-usual and the un-accustomed, the uncanny' (p. 67).

8 WALLACE STEVENS AND AMERICA

1 See David Bennett, 'Defining the "American" Difference: Cultural Nationalism and the Modernist Poetics of William Carlos Williams', *Southern Review* 20:3 (1987), 273; William Carlos Williams, *Prologue* to *Kora in Hell: Improvisations* (1918), rpt in *Imaginations* (New York: New Directions, 1970), p. 27.
2 *The Collected Poems of Wallace Stevens* (New York: Knopf, 1954), p. 345. Further references will be designated parenthetically in the text as *CP*; William Carlos Williams, 'Sample Critical Statement', *Contact* 4 (1921), 18, and *In the American Grain* (1925), rpt (New York: New Directions, 1956). In rebuttal of Stevens' 'Description without Place', Williams wrote his poem 'A Place (Any Place) to Transcend All Places', in *The Collected Poems of William Carlos Williams*, 2 vols. (New York: New Directions, 1988), vol. II, p. 163; see Alan Filreis, *Wallace Stevens and the Actual World* (Princeton University Press, 1991), p. 182.
3 Strom argues that Stevens' 'The Comedian as the Letter C' should be read as a 'reaction against the localists': 'When Stevens refers to "The Comedian" as an "anti-mythological poem", one of the myths he refers to is

surely the sacrosanct Americanism which surrounded him on all sides': Martha Strom, 'Wallace Stevens' Revisions of Crispin's Journal: A Reaction Against the "Local"', in Steven Gould Axelrod and Helen Deese (eds.), *Critical Essays on Wallace Stevens* (Boston: G. K. Hall, 1988), p. 131, p. 134.

4 William Carlos Williams, 'Comment', *Contact* 2 (1921); in his later poemsequence *Paterson*, Williams revises this model, now envisaging the identity of the American poet as emerging from a familial relationship to place – *pater-son*.

5 Yvor Winters, 'Wallace Stevens; Or, The Hedonist's Progress', in *The Anatomy of Nonsense* (New York: New Directions, 1943), p. 99.

6 *Wallace Stevens Journal* 13:2 (1989), 83. See Jacqueline Vaught Brogan, 'Stevens in History and Not in History: The Poet and the Second World War', where Perloff's analysis of Stevens is placed in 'an unbroken tradition regarding Stevens' poetry as socially irrelevant, socially unconcerned, and even (most damningly) socially irresponsible': ibid., p. 168; Marjorie Perloff, 'Revolving in Crystal: The Supreme Fiction and the Impasse of Modernist Lyric', in Albert Gelpi (ed.), *Wallace Stevens: The Poetics of Modernism* (Cambridge University Press, 1985), pp. 41–65, 42.

7 *Letters of Wallace Stevens*, ed. Holly Stevens (New York: Knopf, 1966), p. 26. Lentricchia also cites this letter from 1899, 'in which manhood as an artist is seen as coincidental with major, canonical status'. Arguing that for Stevens 'economic self-making' was necessarily bound up with masculinisation, Lentricchia suggests that 'The only image of himself as woman that [Stevens] can tolerate . . . is an image of female power' as in 'The Idea of Order at Key West': it is Stevens' fear of 'the cultural powerlessness of poetry in a society that masculinized the economic while feminizing the literary' that led him to 'fantasize the potential social authority of the literary as phallic authority': Frank Lentricchia, *Ariel and the Police: Michel Foucault, William James, Wallace Stevens* (Hemel Hempstead: Harvester, 1988), pp. 169, 142, 154, 168. Critical appraisals of *Harmonium* have frequently been negative, at the time of the book's publication and in later criticism. Helen Vendler, for instance, calls attention to the title Stevens originally proposed for *Harmonium*, 'The Grand Poem: Preliminary Minutiae', and, privileging the 'grand' poetry of his later career, she relegates *Harmonium* to preliminaries and to minutiae. Vendler's adverse judgment has proved influential and has distorted the way in which Stevens' *Collected Poems* has been read: Helen Vendler, *On Extended Wings: Wallace Stevens's Longer Poems* (Cambridge, Mass.: Harvard University Press, 1969), p. 1.

8 The sun-men of 'Sunday Morning' are also a prevision of the 'noble' and 'sovereign' imagery Stevens will develop in *Ideas of Order* and will sustain in 'A Thought Revolved' from *The Man with the Blue Guitar*, where the 'Son only of man and sun of men' is a punning example of the pagan cult of the sun with which Stevens' 'hero' and 'major man' are subsequently associated (*CP* 185). Lentricchia describes the 'ring of men' in 'Sunday Morning' as 'a masculine totality, fused in an image of masculine power: Father Nature:' *Ariel and the Police*, p. 158.

9 These themes are also pertinent to Stevens' poem-sequence 'Notes Toward a Supreme Fiction'; first published in 1942, 'Notes' can more suggestively be read in the context of *Parts of a World* and with related prose pieces Stevens wrote at this time than in the context of the 1947 volume *Transport to Summer*, in which 'Notes' appears in the *Collected Poems*.

10 See Eleanor Cook's analysis of Stevens and synecdoche, in her *Poetry, Word Play and Word-War in Wallace Stevens* (Princeton University Press, 1988), p. 153.

11 Harold Bloom, *Wallace Stevens: The Poems of Our Climate* (Ithaca: Cornell University Press, 1977), p. 159.

12 *Letters of Wallace Stevens*, p. 370.

13 The question of belief in the 'hero' is posed with greater urgency in canto VI of 'Examination of the Hero in a Time of War', where Stevens asks, 'Unless we believe in the hero, what is there / To believe?' (*CP* 275).

14 This quotation is taken from the statement on poetry and war which Stevens appended to the first edition of *Parts of a World*: Wallace Stevens, *Opus Posthumous*, ed. Milton J. Bates (New York: Knopf, 1989), p. 242.

15 See Melita Schaum, *Wallace Stevens and the Critical Schools* (Tuscaloosa: University of Alabama Press, 1988). It isn't of course a paradox that both New Critics and proponents of deconstruction should have seized on Stevens for their own purposes. Deconstruction is a new New Criticism, insisting as it does on the self-sufficiency of the text and the separation of the text from the wider context of its production.

16 Vendler, *On Extended Wings*, pp. 144–67; for Hillis Miller, Stevens' is a poetry 'appropriate to the incomplete', and for Riddel, Stevens is the poet of 'openness' and 'incompleteness': J. Hillis Miller, 'Wallace Stevens' Poetry of Being', in Roy Harvey Pearce and J. Hillis Miller (eds.), *The Act of the Mind: Essays on the Poetry of Wallace Stevens* (Baltimore: The Johns Hopkins University Press, 1965), pp. 243–77; Joseph Riddel, 'Metaphoric Staging: Stevens' Beginning Again of the "End of the Book"', in Frank Doggett and Robert Buttel (eds.), *Wallace Stevens: A Celebration* (Princeton University Press, 1980), p. 317.

17 Filreis, *Wallace Stevens and the Actual World*, pp. 3, 6.

18 John Fekete, *The Critical Twilight* (London: Routledge and Kegan Paul, 1977), p. 49.

19 As Fekete points out, however, it was not until the end of the 1940s that the New Criticism 'became established as the dominant pedagogic tradition' in America: ibid., p. 88.

20 Filreis, *Wallace Stevens and the Actual World*, pp. 76, 77; Fekete notes that in the New Criticism, 'All possibilities of reshaping the exterior world are renounced to gain social sanction for the perfection of the interior world', and, with reference to Ransom's criticism, Fekete discusses 'the general indictment of the modern world which . . . can serve as a pretext for casting off systems of reference' and which 'permits the elaboration of an aesthetic that focusses on the isolated work itself': Fekete, *The Critical Twilight*, pp. 45, 73.

21 Stevens was appropriated by the New Critics in other respects, too. Leitch quotes Tate, on the Agrarian ideal of a unified or organic society – the 'point at issue is not whether unity of being in an organic society ever existed, or whether it could exist; we must affirm its necessity' – and comments that 'The strategy here' is 'modelled after Wallace Stevens' celebrated "necessary fictions"': Vincent B. Leitch, *American Literary Criticism from the '30s to the '80s* (New York: Columbia University Press, 1988), p. 34.

22 Filreis, *Wallace Stevens and the Actual World*, pp. 87–9.

23 Wallace Stevens, *Opus Posthumous*, p. 223.

24 See Stanley Burnshaw's hostile review of *Ideas of Order* as a 'record of agitated attitudes toward the present social order', in *New Masses* 17 (1935), 41–2; for Stevens' response to Burnshaw, see his poem 'Mr Burnshaw and the Statue', *Owl's Clover* (1936), rpt *Opus Posthumous*, pp. 78–83.

25 Vendler, *On Extended Wings*, p. 153.

26 Ibid., p. 153.

27 Wallace Stevens, *Opus Posthumous*, p. 108.

28 See, for instance, the passage in 'Montrachet-le-Jardin', concerning 'the root-man and the super-man, / The root-man swarming, tortured by his mass, / The super-man friseured, possessing and possessed' (*CP* 262).

29 *Letters of Wallace Stevens*, p. 409, pp. 431–2, p. 461, p. 462; in another letter from 1942, Stevens acknowledges that he 'had better wait until after the war' to order editions of Nietzsche's work: p. 431.

30 Patrick Bridgwater, 'English Writers and Nietzsche', in Malcolm Pasley (ed.), *Nietzsche: Imagery and Thought* (London: Methuen, 1978), pp. 255, 252.

31 *Letters of Wallace Stevens*, pp. 289–90.

32 Ibid., pp. 371–2.

33 Hi Simons, 'The Humanism of Wallace Stevens' (1942), rpt in Charles Doyle (ed.), *Wallace Stevens: The Critical Heritage* (London: Routledge, 1985), p. 208.

34 The phrase is borrowed from Michel Benamou's description of Stevens in his *Wallace Stevens: and the Symbolist Imagination* (Princeton University Press, 1972), p. 124.

35 Frank Kermode, 'Dwelling Poetically in Connecticut', in Doggett and Buttel, *Wallace Stevens: A Celebration*, p. 273.

36 Wallace Stevens, *Opus Posthumous*, p. 138.

37 Ibid., p. 135.

38 Ibid., p. 141; see the description of Stevens' Crispin in 'The Comedian as the Letter C', as 'Like Candide, / Yeoman' (*CP* 42), and compare Stevens' statement from 1955 that 'we live in the tradition which is the true mythology of the region': Wallace Stevens, *Opus Posthumous*, p. 303.

39 Ibid., p. 248; see the editor's note to the effect that Stevens' typescript suggests some confusion on Stevens' part as to which states – Tennessee and Kentucky – Ransom and Tate came from: ibid., p. 329.

40 Ibid., pp. 303–4. See my 'Thomas MacGreevy and the Pressure of Reality',

Wallace Stevens Journal 18:2 (1994), 146–56, where I argue that Stevens' correspondence with the Irish poet Thomas MacGreevy may have contributed to the 'regionalism', or descriptions *with* places, of Stevens' late poems. In a letter to MacGreevy, Stevens stated that 'Whatever I have comes from Pennsylvania and Connecticut and from nowhere else. That too, no doubt, is why Ireland, green as it is, seems to me so much greener than it is, and why you seem to be the best of all my correspondents': letter to Thomas MacGreevy from Wallace Stevens, 17 April 1953 – Trinity College Dublin 8123/29, quoted with the permission of Margaret Farrington and Elizabeth Ryan.

41 I refer to Charles Olson's and the Black Mountain school's version of localism.

9 LOCATING THE LYRIC: MARIANNE MOORE, ELIZABETH BISHOP AND THE SECOND WORLD WAR

1 Wallace Stevens, *Opus Posthumous*, rev. edn ed. Milton J. Bates (London: Faber and Faber, 1990), p. 229.

2 The network of relationships between Moore, Bishop and Stevens is mapped in David Kalstone, *Becoming a Poet: Elizabeth Bishop with Marianne Moore and Robert Lowell* (London: Hogarth, 1989); *Stevens and Elizabeth Bishop: Special Issue: Wallace Stevens Journal*, 19:2 (1995); and Robin G. Schulze, *The Web of Friendship: Marianne Moore and Wallace Stevens* (Ann Arbor: University of Michigan Press, 1995).

3 For a sequential reading, see Lynn Keller, *Re-Making it New: Contemporary American Poetry and the Modernist Tradition* (Cambridge University Press, 1987).

4 The phrase is Stevens': see 'The Noble Rider and the Sound of Words' (1941), in his *The Necessary Angel: Essays on Reality and the Imagination* (London: Faber and Faber, 1960), p. 36.

5 Elizabeth Bishop, 'Efforts of Affection' (*c.* 1969), in *Collected Prose*, ed. Robert Giroux (London: Hogarth, 1984), p. 137.

6 Marianne Moore, *The Complete Prose of Marianne Moore*, ed. Patricia C. Willis (London: Faber and Faber, 1987), pp. 539, 540.

7 Stevens' regular Florida vacations ended in 1940 when the Navy requisitioned Casa Marina, his favourite Key West resort. See Alan Filreis, *Wallace Stevens and the Actual World* (Princeton University Press, 1991), p. 47.

8 Stevens, *The Necessary Angel*, p. 36.

9 This is the broad contour of Stevens' poetry sketched by Alan Filreis: after America's entry into the Second World War, Filreis reads Stevens' as a poetic of engagement. See his *Wallace Stevens and the Actual World*, chapter 2.

10 See, for example, the spatial metaphors in Allen Tate's 'Tension in Poetry' (1938), in his *Essays of Four Decades* (Oxford University Press, 1970).

11 Elizabeth Bishop, *The Complete Poems, 1927–1979* (London: Hogarth, 1984), p. 4.

12 Stevens, *The Necessary Angel*, p. 36; *Opus Posthumous*, p. 230.

13 According to Randall Jarrell, for example, Moore's substitution of 'abstractions' for the 'real particulars' of a war she had not seen was disastrous: 'Poetry in War and Peace' (1945), in *Kipling, Auden & Co.: Essays and Reviews, 1935–1964* (New York: Farar, Strauss and Giroux, 1980), p. 130. Recent opposition to the negative consensus about the war lyrics has focussed on gender: see, for example, Susan Schweik, *A Gulf So Deeply Cut: American Women Poets and the Second World War* (Madison: University of Wisconsin Press, 1991), p. 39.

14 Marianne Moore, 'In Distrust of Merits', in her *Nevertheless* (New York: Macmillan, 1944), p. 13.

15 Bishop, letter to Ferris Greenslet (literary advisor to Houghton Mifflin), 22 January 1945, in *Elizabeth Bishop, One Art: The Selected Letters*, ed. Robert Giroux (London: Chatto and Windus, 1994), p. 125; hereafter *Letters*. The disclaimer eventually read 'Most of these poems were written, or partly written, before 1942': *North & South* (Boston: Houghton Mifflin, 1946). Susan Schweik astutely points out that in *North & South* there are, in fact, 'naval engagements, border crossings, skirmishes, search missions'. She argues that these 'matters of war literature . . . appear, but only as covert operations. Each takes the form of a lyric trope, interiorized, parabolic, skewed': *A Gulf So Deeply Cut*, p. 213. In Schweik's argument lyricism is thought of as definitively inward facing. I want to consider the possibility that the orientation and parameters of the lyric might themselves be distended by war.

16 See Mark Jancovich, *The Cultural Politics of the New Criticism* (Cambridge University Press, 1993), pp. 108–9.

17 Marianne Moore, 'What Are Years?' *Kenyon Review* 2 (1940), 286. As the title of the 1941 volume, *What Are Years* has no question mark, so reinforcing the question's rhetorical nature.

18 *Kenyon Review* 2 (1940), p. 284.

19 The syllabic timing of the poem is threatened in its final line: 'ity is not now a crime' has seven syllables, but should have only six. In the version published in *What Are Years*, Moore removes the word 'now': it is in keeping with my argument that the adverb that draws the poem into the ambit of contemporary history disturbs its structure, and that the removal of 'now' restores its timeless settled state.

20 Crystal had accrued the figurative sense of inwardness in debates with which Moore was familiar: Stanley Burnshaw's influential 1935 review of *Ideas of Order*, for example, discerned in Stevens a 'scientific objectified sensuousness separated from its kernal of fire and allowed to settle, cool off, and harden in the poet's mind until it emerges a strange amazing crystal': 'Turmoil in the Middle Ground', rpt in Charles Doyle (ed.), *Wallace Stevens: The Critical Heritage* (London: Routledge, 1985), p. 139. My thinking about crystal was prompted by Lee Jenkins, 'Negotiating The Will: A Three Part Study of Wallace Stevens', Ph.D. dissertation, Cambridge 1992, p. 93.

21 Marianne Moore, *What Are Years* (New York: Macmillan, 1941), p. 53.

22 Stevens, *Opus Posthumous*, p. 230.

23 'Une Allocution Radiodiffusée de M. Giraudoux Aux Françaises à Propos de Sainte Catherine', *Figaro*, 26 November 1939, p. 4. My translation and emphases.

24 Moore, *What Are Years*, p. 43.

25 Stevens in 'The Noble Rider' also distrusts the intimacy with foreign parts that the radio enforces: 'we lie in bed and listen to a broadcast from Cairo, and so on. There is no distance. We are intimate with people we have never seen and, unhappily, they are intimate with us.' Like Giraudoux, he also seems nostalgic for the Napoleonic era when political news rang fainter in the ears of poets and novelists: *The Necessary Angel*, pp. 18, 21.

26 Herbert F. Tucker adopts the felicitous term 'punctual spot' to set against the 'historical line' he associates with dramatic monologue: 'Dramatic Monologue and the Overhearing of Lyric', in Chaviva Hosek and Patricia Parker (eds.), *Lyric Poetry: Beyond New Criticism* (Ithaca: Cornell University Press, 1985), p. 232.

27 According to Taffy Martin, Moore's speaking clock represents a 'near Derridean instance of repetition and difference': *Marianne Moore: Subversive Modernist* (Austin: University of Texas Press, 1986), p. 116. Although it certainly anticipates the procedures of deconstruction, this poem also has something particular to say to its time and place.

28 Bishop to Frani Blough, 1 January 1935, *Letters*, p. 29.

29 Brett C. Millier, *Elizabeth Bishop: Life and the Memory of it* (Berkeley: University of California Press, 1993), pp. 75–6.

30 Bishop, *Complete Poems*, p. 3.

31 Ibid., p. 32.

32 Celeste Goodridge points out the 'implicit indictment of colonialism that ['Florida'] offers': 'Elizabeth Bishop and Wallace Stevens: Sustaining the Eye/I', *Wallace Stevens Journal* 19:2 (1995), 147.

33 There is an echo here of the inscrutable (though not predatory) pigeons that 'sink / downward to darkness' at the end of Stevens' 'Sunday Morning'. Bishop is perhaps also influenced by the hawks and airmen in Auden's premonitory aerial poems: see, for example, 'From Scars where Kestrels Hover' (1929) and 'Journal of an Airman', *The Orators* (1931), in *The English Auden*, ed. Edward Mendelson (London: Faber and Faber, 1977), pp. 28, 73.

34 17 October 1940, Bishop, *Letters*, p. 96.

35 Bishop, *Complete Poems*, p. 36.

36 Bishop to Charlotte Russell, 2 April 1942, *Letters*, p. 106.

37 Bishop to Moore, 28 December 1941, *Letters*, p. 104.

38 Stevens, *Opus Posthumous*, pp. 241–2.

39 Bishop to Moore, 1 September 1943, *Letters*, pp. 115–16.

40 The placement appealed to Bishop because it was not classified as feminine: she turned down several clerical jobs because, she said, office workers 'seem to comb their hair and file their nails most of the time'. In contrast the navy yard workers 'worked in their undershirts' and were heavily tattooed: Bishop to Moore, 1 September 1943, *Letters*, p. 115.

41 Bishop's claim to clear-sightedness belies what might be thought of as her blindness to divisions of labour – her assumption of the priority of theory over practice. The discomforting tone of this letter is further compounded by Bishop's reference to optical instruments in the domestic sphere: she writes of 'the purchasing and financing of Flossie's [her friend's black servant's] new glasses', adding that 'glasses are replacing gold teeth as personal decorations with the smarter negroes here': ibid., p. 116.

42 Marianne Moore, 'Walking-Sticks and Paperweights and Watermarks', *Poetry* 49 (1936), 59–64; rpt with revisions in *What Are Years*, pp. 10–14. The poem is not included in any subsequent collection.

43 See Moore's essay 'Feeling and Precision' (1943): 'We must be as clear as our natural reticence allows us to be': *Complete Prose*, p. 396.

44 Moore's prescription of thrift contrasts sharply with Stevens' extravagance. For an account of his detailed instructions regarding the hand-made paper and costly binding of *Notes Toward a Supreme Fiction* in the context of wartime paper shortages, see Filreis, *Wallace Stevens and the Actual World*, pp. 45–6.

45 James A. Mackay, *Postmarks of England and Wales* (Dumfries: priv. printed, 1988), pp. 111–12. The slogan that appears in the 1936 version of Moore's poem, 'trade follows the phone', was current from 1931, while 'Dig for Victory' was introduced in 1939.

46 Moore's and Bishop's letters about 'Roosters' are reproduced in Kalstone, *Becoming a Poet*.

47 The gift was sent by Bishop's partner Louise Crane, heiress of the Crane Paper Company fortune. Crane provided Moore with financial support and eventually served as one of her executors. Both Moore's and Bishop's financial situations depended in part on the fortunes of the paper market. The list of watermarks that identify luxury papers in 'Walking Sticks' (1941) includes 'Crane'.

48 *Kenyon Review* 2 (1940), 287–8.

49 See, for example, Bonnie Costello, 'Marianne Moore and Elizabeth Bishop: Friendship and Influence', *Twentieth Century Literature* 30 (1984), 130–49; Betsy Erkilla, 'Elizabeth Bishop and Marianne Moore: The Dynamics of Female Influence', in Patricia C. Willis (ed.), *Marianne Moore: Woman and Poet* (Orono: National Poetry Foundation, 1990), pp. 335–49.

50 Bishop, *Complete Poems*, p. 34.

51 We can assume that Bishop wrote 'Jerónymo's house' before reading 'A Glass Ribbed Nest'. A letter to Moore implies that she thought Moore's poem owed some debt to hers: 'The whole poem is like a rebuke to me, it suggests so many of the plans for things I want to say about Key West and have scarcely hinted at in "Josés House" [draft title], for example': 21 May 1940, *Letters*, pp. 89–90.

52 Bonnie Costello also considers Bishop's houses as emblems of the lyric. Her distinction is between lyric and narrative, the house standing for a point of suspension in an otherwise linear sequence. See 'Narrative Secrets, Lyric Openings: Stevens and Bishop', *Wallace Stevens Journal* 19:2 (1995), 180–200.

In my analogy the house is an enclosure that delimits an expansive *two-dimensional* cartographic space.

53 In 'Little Exercise' Bishop writes of a storm retreating 'in a series / of small, badly lit battle-scenes': *Complete Poems*, p. 41. Stevens uses storm as a figure for war in 'The Noble Rider', *The Necessary Angel*, p. 20.

54 Randall Jarrell, 'Poets', in his *Poetry and the Age* (London: Faber and Faber, 1955), p. 210.

55 Bishop to Moore, 23 October 1941, *Letters*, p. 104; 9 October 1944, *Letters*, p. 120.

10 'IN THE PUBLISHED CITY': THE NEW YORK SCHOOL OF POETS

1 John Bernard Myers, *The Poets of the New York School* (Pennsylvania University Press, 1969), p. 7.

2 Donald Allen (ed.), *The Collected Poems of Frank O'Hara* (New York: Knopf, 1971), p. 476, p. 307. Further page references to this edition are given parenthetically in the text, prefaced as *CP*.

3 Ron Padgett and David Shapiro (eds.), *An Anthology of New York Poets* (New York: Vintage, 1970), p. xxx.

4 John Ashbery, *Flow Chart* (Manchester: Carcanet, 1991), pp. 216, 3.

5 John Ashbery, *Self-Portrait in a Convex Mirror* (New York: Viking, 1975), p. 75.

6 John Ashbery, *A Wave* (Manchester: Carcanet, 1984), p. 11.

7 Christopher Dewdney, *The Secular Grail: Paradigms of Perception* (Toronto: Sommerville House, 1993), p. 56.

8 Ibid., p. 4.

9 Bonnie Costello, 'John Ashbery's Landscapes', in Susan M. Schultz (ed.), *The Tribe of John: Ashbery and Contemporary Poetry* (Tuscaloosa: Alabama University Press, 1995), p. 61.

10 Ashbery, *Self-Portrait in a Convex Mirror*, p. 21.

11 Brad Gooch, *City Poet: The Life and Times of Frank O'Hara* (New York: Knopf, 1993).

12 Helen Vendler, 'Frank O'Hara: The Virtue of the Alterable', in Jim Elledge (ed.), *Frank O'Hara: To Be True to a City* (Ann Arbor: Michigan University Press, 1990), p. 246.

13 Herbert A. Leibowitz, 'A Pan Piping on the City Streets', in Elledge, *Frank O'Hara*, p. 26.

14 Neil Bowers, 'The City Limits: Frank O'Hara's Poetry', in Elledge, *Frank O'Hara*, p. 329.

15 Paul Carroll, 'An Impure Poem About July 17, 1959', in Elledge, *Frank O'Hara*, p. 376.

16 As given in Gooch, *City Poet*, p. 328.

17 Ashbery, *Self-Portrait in a Convex Mirror*, p. 20.

18 James Schuyler, *Collected Poems* (New York: Farrar, Strauss and Giroux, 1993), p. 255.

II MODERNISM DEFERRED: LANGSTON HUGHES, HARLEM
AND JAZZ MONTAGE

1 See Arnold Rampersad, *The Life of Langston Hughes*, vol. 1: *1902–1941. I, Too, Sing America*, 2 vols. (New York and Oxford: Oxford University Press, 1986), vol. 1, pp. 123–4. I draw on this and the subsequent volume for much of the biographical information which appears in this chapter.

2 See George Hutchinson, *The Harlem Renaissance in Black and White* (Cambridge, Mass.: The Belknap Press of Harvard University Press, 1995), for an extensive discussion of *The New Negro* and a consideration of the differences between this volume and the special issue of the *Survey Graphic*.

3 Alain Locke (ed.), *The New Negro: An Interpretation* (1925) (New York: Johnson Reprint Corporation, 1968), pp. 10, 11.

4 Ibid., pp. 11–12.

5 Rampersad, *The Life of Langston Hughes*, vol. 1, p. 113.

6 Edward J. Mullen (ed.), *Critical Essays on Langston Hughes* (Boston: G. K. Hall, 1986), pp. 37–9.

7 Rampersad, *The Life of Langston Hughes*, vol. 1, p. 63.

8 Du Bois viewed *Nigger Heaven* as 'a caricature ... a mass of half truths ... a blow in the face' and complained that *Home to Harlem* 'nauseates me'. See Amrijit Singh, *The Novels of the Harlem Renaissance* (Pennsylvania State University Press, 1976), pp. 30, 44–5, and Kathy J. Ogren, *The Jazz Revolution: Twenties America and the Meaning of Jazz* (Oxford University Press, 1989), pp. 126–9.

9 Gilroy cites Hughes on these grounds as a symptomatic figure in the 'Black Atlantic'. Paul Gilroy, *The Black Atlantic* (London: Verso, 1994), p. 13.

10 Langston Hughes, *The Big Sea: An Autobiography* (1940) (London: Pluto, 1986), p. 81; and see Christopher Mulvey, 'The Black Capital of the World', in Christopher Mulvey and John Simons (eds.), *New York: City as Text* (London: Macmillan, 1990).

11 Hughes, *The Big Sea*, p. 247.

12 James Weldon Johnson, 'Harlem: The Culture Capital', in Locke, *The New Negro*, p. 301.

13 Wayne F. Cooper, *Claude McKay: Rebel Sojourner in the Harlem Renaissance. A Biography* (Baton Rouge: Louisiana State University Press, 1987), pp. 70–1.

14 Bruce Kellner (ed.), *The Harlem Renaissance: A Historical Dictionary for the Era* (London: Routledge, 1987), p. xv.

15 Ibid., p. xviii.

16 Johnson, in Locke, *The New Negro*, p. 301.

17 Gilbert Osofsky, *Harlem: The Making of a Ghetto, Negro New York, 1890–1930* (New York and Evanston: Harper Torchbooks, 1963), pp. 137–8.

18 Ogren, *The Jazz Revolution*, p. 62; Arnold Shaw, *The Jazz Age: Popular Music in the 1920s* (New York: Oxford University Press, 1987), pp. 59–60.

19 Rampersad, *The Life of Langston Hughes*, vol. 1, p. 107.

20 Ogren, *The Jazz Revolution*, p. 57.

21 Osofsky, *Harlem*, p. 186.
22 Johnson, in Locke, *The New Negro*, p. 310.
23 Rampersad, *The Life of Langston Hughes*, vol. I, p. 123.
24 Locke, *The New Negro*, pp. 210, 199–200.
25 Ibid., p. 199.
26 Hutchinson, *The Harlem Renaissance in Black and White*, p. 423; Gilroy, 'Modern Tones', in *Rhapsodies in Black: Art of the Harlem Renaissance* (London: Hayward Gallery; and University of California Press, 1997), p. 108.
27 J. A. Rogers, 'Jazz at Home', in Locke, *The New Negro*, p. 223.
28 Ibid., pp. 223, 223, 221, 222, 224.
29 Alain Locke, *The Negro and His Music* (1936) (New York: Arno Press, 1969), p.72. See Paul Burgett, 'Vindication as a Thematic Principle in the Writings of Alain Locke on the Music of Black Americans', in Samuel A. Floyd, Jr (ed.), *Black Music in the Harlem Renaissance: A Collection of Essays* (Knoxville: University of Tennessee Press, 1993).
30 Countee Cullen, review of *The Weary Blues*, rpt in Mullen, *Critical Essays on Langston Hughes*, p. 38.
31 Onwuchekwa Jemie, *Langston Hughes: An Introduction to the Poetry* (New York: Columbia University Press, 1973), p. 7.
32 Langston Hughes, 'The Negro Artist and the Racial Mountain' (1926), rpt in August Meier *et al.* (eds.), *Black Protest Thought in the Twentieth Century* (Indianapolis: Bobbs Merrill, 1965), p. 115.
33 Ibid., p. 112, p. 114; and see Peter Brooker, *New York Fictions: Modernity, Postmodernism, The New Modern* (London: Longman, 1996), pp. 181–2, p. 187.
34 Rampersad, *The Life of Langston Hughes*, vol. I, p. 109.
35 Rogers, in Locke, *The New Negro*, p.217.
36 Ibid., p. 220.
37 See Rampersad, *The Life of Langston Hughes*, vol. I, pp. 185–94.
38 Hughes, *The Big Sea*, p. 325.
39 Ibid, p. 325.
40 Rogers, in Locke, *The New Negro*, p. 216, p. 220.
41 See Beeke Sell (ed.), *Envisioning America* (Cambridge, Mass.: Busch-Reisinger Museum, Harvard University, 1990).
42 Nanry confirms the association of jazz, capitalist expansion, the technologies of mass production and the modern city. The 'modernism' of his title, however, refers to these processes of modernity and 'modernization' rather than to aesthetic modernism: Charles Nanry, 'Jazz and Modernism; Twin-Born Children of the Age of Invention', *American Review of Jazz Studies* I (1982), 146–54. Rogers' view is echoed also in Harvey, who identifies the 'modernism' of 1920s jazz with its revolt against tradition: Mark S. Harvey, 'Jazz and Modernism: Changing Conceptions of Innovation and Tradition', in Reginald T. Buckner and Steven Weiland (eds.), *Jazz in Mind* (Detroit: Wayne State University Press, 1991), pp. 128–47.
43 Houston A. Baker, Jr, *Modernism and the Harlem Renaissance* (Chicago University Press, 1987), p.8.

44 Houston A. Baker, Jr, *Afro-American Poetics: Revisions of Harlem and the Black Aesthetic* (Madison: University of Wisconsin Press, 1988), p. 5.

45 Hutchinson, *The Harlem Renaissance in Black and White*, p. 25.

46 Ibid., p. 31.

47 Hutchinson later cites Hughes' poem 'I, Too', included in *The New Negro* as an example of this 'kinship'. This misses the position of disadvantage from which this claim is made in the poem. Where he approaches the question of definition, Hutchinson speaks of Harlem Renaissance modernism as drawing upon traditions of realist and naturalist discourse. This is interesting and relevant to Hughes. But why we should call this or the intellectual traditions he discusses 'modernist' rather than 'modern' is unclear: Hutchinson, *The Harlem Renaissance in Black and White*, pp. 414, 117–20.

48 Hutchinson, *The Harlem Renaissance in Black and White*, pp. 7, 30.

49 Peter Brooker (ed.), *Modernism/Postmodernism* (London: Longman, 1992), pp. 5–13.

50 Arnold Rampersad, *The Life of Langston Hughes*. Vol. II: *1941–1967. I Dream a World*, 2 vols. (New York and Oxford: Oxford University Press, 1988), vol. II, p.151.

51 Quoted in Jemie, *Langston Hughes*, p. 63.

52 Langston Hughes, *Selected Poems* (1959) (London: Pluto, 1986), p. 230.

53 Ibid., pp. 223, 265, 248, 227.

54 See Brooker, *New York Fictions*, pp. 182–7.

55 Ralph Ellison, *Shadow and Act* (London: Secker and Warburg, 1967), p. 234.

56 Harvey, in Buckner and Weiland, *Jazz in Mind*, p. 149.

57 Nanry, 'Jazz and Modernism', p. 149.

58 Hughes, *Selected Poems*, p. 234.

59 Ibid., p. 268.

60 Rampersad, *The Life of Langston Hughes*, vol. II, p. 235, and see 193 and 201.

61 Ibid., p. 235.

62 See Richard Dyer, *White* (London: Routledge, 1997), pp. 2–3.

63 Raymond Williams, 'When Was Modernism?' in his *The Politics of Modernism: Against the New Conformists*, ed. Tony Pinkney (London: Verso, 1989), p. 35.

Index